Revival and Reform in Islam

The Legacy of Muhammad al-Shawkānī

Revival and Reform in Islam is at once an intellectual biography of Muhammad al-Shawkānī, and a history of a vital transitional period in Yemeni history. This was a time when a society dominated by traditional Zaydī Shiᶜism shifted to one characterised instead by Sunnī reformism. Deploying an array of sources, the author traces the origins and outcomes of this transition, presenting the first systematic account of the ways in which the eighteenth- and nineteenth-century reorientation of the Zaydī *madhhab*, and consequent 'sunnification' of Yemeni society, were intricately linked to – and a catalyst for – tensions within the political realm. In advocating juridical systematization and increased uniformity of religious belief and practice, Shawkānī espoused a socio-religious order which in its dominant features echoed certain aspects of Western modernity. Yet he did so in a context bereft of Western ideational influence. This study then presents a textured account of eighteenth-century Islamic reformist thought and challenges our most fundamental understandings of the meaning of modernity in an Islamic context.

Bernard Haykel is Assistant Professor of Middle Eastern Studies and History in the Department of Middle Eastern Studies at New York University.

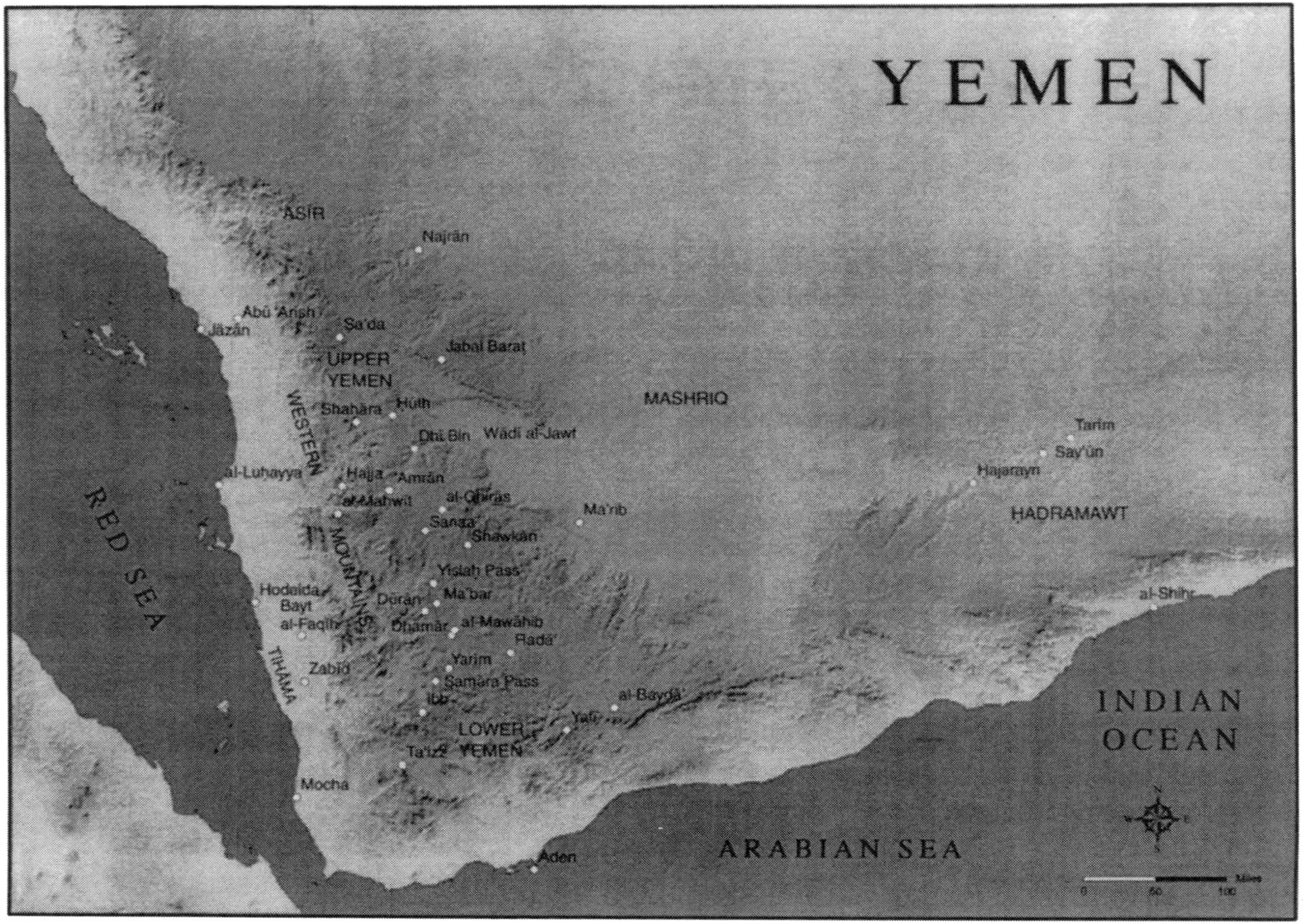

Yemen in the time of Shawkānī

Cambridge Studies in Islamic Civilisation

Published titles in the series are listed at the back of the book

To my Mother and Father

Revival and Reform in Islam

The Legacy of Muhammad al-Shawkānī

BERNARD HAYKEL

New York University

CAMBRIDGE
UNIVERSITY PRESS

CAMBRIDGE
UNIVERSITY PRESS

University Printing House, Cambridge CB2 8BS, United Kingdom

Cambridge University Press is part of the University of Cambridge.

It furthers the University's mission by disseminating knowledge in the pursuit of education, learning and research at the highest international levels of excellence.

www.cambridge.org
Information on this title: www.cambridge.org/9780521528900

First published 2003

A catalogue record for this publication is available from the British Library

National Library of Australia Cataloguing in Publication data
Haykel, Bernard, 1868–.
Revival and reform in Islam: the legacy of
Muhummad al-Shawkānī.
Bibliography.
Includes index.
ISBN 0 521 52890 9 (pbk).
ISBN 0 521 81628 9.
1. Shawkānī, Muhammad ibn Ali, 1759–1839. 2. Islam – Customs and pratices. I. Title.
297

ISBN 978-0-521-81628-1 Hardback
ISBN 978-0-521-52890-0 Paperback

Contents

Acknowledgements

My foremost thanks are due to the supervisors of my doctoral thesis in which this book has its origins: Professor Wilferd Madelung and Dr Paul Dresch of St John's College, Oxford. Studying under Professor Madelung was a humbling experience, and I have benefited enormously from his punctilious treatment of texts and his remarkable knowledge of the Shīᶜite traditions. Paul Dresch opened my eyes to the history of Yemen and imparted to me his love for the country and its people. His unflagging faith in my abilities sustained me, and without his encouragement this work might have languished.

Several institutions provided me with financial and academic support. I was awarded a fellowship at the Institute for Advanced Study in Princeton where I completed most of the manuscript revisions. I would like to thank the faculty of the Institute, and especially Patricia Crone for her support and suggestions on improving this study. Grants from the Fulbright Commission and the American Institute for Yemeni Studies allowed me to do fieldwork in Yemen. The Yemen Centre for Research and Studies (YCRS) provided me with the necessary research permits during my stay in Yemen. YCRS appointed Professor Ḥusayn al-ᶜAmrī as my academic supervisor, and I am grateful for all the advice and help he has offered me over the years. The General Organization for Antiquities and Museums (GOAM) and the Ministry of Religious Trusts in Yemen gave me access to the manuscript collections of the Gharbiyya and Sharqiyya Libraries of the Great Mosque in Sanaa. In particular, I would like to thank GOAM's former director Professor Yūsuf ᶜAbd Allāh as well as Qāḍī ᶜAli Abū ʾl-Rijāl, director of the National Centre for Archives in Sanaa.

Many Yemenis have helped me a great deal and in different capacities over the years and I would like to acknowledge them gratefully here. The doyen of Yemeni history, Mr ᶜAbd Allāh al-Ḥibshī, provided me with copies of numerous manuscripts without which this project would have been impossible. Dr ᶜAlī Muḥammad Zayd, Mr Zayd al-Wazīr and Qāḍī Muḥammad b. Ismāᶜīl al-ᶜAmrānī shared with me their ideas on Shawkānī and provided me with copies of manuscripts and books from their private collections. Among my Zaydī-Hādawī friends, Messrs Muḥammad ᶜIzzān, ᶜAbd al-Salām al-Wajīh, Aḥmad Isḥāq and Dr al-Murtaḍā al-Maḥaṭwarī shared with me insights into aspects of Hādawī law and history without which this work would have been immeasurably poorer. In Bromley, Kent, Sayyid Aḥmad al-Shāmī was kind enough to discuss aspects of his own education and his thoughts on Yemeni intellectual history. Nabīl Darwīsh offered me his friendship during my time in Yemen and I can never repay all the kindness he and his family have shown me.

Among my colleagues in Yemeni studies, I thank François Blukacz, François Burgat, Maria Ellis, Franck Mermier, Thomas Pritzkat, Thomas Stevenson, Yosef Tobi, Daniel Varisco, Shelagh Weir and especially Renaud Detalle, Isaac Hollander, Brinkley Messick and Lucine Taminian who were extremely kind and helpful. I can only gesture at the extent of my gratitude to Eng Seng Ho for his friendship and support. He helped me draw up the genealogical charts, produced the map and read through several chapters in draft form. Aron Zysow offered invaluable insights in the field of *uṣūl al-fiqh*, read drafts of several chapters and encouraged me to keep at it. I thank him for all he has done for me.

In the world of numismatics, Stephen Album taught me how to read coins and answered many of my questions. Michael Cook, Etan Kohlberg, Rudolph Peters, James Piscatori, David Powers, Gabriele vom Bruck and Mark Wagner read through early drafts of this work and I am grateful for the corrections and advice they offered. In the last few years, my colleagues at the Department of Middle Eastern Studies at New York University have provided a wonderfully stimulating environment in which to think and write about the Islamic world. I am particularly grateful to Michael Gilsenan, Philip Kennedy, Adnan Husain and Katherine Fleming for their encouragement and advice on this book. Though friends and colleagues have offered me much assistance, the usual *caveat* holds in that all the infelicities and errors here are my own.

Finally, I would like to thank my in-laws, Salman and Kusum Haidar, for providing me with books and references from India. My mother and father, Albert and Mila Haykel, have been more patient with me than I deserve, and no words can express my gratitude for all they have done for me. By far my greatest debt is owed to my wife, Navina, who patiently put up with me through the completion of this project.

Bernard Haykel
New York, New York

Note on Transliteration and Dates

In transliterating Arabic words, I have followed the system of the *International Journal of Middle East Studies*. I have tried to provide a faithful and consistent transliteration of all Arabic words which have not received a popular Anglicised form as a result of frequent usage. Words as familiar as 'Islam' and 'imam' have been written in their common form, as have known place names such as Mocha, Sanaa, Mecca and Medina. The only exceptions to this, however, have been 'Qurʾān' and 'Sharīʿa', instead of Koran and Sharia, which, I feel, need to be presented in their transliterated form. I have transliterated proper names fully the first time the name is mentioned, thereafter I refer to the person by his commonly known name in Yemen; e.g., Aḥmad b. Yaḥyā al-Murtaḍā becomes Ibn al-Murtaḍā, and al-Hādī Yaḥyā b. al-Ḥusayn becomes al-Hādī. I have dispensed with the article 'al' whenever mentioning Shawkānī. As for less known Zaydī imāms, I have generally referred to them by the first word in their title and then their first name, e.g., al-Mahdī al-ʿAbbās and al-Manṣūr ʿAlī.

In transliterating Hebrew words, I have adopted the system of the *Jewish Quarterly Review* (see vol. 79.1, (1988), iii).

All dates, unless otherwise stated, belong to the Gregorian calendar. Where two dates have been given, the date belonging to the Muslim calendar precedes that belonging to the Gregorian calendar.

Illustrations

Map

Photographs

Abbreviations

Adab al-ṭalab	al-Shawkānī, Muḥammad b. ᶜAlī, *Adab al-ṭalab*, Sanaa: Markaz al-Dirāsāt waʾl-Buḥūth al-Yamaniyya, 1979.
Azhār	al-Murtaḍā, Aḥmad b. Yaḥyā, *Kitāb al-Azhār fī fiqh al-aʾimma al-aṭhār*, Sanaa: n.p., 1982.
Badr	al-Shawkānī, Muḥammad b. ᶜAlī, *al-Badr al-ṭāliᶜ bi-maḥāsin man baᶜd al-qarn al-sābiᶜ*, Muḥammad Zabāra (ed.), 2 vols., photoreprint of 1348/1929 edn, Beirut: Dār al-Maᶜrifa, n.d.
BSOAS	*The Bulletin of the School of Oriental and African Studies.*
EI¹	*The Encyclopedia of Islam*, 1st edition.
EI²	*The Encyclopedia of Islam*, 2nd edition.
Ghaṭamṭam	Muḥammad b. Ṣāliḥ al-Samāwī, *al-Ghaṭamṭam al-zakhkhār al-muṭahhir li-riyāḍ al-azhār min āthār al-Sayl al-Jarrār*, Muḥammad ᶜIzzān (ed.), 6 vols., Amman: Maṭābiᶜ Sharikat al-Mawārid al-Ṣināᶜiyya al-Urduniyya, 1994.
Ḥawliyyāt	Anonymous author, *Ḥawliyyāt Yamāniyya*, ᶜAbd Allāh al-Ḥibshī (ed.), Sanaa: Dār al-Ḥikma al-Yamāniyya, 1991.
Hijar al-ᶜilm	al-Akwaᶜ, Ismāᶜīl b. ᶜAlī, *Hijar al-ᶜilm wa maᶜāqiluh*, 5 vols., Beirut: Dār al-Fikr al-Muᶜāṣir, 1995.
IJMES	*International Journal of Middle Eastern Studies*
Irshād al-fuḥūl	al-Shawkānī, Muḥammad b. ᶜAlī, *Irshād al-fuḥūl ilā taḥqīq al-ḥaqq min ᶜilm al-uṣūl*, Beirut: Dār al-Maᶜrifa, n.d.
Irshād al-ghabī	al-Shawkānī, Muḥammad b. ᶜAlī. *Irshād al-ghabī ilā madhhab ahl al-bayt fī ṣuḥb al-nabī*, ms. personal library of *Qāḍī* Muḥammad b. Ismāᶜīl al-ʿAmrānī.
JAOS	*Journal of the American Oriental Society.*
JSAI	*Jerusalem Studies in Arabic and Islam.*
Maṭlaᶜ al-budūr	Ibn Abī ʾl-Rijāl, Aḥmad b. Ṣāliḥ, *Maṭlaᶜ al-budūr wa majmaᶜ al-buḥūr*, 4 vols., ms. photocopy New Sanaa University Library.

Nashr	Zabāra, Muḥammad b. Muḥammad, *Nashr al-ʿarf li-nubalāʾ al-Yaman baʿd al-alf*, 3 vols., Sanaa: Markaz al-Dirāsāt waʾl-Buḥūth al-Yamanī. (vol. 1, n.d.; vols. 2 and 3, 1985).
Nayl	Zabāra, Muḥammad b. Muḥammad, *Nayl al-waṭar min tarājim rijāl al-Yaman fī ʾl-qarn al-thālith ʿashar*, 2 vols. in one, Sanaa: Markaz al-Dirāṣāt waʾl-Abḥāth al-Yamaniyya, n.d.
Nuzhat al-naẓar	Zabāra, Muḥammad b. Muḥammad, *Nuzhat al-naẓar fī rijāl al-qarn al-rābiʿ ʿashar*, Sanaa: Markaz al-Dirāsāt waʾl-Abḥāth al-Yamaniyya, 1979.
al-Sayf al-bātir	Ismāʿīl b. ʿIzz al-Dīn al-Nuʿmī, *Kitāb al-Sayf al-bātir al-muḍīʾ li-kashf al-īhām waʾl-tamwīh fī Irshād al-Ghabī*, ms. Sanaa, Gharbiyya Library, *majmūʿ* no. 188, fols. 1–36 and *majmūʿ* no. 91, fols. 55–77.
Sharḥ al-Azhār	Ibn Miftāḥ, ʿAbd Allāh, *Kitāb al-Muntazaʿ al-mukhtār min al-gayth al-midrār al-mufattiḥ li-kamāʾim al-Azhār fī fiqh al-aʾimma al-aṭhār*, 4 vols., reprint of Yemeni Ministry of Justice, Cairo: Maṭbaʿat Sharikat al-Tamaddun, 1332/1914.
Ṭabaq al-ḥalwā	al-Wazīr, ʿAbd Allāh b. ʿAlī, *Tārīkh ṭabaq al-ḥalwā wa ṣuḥaf al-mann waʾl-salwā*, Muḥammad Jāzim (ed.), Sanaa: Markaz al-Dirāsāt waʾl-Buḥūth al-Yamanī, 1985.
al-Tiqṣār	al-Shijnī, Muḥammad, *Ḥayāt al-imām al-Shawkānī al-musamma Kitāb al-Tiqṣār*, Muḥammad b. ʿAlī al-Akwaʿ(ed.), Sanaa: Maktabat al-Jīl al-Jadīd, 1990.
Tuḥfat al-ikhwān	al-Jirāfī, ʿAbd Allāh b. ʿAbd al-Karīm, *Tuḥfat al-ikhwān bi-ḥilyat ʿallāmat al-zamān*, Cairo: al-Maṭbaʿa al-Salafiyya, 1365/1946.

All references to the Sunnī ḥadīth collections (e.g., the *Ṣaḥīḥ* of Bukhārī and of Muslim, the *Sunan* of Abū Dā'ūd, al-Tirmidhī, al-Nasā'ī, Ibn Mājah and the *Musnad* of Ibn Ḥanbal) are based on A. J. Wensinck *et al.*, *Concordance et indices de la tradition musulmane*, 8 vols., Leiden: E. J. Brill, 1936–1988.

The Qāsimī Imams

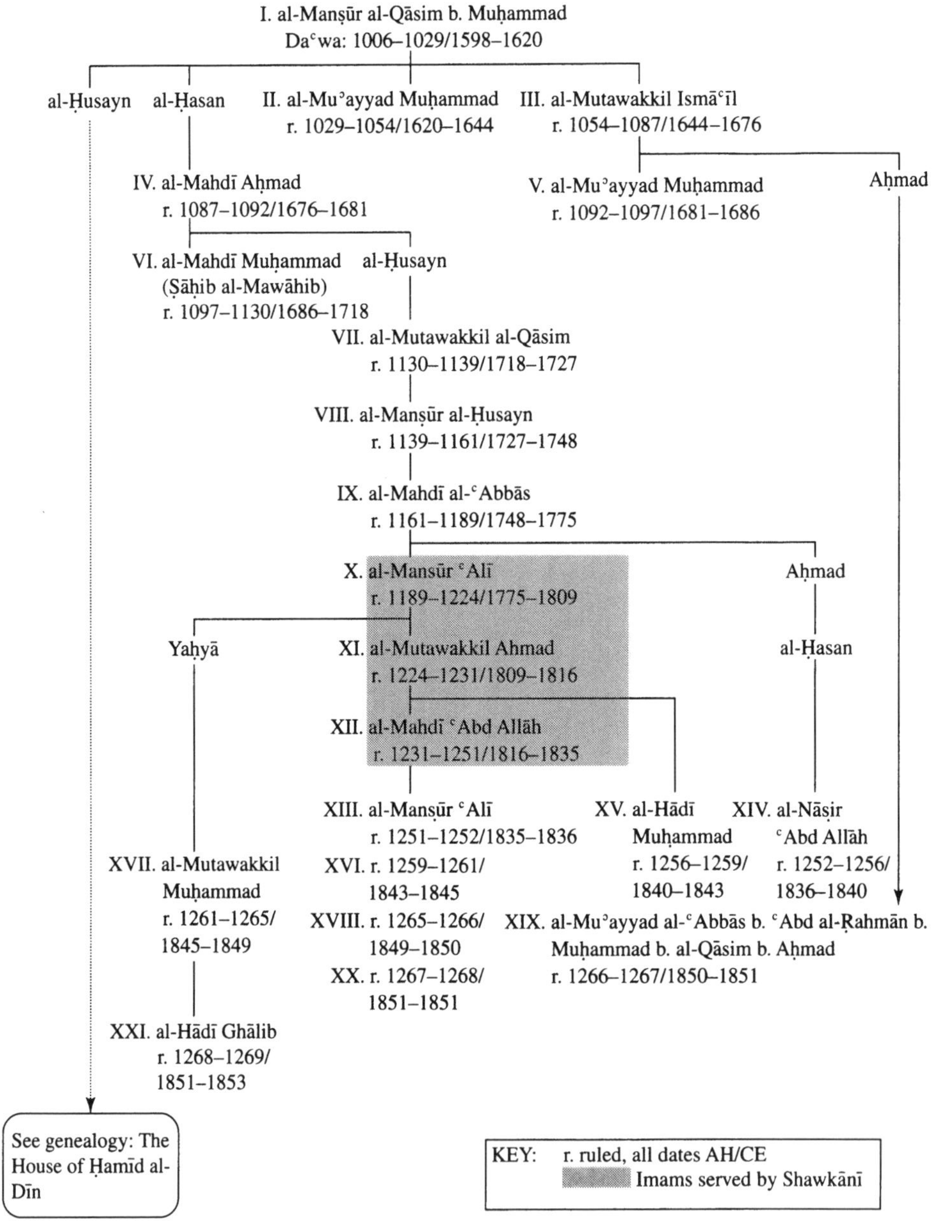

Genealogy of the Qāsimī imams

The House of Ḥamīd al-Dīn

al-Manṣūr al-Qāsim b. Muḥammad

|

al-Ḥusayn (see genealogy: The House of al-Qāsim)

|

Muḥammad

|

Ismāʿīl

|

Yaḥyā

|

Muḥammad

|

Yaḥyā

|

I. al-Manṣūr Muḥammad
Daʿwa: 1307–1322/1890–1904

|

II. al-Mutawakkil Yaḥyā
Daʿwa 1322/1904, effective r. 1918–1948

|

III. al-Nāṣir Aḥmad
r. 1948–1962

|

IV. al-Manṣūr Muḥammad (al-Badr)
r. 1962
Overthrown in September revolution, 1962

Genealogy of the Hamīd al-Dīn imams

Introduction

In 1966, four years after the September revolution that ended the reign of the last imam in Yemen, bulldozers were clearing Sanaa's famous Khuzayma cemetery to build an Officers' Club. When the scholar Muḥammad al-ᶜAmrānī happened to be passing by the site he realised that the graves of the city's most eminent scholars were being destroyed, including that of the jurist Muḥammad b. ᶜAlī al-Shawkānī (d. 1250/1834). Al-ᶜAmrānī immediately informed the minister of education. They located Shawkānī's grave and had his remains exhumed. This done, an official procession and reburial ceremony took place and Shawkānī was interred next to the Filayḥī mosque in the old city, where his present grave-site is precisely indicated as lying to the west of the westernmost dome. So, whilst Republican officers would now mingle over the concrete and asphalt covered remains of past generations of Sanaa's ulema, only Shawkānī was spared this indignity.[1]

Considered to be one the greatest scholars of Islam at the dawn of the modern age, Shawkānī is a towering figure in both Yemeni Islam and modern Islamic reformist thought. His encyclopaedic oeuvre is studied and referred to throughout the Sunnī world today, from Nadwat al-ᶜUlamāᵓ in north India to the *madrasa*s of Kano in Nigeria. One of the most widely used legal texts among contemporary Sunnīs, Sayyid Sābiq's *Fiqh al-sunna*, is essentially an abridgement of Shawkānī's hadīth-based legal commentary, *Nayl al-awṭār*, a text that is itself also universally referred to. His popularity cannot be attributed merely to the synthetic quality and clear exposition of his writings. Rather, it is his formulation of the problems facing the community of Muslims (*umma*) and the solutions he proffered for solving these – his intellectual project – as well as his attempt to put these into practice in his own lifetime that account for his enduring appeal. When describing eighteenth-century Islam, modern studies invariably mention Shawkānī as an important member of a network of reformist scholars that spanned the entire Muslim world, one that included such scholars as Shāh Walī Allāh of Delhi, Muḥammad b. ᶜAbd al-Wahhāb of Najd and ᶜUthmān dan Fodio in northern Nigeria.[2] A reading of these scholars'

[1] Cf. *al-Thawra* (Sanaa, 1966), no. 142, p. 2 and no. 150, p. 2.

[2] See for example John Voll, 'Foundations for renewal and reform', in John L. Esposito (ed.), *The Oxford History of Islam* (Oxford University Press, 1999), pp. 509–47; Daniel Brown, *Rethinking Tradition in Modern Islamic Thought* (Cambridge University Press, 1996), pp. 22–7.

Shawkānī's grave (author)

writings with the aim of creating well-defined typologies may lead one to believe that terminological similarities among these scholars justifies subsuming them under one label. Voll and Levtzion, for example, describe them as operating within a 'fundamentalist mode'. Such generalisations can be misleading. This is because they ignore genuine intellectual differences between the scholars as well as the varied local contexts in which they were elaborating and promulgating their teachings. And, more importantly, the relationship that these scholars maintained with the political authorities of their day and the ways in which this effected their ideas is touched upon in a perfunctory manner. Rather than presenting Shawkānī's ideas interregionally or on the plane of the Muslim world as a whole, this study aims at providing detailed analysis of a specific project initiated by a reformist scholar. Understanding the intellectual and political history of eighteenth-century Yemen and its formative relationship to the present is the proper backdrop for appreciating the importance of Shawkānī and the reformist ideals he so clearly formulated.

This study is an intellectual biography of Shawkānī that is woven through the political history of the Qāsimī imamate (1635–1850s CE) he was born into and which he served. It delineates two fundamental transformations which took place from the seventeenth through the nineteenth centuries in the realm of the state and in the intellectual world of scholars in the period, culminating in the thought and political work of Shawkānī. The first shift pertains to the transformation of Qāsimī structures of rule from their initial charismatic style into dynastic and patrimonial modes of domination.[3] The second, and simultaneous transformation, relates to the rise within the institutions of the imamate of scholars who subscribed to Sunnī Traditionist ideas, men who had abandoned the inherited teachings of the Zaydī-Hadawī school of law (*madhhab*) upon which the imamate in Yemen was founded, preferring instead a non-*madhhab* identity. The imamate patronised the Traditionists, who in turn set about reforming Yemeni society in accordance with their religious ideas. The details of this reformist project are addressed here as well as the intellectual and political reactions it engendered from those who clung to the teachings of the Zaydī-Hādawī school. Finally, the study traces Shawkānī's intellectual legacy into the modern period.

Geography

Yemeni historical works divide the country into well-defined geographical regions one of which, Upper Yemen, coincides with the area in which Zaydīs predominate demographically. Upper Yemen is the highland plateau that stretches from Najrān in the north down to the Sumāra pass south of Yarīm and includes all the major Zaydī centers of learning, such as Ṣaᶜda, Sanaa and Dhamār. In Upper Yemen live the farming tribesmen in whose territories Zaydī imams and scholars have based themselves and who have provided the imams with the military power with which to establish their claim to rule. An elective affinity existed between the tribesmen and the imams and this was displayed robustly when the imams waged campaigns against outside invaders, such as the Ottomans, or when they led wars of conquest into outlying regions such as Lower Yemen. The relationship, however, was always fraught with tensions and as often as not, tribes turned against an imam, supported a contender, or simply refused to acknowledge any imam.

Below the Sumāra pass lies Lower Yemen, a mountainous region and the richest agricultural area in the country. Here lay the tax-base from which surplus could be extracted on which to run a state. The prosperous medieval dynasties, e.g., the Rasūlids and Ṭāhirids, were centered on this region. Lower Yemen includes the

[3] The concepts of charisma and patrimonialism are drawn from a Weberian typology of forms of authority (cf. Max Weber, *Economy and Society* (Berkeley: University of California Press, 1978), vol. I, pp. 1010f., 1111f.). Weber defines charisma as 'a certain quality of an individual personality by virtue of which he is set apart from ordinary men and treated as endowed with supernatural, superhuman, or at least specifically exceptional powers or qualities. These are such as are not accessible to the ordinary person, but are regarded as of divine origin or as exemplary, and on the basis of them the individual concerned is treated as leader'. Weber also saw the charismatic leader as disrupting tradition. The Zaydī imam fits certain aspects of this definition, and it is apt to use the concept to define those among the imams who fulfilled the institution's rigorous qualifications. Patrimonialism, by contrast, was defined by Weber as a form of political domination in which authority rests on the personal and bureaucratic power exercised by a royal household. This power is formally arbitrary and under the direct control of the ruler. Domination in patrimonial states is secured by means of a political apparatus staffed by mercenaries, conscripts, slaves, administrators and, as in our case, jurists and scholars. These groups do not have an independent power-base and are therefore at the mercy of the ruler's whim.

important towns of Ibb, Dhū Jibla and Taᶜizz; its inhabitants, other than the non-Muslims, are Shāfiᶜīs whose social affairs are best described as relations between landlords and peasants.[4] A third region is the Western Mountains. This abuts the highland plateau on the west and consists of numerous villages involved in terraced agriculture where, most notably, coffee was grown and from which tax revenue was also generated but never in the amounts extracted from Lower Yemen. The population of the Western Mountains is mixed between Zaydīs, Shāfiᶜīs and some Ismāᶜīlīs, and though these inhabitants are organized in tribes, these are not as militarily significant as those in Upper Yemen. Finally, there is the Tihāma, the hot sandy plains along the coast of the Red Sea. Here the population is overwhelmingly Shāfiᶜī, enjoying strong links with Africa, the Hijaz as well as the wider world of the Indian Ocean. From the perspective of the Qāsimī imamate, the Tihāma was important primarily because of the revenues generated from the trade that took place in such port towns as Mocha and Luḥayya.[5]

Social stratification[6]

In the period under consideration (from the seventeenth through the twentieth centuries), the society of Upper Yemen was hierarchical and stratified into a number of social groups or estates, each being associated with a professional occupation. The *sāda* (sing. *sayyid*), who claim descent from the Prophet Muḥammad, see themselves as being at the top of the social hierarchy and are engaged ideally in affairs of politics and the interpretation of God's law. Being related to the Prophet, they are descendants of the eponym of the Northern Arabs, ᶜAdnān. Only *sayyid*s can become imams, and learning, piety, humility and courage are all attributes ascribed to the *sayyids*.[7] Below the *sayyid*s are the *quḍāt* ('the judges', sing. *qāḍī*). The *qādī*s claim descent from South Arabian tribes – they are the descendants of Qaḥṭān, the eponym of the Southern Arabs – and had attained their status either by dint of individual scholarly accomplishment in the religious sciences, or by claiming descent from ancestors who were learned and/or had been in some way associated with the rule of a Zaydī imam. The *qāḍī*s cannot aspire to the imamate, but can otherwise hold ministerial, judicial and administrative posts. The *qāḍī*s, along with the *sayyid*s, are the purveyors of the religious sciences and often lived in towns or villages called *hijar* (sing. *hijra*). These are 'protected

[4] Paul Dresch, 'Imams and tribes: the writing and acting of history in Upper Yemen', in Philip S. Khoury and Joseph Kostiner (eds.), *Tribes and State Formation in the Middle East* (Berkeley: University of California Press, 1990), p. 254.

[5] All the other regions of Yemen that are not described here, such as Yāfiᶜ, Aden and Ḥaḍramawt were Shāfiᶜī, and in the case of Yāfiᶜ also tribal. However, since these only fell under Qāsimī rule for a very short span of time, their histories are not within the purview of this study.

[6] For a more detailed description of the social structure of Yemeni society, see the works that are mentioned in the bibliography by Caton, Dresch, Messick, Mundy, Serjeant and Weir.

[7] Cf. al-Ḥusayn b. al-Qāsim, *Ādāb al-ᶜulamāʾ waʾl-mutaᶜallimīn* (Sanaa: al-Dār al-Yamaniyya liʾl-Nashr waʾl-Tawzīᶜ, 1987), pp. 37, 99–109.

enclaves' in otherwise tribal territories in Upper Yemen. Some of the *hijras* were associated with markets and centres of learning. Shawkānī's *nisba* denotes that he was originally from such an enclave, Shawkān.

The next group in the hierarchy are the tribal armed peasants (*qabā'il*), constituting the numerical majority of Upper Yemen's society, and under whose armed protection the other estates live.[8] Below the tribesmen are a number of lowly estates whose members provide a variety of menial and service-oriented jobs for society – such professions as barbers, heralds, butchers, tanners, bloodletters, weavers, musicians – and these are collectively referred to as the *Banū al-Khums*, some of whom (depending on one's professional occupation) are also known as the *mazāyina* (sing. *muzayyin*). The Jews of Yemen, as *dhimmīs* (protected non-Muslim subjects) of an Islamic state, or as 'protected clients' (*jīrān*) of the tribes, inhabit a social space that is properly outside this hierarchy, though they were associated with the *Banū al-Khums* since they often were engaged in the service professions, e.g., silversmiths, cobblers, ironmongers, potters.

Members of these estates could be distinguished sartorially. Among the Muslims, 'two elements, the dagger and the headgear, were of particular significance in social differentiation'.[9] The *sayyids* and the *qāḍīs*, for instance, wore a distinctive slightly curved dagger called the *ᶜasīb* as well as white flowing robes (with long sleeves) and large turbans. Dress, however, was not the only marker of *sayyid* or *qāḍī* identity. A code of conduct and a particular mode of speech were associated with the learned estates, and these were assumed to inhere in their innate dispositions. According to Shawkānī, the *sayyids* and *qāḍīs*, 'as people of nobility (*ahl al-sharaf*) and elevated households (*al-buyūt al-rafīᶜa*)', have a pre-disposition to love learning, an aptitude for the religious sciences and the requisite manners and habits of men of learning.[10] For instance, the *sayyids* were not expected to enter the market-place since engaging in the fray and commotion of trade was considered demeaning and might result in loss of probity (*ᶜadāla*).[11] As descendants of the Prophet, the *sayyids* had an historical, religious and eschatological role to play as guides to the Muslim community.

Zaydism and the Imamate in Yemen

The Zaydīs are a sect of Shīᶜī Islam who supported the revolt of Zayd b. ᶜAlī in 122/740 against Umayyad rule. In 284/897, Zaydīs managed to establish a

[8] The tribesmen did not necessarily accept the social hierarchy in the terms presented here since they were the ones who offered protection to the other estates. Nonetheless, the tribesmen did acknowledge and accord a special place and role for the *sayyids* and the *qāḍīs* as men of learning and noble ancestry.

[9] Martha Mundy, 'Ṣanᶜā' dress', in Robert Serjeant and Ronald Lewcock (eds.), *Ṣanᶜā': An Arabian Islamic City* (London: World of Islam Festival Trust, 1983), p. 532.

[10] Muḥammad b. ᶜAlī al-Shawkānī, *Adab al-ṭalab* (Sanaa: Markaz al-Dirāsāt wa'l-Buḥūth al-Yamaniyya, 1979), pp. 129–31 (hereinafter *Adab al-ṭalab*).

[11] Mundy, 'Ṣanᶜā' dress', p. 531 fn. 13 and Aḥmad b. Muḥammad al-Wazīr, *Ḥayāt al-amīr ᶜAlī b. ᶜAbd Allāh al-Wazīr* (n.p.: Manshūrāt al-ᶜAṣr al-Ḥadīth, 1987), p. 53.

community in Yemen. The main emphasis of their teachings is their insistence on righteous rule through the Ahl al-Bayt (i.e., the descendants of ᶜAlī b. Abī Ṭālib from either al-Ḥasan or al-Ḥusayn) who have a guiding role in both religious and secular affairs. The founder of this community in Yemen was the imam al-Hādī ilā al-Ḥaqq Yaḥya b. al-Ḥusayn (d. 298/911) whose collected legal teachings and judgements are the basis for the Zaydī-Hādawī school of law which has dominated the Yemeni highlands until modern times. His main legal works are the *Kitāb al-Aḥkām* and *Kitāb al-Muntakhab*, in which he supports characteristic Shīᶜite opinions such as the mention of *ḥayya ᶜalā khayr al-ᶜamal* in the call to prayer and the rejection of the wiping over the shoes (*masḥ ᶜalā al-khuffayn*) in the ritual ablution.[12] In addition, many of his views are based on the principle of the consensus (*ijmāᶜ*) of the Ahl al-Bayt. Al-Hādī's works were commented on by successive generations of scholars and it was finally with al-Mahdī Aḥmad b. Yaḥyā al-Murtaḍā (d. 840/1436), in his *Kitāb al-Azhār*, that an authoritative collection of the Hādawī school's doctrine was established.[13] With respect to theological questions, al-Hādī subscribed to the teachings of the Muᶜtazilī school of Baghdād.

Unlike Sunnīs, Zaydīs have continuously insisted on having a just ruler who must fulfil rigorous qualifications and duties. They believe that ᶜAlī was the most excellent of men after the Prophet, and that he and his sons, al-Ḥasan and al-Ḥusayn, were invested by the Prophet as his executors (*waṣī*) through designation (*naṣṣ*), but that the designation was covert (*khafī*) and could only be ascertained after investigation.[14] Zaydīs also contend that after the supreme leadership (*imāma*) of al-Ḥusayn any descendant of his or of his brother, al-Ḥasan, who has the requisite qualifications could become imam after making a 'summons' to allegiance (*daᶜwa*) and then 'rising' (*khurūj*) against illegitimate rulers. According to some Zaydīs, the imam was not chosen by anyone but God. This teaching is already clearly enunciated by al-Hādī, who traces it back to earlier imams. The people are obliged to support the one whom God has chosen.[15] However, other Zaydī theologians are said to have claimed that the selection of the imam is accomplished by consultation (*shūrā*) among the descendants of al-Ḥasan and al-Ḥusayn;[16] this restricted *shūrā* is the one that counts. Unlike the Twelver Shīᶜite imam, the Zaydī imam was not considered impeccable or infallible (*maᶜṣūm*) and therefore his religious authority could be challenged. He was, however, considered a *mujtahid*, and later Zaydīs accepted the doctrine that every *mujtahid* is correct (*kull mujtahid muṣīb*), which in fact allowed for divergence of opinions, especially in matters of law (*furūᶜ*).

[12] al-Hādī Yaḥyā b. al-Ḥusayn, *Kitāb al-Aḥkām fī al-ḥalāl waʾl-ḥarām*, 2 vols. (n.p., 1990), vol. I, pp. 78–80, 83–4.

[13] The *Kitāb al-Azhār* is the functional equivalent of the *mukhtaṣar* in the Mālikī school. On the rise of the *mukhtaṣar* genre see Mohammad Fadel, 'The social logic of *taqlīd* and the rise of the *mukhtaṣar*', *Islamic Law and Society* 3 (1996), 193–233.

[14] *EI²*, art. 'Imāma' (Wilferd Madelung), vol. III, p. 1166. By contrast, the Imāmī Shīᶜīs claim an explicit designation (*naṣṣ jalī*) of the imams.

[15] Cf. al-Hādī Yaḥyā b. al-Ḥusayn, *Kitāb al-Aḥkām*, vol. 2, pp. 460–62.

[16] Abū ʾl-Ḥasan al-Ashᶜarī, *Kitāb Maqālāt al-islāmiyyin*, Helmut Ritter (ed.) (Wiesbaden: Franz Steiner, 1963), p. 67.

Zaydīs did not recognise a hereditary line of imams and were prepared to support any member of Ahl al-Bayt who claimed the imamate by 'rising', and it became incumbent on every Muslim to acknowledge the imam after he had issued his 'summons' to allegiance. The imamate was envisaged in universal Islamic terms and was never presented as being confined to Yemen or the Zaydī community. The imam assumed the title of Commander of the Faithful (*amīr al-muʾminīn*), and Yemen was seen as the base from which the 'summons' would spread to the Muslim world.

In addition to being a member of the Ahl al-Bayt, it was necessary for the imam to have other qualifications: knowledge of religious matters, piety, moral and physical integrity, courage, and an ability to render independent judgement (*ijtihād*) in law. His duties are similar to those envisaged by the Sunnīs and Muᶜtazilīs: he had to 'order the good and prohibit the evil' (*al-amr biʾl-maᶜrūf waʾl-nahy ᶜan al-munkar*), impose the legal punishments (*ḥudūd*), appoint judges, supervise religious endowments, look after orphans, collect the legal alms and other taxes, lead the congregational Friday prayer, 'raise the banner of faith', defend the territory of Islam, and conduct the *jihād*.[17] If after assuming the post the imam was to come to lack one or more of these qualifications or fall short in the performance of his duties, his imamate was forfeit and he was expected to cede it to a more qualified candidate, who in turn would make his 'summons' and 'rise'. Even the loss of a finger, for example, would in theory have meant forfeiture of the post. The imam, in short, had to be an upstanding person, a scholar-warrior of untainted character who acted as an overlord of the Holy House and who judged impartially.[18]

Late Yemeni Zaydism recognized imams who were 'restricted' (*muḥtasibūn*), when no one could be found to fulfil the high requirements of 'full' imams (*sābiqūn*). The *muḥtasib* was expected to defend the community against external aggression, protect the rights of the weak and 'order the good and prohibit the evil'.[19] This constituted a doctrinal compromise allowing for periods in which a full imam could not be found. It should be noted, however, that in Yemeni history it was not always the most qualified contender for the imamate who was given allegiance, but rather, the most powerful. For example, al-Mahdī Aḥmad b. Yāhyā al-Murtaḍā eventually had to forgo his bid because of the more powerful al-Manṣūr ᶜAlī b. Muḥammad Ṣalāḥ al-Dīn (d. 840/1436), despite being more qualified than the latter.[20] Moreover, in historical practice it was the *ahl al-ḥall waʾl-ᶜaqd* ('the people who loose and bind', understood to mean the community of scholars and notables) who gave their *bayᶜa* (oath of allegiance) to the imam, and this oath was

[17] Muḥammad b. al-Ḥasan, *Kitāb Sabīl al-rashād* (Sanaa: Dār al-Ḥikma al-Yamāniyya, 1994), p. 68; cf. *EI*², art. 'Imāma', vol. III, p. 1166.

[18] Cf. *EI*², art. 'Imāma', vol. III, p. 1166; R. B. Serjeant, 'The Zaydīs', in A. J. Arberry (ed.), *Religion in the Middle East*, 2 vols. (Cambridge University Press, 1969), vol. II, p. 292.

[19] Cf. Aḥmad b. Muḥammad al-Sharafī, *Kitāb ᶜUddat al-akyās*, 2 vols. (Sanaa: Dār al-Ḥikma al-Yamāniyya, 1995), vol. II, pp. 223–6.

[20] Muḥammad b. ᶜAlī al-Shawkānī, *al-Badr al-ṭāliᶜ bi-maḥāsin man baᶜd al-qarn al-sābiᶜ*, Muḥammad Zabāra (ed.), 2 vols., photoreprint of 1929 ed. (Beirut: Dār al-Maᶜrifa, n.d.), vol. I, pp. 122–6 (hereinafter *Badr*).

what *de facto* legitimated his rule. *De jure* one could lack this recognition and still be imam.

In his pathbreaking work on al-Hādī's grandfather, al-Qāsim b. Ibrāhīm (d. 246/860), Wilferd Madelung has described in fine detail the intellectual history of Zaydism until the early sixteenth century, ending with the teachings of al-Manṣūr al-Qāsim b. Muḥammad (d. 1029/1620).[21] The early Zaydīs, in the Kūfan period, were composed of two currents, the Jārūdiyya and the Batriyya. The former upheld robust Shīᶜite views, rejecting the imamates of the three caliphs preceding ᶜAlī while condemning most of the Companions for abandoning ᶜAlī's rightful claims as well as rejecting the legal teachings of the Sunnī Traditionists. The Batriyya, by contrast, were more moderate in that they accepted the imamates of the first three caliphs, since ᶜAlī had done so, and did not restrict religious knowledge to the Ahl al-Bayt. Ultimately, however, the Jārudī teachings prevailed within Zaydism, as attested by al-Hādī's unequivocal condemnation of Abū Bakr and ᶜUmar as usurpers.

By the early tenth century CE, the Zaydīs were able to establish communities in the Caspian region but these were divided into two rival schools: the Qāsimiyya (followers of al-Qāsim b. Ibrāhīm's teachings) and the Nāṣiriyya (followers of al-Naṣir al-Ḥasan b. ᶜAlī al-Utrūsh, d. 301/914). In terms of law, al-Qāsim's teachings were consistent with a Medinan moderate Shīᶜī tradition and in matters of theology his views, while distinct from the Muᶜtazila, were anti-determinist and anti-anthropomorphist. However, Madelung has argued that his theological stance enabled later followers to adopt Muᶜtazilī doctrines. Al-Nāṣir, unlike al-Qāsim, held legal opinions closer to the Kūfan Zaydīs and the Imāmīs, and in matters concerning theology was polemically anti-Muᶜtazilī though he also upheld views similar to those of al-Qāsim. A reconciliation took place in the course of the fourth/tenth century on the basis that the legal doctrines of both schools were equally valid. The community in the Caspian, however, declined considerably in the sixth/twelfth century and ultimately disappeared in 933/1526–7 when the last Zaydī ruler converted to Imāmī Shīᶜism.

Strong links were maintained between the Caspian Qāsimiyya and the Zaydīs in Yemen. In this connection, two imams in particular are worth mentioning: al-Muᵓayyad Aḥmad b. al-Ḥusayn (d. 411/1020) and al-Nāṭiq Abū Ṭālib Yaḥyā b. al-Ḥusayn (d. 424/1033). These two brothers were both followers of the Muᶜtazilī al-Qāḍī ᶜAbd al-Jabbār and accepted the doctrines of his Baṣran school. In matters of law, they adhered to the teachings of al-Qāsim and his grandson al-Hādī, which they expounded in important works, most notably the recently published *Kitāb al-Taḥrīr* by al-Nāṭiq. The Yemeni imam al-Mutawakkil Aḥmad b. Sulaymān (r. 532–566/1137–1170) was a strong unifying figure for Zaydism, a staunch supporter of Baṣran Muᶜtazilī doctrines and an advocate of the transfer of Caspian Zaydī books to Yemen. His successor al-Manṣūr ᶜAbd Allāh b. Ḥamza

21 Wilferd Madelung, *Der Imam al-Qāsim ibn Ibrāhīm und die Glaubenslehre der Zaiditen* (Berlin: Walter de Gruyter, 1965); *EI*², art. 'Zaydiyya' (Wilferd Madelung), Vol. XI, pp. 477–81.

(r. 583–614/1185–1217) followed in al-Mutawakkil's footsteps, achieving significant doctrinal consolidation of the Zaydī community and establishing dominance for Muᶜtazilī theology. This theological tendency, however, was challenged by a number of prominent Zaydī scholars who harked back to the teachings of the early imams, viz., al-Qāsim and al-Hādī. Perhaps the first to do this was the sayyid Ḥumaydān b. Yaḥyā (fl. seventh/thirteenth century) and, later, al-Manṣūr al-Qāsim b. Muḥammad, founder of the Qāsimī state, followed the same trajectory. Though admitting that the Zaydīs and Muᶜtazilīs agreed on basic tenets, al-Manṣūr 'maintained that the early imams had confined their teaching to what could be safely established by reason, the unambiguous texts of the Qurʾān and the generally-accepted Sunna. They had not followed the Muᶜtazila in their abstruse speculation and absurd fantasies'.[22] Al-Manṣūr views represent a strong reassertion of Shīᶜī views among the Zaydīs as evinced also by his Jārūdī stance with respect to the imamate.

During the imamate of al-Mutawakkil Aḥmad b. Sulaymān, in the sixth/twelfth century, Zaydīs began citing from the Sunnī canonical ḥadīth collections, as can be seen, for example, in al-Mutawakkil's own work entitled *Uṣūl al-aḥkām fī al-ḥalāl waʾl-ḥarām*.[23] By the time of his successor, al-Manṣūr ᶜAbd Allāh b. Ḥamza, many Zaydī ulema were using the Sunnī collections extensively while continuing to cite Zaydī collections such as the *Amālī* of Aḥmad b. ᶜĪsā or *Kitāb al-Jāmiᶜ al-kāfī* by Abū ᶜAbd Allāh Muḥammad b. ᶜAlī al-ᶜAlawī (d. 445/1053).[24] This trend culminated with such works as Aḥmad b. Yaḥyā al-Murtaḍā's *al-Baḥr al-zakhkhār*, a comparative legal work across the *madhāhib*, and later with al-Manṣūr al-Qāsim's *al-Iᶜtiṣām bi-ḥabl Allāh al-matīn*. Careful reading of these texts, however, indicates that these scholars were using Sunnī ḥadīths selectively to bolster established Zaydī-Hādawī views. Al-Manṣūr himself uses these sources despite his belief, which he attributes to al-Hādī also, that the *Ṣaḥīḥayn* of Bukhārī and Muslim are devoid of sound traditions. This is what is reported about his view.

> Imam al-Mahdī li-Dīn Allāh Aḥmad b. Yaḥyā – peace be upon him – relates that the great imam, the lofty and noble, the Guider to the Clear Truth Yaḥyā b. al-Ḥusayn – God's blessings and peace be upon him and his noble fathers – said: 'A great distance and divide lies between soundness and the *Ṣaḥīḥ*s of Bukhārī and Muslim'. Our lord al-Qāsim b. Muḥammad said: 'This is correct'. By this he meant that most of the ḥadīths in the two books are defective (*muᶜtall*).[25]

This assertion is based on the fact that many of the traditions contained therein are transmitted by those who showed enmity to ᶜAlī – men such as Muᶜāwiya whom al-Manṣūr curses – and therefore are not to be trusted. The early Qāsimī

22 *EI*², art. 'Zaydiyya', vol. XI, p. 480; Madelung, *Der Imam al-Qāsim*, pp. 220–1.

23 Cf. Isḥāq b. Yūsuf, *al-Wajh al-ḥasan al-mudhhib liʾl-ḥazan* (Sanaa: Maktabat Dār al-Turāth, 1990), p. 53. Cf. Aḥmad al-Ḥusaynī, *Muʾallafāt al-Zaydiyya*, 3 vols. (Qom: Maṭbaᶜat Ismāᶜīliyyan, 1413/1993), vol. I, pp. 126–7.

24 For a full list of Zaydī ḥadīth sources see ᶜAbd Allāh al-ᶜIzzī, *Ulūm al-ḥadīth ᶜinda al-Zaydiyya waʾl-muḥaddithīn*, Amman: Muʾassasat al-Imām Zayd b. ᶜAlī al-Thaqāfiyya, 2001), pp. 275–86.

25 Eugenio Griffini (ed.), *'Corpus Iuris' di Zaid ibn ᶜAlī* (Milan: Ulrico Hoepli, 1919), p. lxxix.

imamate therefore represents a moment of traditional Zaydī-Shīʿī assertiveness, one that refers back to the teachings of al-Hādī. This is the backdrop against which Shawkānī views must be understood.

Shawkānī and Traditionist Islam

Shawkānī rejected unequivocally the Zaydī-Hādawī school he was born into and saw himself more properly as the intellectual heir of the Sunnī Traditionists of highland Yemen, scholars who argued that the Sunnī canonical ḥadīth collections were unconditionally authoritative in matters of religion. The first Traditionist scholar in this lineage was Muḥammad b. Ibrāhīm al-Wazīr (commonly known as Ibn al-Wazīr, d. 840/1436), later followed by al-Ḥasan b. Aḥmad al-Jalāl (d. 1084/1673), Ṣāliḥ b. Mahdī al-Maqbalī (d. 1108/1696), Muḥammad b. Ismāʿīl al-Amīr (commonly known as Ibn al-Amīr, d. 1182/1769) and finally Shawkānī. These scholars adopted Traditionist views because they argued greater certainty of God's will could be obtained therein. They felt that the texts of revelation and the science of ḥadīth criticism for evaluating their soundness were more authoritative than the views of the imams or those of the scholars of theology and law. The epistemology and methods of the Sunnī ḥadīth scholars enabled them to identify a more reliable corpus of Traditions on which to base law and theology. Ibn al-Wazīr, for instance, states that his distress at becoming an infidel were he to blindly follow the opinions of others in matters of creed, compounded by his disappointment with the arguments of the *kalām* scholars, was what led him to investigate the Qurʾān and the canonical collections of ḥadīth. In these, he found solace and certainty of his belief in Islam.[26]

In his biography of Ibn al-Wazīr, Shawkānī clearly identifies himself with the Yemeni Traditionists and laments that they had been ignored by those outside Yemen. He says:

> There is no doubt that non-Yemeni scholars do not pay attention to the people of this country [Yemen]. This is because their perception of the Zaydīs is based on those unfamiliar with the conditions [here]. [I say] to those who do not investigate the situation, that in the country of the Zaydīs one can find a limitless number of imams of the Book and the Sunna. These confine themselves to following evidentiary proof-texts (*nuṣūs al-adilla*) [from the Qurʾān and Sunna], and rely on sound Traditions in the canonical ḥadīth collections and other accompanying Islamic compilations which contain the Sunna of the Lord of Mankind [the Prophet Muḥammad]. They do not practise *taqlīd* at all and do not corrupt their religion with reprehensible innovations, which can be found in the other schools. Indeed, they are in the manner of the Pious Ancestors (*al-salaf al-ṣāliḥ*), in practising what the Book of God and the sound Sunna of His Messenger have

[26] Muḥammad b. Ibrāhīm al-Wazīr, *al-ʿAwāṣim waʾl-qawāṣim fī ʾl-dhabbi ʿan sunnati Abī ʾl-Qāsim*, Shuʿayb al-Arnaʾūṭ (ed.), 9 vols. (Beirut: Muʾassasat al-Risāla, 1992), vol. 1, pp. 201–2.

> indicated. They delve extensively into the basic sciences of the Book and Sunna (*ālāt ʿilm al-kitāb waʾl-sunna*), such as grammar, morphology, rhetoric, the principles [of jurisprudence and theology] and language. Nor do they neglect in addition to these the rational sciences. Their merit lies in that they limit themselves to the texts of the Book and the Sunna and cast off *taqlīd*. God has made this the characteristic of the people of this country in recent times, which is rarely found in others.[27]

The Traditionist Yemeni scholars to whom Shawkānī is referring here opposed most forms of human reasoning (*ʿaql*) in dogmatic theology (*kalām*) as well as the use of personal opinion (*raʾy*) in law (*fiqh*). Like Traditionists elsewhere in the Muslim world, they emphasized the literal word of the Qurʾān and its interpretation through the Prophetic Traditions which they equated fully with the Sunna.[28] Theologically, this entailed rejecting most Zaydī *kalām*, which draws heavily on Muʿtazilism as well as the teachings of the imams. Shawkānī, for instance, considered *kalām* as consisting of 'idle talk' (*khuzaʿbalāt*) and felt that its hermeneutic methods and conclusions were being imitated by scholars without reference to revealed texts. Scholars of *kalām*, according to him, had invented a conceptual terminology and vocabulary which they have rendered into a principle (*aṣl*), to which they then refer the Qurʾān and Sunna. Therefore, to partake in the discourse (*maqūlāt*) of the *kalām* scholars, meant for Shawkānī to partake in a type of *taqlīd* and to reject the texts of the Qurʾān and Sunna, which have been made subordinate to the discourse of *kalām*.[29]

In legal matters, the Traditionists stressed the practice of *ijtihād* and the shunning of *taqlīd*. By *ijtihād* they meant a scholar's independent ability to elaborate legal opinions from the principal sources of the Qurʾān and the canonical ḥadīth corpus. They understood *taqlīd* as the acceptance of another person's opinion on a given matter without knowing the texts on which it was based. Their attack was levelled primarily at the established schools of law, and in particular the Hādawī school, whose opinions they said were often textually unfounded. In other words, the process of *ijtihād* by which the school's opinions were arrived at was improper. This was made more pernicious by the prevailing practice and custom which entailed the closest adherence (*taqlīd*) to these opinions. Shawkānī's principal aim vis-à-vis the Zaydī-Hādawī school was to denounce its authoritative legal corpus of opinions which he felt were based on mere opinion (*raʾy*) while promulgating his own views which he asserts are anchored in texts of revelation.

More broadly, Shawkānī's attack involved a depiction of the Zaydīs as parochial scholars, not following serious standards of scholarship and being deficient even in the writing of their own history. Their books, he says, do not follow accepted methodological practices and one of his aims is to redress this failing. Here is what he says:

[27] *Badr*, II: 83. [28] Cf. *EI*[2], art. 'Ahl al-Ḥadīth' (Joseph Schacht), vol. I, pp. 258–9.
[29] Muḥammad b. ʿAlī al-Shawkānī, *al-Tuḥaf fī madhāhib al-salaf*, in *al-Rasāʾil al-salafiyya fī iḥyāʾ sunnat khayr al-bariyya*, photoreprint of 1930 ed. (Beirut: Dār al-Kutub al-ʿIlmiyya, n.d.), pp. 6–7; cf. idem, *Kashf al-shubūhāt ʿan al-mushtabahāt*, pp. 19f.; *Adab al-ṭalab*, pp. 113–5.

> ...despite the virtuous and the eminent persons with every good trait throughout the ages among them, the Zaydīs have a great interest and a plentiful desire to bury the good deeds of the noteworthy among them and to erase the legacy of their most glorious members. They do not transmit the poetry, prose or works of their notable figures, despite their own eagerness to read what was produced by others, their desire to have a full acquaintance with the other sects and schools, and their dedication to the historical and other works of these. I am greatly astonished by this trait in the Zaydīs, which has led to burying the traces of their early and more recent members, and to undervaluing their high ranking scholars, the eminent, the poets and the rest of their most distinguished members. Because of this, historians, who have written biographies of the people of a given century or age, have generally ignored them. The rare biography of a Zaydī which they may mention is useless and lacking in what the person deserves. It makes no mention of his birth, his death, his teachers, the books he studied and taught, his poetry and his news. Those who know a given person, and who are from his country, are the ones who transmit news about him; should they ignore him then others will do so as well and be ignorant of him. It is for this reason that you find me in this book [i.e., *al-Badr al-ṭāliʿ*] when I mention one of them, I do not know what to say because his own generation ignored him. So all I can say is he is so-and-so son of so-and-so. I do not know when he was born, when he died or what he did in his life.[30]

Debates about Eighteenth-Century Islam

A number of scholars have made the argument that the eighteenth century marks a significant moment of internal change in the history of Islamic societies. Peter Gran, for example, sees an Islamic enlightenment taking place in eighteenth-century Egypt, and links the revival of ḥadīth studies both to middle-class empiricism and ultimately to an indigenous capitalist transformation.[31] Building on Gran, Reinhard Schulze has also argued that an Islamic enlightenment (*Aufklärung*) took place in the eighteenth century. Among other things, Schulze adduces evidence for a new subjectivity and an anthropocentrism, as opposed to a theocentrism, among Muslim scholars of this period and which he sees as constitutive of any enlightenment process.[32] The principal appeal of Gran and Schulze's theses is that they reinscribe Muslims as active agents into the processes of modernity, thereby diminishing the role of the West as the purveyor of modernity. These arguments have engendered considerable controversy, however, and Schulze's thesis in particular has been severly criticised for its highly speculative nature and tendentious use of texts.[33] As thought provoking as the idea of an Islamic enlightenment may be, the

30 *Badr*, I: 60.

31 Peter Gran, *Islamic Roots of Capitalism* (Syracuse University Press, 1998), pp. 49–56.

32 Reinhard Schulze, 'Das islamische achtzehnte Jahrhundert: Versuch einer historiographischen Kritik', *Die Welt des Islams* 30 (1990), 140–9; idem, 'Was ist die islamische Aufklärung?' *Die Welt des Islams* 36 (1996), 276–325.

33 Gottfried Hagen and Tilman Seidensticker, 'Reinhard Schulzes Hypothese einer islamischen Aufklärung', *Zeitschrift der Deutschen Morgenländischen Gesellschaft* 148 (1998), 83–110; Bernd Radtke, *Authochthone islamische Aufklärung im 18. Jahrhundert* (Utrecht: Houtsma Stichting, 2000).

Traditionist reform movement in eighteenth-century Yemen does not embody any of the ideals of the European Enlightenment, central to which is the notion that only reason, and not any religious or political authority, is the ultimate arbiter of truth.[34] For Shawkānī, reason, understood as the use of *ᶜaql* in theology and *raᶜy* in law, were unacceptable means by which one arrived at the truth, understood to be God's will in any given matter; rather, to arrive at this one had to adhere to a well defined hermeneutic method centered on a literal interpretation of the texts of revelation.

Another thesis about the history of the eighteenth century has been defended by John Voll. He argues that the eighteenth century is marked by a 'fundamentalist spirit' that is represented by movements of revival and reform which were headed by scholars who were hadīth-oriented and 'neo-Sufi'.[35] These scholars interacted with each other in informal educational networks centered on Mecca and Medina and sought to bring about a socio-moral reconstruction of Islamic society, by among other things ridding Sufism of its antinomian excesses, asserting God's transcendence rather than His immanence. They also advocated *ijtihād* and shunned *taqlīd*. Furthermore, Voll claims these reformist movements spanned the entire Muslim world, from Indonesia and China in the east to Nigeria in the west, and are the ideological precursors of modern Islamic fundamentalism. The principal appeal of this thesis is heuristic because 'it allows the student of modern Islam to analyze and understand a complex set of variables in the context of one coherent whole'.[36] It is, however, misleading. In his important article on the thought of four major eighteenth-century scholars, Ahmad Dallal shows by thoroughly investigating their writings that they cannot be subsumed under one ideological rubric. This study on Shawkānī shares Dallal's view that the substantive content of the ideologies of Islamic revival needs to be thoroughly researched before any broad generalisations can be made about the nature of Islamic thought in a given period or across a vast expanse of geographic space.[37] Furthermore, it is not proven that an identity of views between scholars exists because they may have studied in the same educational circles.[38] Given that ideas are not formed in a vacuum, one must attempt to link a given scholar's ideology with the political and social contexts in which he is developing his views and then compare these with those of his teachers or peers from other regions of the Islamic world. And this has yet to be undertaken for the period in question.

[34] Cf. Jonathan I. Israel, *Radical Enlightenment* (Oxford: Oxford University Press, 2001).

[35] John Voll, *Islam: Continuity and Change in the Modern World* (Syracuse University Press, 1994), pp. 24f.; John L. Esposito, *Islam, the Straight Path* (Oxford University Press, 1988), pp. 117f.; Ira M. Lapidus, *A History of Islamic Societies* (Cambridge University Press, 1988), pp. 258–9, 563–9.

[36] Ahmad Dallal, 'The origins and objectives of Islamic revivalist thought, 1750–1850', *JAOS* 113 (1993), 342.

[37] For a good example of the detailed research that is needed on the scholars of the eighteenth century see R. S. O'Fahey, *Enigmatic Saint: Ahmad Ibn Idris and the Idrisi Tradition* (Evanston, IL: Northwestern University Press, 1990).

[38] Cf. John Voll, 'Linking groups in the networks of eighteenth-century revivalist scholars', in Nehemiah Levtzion and John Voll (eds.), *Eighteenth-Century Renewal and Reform in Islam* (Syracuse University Press, 1987), pp. 69–92; Dallal, 'The Origins and Objectives', 342.

A common misapprehension is to associate Shawkānī with the Wahhābiyya.[39] The rise of the Wahhābī movement in Najd in the second half of the eighteenth century influenced the Yemeni Traditionists by providing them with a successful model of a state which was forged on an alliance between ulema and rulers. More specifically, it was the alliance made in 1744 CE between Muḥammad b. ʿAbd al-Wahhāb (d. 1206/1792) and the emir of the town of Dirʿiyya, Muḥammad b. Saʿūd (d. 1179/1766), which started the movement. By the turn of the nineteenth century, the Wahhābīs constituted a formidable military force in Arabia, promoting a renovative message which emphasized the doctrine of God's unicity (*tawḥīd*) and attacking all whom they felt were derogating from it. In particular, the Wahhābīs attacked the cult of Sufi saints and the practices associated with tomb visitation which they felt were contrary to the law.[40] Initially, scholars like Ibn al-Amīr and Shawkānī welcomed this, seeing a correspondence between their own Traditionist views and those of the Wahhābīs. However, upon hearing that the Wahhābīs were practising indiscriminate excommunication (*takfīr*) of fellow Muslims, the Yemenis soon withdrew their support, levelling severe criticism against the Najd-based movement.[41] The Yemeni Traditionists did not borrow their ideas from the Wahhābīs; rather, they felt the Wahhābīs to be inferior in terms of scholarship and limited by a restrictive interpretation of the Ḥanbalī *madhhab*.

The intellectual context from which Shawkānī emerged and in which he operated is complex, involving local as well as broader geographical influences. His ideas and life cannot easily be subsumed under a wider pan-Islamic movement of reform in the eighteenth century. The local context, namely the cultural and juridical dominance of the Hādawī school and the evolution of Qāsimī rule from charismatic to patrimonial forms of government, underpins his ideas and the reforms he endeavoured to bring about. The subject which took centre stage in Shawkānī's education was ḥadīth and its attendant sciences, and in this regard Ibn al-Amīr and ʿAbd al-Qādir b. Aḥmad al-Kawkabānī (d. 1207/1792) played crucial roles in teaching and promoting these in Sanaa in the eighteenth century. In this context, *ijtihād*, understood here as the scholar's ability to act in accordance with proof-texts (*al-ʿamal biʾl-dalīl*), was intimately related to the ḥadīth sciences. These scholars felt that the canonical ḥadīth collections provided the bulk of proof-texts relating to most, if not all, contingencies. *Ijtihād* was the total methodological and epistemological procedure which enabled them to cite relevant texts, weighing the relative authenticity and authority of each ḥadīth in order to

39 Barbara Metcalf, *Islamic Revival in British India: Deoband, 1860–1900* (Princeton University Press, 1982), p. 278.

40 Cf. George Rentz, 'The Wahhābīs', in A. J. Arberry (ed.), *Religion in the Middle East*, vol. II, pp. 270–84; Henri Laoust, *Essai sur les Doctrines Sociales et Politiques de Taki-D-Din Ahmad b. Taimiya* (Cairo: Imprimerie de l'Institut Français d'Archéologie Orientale, 1939), pp. 506–40.

41 Cf. Muḥammad b. Ismāʿīl al-Amīr, *Irshād dhawī al-albāb ilā ḥaqīqat aqwāl Muḥammad b. ʿAbd al-Wahhāb*, ms. Sanaa, Gharbiyya Library, *majmūʿ* no. 107, fols. 131–42; Ḥamad al-Jāsir, 'al-Ṣilāt bayn Ṣanʿāʾ waʾl-Dirʿiyya', *al-ʿArab* 22 (1987), 433–49.

bolster a legal opinion or judgement. They held that the inherited Hādawī teachings were not properly bolstered by proof-texts in the manuals and commentaries of the school, for example the *Kitāb al-Azhār* or its principal commentary, the *Sharḥ al-Azhār*, and therefore these were to be refuted. Shawkānī excitedly describes how his studies (*qirā'āt*, lit. readings) with his teacher ᶜAbd al-Qādir al-Kawkabānī involved

> investigative discussions which he conducted in the manner of *ijtihād*, in that [proof-texts] were issued and set forth (*kānat al-qirā'āt jamīᶜuhā yajrī fīhā min al-mabāḥith al-jāriya ᶜalā namaṭ al-ijtihād fī 'l-iṣdār wa'l-īrād*).[42]

More traditional Zaydīs and Shāfiᶜīs would have contented themselves with their established law manuals: the Zaydīs had Aḥmad b. Yaḥyā al-Murtaḍā's *Kitāb al-Azhār* and the Shāfiᶜīs used Abū Shujāᶜ's *Mukhtaṣar* and Muḥyī 'al-Dīn al-Nawawī's *Minhāj*. Both schools recognised the possibility of *ijtihād*, especially the Zaydīs who had a continuous tradition of *mujtahid*s, but would have expected their members to adhere to their schools' teachings as set in these authoritative texts.[43] Shawkānī and his Traditionist peers set out to undermine this attitude and ultimately the schools themselves. This is one reason why he is seen as a reformer. The stricter adherents of the Hādawī school rejected his ambitious programme and attacked him in doctrinal as well as political terms. So far, I have not come across any Shāfiᶜī Yemenis criticising Shawkānī or the Traditionists. This is perhaps because they favoured his views and felt these would undermine those of the Hādawī *madhhab*, which they saw as a northern highland imposition.[44]

The Qāsimī Imamate

Since its founding by al-Hādī and until the rise of the Qāsimīs in the late sixteenth century, the Zaydī imamate had been an oppositional power which enjoyed varied fortune, seeing its domain expand and contract. During this period the Zaydī imams rarely held territory beyond the confines of Upper Yemen, and their politics followed a pattern of resistance to the competing Ismāᶜīlī Shīᶜite movement and the Ṣulayḥid state (1047–1140 CE) it had established or to foreign dynasties, such as the Rasūlids (1229–1454 CE) and the Ottomans (1536–1635 CE). Though frequently driven back to the town of Ṣaᶜda or some other highland stronghold like Shahāra, the imamate survived all these dynasties. Its resilience is due to the fact that its authority resides not in what we normally consider institutions of the state – such as an administrative bureaucracy and a standing army – but in the potentials

42 *Badr*, I: 363.
43 For a study of the restricted *ijtihād* that was operable within the Shāfiᶜī school see Norman Calder, 'Al-Nawawī's typology of *muftī*s and its significance for a general theory of Islamic law', *Islamic Law and Society* 3 (1996), 137–64.
44 Brinkley Messick, *The Calligraphic State* (Berkeley: University of California Press, 1993), pp. 41–2, 49.

for righteous rule and a just social order embedded in manuals of law and the Ahl al-Bayt, an ever present source of imams. The affinity that existed between the tribesmen of Upper Yemen and the imams also meant that the latter were able to raise military forces making conquest possible. Once rule was established, however, the imams' energies were absorbed by keeping the tribes loyal to the imamate or divided so as not to threaten it.

The Qāsimī imamate, established by al-Manṣūr Qāsim in 1598 CE, managed to change, for a while at least, what had hitherto been a history of opposition. This was due to the unprecedented power and territory that had accrued to the imamate after the Ottoman Turks were driven out in 1635 CE, when the Zaydīs came to control all of Yemen. The zenith of Qāsimī rule was reached during the reign of the Imam al-Mutawakkil ᶜalā Allāh Ismāᶜīl b. al-Qāsim (r. 1054–1087/1644–1676), when the imamate's influence reached as far as Dhofar in the east, Aden in the south, and ᶜAsīr and Najrān in the north. With this expansion, the imamate acquired control over predominantly Shāfiᶜī territories in Lower Yemen and on the coast. These latter regions provided a rich agricultural tax-base and ports through which moved a burgeoning coffee trade.

Yemen's monopoly on the production of coffee through the seventeenth and the first half of the eighteenth centuries, meant that the coffee trade was the most important source of revenue for the imamate and without it the Qāsimī state might never have succeeded in consolidating its rule. Never before nor after this period (seventeenth and eighteenth centuries) did the Yemeni highlands generate a cash-crop like coffee, a much-prized commodity on the international market. It is therefore not inaccurate to label the Qāsimī state 'The Coffee Imamate'. André Raymond estimates that Yemen was exporting well over 200,000 quintals of coffee at the end of the seventeenth century, and half of this went to Egypt from where it was re-exported to the Ottoman empire.[45] Dutch, English, French and American merchants were engaged also in this trade and competed with each other over preferential treatment by the Yemeni authorities.[46] Indian merchants were also active in bringing goods from South and South East Asia and returning with precious metals in exchange for what they had sold in Yemen.[47] One eighteenth-century merchant describes the nature of this commerce aptly by saying:

[45] André Raymond, 'Le café du Yémen et l'Égypte', *Chroniques Yéménites* 3 (1995), 16–25. Raymond states that by the end of the eighteenth century, coffee represented in real terms one third of all imports into Egypt and a quarter of all its exports to Europe. It was also the single most important economic activity during the period of Ottoman rule over Egypt. For further information on coffee in Yemen see Hans Becker *et al.*, (eds.), *Kaffee aus Arabien* (Wiesbaden: Franz Steiner, 1979) and Michel Tuchscherer (ed.), *Le Commerce du Café avant l'Ère des Plantations Coloniales* (Cairo: Institut Français d'Archéologie Orientale, 2001).

[46] Cf. La Roque, *A Voyage to Arabia the Happy* (London: Golden Ball, for G. Strathan and R. Williamson, 1726), pp. 94f.; George, Viscount Valentia, *Voyages and Travels to India, Ceylon, the Red Sea, Abyssinia and Egypt*, 3 vols., (London: printed for William Miller, 1809), vol. II, pp. 212–13, 363–78.

[47] Ashin Das Gupta, *Indian Merchants and the Decline of Surat c. 1700–1750* (New Delhi: Manohar Publishers, 1994), p. 73 and passim.

> The riches of Yemen may be considered as solely owing to its coffee, for it is from the sale of that article, that its merchants receive [Spanish] dollars in Egypt, with which they purchase the manufactures and spices of India.[48]

The rates of taxation on both imports and exports during the Qāsimī period varied considerably, privileging at times European merchants in order to encourage greater export of coffee. The historical sources are not precise about the amounts accruing to the state coffers or whether these sums were stable. Yemen was clearly important regionally at this historical juncture and the imams behaved as regional potentates, maintaining relations with a number of pre-modern imperial powers, like the Mughals in India and the Ottomans.

The imamate, which had largely relied on the northern tribes in its expansion, had to link the newly acquired regions to the tribal north, where lay the armed force on which the imamate depended.[49] The link proved hard to sustain and preoccupied every Qāsimī imam. Despite these difficulties, administrative, tax collecting and judicial systems had to be devised which gave the imamate state-like qualities it had never before developed fully. A direct borrowing from Ottoman administrative structures is difficult to identify from the sources, but these were probably the models for the infrastructure the Qāsimīs established.[50] In the process, a change in the nature of imamic authority and rule took place. The imams became, as their detractors said, more like kings, and a discernible shift occurred from what had hitherto been a 'summons' (*da^c^wa*) to something more like a state (*dawla*). The imams, for example, began paying for a standing army. Carsten Niebuhr, a Danish traveller who visited Yemen in 1762–3 CE, reports that the imam of the time maintained a standing army of 4,000 infantry and 1,000 cavalry.[51] Many of the commanders (*amīrs*) of the imamic forces were slaves of Abyssinian origin, which gave the imams some degree of autonomy and lessened their dependence on tribal arms. For important military operations, however, they were still dependent on the tribes and continued to pay them important subsidies.

The Qāsimī imams also established an administrative system in which ministers were given their own jurisdictions, and under whom operated a number of appointed governors (*^c^āmil* or *wālī*). These governors in turn were responsible for collecting taxes and the duties from the ports and the regions they administered. Control over taxation, however, was problematic for the imams because of their inability to control tax-collectors. The administrative system was characterised by

48 Valentia, *Voyages and Travels*, vol. II, p. 378.

49 Paul Dresch, *Tribes, Government and History in Yemen* (Oxford: Clarendon Press, 1989), p. 200.

50 For an excellent study on the history of Ottoman rule in Yemen until their expulsion, see Frédérique Soudan, *Le Yémen Ottoman* (Cairo: Institut Français d'Archéologie Orientale, 1999). One borrowing from the Ottomans by the Qāsimīs, for example, was the creation of the post of Commander of the Pilgrimage to Mecca (*amīr al-ḥajj*), cf. Soudan, pp. 325–7 and ^c^Abd Allāh al-Jirāfī, *al-Muqtaṭaf min tārīkh al-Yaman* (Beirut: Manshūrāt al-^c^Aṣr al-Ḥadīth, 1987), p. 227.

51 M. Niebuhr, *Travels through Arabia and Other Countries in the East*, Robert Heron (trans.), 2 vols. (Edinburgh: R. Morison and Son, 1792), vol. II, p. 89. Reporting in the early 1800s, or some forty years after Niebuhr, Valentia estimates the imam's forces at 3,000 infantry and 600 cavalry, cf. Valentia, *Voyages and Travels*, vol. II, p. 381.

nepotism and exploitation of the peasantry (*raᶜāyā*), as well as constant rebellions by either appointed governors – many of whom were close relatives of the imams – or local potentates against the central authority. A judicial system was also organised under the direction of a chief judge (*qāḍī al-quḍāt*). The changes and developments which the Qāsimīs brought to the imamate gave it 'the form of an elaborate dynastic state' without securing 'the means to support itself or to transmit authority without dispute'.[52]

Shawkānī's biography

Muḥammad b. ᶜAlī b. Muḥammad al-Shawkānī was born a Zaydī-Hādawī in the village of Hijrat Shawkān, a day's walk south-east of Sanaa on 28 Dhū al-Qaᶜda 1173/12 July 1760. A scion of a scholarly family of the tribe of Khawlān, he belonged to the *qaḍī* estate. In the biography he wrote on his father, Shawkānī proudly traces his family back to Qaḥṭān, the eponym of the Southern Arabs, while emphasising that his ancestors had been among al-Hādī's supporters and had valiantly supported the Qāsimī imams in their war (*jihād*) against the Ottomans.

Shawkānī's father, ᶜAlī b. Muḥammad (d. 1211/1797), was a learned man who was appointed by Imam al-Mahdī al-ᶜAbbās as a judge in the lands of Khawlān and later given a post in Sanaa.[53] He served as a judge of the imamate for forty years, and supported his son financially until the latter became a court official in his own right. By all accounts, Shawkānī's father was committed to Hādawī legal teachings, but later in life, under the tutelage of his son, he was converted to Traditionist views. A story is narrated by al-Shijnī (one of Shawkānī's biographers) about a precocious young Shawkānī, who, when studying with his father the *Sharḥ al-Azhār* asked him which of the conflicting opinions listed in the work was the one to follow. His father answered that Ibn al-Murtaḍā's opinion, i.e., that of the Zaydī-Hādawī author, was the accepted one. It is reported that Shawkānī was not satisfied with this answer and therefore sought to study with the most learned scholar of the age, Sayyid ᶜAbd al-Qādir b. Aḥmad al-Kawkabānī,[54] to learn for himself how to distinguish between various opinions.[55]

Unlike other scholars who attained his rank, Shawkānī never left Sanaa in pursuit of knowledge, and, surprisingly, he did not perform the pilgrimage to Mecca. He explains that his parents never gave him permission. His principal teacher ᶜAbd al-Qādir al-Kawkabānī, however, had traveled throughout Yemen and spent two years studying in Mecca and Medina. Ibn al-Amīr, who had been ᶜAbd al-Qādir al-Kawkabānī's teacher, had also studied in the Hijaz, where he was exposed to ideas

[52] Dresch, *Tribes*, p. 217. [53] *Badr*, I: 478–85.
[54] Cf. *Badr*, I: 360–9.
[55] Muḥammad al-Shijnī, *Ḥayāt al-imām al-Shawkānī al-musammā Kitāb al-Tiqṣār*, Muḥammad b. ᶜAlī al-Akwaᶜ(ed.) (Sanaa: Maktabat al-Jīl al-Jadīd, 1990), p. 143 (hereinafter *al-Tiqṣār*).

and circles of teachers and students from all over the Islamic world. Shawkānī's exposure, therefore, was not parochial by the standards of his time; rather, through his teachers he was aware of the most contemporary ideas and trends in the wider Muslim world.

At the age of twenty Shawkānī was living in Sanaa and was issuing *fatwā*s (consultative legal opinions) to those who came to him from far and wide, most notably from the Tihāma. It is my conjecture that in doing this, Traditionist scholars like him were juridically and religiously knitting together the Shāfiᶜī regions of Yemen with the Zaydī highlands, and more specifically with the seat of government in Sanaa. Shawkānī makes the point in his autobiography that he did not charge for issuing *fatwā*s, 'as he had received knowledge freely and would impart it likewise'. He also started teaching students from an early age, mainly through the instruction methods of *qirāʾa* (recitational-reading) or *samāᶜ* (audition).[56] The image he conveys of himself is a traditional one: that of being a node or link in a multitude of chains of transmission emanating from the Prophet, in the case of ḥadīth, but also from authors of many books in the numerous sciences, all of which he could transmit and which collectively constituted the living body of Islamic and human knowledge.

Speaking in the third person, Shawkānī says of himself that he dispensed with *taqlīd* and became a *mujtahid muṭlaq* (an unrestricted religious authority) before reaching the age of thirty. At thirty-four, he was still living in his father's house, involved mainly with teaching, issuing *fatwā*s and writing. ᶜAbd Allāh al-Ḥibshī has compiled a list of 250 titles attributed to him.[57] Amongst these are short and long treatises, letters, *fatwā*s, and multi-volume compendia many of which have now been edited and published. The most famous of these compendia are:

1) *Nayl al-awṭār fī sharḥ muntaqā al-akhbār* (Attaining the Aims in Commenting on the Choicest Traditions). This was completed in 1210/1795 and consists of a law manual based on ḥadīth.
2) *Wabl al-ghamām* (Torrent of the Clouds) which was completed in 1213/1798 and represents a critical legal commentary on an important Zaydī ḥadīth-based legal work.
3) *Fatḥ al-qadīr* (Victory of the Almighty) which was completed in 1229/1814 and represents his Qurʾānic exegesis.
4) *al-Sayl al-jarrār* (The Raging Torrent) which was completed in 1235/1819–20 and consists of a critical legal commentary on *Kitāb al-Azhār*.

As for teaching, Shawkānī claims he taught thirteen separate lessons per day in such disciplines as Qurʾānic exegesis (*tafsīr*), principles of jurisprudence (*uṣūl al-fiqh*), rhetoric (*maᶜānī wa bayān*), grammar (*naḥw*), and law (*fiqh*).

[56] Cf. Messick, *Calligraphic State*, pp. 90–2.
[57] Cf. ᶜAbd Allāh al-Ḥibshī, 'Thabat bi-muʾallafāt al-ᶜallāma Muḥammad b. ᶜAlī al-Shawkānī', *Dirāsāt Yamaniyya* 3 (Sanaa: Markaz al-Dirāsāt wa ʾl-Buḥūth al-Yamanī, 1979), pp. 65–86.

On 1 Rajab 1209/22 January 1795 the chief judge (*qāḍī al-quḍāt*) of the imamate, Yaḥyā b. Ṣāliḥ al-Saḥūlī, died and Shawkānī was called upon by the Imam al-Manṣūr ᶜAlī to assume the chief judgeship.[58] His candidacy seems to have been based on the general recognition of his precedence in the scholarly community, and the sources make no mention of other candidates. For a week, Shawkānī says, he dithered about this offer, partly because of the time it would take away from his teaching and studies. Another factor may have been the widespread sentiment amongst Islamic scholars which disapproved of ulema associating with or accepting employment from rulers.[59] However, after the persistent insistence of peers and colleagues that he should accept, lest someone less capable take up the post, Shawkānī says he relented and became *qāḍī al-quḍāt*, a position he held for nearly forty years, from 1795 CE until his death in 1834 CE. In this time he became the supreme judge in the imamate (*marjiᶜ*), and the *fatwā*s and judgements he issued set precedents which other judges were meant to follow. He became responsible for appointing judges throughout the realm and for supervising them. Acting as the imam's secretary, he answered all correspondence on the latter's behalf and seems to have determined doctrinal and juridical orthodoxy. Politically, too, he played a very important role by mediating in disputes between various members of the ruling house and making policy recommendations to imams.[60]

Despite his official obligations, Shawkānī continued teaching, particularly his own works, and established a reputation as a reformist scholar who had garnered an impressive number of *ijāza*s and transmission chains (*isnād*s) for a multitude of written works. This led students, from Yemen as well as from other places, to flock to Sanaa to study with him and receive certificates. He was proud of Sanaa's scholarly community and claims that it was unlike other places, where *ijtihād* was no longer practised. In praising Sanaa and its scholars he says:

> It is rare to find in a city what can now be found in Sanaa, namely the return of its scholars to the sound [texts] of the Legislator, their not relying upon mere opinion (*raʾy*) and their rejection of the schools (*madhāhib*) when clear evidence is provided. This is a merit and a virtue which is hardly known in other countries, except in the odd individual.[61]

Sanaa's closeness to Mecca must have played a role in attracting foreign scholars who were either on their way to or returning from the pilgrimage. The Indian scholar, Shaykh ᶜAbd al-Ḥaqq al-Banārisī (d. 1276/1860), describes coming to Sanaa in 1238/1823 specifically to study with Shawkānī and to receive certificates from him. He says:

58 For al-Saḥūlī's biography see *Badr*, II: 333–8.

59 In the biographical dictionaries and historical chronicles it is considered praiseworthy not to have accepted the blandishments of rulers as these are considered corrupting influences which can compromise a scholar's character, credibility and reputation. See for example the biography of al-Ḥasan b. Aḥmad al-Jalāl in Ismāᶜīl b. al-Akwaᶜ, *Hijar al-ᶜilm wa maᶜāqiluh fī ʾl-Yaman*, 5 vols. (Beirut: Dār al-Fikr al-Muᶜāṣir, 1995), vol. I, p. 345 (hereinafter *Hijar al-ᶜilm*). Cf. A. J. Wensinck, 'The refused dignity', in T. W. Arnold and Reynold A. Nicholson (eds.), *A Volume of Oriental Studies presented to Edward G. Browne* (Cambridge University Press, 1922), pp. 491–9.

60 Cf. *Badr*, I: 465–7.

61 *Adab al-ṭalab*, p. 78.

> I left the city of God's Messenger [Medina] – may God's peace and blessings be upon him – heading for Sanaa the Preserved in order to visit the lordly scholar Muḥammad b. ᶜAlī al-Shawkānī. I endured the travails of travel and traversed the wildernesses, seas and [endured] the calamities of rain until I reached the mentioned city. I entered one of its houses and then wrote him a letter and sent it to him with some people. He beckoned me immediately and treated me with great honour and asked me about my age and what I had studied. Then he gave me copies of his works and asked me to read these. I read most of them and would visit him on the two days he gave lessons, Mondays and Thursdays, and would 'hear from him' (*asmaᶜ min-hu*). The Shaykh [Shawkānī] would solve all the obscure and difficult matters in a correct manner. Whilst I was in this state, I was overcome with fever and remained so for a long time. Then God – the Exalted – cured me of my illness. The Shaykh [Shawkānī] then decided to travel, so I went to him and bid him farewell and this was on Friday 10 Jumāda al-Ākhira 1238 [21 February 1823]. He was friendly towards me and sympathized with me so that I read with him most of his *musalsalāt* [ḥadīths with a shared special feature in each link of the chain of transmission back to the Prophet]. Then he issued me with a certificate for all his *marwiyyāt* [works which he could transmit], and he wrote me a certificate in his own noble hand and gave me his register (*thabat*) [of *isnāds* entitled] *Itḥāf al-akābir fī isnād al-dafātir* and told me to copy it.[62]

Fortunately, al-Banārisī has also left a copy of the *ijāza* given him by Shawkānī which shows the modalities of this system of education and transmission.

> In the name of God the Merciful the Compassionate. Praise be to God. Muḥammad b. ᶜAlī Shawkānī – may God pardon them both [i.e., Muḥammad and his father ᶜAlī] – says while praising God the Exalted and asking for blessings on His Messenger, his Family and Companions: I have given an *ijāza* to the Shaykh, the scholar, Abū ᵓal-Faḍl ᶜAbd al-Ḥaqq son of the Shaykh, the scholar, Muḥammad Faḍl Allāh al-Muḥammadī al-Hindī – may God through his kindness and generosity increase his benefits and make useful his knowledge – all that is contained in this register, which I have compiled and called *Itḥāf al-akābir bi-isnād al-dafātir*. Let him transmit from me all that is in it of the books of Islam, regardless of the different genres which he sees therein. He is capable of doing this, and I do not place on him any condition for he is more worthy and lofty than that. I have asked him to include me in his future invocations, during my lifetime and after I die. I have written this on Friday Jumāda al-Ākhira of the year 1238 of the Prophet's hijra – on him be the best of blessings and salutations.[63]

Shawkānī was perhaps most active politically during the reign of the last imam under whom he served, al-Mahdī ᶜAbd Allāh. He accompanied this imam on a number of military campaigns, mainly in Lower Yemen, where Shāfiᶜī scholars, as well as like-minded Traditionists, took delight in studying with and receiving

62 ᶜAbd al-Ḥayy al-Laknawī, *al-Iᶜlām bi-man fī tārīkh al-Hind min al-aᶜlām* (Rāᵓī Barīlī: Maktabat Dār ᶜArafāt, 1413/1992–3), vol. VII, p. 268 (= *Nuzhat al-khawāṭir wa-bahjat al-masāmiᶜ waᵓl-nawāẓir*).

63 al-Laknawī, *Nuzhat al-khawāṭir*, pp. 268–9. Al-Banārisī also received an *ijāza* from Sayyid ᶜAbd Allāh b. Muḥammad al-Amīr (Ibn al-Amīr's son) in Sanaa which is quoted on the following pages. Its emphasis is on the transmission of the canonical ḥadīth collections, highlighting the principal disciplinary concerns of these scholars.

ijāzas from him. It is to one of these outings that al-Banārisī was referring when he said that Shawkānī had decided to travel.

Shawkānī died in Jumādā al-Ākhira 1250/October 1834, one year before Imam al-Mahdī ᶜAbd Allāh passed away. He left behind one son, Aḥmad (d. 1281/1864), who later took over as *qāḍī al-quḍat* but led a more turbulent life than his father did, a reflection of the troubled political situation in Yemen in the latter half of the nineteenth century. Aḥmad was imprisoned by the strict Hādawī imam al-Nāṣīr ᶜAbd Allāh b. al-Ḥasan (d. 1256/1840), who rose to power in 1252/1837. Later he became *qāḍī al-quḍāt* again but eventually the political situation led him to give up the post to become an independent authority in his own right in the village of al-Rawḍa without any imamic sanction. He did not have his father's scholarly abilities or stature and is known to have produced only one short treatise.[64] It is noteworthy, however, that the hereditary model of imamic succession, with son succeeding father, now replicated itself in official posts, regardless of qualification or merit. Shawkānī's lineage died out because Aḥmad did not leave surviving sons. His books, however, have been transmitted diligently to the present and the role he played in the imamate continues to animate and inspire much discussion among Yemenis today.

The chapters that follow are organised in chronological order and around particular aspects of Shawkānī's life and thought. Chapter one is a detailed account of the rise of the seventeenth-century Qāsimī state and its relationship to traditional Zaydī forms of rule. Here, I argue that seventeenth-century imams lived up to the ideal posited by Zaydī law: they were learned men and able military commanders. Their authority was largely based on their ability to personify convincingly Zaydī political theory, with its demand that imams be men of the pen and the sword. This period (1635–86 CE) represents the pinnacle of Zaydi power since the arrival of Zaydism in the country in the early tenth century CE.

Chapter two looks to the eighteenth century, a period of marked social, political and institutional change. The eighteenth-century Qāsimī imams lacked the qualities evident in their seventeenth-century predecessors; they behaved more like kings than imams. They sought religious and legal sanction to establish dynastic and patrimonial forms of rule but Zaydī scholarly circles were unwilling to provide this. The sanction materialised from within Sunnī Traditionist scholarly circles who were willing to uphold dynastic rule and to maintain and operate a bureaucracy. With this established, the Qāsimī imamate shed to a considerable extent its Zaydī identity and adopted more mainstream Islamic attitudes regarding authority and governance.

Chapter three is a detailed study of Shawkānī's legal and pedagogical ideas. I situate him within several distinct intellectual traditions, local and pan-Islamic, but illustrate how his particular synthesis of these streams places him firmly within

[64] Muḥammad b. Muḥammad Zabāra, *Nayl al-waṭar min tarājim rijāl al-Yaman fī ʾl-qarn al-thālith ᶜashar*, 2 vols. in one, (Sanaa: Markaz al-Dirāsāt wa ʾl-Abḥāth al-Yamaniyya, n.d.), vol. I, pp. 215–23 (hereinafter *Nayl*).

the Sunnī Traditionist camp. His distinctive vision of social order is highlighted through the hermeneutic and pedagogical systems he elaborated and which were aimed at reproducing *mujtahid*s in serial fashion – men who could run the judicial administration of his ideal Muslim polity.

Chapter four delineates how Shawkānī went about implementing this vision upon acceding to the post of chief judge. He promoted like-minded jurists to positions of authority and sought to reform Yemeni society. Two examples of this reform project are provided. The first involved repeated attempts to expel the Jews from Yemen, upon the failure of which he argued for the imposition of legal restrictions on them. The second example concerns his condemnation of the cult of saints and the practice of visiting graves, prominent features in the Shāfiᶜī regions.

Chapter five is the first of two chapters which deal with the clashes which took place between the Zaydīs and the Sunnī Traditionists as a consequence of the power the latter now wielded in the imamate. The initial encounter centres on a dispute over whether a Muslim may curse certain Companions of the Prophet Muḥammad, namely those who did not side with ᶜAlī b. Abī Ṭālib in the matter of the succession. The history of the doctrines pertaining to this issue is presented as well as a treatise Shawkānī wrote in which he sought to establish that the Zaydī position was against cursing any of the Companions.

Chapter six describes a vituperative reponse by a strict Zaydī to Shawkānī's treatise and the political and social turmoil that ensued from the clash between Shawkānī and his strict Zaydī detractors.

Chapter seven traces Shawkani's legacy into the modern period and shows how his students and later adherents of his views perpetuated it until the present day. I illustrate how the imams of the Ḥamīd al-Dīn dynasty, who ruled Yemen from 1918 till 1962 after the Turkish interregnum, continued many of the Qāsimī forms of rule initiated by Shawkānī. More important, perhaps, was the fact that these imams realised Shawkānī's appeal amongst Muslims outside Yemen, and the potential for presenting his teachings as a Zaydī form of Sunnism, thereby making Zaydism appear more normative. With respect to Shawkānī, the republican regime that has ruled Yemen since 1962 followed some of the trajectories initiated by the imams they overthrew, but it has gone further by giving him iconic status for reasons which are described here too.

Yemeni studies

The history of Yemen, be it political, social or intellectual, and in particular during the Qāsimī period, remains understudied. Most of the primary sources are still unedited manuscripts distributed in private and public libraries and many of these are difficult of access. The existing historical works, whether by western or Arab authors, fall largely into the category of *histoire événementielle*, that is, annalistic histories with screed presentations of facts about kings, battles, droughts, earthquakes and monetary fluctuations etc. Yemen did not open up to researchers until the 1970s after the civil war that raged during the 1960s had ended. Recent studies have been undertaken mainly by anthropologists, some of whom, such as Dresch and Messick, have strong historical and documentary sensibilities. Historians, however, have yet to engage with the history of Yemen for the period from the seventeenth century, and it is my hope that this study will offer a preliminary roadmap for the country's political and religious history.

CHAPTER 1

Charismatic Authority: the Qāsimī Imamate in the Seventeenth Century

By the late eighteenth century, two separate shifts in the Qāsimī state had become fully actualised. The first was the institutionalisation of imamic authority through formalised customs and practices and the development of bureaucratic structures. Patrimonial forms of rule evolved and replaced a system of government in which authority had been based on, and had emanated from, the charismatic presence of an imam as the embodiment of the Zaydī ideal. The second and related shift was a gradual doctrinal and ideological move away from Zaydism in its Hādawī guise towards Sunnism. By the eighteenth century, the imamate cultivated Traditionist scholars like Shawkānī and offered them patronage, whilst Hādawī scholars, especially staunch ones, lost favour.

Although the factors impelling these two shifts may not necessarily have been the same, the shifts themselves are not separate. The 'routinisation' of imamic authority was brought about in part because the imams no longer lived up to the ideal posited in Hādawī teachings. They became more like sultans and less like imams. The doctrinal shift to Sunnī views probably came about as a result of increased interaction between Zaydīs and Shāfiᶜī Sunnīs, who were the majority subjects in the realm. Sunnī teachings, unlike those of Hādawī Zaydism, countenanced the rule of less than ideal men and forbad revolt or rebellion against them. In addition, the resource-base of the imamate was now centered primarily on the Shāfiᶜī regions, and through trade in the Indian Ocean and Red Sea, on a wider world in which traditional Zaydism held little currency.

This chapter aims to show what the Qāsimī rulers were like in the seventeenth century and contrast them with their eighteenth century counterparts, thereby highlighting the first shift mentioned above. Until the beginning of the eighteenth century, Traditionist scholars like Shawkānī represented a small minority of Zaydī-born scholars, whereas by the close of that century they had become numerous and were powerful in determining religious doctrine through the judicial and religious structures of the state.

The Archetype of the Zaydī Imam

In historical Zaydism, before the Qāsimīs, the imam, in his capacity as a learned, pious, courageous and militarily effective leader, was the focus of all political authority. Indeed, much of the support he could garner, whether from the tribes or scholars, rested on those qualities. The life chronicles (*siyar*) and biographical dictionaries (*tarājim*) illustrate this point well. The classical archetype was, of course, al-Hādī ilā al-Ḥaqq Yaḥyā b. al-Ḥusayn, the first Zaydī imam in Yemen. One of al-Hādī's poems reveals the bases of his claim to being imam and reflects the nature of the institution.

> The horse and every spear // testify to my tenacity, prowess and courage
> Truly Dhū ᵓal-Faqār bears witness that I // gave its two blades to drink of the blood of vile folk
> Time and time again I quenched its thirst in every confrontation, // seeking to avenge the Faith and Islam
> So that Dhū ᵓal-Faqār recalled battles waged // by him who possessed power, the leader, the noble one
> My grandfather is ᶜAlī, he of transcendent virtues and perspicacity, // the sword of God and the smasher of the idols
> The true brother of the Apostle and the best whom the earth ever covered up, // after the Prophet, the imam of every imam[1]

In addition to describing al-Hādī's military campaigns, his *sīra* describes the nature of his rule, emphasizing in particular his humility (*tawāḍuᶜ*) and piety (*waraᶜ*). It is reported, for example, that he would salute all people he encountered, regardless of age, social class or origin, and he would personally listen and attend to the complaints of aged women and *dhimmī*s. In terms of piety it is reported that al-Hādī refused to consume any monies collected as taxes in Yemen, and was diligent in making sure that his people committed no financial misdeeds or mismanagement. According to Islamic law, *sayyid*s were prohibited from consuming the *zakāt*, because it was felt that they would be polluted in so doing.[2] This element of probity is reflected in a report about one of al-Hādī's tax collectors, Muḥammad b. Sulaymān, who came to him one evening with a bag full of dinars and dirhams from the *zakāt* tax and asked him to keep this in safe keeping under his bed. When al-Hādī discovered the contents of the bag, he quickly said: 'Keep it away from me...; by God should I ever become needy of what is collected from the *ṣadaqa*

[1] ᶜAlī b. Muḥammad al-ᶜAlawī, *Sīrat al-Hādī ilā al-ḥaqq Yaḥyā b. al-Ḥusayn*, Suhayl Zakkār (ed.) (Beirut: Dār al-Fikr, 1981), pp. 223–4. The poem was translated by A. B. R. D. Eagle, *Ghāyat al-amānī and the life and times of al-Hādī Yaḥyā b. al-Ḥusayn*, M.Litt thesis, University of Durham (1990), p. 9.

[2] Cf. Wilferd Madelung, 'The Hāshimiyyāt of al-Kumayt and Hāshimī Shiᶜism', *Studia Islamica* 70 (1989), 24–6. Receiving the *zakāt* is considered polluting because the *zakāt* is perceived to be 'the filth of the people' (*min awsākh al-nās*), since Muslims purify themselves by paying it as a religious duty. The issue of whether *sayyid*s are allowed to take from the *zakāt* for their personal use is a recurring issue of controversy in Yemeni history. The more upright imams would habitually condemn it, but it was obviously a common practice.

or *ᶜushr* and I were then to find carrion, I would consume the carrion and never consume anything from the former'.[3]

A succinct doctrinal statement about the qualities a Zaydī imam must have can be found in a legal work by the Caspian imam Abū Ṭālib al-Nāṭiq (d. 424/1033), one of al-Hādī's followers, who says:

> After [the rule of] the Commander of the faithful, 'Alī (peace be upon him), the imam, whose commands must be obeyed by Muslims, has to be from the offspring of the Messenger of God (peace and blessings be upon him). These offspring are [those who descend from] al-Ḥasan and al-Ḥusayn... He must be learned (*ᶜālim*) in the principles of religion (*uṣūl al-dīn*) and its branches (*furūᶜ*), by which is meant that in addition to his knowledge of the principles of religion he must be a *mujtahid* in branches [of the law]. He must be pious and God-fearing (*wariᶜ wa taqī*), by which is meant he must fulfil the canonical obligations and desist from all that is prohibited. He must be upright (*ᶜadl*) and pleasing in his ways [to God]. He must be courageous and a leader, and by this is meant that he must be brave and knowledgeable in the arts of war and in leading the people, in addition to being capable of raising armies and leading these in battle. He must be independent in arranging the interests of the subjects (*raᶜiyya*). He must be generous in allocating rights properly. He is not to be stingy in spending money in the areas which are advantageous for Muslims and must not hinder this from happening. He who combines in himself all these attributes can be a candidate for the imamate. If he opposes the evildoers (*ẓālimūn*) and presents himself to undertake the duties of the imams in leading the community (*umma*) and he makes a summons to support and pay allegiance to him, then let him rise to accomplish this as best as possible, for his imamate has been confirmed and Muslims are bound to give him their allegiance and to obey him in all matters in which an imam may command his followers.

Once in power, Abū Ṭālib al-Nāṭiq describes the imam's obligations and duties in the following manner:

> The imam must command the good and forbid evil and provide justice to the wronged against the wrongdoer. He must enforce the canonical penalties (*ḥudūd*) on the one who is deserving regardless of whether the person is of high or low status, a relative or a stranger. He must show anger to those who disobey God, even if it is his father, son or some other relative or stranger. He must collect the canonical taxes (*amwāl Allāh*) from all who should pay these and then spend it appropriately without tyranny or partiality. He must judge his subjects according to the laws of God Almighty, be just in his judgement and be impartial in distributing the booty (*fayʾ*) amongst them... He must bring close to him the people of religion and virtue and attend to the weak and poor, protecting and teaching them enough about religion. He must allow easy access to himself for his subjects and must not screen himself from them (*yusahhil ḥijābahu ᶜalā raᶜiyyatihi wa lā yaḥtajib ᶜanhum*) to the extent that this may result in harming their affairs...[4]

[3] al-ᶜAlawī, *Sīrat al-hādī*, p. 61.

[4] Al-Nāṭiq biʾl-Ḥaqq Yaḥyā b. al-Ḥusayn al-Hārūnī, *Kitāb al-Taḥrīr*, Muḥammad ᶜIzzān (ed.), 2vols. (Sanaa: Maktabat Badr, 1997), vol. II, pp. 653–5 and R. Strothmann, *Das Staatsrecht der Zaiditen* (Strassburg: Karl J. Trübner, 1912), pp. 104–5.

Imams were expected to live up to this ideal of probity, humility and charismatic authority. It is reported that some did. For example, Imam al-Qāsim b. ᶜAlī al-ᶜIyānī (d. 393/1003) is said to have died without bequeathing a single dinar or dirham as inheritance, except for his weapons, pack animals and clothes, all of which would not cover his debts.[5] Another imam, al-Muṭahhar b. Yaḥyā al-Murtaḍā (d. 697/1298), is said to have eaten coarse food and to have worn rough clothing. After teaching his students, al-Muṭahhar would go with them to gather firewood and would carry some of it back himself.[6]

Yet another example of a Zaydī imam fitting the classical archetype is al-Nāṣir Muḥammad Ṣalāḥ al-Dīn (d. 793/1390). He assumed the reins of power when his father, al-Mahdī ᶜAlī b. Muḥammad (d. 773/1371), became hemiplegic (*fālij*) and therefore lost the qualification to remain imam (*saqaṭa ᶜanhu al-taklīf*). After his father's death a year later, al-Nāṣir 'made a summons in his own name' (*daᶜā ilā nafsih*) and met with the ulema and called upon them to recognise him as imam. One thousand three hundred of the ulema met with him, tested him and upon finding him 'complete' (*kāmil*) decided unanimously to accept him as imam and follow his opinions (*ajmaᶜ raʾyuhum ᶜalā taqlīdihi*).[7] By declaring al-Nāṣir *kāmil*, the ulema found him to have all the necessary qualifications stipulated by Hādawī law – these are usually considered to be fourteen in number.[8] However, their recognition was not in and of itself the deciding factor in establishing his imamate. According to the Hādawī view, a candidate becomes imam by virtue of his own perception or, as Messick has put it:

> an imam is meant to be the sort of man who, upon recognizing his own exemplary qualities and perhaps on the urging of his fellows, rises up and makes himself known, actively and even aggressively asserting his call and claim (*daᶜwa*) to be the imam.[9]

The Zaydī chronicles and biographical dictionaries stress the personal attributes of the imams, most notably their learning, piety, probity and courage. For example, a contemporary supporter of al-Nāṣir's describes him as having attained in the sciences a rank above that of *ijtihād*, as attested in part by his many written works.[10] He also tells us that al-Nāṣir's daily routine consisted of spending at least two-thirds

[5] Muḥammad b. Muḥammad Zabāra, *Aʾimmat al-Yaman* (Taᶜizz: Matbaᶜat al-Nāṣir al-Nāṣiriyya, 1952), p. 82.

[6] Ibid., p. 198. [7] Ibid., pp. 260f.

[8] Cf. Aḥmad b. Yaḥyā al-Murtaḍā, *Kitāb al-Azhār fī fiqh al-aʾimma al-aṭhār*, 5th ed. (n.p., 1982), pp. 313–15 (hereinafter *Azhār*).

[9] Messick, *Calligraphic State*, p. 38.

[10] Al-Nāṣir is noted for a commentary on one of Zamakhsharī's works in which he elaborated on its linguistic aspects. Cf. Zabāra, *Aʾimmat al-Yaman*, p. 261–2 citing al-Hādī b. Ibrāhīm al-Wazīr's work *Kāshif al-ghumma fī ʾl-dhabb ᶜan sīrat imām al-umma*. Al-Nāṣir's works are not extant according to Ḥibshī, cf. ᶜAbd Allāh b. Muḥammad al-Ḥibshī, *Maṣādir al-fikr al-ᶜArabī al-Islāmī fī ʾl-Yaman* (Sanaa: Markaz al-Dirāsāt al-Yamaniyya, n.d.), pp. 577–8. Interestingly, al-Naṣir insisted on the use of the Sunnī ḥadīth works, viz. the *Ṣaḥīḥayn*. The issue of qualification arose after al-Nāṣir's death when his son, al-Manṣūr ᶜAlī b. Muḥammad, claimed the imamate for himself despite being less qualified in religious learning than another contender, the famous Aḥmad b. Yaḥyā al-Murtaḍā (d. 840/1436). Al-Manṣūr only became imam after defeating his opponents in battle. Cf. Zabāra, *Aʾimmat al-Yaman*, pp. 280–2; *Badr*, I: 487.

of the night in prayer; at daybreak, he would pray the supererogatory prayers followed by the obligatory ones and then sit facing Mecca in prayer and recitation. At sunrise, he would embark on dealing with the affairs of the Muslims and other religious matters, which involved studying the religious sciences. At noon, he would perform the supererogatory prayers followed by the obligatory ones. He would then look into the affairs of Islam (*maṣāliḥ al-islām*) and the defence of its borders (*sadd al-thughūr*) and answer any letters which he had received. He would perform the remaining prayers, at their alloted times, and continue dealing with affairs of *jihād* and those of the believers. He would sleep after nightfall, but only for a short period, rising to repeat the routine. Al-Nāṣir was, besides, a warrior. He defeated the Rasūlids in Zabīd in 777/1376 and later took hostage their leading officer.[11] According to Shawkānī, he also fought the Ismāʿīlīs (referred to by the Zaydīs as al-Bāṭiniyya, and considered by them to be heretics), 'destroying their foundations, shedding their blood and looting their property'.[12] Another source, Yaḥyā b. al-Ḥusayn's *Anbāʾal-zaman*, attributes to al-Nāṣir the construction of the ablution areas in the Great Mosque of Sanaa as well as providing for its carpeting (*firāsh*). The *Anbāʾ* also says that he would go for outings on some nights with his companions to check on the condition of the people, and if he found that someone was deserving of the legal punishment (*ḥadd*) he would carry it out.[13]

The image one gets from the Zaydī sources of an imam like al-Nāṣir is perhaps in part idealised, but central to their description of a 'summons' is the personality of the imam whose attributes count for both its legitimacy and effectiveness. The political structures they established are not to be understood in terms of a state (*dawla*); rather, theirs was a *daʿwa* whose fortunes followed those of the imam. As a result, these *daʿwa*s had an evanescent and terminal quality. Sometimes they disappeared as quickly as they were established, e.g., if the imam fell short of a qualification or if a more qualified candidate challenged successfully the incumbent's claim to rule. One sees in the case of al-Nāṣir that it is through his piety, knowledge and courage that Islam is safeguarded and defended; the Sharīʿa is imposed through his personal vigilance, as exemplified by his nightly outings. It is the quality of the man which is stressed and no mention is made of the trappings of state. There are, for example, no mentions of formal processions, ceremonies and no retinue of guards or bureaucrats to administer the state and enforce its injunctions, no emblems or symbols of sovereignty. Mention is made of judges of the imams in the various areas and towns of Yemen, but their influence depended as much on their own piety and learning as on their relationship with the imam.[14]

The institution of the imamate was inherently unstable. The establishment of localised dynasties was attempted by the descendants of a number of noted imams,

[11] Cf. al-Ḥibshī, *Maṣādir al-fikr*, p. 577. [12] *Badr*, II: 226.

[13] Cited in Zabāra, *Aʾimmat al-Yaman*, pp. 262–3.

[14] The most notable example of one of al-Nāṣir's representatives was ʿAbd Allāh b. al-Ḥasan al-Dawwārī (d. 800/1397) who was based in Ṣaʿda. Al-Dawwārī was one of the most learned men of his day and was nicknamed the 'Sultan of the ulema'. His recognition of both imams al-Nāṣir and his son al-Manṣūr counted for more than that of any other scholar in the validation of their respective rules as imams.

who refused to recognize the *da^c was* made by other imams. An early example of this were the descendants of al-Hādī who based themselves in Ṣa^cda and resisted Imam al-Qāsim b. ^cAlī al-^cIyānī's 'summons'. Al-^cIyānī's descendants, in turn, based themselves at Shahāra and from there sought the leadership of the Zaydīs.[15] Another example of a local dynasty were the Banū Ḥamza, the descendants of Imam al-Manṣūr ^cAbd Allāh b. Ḥamzā (d. 614/1217), who based themselves in Ẓafār al-Ẓāhir.[16] From here they continued to mint coins in the name of their deceased father, taking on the titles of *amīr* and *muḥtasib*, but they refrained from making a proper 'summons'.[17] Yet another local dynasty was established by the Sharaf al-Dīn family in the area in and around Kawkabān. The founder was Imam al-Mutawakkil Yaḥyā Sharaf al-Dīn (d. 965/1557) who led a vigorous military campaign in the name of greater Zaydī legitimacy against the Circassian Mamlūks and later against the Ottomans.[18] None of these dynasties, however, managed to institutionalise its structures of rule or to give these perdurable forms.

The example of the Sharaf al-Dīn imams, and later that of the Qāsimīs, illustrates the oppositional quality of the Zaydī *da^cwa*. It was most effective when its attention was focused on an enemy who was both foreign and doctrinally at odds with Zaydī tenets. The Ottomans had come to Yemen as the successors of the Mamlūks with the intention of restraining the influence which the Portuguese had gained in the Red Sea and Indian Ocean. Locally, the Ottomans courted Yemeni Sufis, who initially welcomed them, as did many of the Shāfi^cīs in Lower Yemen.[19] Zaydism's relationship with Sufism has been predominantly antagonistic, though there were important imams, such as al-Mu^oayyad Yaḥyā b. Ḥamza, who tolerated certain pietistic aspects of the *Sufiyya* and there were periods when Sufis were active in the Zaydī highlands.[20] However, the alliance which was now struck between the Ottomans and the Sufis engendered a reaction from the Zaydīs, starting with al-Mutawakkil Yaḥyā Sharaf al-Dīn, who initiated a policy of systematic persecution of Sufis.

The Zaydīs also reacted by levelling polemical attacks against Sufism and its adherents. The most vociferous opponent was Imam al-Manṣūr al-Qāsim b. Muḥammad (d. 1029/1620) who describes the Sufis as a sect of the *Bāṭiniyya* whose roots lay in the religion of the *Majūs*, thereby applying to them an old accusation against the Ismā^cīlīs as being a Mazdakite conspiracy against Islam.[21] These polemical works can be seen as forming part of the ongoing war the Zaydīs

[15] Cf. Mufarriḥ b. Aḥmad al-Raba^cī, *Sīrat al-amīrayn al-jalīlāyn al-sharīfayn al-fāḍilayn*, Riḍwān al-Sayyid and ^cAbd al-Ghanī ^cAbd al-^cĀṭī (eds.), (Beirut: Dār al-Muntakhab al-^cArabī, 1993).

[16] Cf. S. M. Stern, 'Some unrecognized dirhems of the Zaidis of the Yemen', *Numismatic Chronicle* 9 (1949), 180–8; Nicholas Lowick, 'The Manṣūrī and the Mahdawī Dirham', in *Coinage and History of the Islamic World*, (Aldershot: Variorum 1990), art. IV.

[17] Cf. Zabāra, *A^oimmat al-Yaman*, pp. 143f.

[18] Cf. Zabāra, *A^oimmat al-Yaman*, pp. 369f.

[19] ^cAbd Allāh b. Muḥammad al-Ḥibshī, *al-Ṣufiyya wa^ol-fuqahā^o fī ^ol-Yaman* (Sanaa: Maktabat al-Jīl al-Jadīd, 1976), pp. 52–3.

[20] Cf. Wilferd Madelung, 'Zaydī attitudes to Sufism', in Frederick De Jong and Bernd Radtke (eds.), *Islamic Mysticism Contested* (Leiden: Brill, 1999), pp. 124–44.

[21] al-Manṣūr al-Qāsim b. Muḥammad, *Kitāb Ḥatf anf al-āfik*, ms. private library of Sayyid Muḥammad b. al-Ḥasan al-^cUjrī in Ḍaḥyān, fol. 1.

waged against the Ottomans and which raged intermittently under Qāsimī leadership from 1598 until 1635, when the Ottomans were finally evicted from Yemen. The Sufis did not make a come-back in the highlands until the eighteenth century with the arrival of Egyptian Sufis who initiated a succession of ulema there.[22] The phenomenon remained marginal and elitist, and no large scale movement or brotherhood was ever established.

The Seventeenth Century Imams: charismatic leadership and righteous rule

The Qāsimī imamate which emerged after the expulsion of the Ottomans in 1635 was different in some respects from the earlier Zaydī imamates. For one thing, it was no longer an oppositional power confined to the northern highlands of Upper Yemen; instead, it was an aggressive expansionist force with whom all the regional South Arabian leaderships had to come to terms. It was the first time in the history of Yemen that the Zaydīs successfully managed to conquer and claim sovereignty over the whole of South-West Arabia from Dhofar to ᶜAsīr, and they remained in control for nearly a century.[23] Despite the fact that their hold on this territory was at times tenuous and their sovereignty nominal, the historic mission of the Zaydīs, which was to establish righteous rule over the *umma* by a member of the House of the Prophet, seemed finally attainable, at least in Yemen.

The best evidence for the terms in which the Qāsimī imams articulated the legitimacy of their rule can be found in the separate chronicles covering the reigns of the first three imams by the historian al-Muṭahhar b. Muḥammad al-Jarmūzī (d. 1077/1667).[24] Drawing on al-Jarmūzī, Blukacz has examined the role of these imams in unifying Yemen in the seventeenth century.[25] In this study, he cites a correspondence between al-Muʾayyad bi-Allāh Muḥammad b. al-Qāsim (d. 1054/1644), the second Qāsimī imam who finally expelled the Ottomans from Yemen in 1635, and the Ottoman governor of al-Ḥasāʾ, ᶜAlī Pasha. This exchange took place in 1630–1, and each side presented arguments for the political legitimacy of its own regime. At this time, the Zaydīs had renewed their war against

22 Cf. Muḥammad b. Muḥammad Zabāra, *Nashr al-ᶜarf li-nubalāʾ al-Yaman baᶜd al-alf*, 3 vols. (Sanaa: Markaz al-Dirāsāt waʾl-Buḥūth al-Yamanī, 1985), vol. II, pp. 230–1 (hereinafter *Nashr*); *Badr*, II: 285.

23 A short-lived domination over much of Yemen was accomplished by Imam al-Mutawakkil Yaḥyā Sharaf al-Dīn (r. 912–965/1506–1557) and his son al-Muṭahhar in the sixteenth century after the Ottoman Sultan Salīm I took Egypt leaving the Mamlūks, who were then ruling Yemen, cut off from their home base and stranded in Zabīd. After considerable difficulty, the Ottomans were able to put an end to Sharaf al-Dīn's imamate once they themselves arrived in Yemen. Cf. *Badr*, I: 278f; Zabāra, *Aʾimmat al-Yaman*, pp. 369–453; Richard Blackburn, 'The era of Imām Sharaf al-Dīn Yaḥyā and his son al-Muṭahhar', *Yemen Update* 42 (2000), 4–8; idem, 'The collapse of Ottoman authority in Yemen', *Die Welt des Islams* 19 (1979), 119–76.

24 These are still manuscript sources. Cf. Ayman Fuʾād al-Sayyid, *Maṣādir tārīkh al-Yaman fī al-ᶜaṣr al-Islāmī* (Cairo: Institut Français d'Archéologie Orientale, 1974), pp. 236–8.

25 François Blukacz, 'Le Yémen sous l'autorité des imams zaidites au XVIIe siècle: une éphémère unité', *Revue du Monde Musulman et de la Méditerranée* 67 (1993), 39–51.

the Ottomans, who found themselves in a dire situation, with the entire population of Yemen, Shāfiᶜīs and Zaydīs, set against them. This was due to the corrupt and oppressive nature of their administration.[26] In this light, the letter by ᶜAlī Pasha can be seen as a desperate attempt by the Ottomans to persuade al-Muᵓayyad to stop fighting them, both by presenting Ottoman claims to legitimacy and by boasting about Ottoman military prowess, no doubt so as to intimidate the imam. ᶜAlī Pasha addresses his letter to 'Muḥammad, member of the Prophet's House', and begins by affirming his love for the Prophet's descendants, declaring that his own intention is merely to provide good counsel. He says:

> It is not a secret to one so knowledgeable as you, that we know about the war, the conflict and the disagreement which exists between you and the Ottoman state, the seat of the Khānate. [You are also not unaware] that the one who loves you will point out what he deems good for you in matters of this lowly world and matters religious; [Heed this] and the affairs of Muslims will be well ordered. It is good that you should be in agreement with the Ottoman state, that you acquiesce to its [representatives], that you obey their orders and that you improve your relations with them. Does not the ḥadīth say: 'that discord is asleep; may God curse the one who wakes it up'. You know that an accommodation has much good to offer, namely ordering the interests of Muslims and Islam. God, may He be exalted, says 'set things right between you' (VIII: 1). He, may He be exalted, has explained cessation in its most complete sense when He says: 'right settlement is better' (IV: 128). You know that His Excellence our Master the Sultan has based religion on this principle, and because of this the interests of the believers are in good order. [You know too] that the sultans are the Servants of the Two Holy Sanctuaries (*khuddām al-ḥaramayn al-sharīfayn*). The efforts they expend in fighting the unbelievers and in waging war against those who are evil are known to you, as is the fact that Yemen is the fount of belief, in accordance with the ḥadīth: 'belief is Yemenite'. It is not becoming that you should be the cause of discord and the expulsion of the people of belief and peace... As for the descendants of ᶜUthmān [i.e., the Ottoman sultans], may God grant them aid, their only desire is the welfare of God's worshippers and that of their countries as well as their spiritual and material well being. All the world knows that they will not abandon the Yemen, and it would be best if you, who are members of the Ahl al-Bayt, are not the cause of troubles.[27]

Al-Muᵓayyad had no intention of stopping a war he was about to win. The Ottomans were routed, having lost Sanaa and Taᶜizz in 1629, and by this date were confined to the towns of the Tihāma. Al-Muᵓayyad's response says as much. It also reveals Zaydī perceptions of the Ottomans as falling beyond the pale of Islam and proffers the reasons for which the Ahl al-Bayt are more fit to rule than the Ottomans, while nonetheless admitting Ottoman right in its own sphere. In his response to ᶜAlī Pasha, al-Muᵓayyad says the following:

[26] Cf. Sayyid Muṣṭafā Sālim, *al-Fatḥ al-ᶜUthmānī al-awwal liᵓl-Yaman*, 3rd ed. (Cairo: Maṭbaᶜat al-Jabalāwī, 1977), pp. 359–68.

[27] Blukacz, 'Le Yémen sous l'autorité des imams', 41, citing al-Muṭahhar al-Jarmūzī, *al-Jawhara al-munīra fī akhbār mawlāna wa-imāminā al-imām al-Muᵓayyad bi-Allāh Muḥammad*, fol. 176b. For Ottoman use of religious titles on their coins, see Kenneth MacKenzie, 'Ottoman coins inscribed with a religious title', *Numismatics International Bulletin*, 21.7 (1987), 157–9.

> What an excellent thing it is that you have received the news of what has taken place between us and those who depend on the powerful Authority, may God strengthen Islam through it. They do not belong to those who adhere to the Truth which comes from God. They do not respect any of God's interdictions and never get angry at those who rebel against Him; rather, they authorize luxurious living, perform evil, drink alcohol in the sight and knowledge of all, and commit abomination amongst the community of Muḥammad – may God's blessings and prayers be upon him and his family – and [they do this] in the proximity of mosques... They refuse what was ordained in favour of the Ahl al-Bayt: to honour them, to take them as guides, to give them the place of honour, to adhere to them as God, may He be exalted, has ordained through the intermediary of his Prophet. They [the Ottoman officials] have opposed our call to God and our practices which are in accordance with what He has commanded us to do, and our ancestors – the pure – and the eminent imams of the House of Muḥammad – may God's blessings and prayers be upon him and his family... [They have refused] to join us in establishing equity, instituting justice, abolishing injustice and obliterating disobedience to God, imposing the legal punishments and punishing those who commit evil.... Since [the Ottoman officials] do not renounce their error and do not perform what God has commanded, we have stopped trying to change them with peaceful means (*biʾllatī hiya al-aḥsan*, XVI: 125)... We have reminded them of God, Judgement Day, and obedience to God, to His messenger, and to those among the Ahl al-Bayt – the pure – who have authority in accordance with what the Almighty, the Majestic has prescribed when He says: 'O believers, obey God, and obey the Messenger and those in authority among you. If you should quarrel on anything, refer it to God and the Messenger, if you believe in God and the Last Day; that is better, and fairer in the issue' (IV: 59). Their refusal of God has now led us to consider them like those who get carried away by their passions, break their promises, violate their oaths and do not respect the obligations or interests of the believer and show no pity or compassion towards the Muslim. We have continuously found excuses for them until such time as the patience of Muslims has reached its end. Whereas their arrogance has merely increased... As we have found no way but to obey God's commandments, we have sought His aid, and placed our trust in Him and applied all our efforts in the accomplishment of the *jihād* so as to conform to the sayings of God, the Omnipotent, the Majestic: 'fight them, till there is no persecution and the religion is God's' (II: 193).[28]

The terms of the response show that the Zaydī-Qāsimī 'summons' was concerned with Muslim legitimacy writ large. The Zaydīs had the capacity to rule the Muslim world and could justify this in ideological and doctrinal terms deriving from their first imam in Yemen.

The triumphalist spirit of the early Qāsimī imams has been mentioned in a number of other studies. The first is an annotated edition by Sayyid Muṣṭafā Sālim of a number of letters by various Qāsimī and Ḥamīd al-Dīn imams. Sālim remarks that letters from the early Qāsimīs (i.e., al-Muʾayyad Muḥammad and

[28] Blukacz, 'Le Yémen sous l'autorité des imams', 42–3, citing al-Jarmūzī, *al-Jawhara al-munīra*, fols. 178–179a. The Ḥamīd al-Dīn imams of the twentieth century attacked the Ottomans in very similar terms, viz., that the latter contravene the prescriptions of Islamic law by drinking alcohol, performing homosexual acts and permitting prostitution. Cf. Hans Kruse, 'Takfīr und Gihād bei den Zaiditen des Jemen', *Die Welt des Islams* 13–14 (1984), 437–57.

al-Mutawakkil Ismāᶜīl) had always an exhortatory tone, demanding the application of the Law of God, stressing the special role of the imams as rulers from the Ahl al-Bayt and the importance of obedience to them.[29] They also refrained from according financial privileges in return for allegiance; rather, in the letters published by Sālim at least, they tend to acknowledge the receipt of taxes from their representatives or the individuals with whom they are corresponding.

With Qāsimī rule moving into coastal and Lower Yemen,[30] the imamate became a regional trading power, particularly because of the imams' control over the trade of coffee and other commodities such as horses. Yemen took part in a network of pre-modern dynasties such as the Mughals in India, with whom, for example, they maintained a correpondence and exchanged gifts and goods. Qāsimī pretensions were grand, as evinced in the imams' letters, but the means at their disposal remained paltry in comparison with those of other empires. A late but poignant example of this is when the Ottoman Sultan ᶜAbd al-Ḥamīd I sent al-Mutawakkil Aḥmad (d. 1231/1816) a young elephant along with other gifts in 1229/1813. Three years later, al-Mutawakkil's successor, al-Mahdī ᶜAbd Allāh (d. 1251/1835) sent the elephant back to Muḥammad ᶜAlī of Egypt, explaining that 'Yemen's poor soil' could not sustain it.[31]

Two further studies by Blukacz also show the earlier Qāsimī self-image as righteous Zaydī rulers. The first details the correspondence between Imam al-Mutawakkil ᶜalā Allāh Ismāᶜīl (d. 1087/1676) and the Mughal Emperor Awrangzīb (d. 1118/1707) in the years from 1657 to 1661.[32] The essence of the correspondence was al-Mutawakkil's bid to have Awrangzīb recognize him as imam of the *umma* and Commander of the Faithful (*amīr al-muʾminīn*) on the basis of his being an imam of Ahl al-Bayt. In return Awrangzīb would be recognised as al-Mutawakkil's legal representative or governor (*wālī*) over India. Awrangzīb had just emerged victorious over his brother Dārā Shikoh in a series of battles over the succession to their father, Emperor Shāh Jahān (d. 1076/1666). Claiming the title of emperor, Awrangzīb wanted to legitimise his accession religiously and (surprisingly

[29] Cf. Sayyid Muṣṭafā Sālim, *Wathāʾiq Yamaniyya*, 2nd ed. (Cairo: al-Maṭbaᶜa al-Faniyya, 1985), pp. 29, 43–54, 73–7. The contents of the letters edited by Sālim pertained to such matters as the nomination of individuals to posts, according privileges to certain families which had fought against the Ottomans on the side of the Qāsimīs, and the resolution of legal disputes among other matters.

[30] The move into these areas is reflected by the successive towns the imams chose to base themselves in (see map). The *daᶜwa* was initially based in the fortified hamlet of Shahāra which remained the capital until al-Mutawakkil Ismāᶜīl chose Ḍūrān, a village in Qāᶜ Jahrān north-west of Dhamār, as his capital. His successor, al-Mahdī Aḥmad chose the village of al-Ghirās, fifteen miles or so north-east of Sanaa. Al-Muʾayyad Muḥammad b. Ismāᶜīl chose Hijrat Maᶜbar, which is again in Qāᶜ Jahrān and just north of Dhamār. Al-Mahdī Muḥammad settled in al-Mawāhib, a village he had built three miles east of Dhamār. After him the imams settled on Sanaa, which remained the capital until 1850s. The successive moves, all of which were south of their original stronghold of Shahāra, indicate that the imams were drawn into a pan-Yemeni economic and political world.

[31] Anonymous, *Ḥawliyyāt Yamāniyya*, ᶜAbd Allāh al-Ḥibshī (ed.) (Sanaa: Dār al-Ḥikma al-Yamāniyya, 1991), pp. 24, 28 (hereinafter *Ḥawliyyāt Yamāniyya*); *Badr*, II: 227.

[32] François Blukacz, 'Les relations entre le Yémen et l'Inde au XVIIe siècle, extraits de la correspondance entre l'imam zaidite et al-Mutawakkil ᶜalā Llāh Ismāᶜīl b. al-Qāsim et le sultan moghol Awrangzib', mémoire de maîtrise, (Université de Paris-Sorbonne, Paris IV, 1992).

perhaps) sought the recognition of the House of Qāsim, as leading members of the Ahl al-Bayt. He therefore accepted al-Mutawakkil's offer. The exchange was symbolic and obviously mutually beneficial, leading to no other measures being taken by either side, except the occasional exchange of gifts, as when al-Mutawakkil Ismāᶜīl sent the Mughal nine Arab steeds in 1075/1665.[33] Blukacz's other study shows that al-Mutawakkil's ambitions did not stop with his attempts in India since he engaged in an activist policy with the Sharīfs in Mecca, from whom he also sought recognition of his religious claims.[34] The importance of the correspondence lies in al-Mutawakkil's perception and presentation of himself as *Amīr al-Muʾminīn*. In an age when neither the Umayyads nor the ᶜAbbāsids were present to thwart the political ambitions of Zaydīs, and with few other major ruling dynasties credibly claiming ᶜAlid descent – the Sharīfs of Morocco being a notable exception – the Qāsimīs could perhaps taste the victory, however nominal, which had long eluded them.

Another example of these religious policies was when al-Muʾayyad Muḥammad, and later al-Mutawakkil Ismāᶜīl, tried to convert to Islam the Christian king of Ethiopia, Fāsiladas (r. 1632–1667). The latter was trying to garner the aid of the Qāsimī imams to open a new trade route on the Red Sea via Baylūl, thereby circumventing the port of Masawwaᶜ which the Ottomans controlled. The Qāsimīs, it seems, were the only source of firearms for the Ethiopians at this time. Fāsiladas sent a letter to al-Muʾayyad about this and al-Muʾayyad responded in 1052/1643. In his rejoinder al-Muʾayyad says the following:

> We are heirs to the Book and the Wisdom, and We honour the birth of His Prophet Muḥammad, the Seal of the Prophets, and therefore We take his place in his Community, in the same way as Abraham . . . It is Our duty to eliminate abomination, for, among the good tidings which He revealed to Our ancestor, He revealed: 'God only desires to put away from you abomination, People of the House, and to cleanse you' (XXXIII: 33), and may He make our love for Muḥammad – God bless him and his family and grant them salvation – a wage in the worlds and for them good tidings in Paradise . . . And the People of the House of Muḥammad – God bless him and his family and grant them salvation – will continue to preserve for us his religion and his legacy, stand up for the right of his call to all mankind, in order to bring the proof for him; they will draw the sword of Holy War in the face of those who are opposed to his command; among his servants they will give good advice [towards God], secretly and openly.[35]

Al-Muʾayyad was trying perhaps to evoke a common lineage with Fāsiladas by referring to a shared Abrahamic tradition. However, his claims lie firmly within Zaydī teachings. By emphasising that he was the leading member of the Family of

[33] Cf. Sāqi Mustᶜad Khan [sic], *Maāsir-i-ᶜālamgiri* [sic], Jadunath Sarkar (trans.) (New Delhi: Munshiram Manoharlal, 1986), p. 32. This is Muḥammad Sāqī Mustaᶜidd Khān's history of Emperor Aurangzīb's reign entitled *Maᶜāsir-i ᶜĀlamgīrī*.

[34] François Blukacz, 'Les relations politiques des imams zaidites du Yémen avec le Hedjaz au XVIIe siècle', mémoire de D.E.A., (Université de Paris-Sorbonne, Paris IV, 1993).

[35] E. J. van Donzel, *A Yemenite Embassy to Ethiopia 1647–1649: al-Ḥaymī's Sīrat al-Ḥabasha* (Stuttgart: Steiner Verlag, 1986), p. 49.

the Prophet and therefore leader of the *umma*, he was promoting the Zaydī view that the Ahl al-Bayt were the ultimate locus of religious and temporal authority in Islam.

The matter did not go further until 1057/1647, at which time Fāsiladas sent another letter in which he raised the subject of the trade route again, but this time intimated an interest in Islam. Al-Muʾayyad had died by now and al-Mutawakkil was the reigning imam. The possibility of converting the Negus of Ethiopia to Islam led al-Mutawakkil in that same year to send a mission to Gondar, headed by Qāḍī Ḥasan b. Aḥmad al-Ḥaymī (d. 1070/1660).[36] Ultimately, however, both efforts failed. The king was not seriously interested in converting, as al-Ḥaymī was to discover after an arduous journey, nor were the Yemenis interested in antagonising the Ottomans by helping the Negus at this juncture.[37]

Men of the Pen and the Sword

The first five Qāsimī imams (their *daʿwa*s being from 1598–1686) lived up to the reputation of being men of the pen and the sword. Their written works testify to the former quality. ʿAbd Allāh al-Ḥibshī has collated a list of these for each of the Zaydī imams and names forty-one titles by al-Qāsim b. Muḥammad, thirteen by al-Muʾayyad Muḥammad and twenty-three by al-Mutawakkil; these are mostly in law, theology and jurisprudence.[38] The fourth imam, al-Mahdī Aḥmad b. al-Ḥasan, appears to have written nothing, though he was the strictest Hādawī among the early Qāsimīs. The fifth imam, al-Muʾayyad Muḥammad b. Ismāʿīl (d. 1097/1686) produced four works. It is reported that this last imam 'only consumed what his hand produced' (*lā yaʾkul illā min ʿamal yadih*).[39] In his biographical entry on this same imam, Shawkānī gives a description reminiscent of the early Zaydī imams when he says:

> He was from among God's friends (*awliyāʾ Allāh*) and was one of the most just caliphs. No mention has ever been made of his injustice in any matter. He prayed and wept a great deal and was always fearful of God. He would only consume votive offerings (*nudhūr*) after ascertaining that these were legally allowed to him, and would not touch anything from the public treasury. His gatherings had many ulema and pious people in attendance and here readings in the sciences and recitation of the Qurʾān took place ... His justice among the subjects is an oft cited example, and the people of his age nicknamed him the

36 Van Donzel, *A Yemenite embassy*, pp. 52–3.
37 Cf. Mordechai Abir, *Ethiopia and the Red Sea* (London: Frank Cass, 1980), p. 226, fn. 36.
38 ʿAbd Allāh b. Muḥammad al-Ḥabshī, *Muʾallafāt ḥukkām al-Yaman*, Elke Niewohner-Eberhard (ed.) (Weisbaden: Otto Harrassowitz, 1979), pp. 126–43. Traini has shown in his study of Zaydī biographical dictionaries that this period, the eleventh/seventeenth century, is one of the most productive in terms of data, second only to the seventh/thirteenth century, cf. Renato Traini, *Sources Biographiques des Zaidites* (Paris: Centre National de la Recherche Scientifique, 1977), pp. xii–xiii.
39 ʿAbd al-Wāsiʿ b. Yaḥyā al-Wāsiʿī, *Tārīkh al-Yaman*, reprint 1367/1948 ed. (Sanaa: Maktabat al-Yaman al-Kubrā, 1991), p. 230.

> father of modesty (*Abū ʾl-ʿAfiya*) because he never harmed anyone either monetarily or bodily. Indeed, at times of misfortune he became needy and would ask the people with fortunes among the merchants, who had plenty, to give him a loan, but they would refuse because they did not fear him in the present or the future.[40]

Al-Ḥibshī's lists of imamic works then taper off dramatically with al-Mahdī Ṣāḥib al-Mawāhib (d. 1130/1718) writing one work, described by Shawkānī as being incomprehensible and devoid of knowledge.[41]

The early Qāsimīs combined in themselves military and scholarly abilities. Their military exploits have been described in a number of studies, as have the intestine conflicts within the Qāsimī House that eventually played a role in the breakup of their power and control over Yemen.[42] The sons of al-Qāsim himself are described in the histories as being exceptionally gifted, and their lives were considered by later generations in Yemen as exemplary for the way they matched the requirements set forth in the manuals of law. A good example is al-Ḥusayn b. al-Qāsim (d. 1050/1640), who like his brother al-Ḥasan (d. 1048/1639), was one of the leading commanders of the Zaydī armies which expelled the Ottomans.

By all accounts, al-Ḥusayn was remarkable: he was a scholar of the first rank and a great military leader. His two-volume work in *uṣūl al-fiqh* entitled *Hidāyat al-ʿuqūl ilā ghāyat al-sūl*, which has now been published, ranks among the best works in the field produced by a Zaydī and has become the most referred to and studied work of its kind.[43] Drawing on al-Ḥusayn's biography in *Maṭlaʿal-budūr*, Shawkānī describes him in this way:

> He wrote it [*Hidāyat al-ʿuqūl*] while leading the armies and laying siege to the Turks in all areas. He harrassed them, bringing to them ruination and launching raids on them. His battles with them would [normally] cause one to be diverted from looking at a book in the sciences. How amazing it is that he – may God's mercy be upon him – whilst leading armies, commanding soldiers and being the one who is referred to ... in all that took place in matters of the Holy War ... could write on scholastic and legal matters, [to the extent] that he could compete with ʿAḍud al-Dīn and al-Saʿd al-Taftazānī and correct them! ... What is this bravery from which the brave would hesitate ... and this inner strength which baffles comprehension and this grounding in the sciences which none other was reckoned to have![44]

[40] *Badr*, II: 139–40. [41] Cf. *Badr*, II: 98; al-Ḥabshī, *Muʾallafāt*, pp. 145–46.

[42] Cf. Sālim, *al-Fatḥ al-ʿUthmānī al-awwal*, pp. 354–411; ʿAbd Allāh Ḥāmid al-Ḥiyed, 'Relations between the Yaman and South Arabia during the Zaydī imāmate of Āl al-Qāsim 1626–1732', D.Phil. thesis, (University of Edinburgh, 1973), pp. 19–122; A. S. Tritton, *The Rise of the Imams of Sanaa* (Oxford University Press, 1925); R. B. Serjeant, 'The post-medieval and modern history of Ṣanʿāʾand the Yemen, ca. 953–1382/1515–1962', in R. B. Serjeant and R. Lewcock (eds.), *Ṣanʿāʾ: An Arabian Islamic City* (London: World of Islam Festival Trust, 1983), pp. 71–81.

[43] al-Ḥusayn b. al-Qāsim, *Kitāb Hidāyat al-ʿuqūl ilā ghāyat al-sūl fī ʿilm al-uṣūl*, 2 vols. (n.p.: al-Maktaba al-Islāmiyya, 1401/1981.)

[44] *Badr*, I: 226–7; cf. Aḥmad b. Ṣāliḥ Ibn Abī ʾl-Rijāl, *Maṭlaʿ al-budūr wa majmaʿ al-buḥūr*, ms. New Sanaa University Library, photocopy, vol. II, pp. 87–91 (hereinafter *Maṭlaʿ al-budūr*). The two scholars who are mentioned here are the famous theologians ʿAḍud al-Dīn ʿAbd al-Raḥmān b. Aḥmad al-Ījī (d. 756/1355) and Saʿd al-Dīn Masʿūd b. ʿUmar al-Taftazānī (d. 792/1390).

Al-Ḥusayn never claimed the imamate but probably had the qualifications for it. His reputation, which can be gleaned from the above quotation, became legendary as he was someone who embodied the ideal on which the Zaydī *daʿwa* had been founded. The feats of his contemporaries became part of the historical consciousness of later Zaydīs who would hark back to this early period of the imamate while lamenting the decline which later set in.

The Religious Policies of the Early Qāsimīs

The early Qāsimīs pursued activist Zaydī religious policies and sought to have Hādawī teachings accepted by the Shāfiʿīs in the lands they conquered. The Ottomans had established close links with the Shāfiʿī populations during their period of rule. This led the Qāsimīs to perceive the Shāfiʿīs as collaborators with an enemy whose adherence to Islam was at best tenuous and gave the Qāsimīs justification to continue the war effort in the Shāfiʿī areas even after the Ottomans had been expelled. The Qāsimīs, therefore, waged wars against the rulers of Laḥj, Aden, and Abyan among others, and declared these wars a *jihād*, enabling them to press into service tribal conscripts and impose special taxes in support of the war effort.[45] The greatest military victories were achieved in the reign of al-Mutawakkil Ismāʿīl, who declared the Turks and the Shāfiʿīs of Yemen to be 'infidels by interpretation' (*kuffār taʾwīl*, i.e., their beliefs were based on an incorrect interpretation of Islam). Yemeni Shāfiʿīs upheld Ashʿarī theological doctrines, some of which were at odds with the Muʿtazilī ones then upheld by Zaydīs. More specifically, al-Mutawakkil, following an old Zaydī tradition, accused the Shāfiʿīs of being predestinarians (*mujbira*) and anthropomorphists (*mushabbiha*), whereas Zaydīs believe both that man is free to act according to his own will and that God is denuded of any physical human attributes. In practice, this meant that attacking Shāfiʿīs was legitimate and their territories were to be considered the 'abode of war' (*dār al-ḥarb*). It also meant that the imam had discretionary powers over whether to expropriate their lands after conquest as war booty and to consider these as conquered lands, taxed at a higher rate of the land tax (*kharāj*). By garnering this power, al-Mutawakkil could grant land holdings to those fighting in his support.[46] Indeed, Dresch has pointed out that the ascension of a number of prominent tribal families in the northern highlands can be traced to this period when they became large land owners in Lower Yemen and the Western Mountains.[47]

Some scholars did not approve of al-Mutawakkil's policies and argued that these were arbitrary decisions which had no basis in the Sharīʿa or in the teachings of the Zaydī school. Perhaps, the most famous of those who objected were al-Hādī b. Aḥmad al-Jalāl (d. 1079/1668), his brother al-Ḥasan b. Aḥmad al-Jalāl

[45] Cf. *Nashr*, III: 98.
[46] Cf. al-Ḥiyed, 'Relations between the Yaman and South Arabia', pp. 57–60.
[47] Dresch, *Tribes*, pp. 202f.

(d. 1084/1673) and the historian Yaḥyā b. al-Ḥusayn (d. 1100/1688).[48] In defending his policies, which were obviously sustaining the war effort, al-Mutawakkil responded to Yaḥyā b. al-Ḥusayn's criticism as follows:

> What proves [my opinion in the matter] is that the school of *Ahl al-ᶜAdl* [read: Muᶜtazila] – may God increase their numbers – says that the *mujbira* and the *mushabbiha* are infidels, and [also] that if infidels [read: Turks] occupy a land, they own it (*malakūhā*), even though these lands may [already] belong to Muslims and the *Ahl al-ᶜAdl*. [Furthermore, the school states] that the same rule [of *takfīr*] applies to those who support them or belong to them [read: Shāfiᶜīs], even if their beliefs are different from theirs. [The school further holds] that any land in which infidelity is manifested becomes itself a land of infidelity (*jiwār kufriyya*), though it may be inhabited by some who are not infidels themselves and who do not partake in this. These principles are well known to us through definite proofs (*adilla qaṭᶜiyya*) and are recorded in the books of our imams and ancestors – may God be pleased with us and them. No one who has the least insight and knowledge about their works can deny this.[49]

Al-Mutawakkil was also responsible for sending Hādawī scholars to various Shāfiᶜī areas to establish *hijra*s and to spread the school's teachings. This seems to have resulted in the conversion of people to Hādawism *en masse*, namely in Jabal al-Sharq (Ānis), Mikhlāf Samāh (ᶜUtma) and al-Ḥadā.[50] Another example, yet, of al-Mutawakkil's Shīᶜite policies was his approval of the institutionalisation of the public celebration of *Yawm al-Ghadīr* on the 18 Dhū al-Ḥijja 1073/23 July 1663.[51] Shīᶜites generally believe that after the Prophet performed his last pilgrimage in 9 AH he stopped on his way back to Medina in a place called Ghadīr Khumm on the 18 of Dhū al-Ḥijja. Here it is reported that the Prophet made an invocation for ᶜAlī, saying: 'O God, be a friend of whomever he [ᶜAlī] befriends and an enemy of whomever he takes as an enemy'.[52] This ḥadīth is adduced by Shīᶜites as proof of ᶜAlī's designation as the successor to the Prophet and hence they celebrate the day. Aḥmad b. al-Ḥasan, who was later to become al-Mutawakkil's successor taking the title al-Mahdī li-Dīn Allāh, was the first who started the celebratory practice

48 *Nashr*, III: 98–101; cf. Ḥusayn b. ᶜAbd Allāh al-ᶜAmrī and Muḥammad b. Aḥmad al-Jirāfī, *al-ᶜAllāma wa'l-mujtahid al-muṭlaq al-Ḥasan b. Aḥmad al-Jalāl* (Beirut: Dār al-Fikr al-Muᶜāṣir, 2000), pp. 436–43; ᶜAbd Allāh b. ᶜAlī al-Wazīr, *Tārīkh ṭabaq al-ḥalwā wa ṣuḥāf al-mann wa'l-salwā*, Muḥammad Jāzim (ed.) (Sanaa: Markaz al-Dirāsāt wa'l-Buḥūth al-Yamanī, 1985), p. 145 (hereinafter *Ṭabaq al-ḥalwā*); al-Ḥiyed, 'Relations between the Yaman and South Arabia', pp. 60–3; al-Ḥibshī, *Maṣādir al-fikr*, p. 221.

49 *Hijar al-ᶜilm*, II: 1075–6 here quoting Yaḥyā b. al-Ḥusayn's *Bahjat al-zaman* (the events of year 1058 AH). Al-Mutawakkil Ismāᶜīl's main treatise on this subject is *al-Jawāb al-mu'ayyad bi'l-burhān al-ṣarīḥ ᶜalā ᶜadam al-farq bayna kufr al-ta'wīl wa'l-taṣrīḥ wa ḥukm al-bughāt ᶜalā 'l-madhhab al-ṣarīḥ*, ms. Milan, Ambrosiana, no. D 244, IX, fols. 115a–131a. For the standard Hādawī view see *Azhār*, p. 323 and ᶜAbd Allāh Ibn Miftāḥ, *Kitāb al-Muntazaᶜ al-mukhtār min al-ghayth al-midrār al-mufattiḥ li-kamā'im al-Azhār fī fiqh al-a'imma al-aṭhār*, 4 vols., reprinted by the Yemeni Ministry of Justice, (Cairo: Maṭbaᶜat Sharikat al-Tamaddun, 1332/1914), vol. 4, pp. 571–72, (a.k.a. *Sharḥ al-Azhār* and will hereinafter be referred to as such).

50 *Hijar al-ᶜilm*, III: 1244; *Ṭabaq al-ḥalwā*, pp. 50–1.

51 *Ṭabaq al-ḥalwā*, pp. 185, 314.

52 Cf. Madelung, *The Succession to Muḥammad* (Cambridge: Cambridge University Press, 1997), p. 253.

which has lasted till today in Yemen, eliciting in the interim much censure from Traditionist scholars who claim it to be a reprehensible innovation started by the *Rāfiḍa* (Shīᶜite extremists).[53]

After subduing much of Lower, South and South-Eastern Yemen, al-Mutawakkil turned his attention to Ḥaḍramawt where the Kathīrī dynasty was in power. In 1045/1635 the Kathīrī Sultan recognised that the Qāsimīs were a force to be reckoned with after their defeat of the Ottomans and offered his submission to al-Muᵓayyad.[54] And in 1067/1656–7 al-Mutawakkil sent Qāḍī Ḥasan b. Aḥmad al-Ḥaymī as his emissary to Ḥaḍramawt in order to impose a formal treaty and to regularize the payment of tribute with Sultan Badr b. ᶜAbd Allāh, who was then ruling there under nominal Qāsimī suzerainty.[55] The terms of the treaty stipulated that the Sultan was to make an oath of allegiance to the imam and gave al-Ḥaymī great powers over the judicial, penal, fiscal and religious policies of the Kathīrī state.[56] By 1069/1659, however, Kāthirī machinations led al-Mutawakkil to doubt the Sultan's loyalty and he decided to invade Ḥaḍramawt, nominating his nephew Aḥmad b. al-Ḥasan as commander of the campaign. Along the way, in Biᵓr Ḥalīma, Aḥmad tried to convince Sultan Munaṣṣar al-ᶜAwlaqī, the leader of the ᶜAwlaqī region, to adopt the Zaydī call to prayer, which includes the statement 'come to the best of works' (*ḥayya ᶜalā khayr al-ᶜamal*) which is not said by Sunnīs.[57] He was not successful in this. Eventually, he led his army into Wādī Ḥaḍramawt, defeated the Kathīrī forces and imposed Zaydī teachings, especially in Tarīm which was the main religious centre. He prohibited the use of the reed-flute (*yarāᶜ*) and the tambourine (*daff*) in the famous Sufi ritual (*ḥaḍra*) of Sayyid ᶜAbd al-Raḥmān al-Saqqāf, and forced the inclusion of *ḥayya ᶜalā khayr al-ᶜamal* in the call to prayer.[58] He also appointed judges and governors who had accepted Zaydī doctrines.[59]

Aḥmad al-Ḥaymī returned to the highlands in 1070/1660, after which Qāsimī authority quickly declined. By 1080/1669, only the port of al-Shiḥr remained under Qāsimī suzerainty, and the imam's only remaining prerogative was the appointment of Kathīrī Sultans upon the death of an incumbent.[60] As this happened Zaydī teachings were done away with. The distances involved were simply too great to allow the Qāsimīs more control over Ḥaḍramawt, besides which they were now involved with internal fights and local rebellions, all of which meant their doctrines

[53] Cf. Muḥammad b. ᶜAlī al-Akwaᶜ, *Ṣifa min tārīkh al-Yaman al-ijtimāᶜī wa qiṣṣat ḥayātī* (n.p., n.d.), pp. 137–8; Franck Mermier, *Le Cheikh de la Nuit* (Paris: Sindbad, 1997), pp. 49–50; Renaud Detalle, 'Ghadir and Nushoor in Yemen: Zaydistan votes for Imam Ali', *Yemen Times*, no. 17 (1997), April 28th–4th May.

[54] al-Ḥiyed, 'Relations between the Yaman and South Arabia', pp. 36–7; cf. Ṣalāḥ al-Bakrī, *Tārīkh Ḥaḍramawt al-siyāsī* (Cairo: Maṭbaᶜat Muṣṭafā al-Bābī al-Ḥalabī, 1956), vol. I, pp. 103–10.

[55] *Ṭabaq al-ḥalwā*, p. 147.

[56] Cf. al-Ḥiyed, 'Relations between the Yaman and South Arabia', p. 94.

[57] al-Ḥiyed, 'Relations between the Yaman and South Arabia', p. 101.

[58] On the prohibition of musical instruments see Michael Cook, *Commanding Right and Forbidding Wrong in Islamic Thought* (Cambridge University Press, 2000), p. 90 and passim.

[59] al-Ḥiyed, 'Relations between the Yaman and South Arabia', pp. 109–11.

[60] Ibid., pp. 119–20.

did not take hold. Despite the effective loss of Ḥaḍramawt by the Qāsimīs, it is reported that the mention of the imam's name in the Friday sermon lingered on for a time as a symbol without any political substance.

Zaydī Scholars are Exposed to Shāfiᶜī Sunnism

The expansion of the Qāsimī state into Sunnī areas led to unprecedented levels of interaction between Zaydī and Shāfiᶜī scholars. The effect was that Zaydīs acquired greater awareness of the wider Sunnī world and began studying Sunnī works, especially the collections of ḥadīth, with an intensity never before seen. Some even adopted Sunnī views. This awareness is reflected in the introduction of *Kitāb al-Mustaṭāb fī tārīkh ᶜulamā al-Zaydiyya al-aṭyāb* (otherwise known as *Ṭabaqāt al-Zaydiyya al-ṣughrā*), an important historical work by Yaḥyā b. al-Ḥusayn (d. 1100/1688), who, as noted earlier, had objected to al-Mutawakkil's policies of declaring Shāfiᶜīs *kuffār taʾwīl*. In it he makes a plea to Sunnīs to find Zaydīs juridically acceptable and laments that Sunnīs consider Zaydīs to be outside the Sharīᶜa because of such things as the *ḥayya ᶜalā khayr al-ᶜamal*, or not placing one hand over the other (*ḍamm*) and not raising them (*rafᶜ*) during prayer. After all, he says, these are subsidiary legal matters (*masāʾil furūᶜiyya*) in which every *mujtahid* is correct (*kull mujtahid muṣīb*) and should he be wrong this still would not count against him.[61] Yaḥyā b. al-Ḥusayn is basing his call to overcome legal differences on principles in *uṣūl al-fiqh* about *ijtihād*, all of which is intended to make Zaydism acceptable to Sunnīs. In itself, this is an interesting claim for a Zaydī to be making, especially since it occurred at a time when Zaydīs had recently triumphed (albeit locally) over Sunnīs.

Though the influence of Sunnism was already present in the Zaydī highlands, most notably in the teachings of Muḥammad b. Ibrāhīm al-Wazīr (d. 840/1436), it was not sustained until the period of the first Ottoman occupation. An example of this is Sayyid Muḥammad b. ᶜIzz al-Dīn al-Muftī (d. 1050/1640), who studied ḥadīth and other subjects with leading Sunnī scholars in Mecca. He was originally from Hijrat Falalla, was appointed *muftī* in Sanaa by the Ottoman governor and was known to issue his *fatwā*s in accordance with the four Sunnī schools (*aftā ᶜalā al-madhāhib al-arbaᶜa*). It is also reported that he followed the path of Muḥammad b. Ibrāhīm al-Wazīr, the first Traditionist scholar among the Zaydīs, and did not declare which school he belonged to.[62] Thus some Zaydī scholars were accommodating the Ottoman presence in Yemen by adopting Sunnī views and forgoing the legal opinions of their own school. They could do this by appealing to an

61 Yaḥyā b. al-Ḥusayn, *Kitāb al-Mustaṭāb fī tārīkh ᶜulamā al-Zaydiyya al-aṭyāb*, ms. New Sanaa University Library, photocopy, pp. 11–13.

62 *Ṭabaq al-ḥalwā*, pp. 81–2; *Badr*, II: 203–4; *Maṭlaᶜal-budūr*, IV: 179–80; *Hijar al-ᶜilm*, III: 1635–6. Another example of such a scholar is ᶜAbd al-Raḥmān b. Muḥammad al-Ḥaymī (d. 1068/1658), see *Badr*, I: 340.

established tendency among Zaydī scholars which lacked sectarian zeal and evinced great openness to Sunnism, as is evident in the works of Ibn al-Wazīr.

An accommodation to Sunnism can also be seen with the Zaydī commander, al-Ḥusayn b. al-Qāsim (mentioned earlier), who studied Muslim's *Ṣaḥīḥ* in his later years and wrote treatises corroborating certain Sunnī views. It is not clear what motivated him to do this. He wanted, however, to make the Shāfiᶜīs appear more acceptable to Zaydīs, in order perhaps to establish better relations between the two communities. In one of his treatises, for example, al-Ḥusayn held that the presence of the supreme imam (*al-imām al-aᶜẓam*) during the Friday congregational prayers was not mandatory, a view which stricter Hādawīs would reject. In a second treatise he argued against preventing Shāfiᶜīs from joining prayers which were being led by Zaydīs.[63] It seems that Qāsimī governors were preventing Shāfiᶜīs praying with them in the areas they had conquered in Lower Yemen; perhaps, this was one consequence of the view which held Shāfiᶜīs to be *kuffār taʾwīl*.

However, some Zaydī-born scholars went beyond al-Ḥusayn b. al-Qāsim's views, according Shāfiᶜīs equal religious status with Zaydīs. They did so by identifying more fully with Sunnism and forgoing many Zaydī teachings. Al-Hādī b. Aḥmad al-Jalāl, who was mentioned earlier, is a good example. It is reported that he went to Ibb and Taᶜizz in 1061–2/1651–2, where he studied the Sunnī canonical ḥadīth collections with Shāfiᶜī scholars, and it is even said he had become a Sufi. At the time, al-Hādī was receiving a stipend (*maᶜlūm*) from the Qāsimī governor of Lower Yemen, Muḥammad b. al-Ḥasan b. al-Qāsim (d. 1079/1668),[64] and this eventually led him to settle there with his family. He adopted certain Ashᶜarī and Sunnī views, such as the belief in the *visio beatifica*.[65] His brother al-Ḥasan b. Aḥmad al-Jalāl is also a notable example of someone who appears to have departed from Zaydī teachings in many respects, adopting the belief that any Muslim, regardless of family or national origin, could become imam.[66]

The latter half of the seventeenth century was a period of great intellectual ferment in the Yemeni highlands. Some scholars were crossing traditional sectarian and school boundaries, making it difficult to pigeonhole them according to the accepted categories of Hādawī and Shāfiᶜī. Study of and reliance on ḥadīth and its attendant sciences, however, appears to have united these scholars. Their arguments are more often than not bolstered by extensive quotations from ḥadīth and are formulated using the conceptual tools of the ḥadīth sciences. The

63 *Ṭabaq al-ḥalwā*, pp. 79–80; cf. al-Ḥibshī, *Maṣādir al-fikr*, p. 217.

64 Cf. *Badr*, II: 159–60. He is the author of a published credal work entitled *Kitāb Sabīl al-rashād ilā maᶜrifat rabb al-ᶜibād* (Sanaa: Dār al-Ḥikma al-Yamāniyya, 1994).

65 *Nashr*, III: 97; *Ṭabaq al-ḥalwā*, p. 243.

66 Cf. *Badr*, I: 191–4; *Hijar al-ᶜilm*, I: 342–50; *Nashr*, III: 83–96; *Ṭabaq al-ḥalwa*, pp. 124–5; al-ᶜAmrī, *al-ᶜAllāma waʾl-mujtahid*, pp. 62–5. Zaydīs commenting on this would label Jalāl a Khārijī in this matter. However, it appears his position reflected, possibly, the position of the Zaydī Batriyya, and was certainly part of his rejection of the Hādawī view on the matter. For a similar position taken by another Yemeni Traditionist, see Ṣāliḥ al-Maqbalī, *al-Manār fī ʾal-mukhtār min jawāhir al-Baḥr al-zakhkhār*, 2 vols. (Beirut: Muʾassasat al-Risāla, 1988), vol. II, p. 464. Patricia Crone kindly clarified this matter for me and alerted me to al-Maqbalī's opinion.

relative ambivalence of the Qāsimī authorities to these developments deserves greater study. The Qāsimīs, however, were on the whole willing to argue their case with the Traditionist scholars without resorting to punitive measures against them. The experience of the scholars who criticised the state a century or so later was very different, as will be seen later.

Imamic Succession

The eighteenth-century Qāsimī imams did not have the qualifications of their predecessors, al-Muʾayyad Muḥammad or al-Mutawakkil Ismāʿīl, nor did they have the same financial and military means at their disposal. Less than ten years after al-Mutawakkil's death the imamate began losing its territorial acquisitions. The important revenue-generating port of al-Shiḥr was lost in 1680 and with it the areas of Dhofar and Ḥaḍramawt. The revenues generated from the ports in the seventeenth century, particularly due to the coffee trade but also the trade with Iran and India, provided the imamic treasury with unprecedented capital wealth.[67] This perhaps explains, in part, why the imamate was able to maintain control for as long as it did over such a vast area of inhospitable terrain. Aden and Abyan, for example, were ruled by the Qāsimīs for close to a century, from 1635–1727. However, the loss of the port taxes must have hurt the imamate's treasury considerably, and this fact is invariably mentioned in the histories as a main source for the decline of power.

Another reason the far-flung state began to unravel was disputes and wars over leadership within the House of Qāsim. Disputes over the imamate have been a constant feature in Zaydī history, for the theory of accession stated that the one who possesses in him all the requirements for the imamate (*jāmiʿan li-shurūṭ al-imāma al-muʿtabara*) should become imam. In the successions of al-Muʾayyad Muḥammad (d. 1054/1644), his brother al-Mutawakkil Ismāʿīl (d. 1087/1676), al-Mahdī Aḥmad b. al-Ḥasan (d. 1092/1681) and al-Muʾayyad Muḥammad b. Ismāʿīl (d. 1097/1686) – respectively the second, third, fourth and fifth imams of the House of Qāsim – other contenders stood down in acknowledgement of the superior qualification for the post of the abovementioned imams. However, the contenders, who were sometimes defeated on the field of battle, were placated through appointments as governors of districts. Shawkānī's biographical entry on al-Mutawakkil Ismāʿīl is notable because of its portrayal of the 'ideal-type' Zaydī imam and for providing the outlines of the way the succession issue was resolved after al-Muʾayyad Muḥammad's death.

Shawkānī tells us that one of al-Qāsim b. Muḥammad's sons, a brother to al-Mutawakkil and al-Muʾayyad who was called Aḥmad, was the first to claim the

[67] Cf. Michel Tuchscherer, 'Des épices au café, le Yémen dans le commerce international (XVIe–XVIIe siècles)', *Chroniques Yéménites* 4–5 (1996–7), 92–102; idem, 'Le commerce en Mer Rouge aux alentours de 1700', in Yves Thoraval *et al.* (eds.), *Le Yémen et la Mer Rouge* (Paris: L'Harmattan, 1995), pp. 39, 46–8, 51–7; *EI*², art. 'Kahwa' (K. N. Chaudhuri), vol. IV, pp. 453–5.

imamate upon al-Muʾayyad's death, despite not being a *mujtahid*. Al-Mutawakkil, who was in Ḍūrān at this time, heard only belatedly about the imam's death, upon which he also claimed the imamate by making a *daᶜwa*. Al-Mutawakkil felt justified since he was more qualified than his brother Aḥmad.[68] Initially, Aḥmad would not stand down and started making military preparations. The matter was finally resolved after Aḥmad was defeated militarily by being penned up in Thulā by al-Mutawakkil's forces; but this came about only after al-Mutawakkil was able to garner support and acknowledgement of the superiority of his candidacy from key members of the House of Qāsim and other noted scholars and tribal shaykhs. The two brothers eventually met upon the agreement that 'he who defeated the other in knowledge (*ᶜilm*) would take the imamate'. Al-Mutawakkil was the obvious winner and Aḥmad gave him his allegiance.[69] Aḥmad was later appointed governor over Ṣaᶜda. One could argue that Aḥmad had no choice but to concede the imamate, given his military defeat. However, in this instance, it is nonetheless important that 'qualification', i.e., religious knowledge, was accepted by all the parties as the only justification for proper accession. This ceased being the case a little over ten years after al-Mutawakkil's death, when al-Mahdī Muḥammad b. Aḥmad, otherwise known as Ṣāḥib al-Mawāhib (d. 1130/1718), acceded to the imamate through sheer military force. The historical sources mark his accession as a definite rupture with past tradition; for, among other things, he developed institutional and personal practices which had hitherto not been seen in Zaydī imamates. Shawkānī describes him as follows:

> He was a king from among the grandest. He took money from the subjects without understanding and would spend it likewise [i.e., he taxed and spent revenues regardless of canonical stipulations]. From the time of the withdrawal of the Turks till he became its king, Yemen was protected from oppression and the non-canonical taxes [*jibāyāt*] and the taking of what the Law does not allow. When he ascended he took money from its rightful place as well as from the wrongful, so that his government and the reverence paid to him became great, his power became firm and his troops multiplied. He was more like a king than a caliph. Despite this, he was austere in his dress and would not wear silk . . . He inclined to the scholars, sitting with them and imitating them . . . He was not a scholar, [however], but liked to pretend he was one. So the scholars in his court would help him in this, both out of desire and fear.[70]

Accompanying the development of state-like institutions was a serious decline in state revenues due to a decline in world coffee prices, as new sources of coffee undermined the monopoly Yemen previously had on the supply of this precious commodity.[71] This led the state to rely even more on the only other major source of

[68] Aḥmad seems to have claimed the imamate because he was present when al-Muʾayyad died in Shahāra and because he was encouraged to do this by Aḥmad b. Saᶜd al-Dīn al-Maswarī, a leading scholar of the time.

[69] *Badr*, I: 147–8; also *Ṭabaq al-ḥalwā*, pp. 99–104.

[70] *Badr*, II: 97–8.

[71] Cf. Ṣāliḥ Ramaḍān Maḥmūd (ed.), *Dhikrayāt al-Shawkānī: rasāʾil liʾl-muʾarrikh al-Yamanī Muḥammad b. ᶜAlī al-Shawkānī* (Beirut: Dār al-ᶜAwda, 1983), p. 184; Ḥusayn b. ᶜAbd Allāh al-ᶜAmrī, *Miʾat ᶜām min tārīkh al-Yaman al-ḥadīth* (Damascus: Dār al-Fikr, 1988), p. 226; Dresch,

revenue available to it, namely the tax-base represented by Shāfiᶜī Lower Yemen and areas of the Western Mountains, like Wuṣāb, where agriculture generating sizeable surplus was historically to be found.[72] The increased importance of Lower Yemen can be seen clearly in the chronicles of the period, which portray the imams constantly waging campaigns in Lower Yemen in an attempt to maintain their control of the area, while tribes from Upper Yemen, especially the Dhū Muḥammad and Dhū Ḥusayn of Bakīl, tried to wrest control for themselves.[73] The Tihāma also formed an important tax-base for the imamate, mainly because of the ports, where imports and exports were taxed. But even these areas were eventually lost when the Wahhābīs invaded in the early years of the nineteenth century. The Tihāma was only to return to the imamate for a period of about thirteen years between the withdrawal of Muḥammad ᶜAlī's forces in 1819 and the arrival in 1832 of another Egyptian force headed by a renegade nicknamed 'Türkçe Bilmez'.[74]

Imamic rule depended on an intricate system of patronage that tied groups and families of northern highland tribal origin into the imamate's network of interests. The tribes acted as the military arm of the state and, in return, some were accorded tax privileges, some were given land in Lower Yemen, and some were given *iqṭā*ᶜs (these were designated regions from which they could collect the canonical taxes on behalf of the state, keeping some portion for themselves).[75] The relationship between the Qāsimī imams and those who had fought with them against the Ottomans lasted until well after the expulsion and is attested in imamic documents, called *al-jabbūriyya*, which gave these allies (called *mujabbarūn*) certain privileges, both financial and moral, in seeming perpetuity.[76] The system broke down, especially as revenues declined from the loss of the coffee trade and the imams ceased to live up to the ideal. As Sālim's work on imamic letters and documents shows, the imams could no longer demand obedience on the basis of religious authority and legitimacy; increasingly, imams had to find, from ever dwindling resources, emoluments to secure support. The system of granting fiefs, expropriating them only to grant them again, appears to have become increasingly difficult for imams to maintain.

In the period following the death of al-Mutawakkil Ismāᶜīl, a pattern emerged whereby the victorious imam would have to acknowledge the political and fiscal authority of other contenders over given areas, and in return the contender would formally acknowledge the imam's position. This was generally done by mentioning

Tribes, p. 200; P. Boxhall, 'The diary of a Mocha coffee agent', *Arabian Studies* 1 (1974), 102–18. This appears to have happened in the second decade of the eighteenth century when the Dutch, and later the French, were able to cultivate coffee in their colonies, cf. Tuchscherer, 'Le commerce en Mer Rouge aux alentours de 1700', p. 56.

72 On the importance of Lower Yemen, Shawkānī states that 'Lower Yemen consists of many towns and the resources of the kingdom (*mawādd al-mamlaka*) come from it', cf. *Badr*, II: 159.

73 Ḥusayn al-ᶜAmrī's *Mi'at ᶜām min tārīkh al-Yaman* depicts many of these campaigns in great detail. Also Dresch's *Tribes* (especially chapter 6) offers an excellent discussion of the role tribes, and tribal shaykhs, played in Lower Yemen and in the taxation policies of the Qāsimī imamate.

74 Cf. al-ᶜAmrī, *Mi'at ᶜām*, pp. 220–9; R. Baily Winder, *Saudi Arabia in the Nineteenth Century* (New York: St. Martin's Press, 1965), pp. 71–5.

75 Cf. Dresch, *Tribes*, p. 209.

76 Sālim, *Wathā'iq Yamaniyya*, p. 76.

his name in the Friday sermon and minting coins in his name (*sikka*). The imam's religious knowledge and character mattered less, and this may have been a factor in the increasing influence a cohort of ulema were to garner throughout the eighteenth century, culminating in the rise of Shawkānī to pre-eminence. With their need to issue judgements, the imams, who were no longer acknowledged as *mujtahid*s themselves, became dependent on scholars who could provide these for them.

CHAPTER 2

Becoming a Dynasty: the Qāsimī Imamate in the Eighteenth and Nineteenth Centuries

The eighteenth century in Yemen constitutes a *conjoncture* in the Braudelian sense in which a host of social, economic, political and especially ideological changes came together.[1] The Qāsimī imams had by the eighteenth century clearly become a ruling dynasty with power being handed down from father to son regardless of personal qualifications or abilities. Whereas, in the seventeenth century, the position of imam remained confined to the descendants of al-Qāsim b. Muḥammad, succession appears to have been based on precedence in terms of merit (i.e., learning and leadership qualities). During the eighteenth century and part of the nineteenth century, however, the descendants of al-Qāsim succeeded each other in an uninterrupted line from father to son from 1716 until 1836, i.e., from al-Mutawakkil al-Qāsim b. al-Ḥusayn (d. 1139/1727) until al-Manṣūr ᶜAlī b. ᶜAbd Allāh (d. 1288/1871).[2] A tradition was instituted whereby the reigning imam nominated his successor by appointing him governor of Sanaa (*ᶜāmil Ṣanᶜāᵓ*) and Commander of the Troops (*amīr al-ajnād*) – these were appointments which all men of rank understood to mean the nomination of a successor. The sons of the imams were given the title 'Sword of Islam' (*Sayf al-Islām*). Previously, epithets were accorded to eminent persons through an informal process and generally by popular consensus (e.g., *faqīh* or *ᶜallāma*), whereas now titles (e.g., *sayf al-islām*, *wazīr* and *amīr*) were given by the imam and denoted a rank which did not necessarily reflect the personal qualities of the person holding it.

The eighteenth century imams no longer fulfilled the requirements of leadership and scholarship prescribed by the original Zaydī doctrine of the imamate,

[1] Fernand Braudel, the famous French historian of the Annales School, claimed that historical time can be divided into three distinct time-spans of different duration. The first and shortest time-span is that of the event, which has been the concern of traditional narrative and certainly that of all Yemeni historical chronicles and biographical dictionaries. The intermediate time span is that of the *conjoncture* where the focus is on broader movements of demography, social structures, economies and political institutions. A *conjoncture* can be as long as fifty years or more. Finally, the longest time-span is that of the *longue durée*, and typically here the historian is looking at a time-span several centuries long in which time is almost stationary and where the focus can be on geo-physical, climatic and biological change. See Stuart Clark, 'The *Annales* historians', in Quentin Skinner (ed.), *The Return of Grand Theory in the Human Sciences* (Cambridge University Press, 1985).

[2] See the genealogical chart of the Qāsimī imams in which the direct father-to-son succession is clearly represented by a straight line.

and made no pretence of doing so. None claimed to be a *muḥtasib* imam, i.e., a leader who did not fulfil the range of requirements for full imam status and who would act as substitute until such time as a full-fledged imam would rise to claim the position.[3] Had they claimed to be *muḥtasib* imams, they would have at least remained consistent with the later Zaydī doctrine of the imamate since it acknowledged the rule of such 'restricted' leaders. However, from the reign of al-Mahdī Muḥammad b. Aḥmad (d. 1130/1718), known in the histories as Ṣāḥib al-Mawāhib for choosing al-Mawāhib as his base, down to that of al-Mansūr ᶜAlī b. al-Mahdī ᶜAbd Allāh (r. till 1851), a period of about 150 years, Zaydī doctrine on the issue appears to have remained in abeyance.

The imamate in this period acquired many of the institutions of other Middle Eastern and Islamic states of the time, such as a standing army, some of whose soldiers were slaves. Futhermore, this was often led by slave 'commanders' who were given the title *Amīr al-jund*.[4] The establishment of a standing army signalled an attempt by the imams to lessen their dependence on the tribes and to acquire a force with which to withstand challenges from rival claimants. The sources mention that the first imam to have recruited slave soldiers from Africa was al-Mahdī Ṣāḥib al-Mawāhib, who did so in order to ward off a challenge from his cousin al-Ḥusayn b. al-Qāsim b. al-Muʾayyad in 1124/1712.[5] Independence from tribal military support was never fully achieved, however.

An official court (*dīwān*) was instituted in which officials charged with specific ministerial affairs served.[6] It was in the *dīwān* that Shawkānī was later to wield great influence. Sanaa, moreover, became a capital city after the reign of al-Mahdī Ṣāḥib al-Mawāhib, which meant that it became the locus of power and patronage until at least 1850, after which a period of political instability set in.[7] In Sanaa, the Great Mosque (*al-Jāmiᶜ al-Kabīr*) became the most important centre of learning, perhaps in a way it had never been hitherto, and Traditionist scholars vied with Hādawīs over what could or could not be taught or read there.

From the early eighteenth century, the mint was run by the leading Jewish family in Sanaa and remained in Jewish hands until well into the nineteenth century.[8]

[3] For an elaboration on the *muḥtasib* see al-Manṣūr al-Qāsim b. Muḥammad, *Kitāb al-Asās li-ᶜaqāʾid al-akyās*, Muḥammad al-Hāshimī (ed.) (Ṣaᶜda: Maktabat al-Turāth al-Islāmī, 1994), pp. 173f.; also al-Sharafī, *Kitāb ᶜUddat al-akyās*, vol. II, pp. 618f.

[4] Cf. Niebuhr, *Travels*, vol. II, pp. 51, 89–92. The Zaydī imamate has historically relied on tribal forces and levies in its military actions. Niebuhr recounts that the imams had tribal regiments who were better paid than the regular soldiers. The regulars were presumably either Ethiopian slaves or men from Lower Yemen and the Tihāma.

[5] Cf. al-Ḥiyed, 'Relations between the Yaman and South Arabia', p. 156. It should be noted that some earlier Zaydī imams, such as al-Mutawakkil Ismāᶜīl, did own slaves but these were few in number and did not constitute a military force, though some did lead campaigns, cf. Ḥusayn al-ᶜAmrī, *al-Umarāʾ al-ᶜabīd waʾl-mamālīk fīʾl-Yaman* (Beirut: Dār al-Fikr al-Muᶜāṣir, 1989), pp. 53–6.

[6] Cf. Niebuhr, *Travels*, vol. II, pp. 83–5.

[7] From this time on Sanaa acquired a status as the seat of government which has endured to this day, except for the brief period when Imam Aḥmad Ḥamīd al-Dīn (d. 1962) made Taᶜizz his capital.

[8] Cf. Yosef Tobi, 'ha-Nisyōnōt le-Garesh et ha-Yehūdīm mi-Teyman be-Meʾa ha-18', in Yosef Tobi (ed.), *Le-Rosh Yosef* (Jerusalem: Afikim, 1995), pp. 459–74; also see Yehuda Nini, *The Jews of the Yemen: 1800–1914* (London: Harwood Academic Publishers, 1991).

Urban Jews were probably chosen for this job because of their weak and subservient political and social position in Yemeni society, and hence the imams were able to control and punish them with impunity should the need arise and without fear of retribution.

On Friday 3 Jumādā al-Ūlā 1166/9 March 1753 Ibn al-Amīr gave a lengthy sermon in Sanaa's Great Mosque and because of this he omitted the mention of Imam al-Qāsim b. Muḥammad, the founder of the Qāsimī *daᶜwa*, in his invocations. This constituted a break with the Qāsimī practice, instituted in the seventeenth century, possibly at the instigation of Qāḍī Saᶜd al-Dīn al-Maswarī (d. 1079/1668). Ibn al-Amīr justified his action by saying that Islamic custom allowed for such omissions in the event of long sermons. Some members of the Qāsimī family were angered by this omission, seeing it as part of a larger conspiracy to undermine Zaydism, and they asked Imam al-Mahdī al-ᶜAbbās to imprison Ibn al-Amīr or else they threatened to kill him. The imam reacted by imprisoning all the Qāsimī agitators, including their leader Muḥammad b. ᶜAlī (d. 1170/1757), whose 'fief' (*iqtāᶜ*) in Ḍūrān he also confiscated. Ibn al-Amīr was also imprisoned in the citadel, next to the mint, where he remained for two months under relatively lenient conditions. Muḥammad b. ᶜAlī, by contrast, was still languishing in prison, seventeen years later when he died.[9] While in prison, Ibn al-Amīr wrote a poem in praise of Saturdays, since these were the only days on which the continuous hammering of the mint would cease, affording him undisturbed sleep. The poem underscores the predominance of the Jews in the mint as well as the favoured position the Traditionist scholars had at this time.

> I dwelt close to the mint under compulsion and suffering // This proximity to the Jews who have no standing on the straight path
> Their hammers are calamities for me // And eye's slumber has no fortune in their midst
> I built a house whose time has passed // Nothing perverted therein for me nor doubt
> One of the strangest things is that I am a devout Muslim // Yet my very best day is – the Sabbath[10]

The imams acquired many of the symbolic trappings of sovereign rulers, namely the imamic umbrella or the parasol,[11] and they instituted such customs as the

[9] Muḥammad b. Ismāᶜīl al-Amīr, *Dīwān al-Amīr al-Ṣanᶜānī*, 2nd edn (Beirut: Manshūrāt al-Madīna, 1986), pp. 357–9; *Nashr*, III: 182–3.

[10] al-Amīr, *Dīwān al-Amīr al-Ṣanᶜānī*, p. 117.

[11] Cf. Niebuhr, *Travels*, vol. I, pp. 380–2. It is reported that one of al-Manṣūr ᶜAlī's governors over Mocha, Sayyid Ibrāhīm b. ᶜAbd Allāh al-Jarmūzī, offered the imam a parasol which astonished everyone (presumably because of its beauty) and which became known as the *Jarmuziyya*, cf. *Nayl*, I: 16–17. Another example of the umbrella becoming a symbol for the imamate can be seen in the chronicle *Ḥawliyāt Yamāniyya* where we are told that when the staunch Zaydī contender Aḥmad b. ᶜAlī al-Sirājī (d. 1250/1834) was recognised as imam 'the umbrella was placed over his head' (*nuṣibat al-miẓalla ᶜalā raʾsihi*), cf. *Ḥawliyāt Yamāniyya*, p. 61. The umbrella is a long established symbol of sovereignty and kingship in India and during the rule of the Fāṭimids in Egypt among other places, cf. *EI*², art. 'Miẓalla'. The use of the umbrella as an imperial symbol is also to be found in the later Muslim dynasties of India, particularly in the Mughal period. It was one of the eight ensigns of royalty and amongst those reserved exclusively for the sovereign (cf. Abul Aziz, *Arms and Jewelry of the Indian Mughals* (Lahore: n.p., 1947), pp. 77–84).

Gold coin of al-Mahdī Aḥmad b. al-Ḥasan, obverse (author)

Gold coin of al-Mahdī Aḥmad b. al-Ḥasan, reverse (author)

ceremonial procession of the imam, with full retinue, from the palace to the Great Mosque for Friday prayers which was invariably followed by a military display in the courtyard of the palace.[12]

Numismatic Evidence for the Doctrinal Shifts

The shifts in doctrine and self-presentation of the Qāsimī imams are substantiated by numismatic evidence.[13] The Qāsimīs did not mint many gold coins because

[12] Imamic processions were probably modelled on those of the Ottoman governor-general of Yemen province, the *Beylerbeyi*. Like the imams, they also led Friday processions to the main mosque, surrounded with troops and musicians, cf. C. G. Brouwer, *al-Mukhā* (Amsterdam: D'Fluyte Rarob, 1997), p. 158 and more generally chapter 5 for Ottoman administrative practice.

[13] Qāsimī coinage is extremely varied and complex and there are no studies of its metrology or of the monetary system of the imamate. One can find only disparate articles about discrete issues in

they tended to use Ottoman or Venetian issues in the higher denominations and for important transactions. They did, however, strike a great number of silver and copper coins, as these were used locally for most transactions. An example of what is probably the first gold coin to be struck by a Qāsimī imam can be found in the British Museum.[14] This coin was called a *ḥarf* and was struck in 1091/1680 by al-Mahdī Aḥmad b. al-Ḥasan (d. 1092/1681), the fourth Qāsimī imam. It was probably intended as a donative or ceremonial coin and very few examples are known. For our purposes, however, it is the inscriptions on it which are important because they reveal the prevailing doctrinal beliefs and the modalities of this imam's claim to legitimate rule. The obverse of the coin contains the following version of the Muslim *credo* (*shahāda*):

> There is no God but God; Muḥammad is the Messenger of God; ᶜAlī is rightfully his Successor (*lā illāha ilā Allāh; Mūḥammadun rasūlu Allāh; ᶜAliyyun khalīfatu-hu ḥaqqan*)

And the reverse has this inscription:

> The Rightly Guided to God's Religion (al-Mahdī li-Dīn Allāh) Aḥmad b. al-Ḥasan b. al-Qāsim 1091 [the year the coin was struck]

With its insistence that ᶜAlī is 'rightfully' the caliph after the Prophet, the *shahāda* inscribed here reaffirms the Shīᶜite credentials of the state and the legitimacy on which its imams based their rule, namely descent from ᶜAlī who was designated by the Prophet as his successor. The Zaydī doctrine of the imamate is confirmed as the only basis for rule. The reverse gives the honorific title of the imam and traces his descent from al-Qāsim b. Muḥammad, the state's founder. It must be pointed out, however, that al-Mahdī's father, al-Ḥasan (d. 1048/1639), who is mentioned here, was one of the most successful commanders of the Qāsimī armies and a scholar in his own right who never became imam.[15] Thus, whilst Qāsimī credentials are being affirmed here, the claim to legitimate rule is not derived from strict patrilineal descent, i.e., father to son.

In 1176/1762–3, eighty-five years later, al-Mahdī al-ᶜAbbās (d. 1189/1775), the ninth imam in the Qāsimī line, struck a gold coin which again appears to have been ceremonial or donative. This is so far a unique piece which was exhibited in the Museum für Völkerkunde in Vienna in 1989–90.[16] The inscriptional style

a variety of numismatic journals. Cf. Stephen Album, *Sylloge of Islamic Coins in the Ashmolean* (Oxford: Ashmolean Museum, 1999), vol. X, pp. xi–xii.

14 Cf. Nicholas Lowick, 'The mint of Ṣanᶜāʾ: a historical outline', in R. B. Serjeant and R. Lewcock (eds.), *Ṣanᶜāʾ: An Arabian Islamic City* (London: World of Islam Festival Trust, 1983), p. 307; Samuel Lachman, 'The Zaidī Imām al-Mahdī Aḥmad b. al-Ḥasan', and 'The gold coins of the Zaidī imāms of the 17th to the 19th centuries', *Numismatic Circular* 96 (1988), 143–6, 211–12.

15 Cf. *Maṭlaᶜ al-budūr*, II: 48–54; *Badr*, I: 205–7.

16 Cf. Samuel Lachman, 'A Ṭughrāʾ on a gold coin of the Zaidī Imām al-Mahdī al-ᶜAbbās', *Numismatic Circular* 98 (1990), 351; Stefan Nebehay, 'Muslimische Münzen aus dem Jemen', in *Jemen: Im Lande der Königen von Saba* (Vienna: Museum für Völkerkunde, 1989), p. 149. I would like to thank the Kunsthistorisches Museum in Vienna for allowing me to reproduce a photograph of this coin.

Gold coin of al-Mahdī al-ᶜAbbās, obverse (Kunsthistorisches Museum, Vienna)

Gold coin of al-Mahdī al-ᶜAbbās, reverse (Kunsthistorisches Museum, Vienna)

is radically different from the coin described above. The reverse has a cartouche which reads:

> Commander of the Faithful son of Commander of the Faithful son of Commander of the Faithful the Imam (*amīr al-muʾminīn b. amīr al-muʾminīn b. amīr al-muʾminīn al-imām*)

On the obverse is a *ṭughrā*, which is identical to the ones found on Egyptian-Ottoman coinage of the period (e.g., the *zar-i maḥbūb*), and which consists of the imam's title and name, 'al-Mahdī al-ᶜAbbās'. Outside the *ṭughrā* is inscribed 'struck in Sanaa 1176' (*ḍuribat fī Ṣanᶜāʾ*).[17] The fact that no *credo* is inscribed

[17] For a comparison with Egyptian coinage of the period see Samuel Lachman, 'The Egyptian coinage of the 18th century', *Numismatics International Bulletin* 13.1 (1979), 11–14.

on the reverse is not important since many Qāsimī coins do not have it.[18] Several aspects, however, are notable about this last coin when contrasted with the earlier one. First, it is striking that the claim to rightful rule here is based on strict patrilineal descent. In other words, al-Mahdī's rule is legitimate because he is the son of a ruler who was the son of a ruler, and the list significantly leads up to the word 'imam'. Here too we note the influence of Ottomanisation on the House of al-Qāsim since Ottoman akçes of the same period have inscriptions which read: 'al-sulṭān ibn al-sulṭān'.[19] Second, the use of the *ṭughrā* is significant since it is emulating in presentational style the Ottoman Sultans, who appear to have become the model on which to base one's rule. The shift away from Zaydism, and the tradition of the early Qāsimī imams, appears to be definitive in the second coin. One final point about these two coins deserves noting, namely that the calligraphy on the first coin is in texture and style much like Mughal and Safavid coins of the period.[20] The second coin is, as we have observed, modelled on Egyptian-Ottoman coinage. This may be an indication of Egypt's greater importance for Yemen in the eighteenth century.

Displaying Power

In this last coin a different conception of legitimate power is suggested from that conventionally attributed to Zaydī imams. In earlier Zaydī thought, as in Shāfiᶜī thought, a certain tolerance or caution is apparent whereby family and personal concerns are brought to the attention of rulers only by the parties' consent. Several possible solutions of a given dispute may be acceptable, while the ruler acts more fully in the public gaze as mediator. In the eighteenth century, however, the Qāsimī ruler becomes secluded. Appearances are more important, and the public display of the ruler to his subjects becomes properly a matter of calculated form and ceremony. In addition, access to the imam in this period becomes problematic even for the elites (*al-khaṣṣa*), such as ministers and public administrators: the eighteenth-century imams, like the Ottoman sultans, now acquire a 'gate keeper' (*bawwāb*) who, as his name suggests, controls access to the ruler. As for the laymen (*al-ᶜawāmm*), the only time at which they may see their ruler is during the

18 Cf. Samuel Lachman, 'The period of the early Qāsimid imāms of the Yemen', *Numismatic Circular* 96 (1988), 39–43; idem, 'The coins of the Zaidī imām al-Mutawakkil ᶜala allāh Ismāᶜīl b. al-Qāsim', *Numismatic Circular* 97 (1989), 147–50, 183–5; idem, 'The coins of the Zaidī imāms of the period 1224–1265 H/1809–1849', *Numismatic Circular* 98, 1–7, and 'A gold coin of the Zaidī imām al-Mutawakkil al-Qāsim b. al-Ḥusayn', *Numismatic Circular* 98 (1990), 84.

19 According to the noted numismatist Stephen Album, the coin of al-Mahdī al-ᶜAbbās is derived from the *zar-i maḥbūb* of the Ottoman sultan Maḥmūd I that is always dated with the accession year 1143 AH, see Chester L. Krause *et al.* (eds.), *Standard Catalog of World Coins: Eighteenth Century, 1701–1800*, 2nd edn (Iola, Wisconsin: Krause Publications, 1997), p. 1056 (cat. no. KM-222).

20 In its inscriptional style and general layout, al-Mahdī Aḥmad b. al-Ḥasan's coin resembles closely a gold issue of Burhān Nizām Shāh II (r. 999 or 1000–3/1591–5) of the Aḥmadnagar Sultanate in India. Cf. Stan Goron, *The Coins of the Indian Sultanate* (New Delhi: Munshiram Manoharlal, 2001), p. 327 (no. N10, Pagoda, Burhanabad, 3.5 g). This is another indication of the influence the global network of trade and ideas had on the Qāsimīs in this period.

elaborate procession accompanying the Friday prayer. A telling account of this is given by Jean de La Roque, a Frenchman who recounts the visit in 1712 of Mr de la Grelaudière and a surgeon named Sieur Barbier to the court of Imam al-Mahdī Ṣāḥib al-Mawāhib.

> The King of Yemen himself lives very regularly; he rises at day-break, dines at nine, and sleeps at eleven, and at two a-clock in the afternoon the drums beat, and the hautboys play. He whom they call chief of the drums, or the drum-major, only has the privilege of entering into the King's apartment at all hours: he is a *Turk* by nation, and very pleasantly equipped: he wears a belt of a monstrous size, set thick with large silver plates and knobs; and his turban has an embroidery of above a hand's breadth on the fore-part of it, and a silver chain which goes several times round it in a whimsical manner. As soon as this officer has given notice of the King's being awake, he is visited by the Princes and Grandees, who entertain him till the usual hour for prayer or business: his great men never approach him but they take his right-hand, which he holds upon his knee, and kiss it with a most profound respect. There are likewise certain hours set apart for taking the air, and visiting his women: after this he sups at five, and concludes the day by going to bed constantly at eleven. But if any thing can be said to be less suitable to this simplicity, and make an appearance of Royal Majesty, it is without doubt the march the King makes out of *Mouab* [i.e., al-Mawāhib] every *Friday* at two in the afternoon, to the place of public worship.[21]

Male slaves, who were generally referred to as *amīr* or *naqīb*, figure prominently in the records of the eighteenth century. They acted as retainers and were sent as leaders of troops to quell insurrections or to insure the collection of revenues. They also were appointed as governors of districts and administrators in the port towns on the Red Sea coast. Furthermore, they played a role in court intrigues and politics. Though the historical records are silent about the lives of slave women, the imams had a number of them as concubines. Carsten Niebuhr, who visited the court of al-Mahdī al-ᶜAbbās in 1762, says that the imam himself

> was of a dark complexion, like his ancestors by the mother's side, and did not at all resemble the other descendants of Mahomet. Had it not been for some negro traits, his countenance might have been thought a good one. He had twenty brothers, of whom some that I saw were black as ebony, flat-nosed, and thick-lipped, like the Caffres of the South of Africa.[22]

It is interesting to note that in this period the natural figures of prominence, the tribal shaykhs, are not given titles or accorded ranks and do not figure as officials in the court. Moreover, one sees an equivalence in the nomenclature between the slave commanders and the members of the ruling household. The army now

[21] La Roque, *A Voyage to Arabia the Happy* (London: Golden Ball (for G. Strathan and R. Williamson), 1726), pp. 194–5. La Roque wrote up the journey of the French expeditions of 1708 and 1711 to the Yemen on the basis of the notes and letters of the participants of these expeditions. The French had come to Yemen to buy coffee and establish treaty relations with the imam; the ulterior motive being to avoid the Egyptian and Turkish middle-men who were supplying the French with coffee in Egypt.

[22] Niebuhr, *Travels*, vol. II, pp. 76–7.

plays an important role, as do the numerous attendants who carry banners, beat drums and blow bugles. The image of power becomes divorced from the personal qualities of the ruler and becomes evident only in public displays, such as the imam's procession in which an elaborate ceremony is displayed. La Roque goes on to describe the procession as follows:

> The procession is begun by a thousand foot soldiers marching in good order, who make a discharge at their coming out of the palace. Among these soldiers there are two ranks carrying the colours, which are scalloped, called the colours of *Mahomet* and *Aly*; these are followed by two hundred cavaliers of the King's guards, mounted upon very fine horses, with handsome furniture; besides the ordinary arms, the sabre and the carbine, they have half pikes, the heads being adorned with [a] fringe. The officers of the King's household, and his courtiers all gallantly mounted, follow this troop; and at some distance from them appears the King on a fine white horse, very gentle, and used only to carry his majesty. On each side are the two Princes his sons, mounted likewise on horses of great price, with rich trappings. An officer carries a large umbrella or rather canopy, under which the King rides shaded from the heat of the sun. This canopy is of green damask, with [a] sort of furbeloe of red silk eight inches deep, running round it, enriched with a gold-lace; on the top of the canopy there is a globe of silver gilt, and upon the globe a pyramid of the same.
>
> Immediately before the King, one of his officers on horseback carries the *Alcoran* in a bag of red-cloth; another carries a standard of green damask, of a square form, which is called the King's standard: this is garnished with gold fringe, and has no figure in it as the others, but only some *Arabick* characters embroidered: and lastly behind the King, another officer on horseback carries his sabre, the handle and sheath of which are very rich, the sheath being covered with another of scarlet. All the time the procession lasts, the drums and kettle-drums never cease beating, nor the hautboys playing.[23]

The nature of imamic authority had obviously changed from that described in Zaydī legal manuals. The European who witnessed the Friday procession was correct in seeing the imam as King of Yemen. In his work *Wathāʾiq Yamāniyya*, Sālim notes that the first Qāsimī imam to use a seal on his letters, perhaps in emulation of the Ottoman Sultans or more probably of the Mughal emperors of India, was Ṣāḥib al-Mawāhib.[24] Until then, the imams would normally just sign their names, generally above the text of a letter and just below the *basmallah* in order, Sālim says, to indicate the exalted status of the imam.

Ṣāḥib al-Mawāhib's reign appears to have been brutal.[25] A number of *sayyids*, many of whom were from the House of Qāsim, fled Yemen in fear of him. For

[23] La Roque, *A Voyage to Arabia*, pp. 195–7. Niebuhr and Valentia describe similar Friday processions, cf. Niebuhr, *Travels*, vol. I, pp. 380–2; Valentia, *Voyages and Travels*, vol. II, p. 349. According to Valentia, the governor of Mocha performed the ceremony of the Friday procession in emulation of the imam.

[24] Cf. Sālim, *Wathāʾiq Yamaniyya*, pp. 40, 71, 76. It is more likely that the imams were emulating the Mughals of India whose seals are identical to those of the imams in Yemen (cf. B. N. Goswamy and J. S. Grewal, *The Mughals and the Jogis of Jakhbar* (Simla: The Indian Institute of Advanced Study, 1967), see especially appendix of seals. The *tughrā*, which is most often associated with Ottoman documents, but Mughal ones as well, appears to have been used first by al-Mahdī al-ʿAbbās.

[25] Cf. *Nashr*, I: 736–7, *Nashr*, II: 402–9.

example, the sons of al-Mutawakkil Ismāʿīl, al-Ḥasan and al-Ḥusayn, fled with their families to Mecca. Another of the imam's retainers, Iṣḥāq b. Muḥammad al-ʿAbdī (d. 1115/1704), fled to India after an incident in which he forgot to mention the imam's title when reading out a letter addressed to the latter.[26] Futhermore, Ṣāḥib al-Mawāhib was accused by Ṣāliḥ b. Mahdī al-Maqbalī of having instituted uncanonical taxation practices. More specifically, he would send his troops to the tribes in order to secure levies, but the tribes would offer payments instead to absolve themselves of the obligation. This then became a form of customary tribute in which certain tribal shaykhs would collude with the imam. Al-Maqbalī adds that no one dared raise a matter of dispute with the imam because he would systematically take money from the plaintiff. Al-Maqbalī gives the example of Kawkabān, his home region, which did not raise enough taxes to cover its own expenses, so that, in the past, imams such as al-Mutawakkil Ismāʿīl would pay whatever debts had accrued from the public treasury. Now, however, Ṣāḥib al-Mawāhib was extracting revenue from the area for himself and his retainers, and it was no longer spent on any of the deserving locals.[27]

The process of establishing patrimonial forms of rule which began mainly with Ṣāḥib al-Mawāhib was continued in the reigns of his eighteenth-century successors. They established more formalised administrative structures which employed judges, *awqāf* administrators, governors (*ʿāmil*, pl. *ʿummāl*), tax collectors, weights/standards officials, and port officials. The imams now had an official who acted like a prime minister, as well as a number of other ministers responsible for, among other things, tribal affairs, *awqāf* and taxation. Each region also had a minister. With the state no longer relying on the courage and erudition of its imam, the personal qualities of the leader no longer seemed formal prerequisites to his rule.

Shawkānī Becomes Chief Judge (*qāḍī al-quḍāt*)

When Yaḥyā al-Saḥūlī died in 1209/1795, Imam al-Manṣūr ʿAlī (d. 1224/1809) requested Shawkānī to assume the position of chief judge. For about a week, Shawkānī vacillated; in his autobiography, he claims that he did not want to accept the position because it would detract from his scholarly activities.[28] He was undoubtedly well aware of the dangers of getting involved with rulers, not to mention the stigma of corruption and unrighteousness, which led most scholars to avoid such associations.[29] However, he claims that he was persuaded ultimately by his students and other scholars to take up the position for fear that someone less capable, or perhaps of a different orientation, would do so. In accepting the appointment, Shawkānī may have been swayed by the promise of the 'fief' (*iqṭāʿ*) he was later granted by the imam from which he could collect taxes or revenues,

[26] Cf. *Nashr*, I: 319–20; *Hijar al-ʿilm*, III: 1425.
[27] Cf. *Hijar al-ʿilm*, III: 1571–4.
[28] See *al-Tiqṣār*, pp. 423–5; *Badr*, I: 464–5.
[29] See, for example, *Nashr*, I: 153.

such as the *zakāt*, *ṣadaqa* (legal alms), and *waṣāya* (testamentary disposition).[30] The official justification for his having an *iqṭāᶜ* was to insure the probity of the judicial system as this removed all incentives for accepting bribes. The author of *Ḥawliyyāt Yamāniyya*, who was writing at least fifty years after the events he describes here, states:

> The Shaykh al-Islām was respected (*mahāban*) for applying the Book of God and the Sunna of His Prophet – peace be upon him. No one has witnessed against him for having taken a little or a lot from legal disputants (*al-mutashājirūn*). The reason for this is that he has fiefs (*anna maᶜahu qiṭaᶜ*) like Ruṣāba, al-Rawna, and other places which provide him with at least one thousand *qadaḥ* of wheat (*ṭaᶜām*), and as many sheep. And from Ḥayma he has a monthly revenue of one hundred silver pieces (*qirsh ḥajar*). All who are with him and know him eat with him [i.e., live off him]. He did not save for himself (*yaddakhir*) anything from what accrued.[31]

Here is another reference to the 'fiefs' which were accorded to Shawkānī by the imam upon becoming his chief judge:

> The imam gave him as a fief the *ṣadaqāt* of Ruṣāba, Jabal al-Lawz, al-Rawna, Saᶜwān, Shawkān, Shawbān and a lot besides this. [Also] part of the *ṣadaqa* of Bayt Rājiḥ, and added to it the *ṣadaqa* of Bayt Qubbān and Bayt al-Ḥaymī and the testamentary disposition (*waṣiyya*) of al-Tawhamī and Tanᶜim.[32]

Shawkānī was undoubtedly a very rich and influential man as a result of these privileges, since the yearly revenues from Ḥayma alone amounted to 1200 Spanish dollars (*qirsh ḥajar*).[33] It is not clear how he spent this money. It is reported that he enjoyed opulent clothing and an elegant lifestyle, however.[34] He undoubtedly spent some of these funds on his students, which may, in part, account for his great popularity and the influence he gained in the scholarly community. The late *muftī* of the Republic of Yemen, Sayyid Aḥmad Zabāra, reports that the falling out which took place between Shawkānī and his prized student, Muḥammad b. ᶜAlī al-ᶜAmrānī (d. 1264/1848), was over the supervision of his 'fiefs'. Al-ᶜAmrānī had the job of looking after them until sometime in the early 1830s when Shawkānī asked him to hand it over to his sons who had reached the age of maturity. As a result, the two men had a falling-out which led to al-ᶜAmrānī's imprisonment and near execution. Sometime in 1250/1834, al-ᶜAmrānī was released and he immediately fled Sanaa to Zabīd, where he was later to die in a raid on the town by the Ismāᶜīlī tribe of Yām.[35]

[30] It is not clear to me what the *waṣāya* were. Perhaps these were testamentary trusts (*awqāf*) that were managed by the imams.
[31] *Ḥawliyyāt Yamāniyya*, pp. 278–9.
[32] *Nayl*, II: 298; cf. ᶜAbd Allāh b. Muḥammad al-Ḥibshī, *Dirāsāt fī ʾl-turāth al-Yamanī* (Beirut: Dār al-ᶜAwda, 1977), p. 64. Much has been made of these 'fiefs' in recent times by Hādawīs in Yemen who claim that they highlight the extent to which Shawkānī was co-opted and worked in concert with corrupt and unrighteous rulers.
[33] For the relative purchasing power of the various denominations at this time see al-ᶜAmrī, *Miʾat ᶜām*, pp. 150, 208–9.
[34] Ḥusayn al-ᶜAmrī, *al-Imām al-Shawkānī rāʾid ᶜaṣrih* (Damascus: Dār al-Fikr, 1990), p. 434.
[35] Cf. *Nayl*, II: 289–93.

While in Zabīd, al-ᶜAmrānī wrote a historical work entitled *Itḥāf al-nabīh bi-taʾrīkh al-Qāsim wa banīh* (The Gifts to the Judicious of the History of al-Qāsim and His Sons) in which he rebukes Shawkānī for a number of things. Amongst these is his claim to be an absolute religious authority (*mujtahid muṭlaq*). This, he says, made the judicial situation worse in Yemen since 'many unintelligent and unaccomplished students answered his summons' and Shawkānī provided them the means to acquire public funds dishonestly. Al-ᶜAmrānī goes on to say:

> And that which encouraged him [Shawkānī] to be excessive in concocting this stagnant trade was that he permitted himself to obliterate the Zaydī *madhhab*, at which point what he decided would become the reference in all parts of Yemen. He competes with al-Shāfiᶜī in the spread of his school, and he participates with Abū Ḥanīfa in taking as religion what he determines in his books... He created discord and hatred among the people of the country.[36]

Contemporary Zaydīs also deride Shawkānī as having benefitted greatly from his association with the imams. Zayd al-Wazīr, for example, narrates that his wealth manifested itself in his corpulence. Indeed, a confection sold in Sanaa today still bears his name: it is called 'Shawkānī's cheeks' (*malājiᶜ al-Shawkānī*).

Shawkānī's Students and His Influence

After Shawkānī became *qāḍī al-quḍāt* he acquired the ability to appoint his students to various postings throughout the realm. This newly acquired power in addition to Shawkānī's already formidable reputation as a purveyor of knowledge and a key personality in chains of transmission which encompassed over five hundred works in all disciplines, Islamic and otherwise – as enumerated in his famous *Itḥāf al-akābir bi-isnād al-dafātir* – led a large group of men to coalesce around him, seeking his instruction and patronage. These students were to help assure the perpetuation of his intellectual legacy and the spread of Traditionist views among the scholars of the Zaydī highlands and beyond.

The most detailed list of Shawkānī's students is contained in a eulogistic work by one of them, which is in the form of an extended biography of Shawkānī, enumerating his virtues and good deeds as well as listing his teachers and students with a biographical note on each.[37] The author of this work, entitled *Kitāb al-Tiqṣār fī jīd zamān ᶜallāmat al-aqālīm waʾl-amṣār* (The Necklace on the Neck of the Life of the Scholar of the Districts and the Towns), is Muḥammad b. al-Ḥasan al-Shijnī.[38] Throughout, al-Shijnī refers to Shawkānī by the honorific title of

[36] Muḥammad b. ᶜAlī al-ᶜAmrānī, *Itḥāf al-nabīh bi-taʾ rīkh al-Qāsim wa banīh*, ms. personal library of Muḥammad al-ᶜAmrānī in Sanaa, fol. 46. A different copy of the same work, with some additions, can be found in Sanaa, ms. Sanaa, Gharbiyya Library, *tārīkh* no. 77.

[37] The list is not exhaustive, but includes the most important persons who came into contact with Shawkānī.

[38] This work has now been edited by Muḥammad b. ᶜAlī al-Akwaᶜ and published under the title *Ḥayāt al-imām al-Shawkānī al-musammā Kitāb al-Tiqṣār*.

Shaykh al-Islām. This is the first time a Yemeni scholar of Zaydī origin is referred to in this way and it may reflect an attempt at emulating Ottoman practice. Al-Shijnī also claims that Shawkānī was the Renewer of the Thirteenth century AH (*mujaddid al-qarn al-thālith ᶜashar*).[39] According to the author's account, Shawkānī was already a widely recognised authority (*marjiᶜ*) well before being appointed chief judge, and, indeed, it was his paramount position among the scholars which made the imam seek him as a replacement for Qāḍī Yaḥyā al-Saḥūlī.

> He [i.e., Shawkānī] attained a degree [of knowledge] in the sciences of *ijtihād* which none of the other *mujtahid*s of his time had attained. The job of teaching and issuing *fatwā*s revolved around him and students came to him from far off places. Questions addressed to him were sent from the ulema of the [various] towns about problematic issues. Also, those close to Sanaa and its environs realized that the judges of Sanaa referred to his *fatwā*s in whatever they quarreled about, and they heard that he forbad taking money for issuing *fatwā*s and that he would censure those who did [take money]. Therefore this [i.e., issuing *fatwā*s] would take up all his time. [When] the Qāḍī, the leading scholar and chief judge of Sanaa Yaḥyā b. Ṣāliḥ al-Saḥūlī – God have mercy on him – died, Imam al-Manṣūr – God have mercy on him – ordered the closure of the judicial council (*dīwān al-ḥukm*) in which the leading judges would meet in the square [in front of] the imam's house (*dār al-imām*). [The imam] inquired with his ministers about Shaykh al-Islām [i.e., Shawkānī] in order to know about him. All said that we do not know him personally, but we know his writings and his reputation and that he has become now the one referred to among the scholars (*marjiᶜ al-ᶜulamāʾ*) in your presence [i.e., even those on the council deferred to him]. This is because Shaykh al-Islām kept away (*taqabbaḍ*) from all the lords of the government (*arbāb al-dawla*), not to mention those who were not people of knowledge at all. It became apparent to the imam – God have mercy on him – that he [i.e., Shawkānī] had [qualities] which no other lord of his government had, so he sent for him . . .[40]

Once in power, Shawkānī became pivotal in the imamic government. He, thus, assured the peaceful transition of power from al-Manṣūr ᶜAlī to al-Mutawakkil Aḥmad, by helping to organise a palace coup by which al-Manṣūr was deprived of his powers and Aḥmad took over.[41] He corresponded with the Wahhābīs on behalf of the imam, defending the doctrinal orthodoxy of the imamate. Later, he was reponsible for negotiating the treaty with Muḥammad ᶜAlī's Egyptian troops by which the imamate recovered control over the Tihāma after the defeat of the Wahhābī movement and its semi-vassal state led by the Sharīfs of Abū ᶜArīsh. Al-Shijnī tell us that no governmental decision was taken without his consultation.[42]

A sense of the influence Shawkānī had on individual members of the ruling family and the extent to which the imams, in particular al-Mutawakkil Aḥmad

[39] *al-Tiqṣār*, p. 417. Similar claims to *mujaddid* status were made by the students of such famous scholars as Ibn Ḥajar and Suyūṭī in medieval Egypt, and it appears that it was only through such recognition by students that the teachers acquired these honorifics; cf. Ella Landau-Tasseron, 'The "Cyclical Reform": a study of the *mujaddid* tradition', *Studia Islamica* 70 (1989), 79–117.

[40] *al-Tiqṣār*, p. 423–4. [41] *Badr*, I: 466–7. [42] *al-Tiqṣār*, p. 425.

and al-Mahdī ᶜAbd Allāh, now identified with his juridical and religious views can be had from the scholarly pursuits of one of the princes. Al-Shijnī reports the story of Imam al-Mutawakkil Aḥmad's son al-Qāsim, who was born in 1211/1796 and was brought up in the palace where he first studied the reading of the Qur'ān and then the ḥadīth sciences. The first ḥadīth work he studied was Ibn Ḥajar's *Bulūgh al-marām* which he read with Muḥammad ᶜĀbid al-Sindī (d. 1257/1841), the grandson of the famous scholar of ḥadīth, who was at the time visiting Sanaa and in the employ of the imam for his medical skills.[43] Memorising the *Bulūgh* by heart, al-Qāsim then spent many days with Shawkānī reciting it numerous times from beginning to end. There follows a description of his studies with Shawkānī and his love for the ḥadīth sciences.

> He studied with Shaykh al-Islām [i.e., Shawkānī] some of *Ṣaḥīḥ* Bukhārī and *Ṣaḥīḥ* Muslim... He had an ardent passion for the science of the pure Sunna [i.e., ḥadīth] and for displaying it in the days of his father al-Mutawakkil – may God have mercy on him – as well as avidly reading the collections of ḥadīth... He did not pay attention to anything else, and the Imam – may God have mercy on him – would encourage him in this regard. He sought to make him interested and would give him all that he asked for of these books in order to make him like it, so that now he [i.e., Prince Qāsim] has a collection of ḥadīth works and commentaries greater than that of anyone else...[44]

Another report which highlights Shawkānī's influence in the reign of al-Mahdī ᶜAbd Allāh relates to Ibn Masᶜad, the tribal shaykh of Rijām, a village in Banū Ḥushaysh, north-east of Sanaa. For some infraction, Shawkānī had summoned Ibn Masᶜad to come to court, but the shaykh refused. Shawkānī took this as an act of defiance against the Sharīᶜa and in anger sent his pens and writing utensils to al-Mahdī ᶜAbd Allāh, who was then resting at Wādī Ẓahr a few kilometers from Sanaa. Upon receiving this news the imam

> rose immediately and ordered the attack on the one who had breached the Sharīᶜa. He did not return to Sanaa but went to al-Rawḍa which was the way to Rijām. There a large group met him with artillery and they surrounded Rijām, ate its grapes, grazed its crop and bombarded it with artillery. Sharīf ᶜAlī and Ghānim b. Mahdī mediated on his [i.e., Ibn Masᶜad's] behalf and he was brought [back to Sanaa] manacled in iron chains. His punishment was greater than what is deserved for breaking the Sharīᶜa...[45]

This account, and others like it, have become proverbial among modern Yemeni judges, who see in the power Shawkānī wielded an exemplary model of the authority and power of jurists, one which ought to be emulated.[46]

[43] For Muḥammad ᶜĀbid al-Sindī's biography see *Badr*, II: 227–8; *Nayl*, II: 279–81. After returning from Egypt where he was an emissary of the imam, al-Sindī famously reported back to Shawkānī that no knowledge of the religious sciences was to be found in Egypt and all that was left was *taqlīd* and sufism.

[44] *al-Tiqṣār*, p. 389. [45] *Ḥawliyyāt Yamāniyya*, p. 50.

[46] Cf. Muḥammad Ismāᶜīl al-ᶜAmrānī, *Niẓām al-qaḍā' fī 'l-islām* (Sanaa: Maktabat Dār al-Jīl, 1984), pp. 244–5, 272–3; Muḥammad b. ᶜAlī al-Akwaᶜ, *Ḥayāt ᶜālim wa amīr* (Sanaa: Maktabat al-Jīl al-Jadīd, 1987), pp. 60–2.

Judicial Appointments

Shawkānī's judicial appointments deserve special mention for they explain how he was able to perpetuate his influence not only in his lifetime but well beyond it. These are too many to enumerate and a few examples will suffice to offer a sense of his patronage and of the terms used in the historical sources to describe his powers. Al-Shijnī states that Qāḍī Ḥusayn b. Muḥammad al-ᶜAnsī (d. 1235/1820) was appointed to the judgeship (*ḥukūmat*) of Zabīd, the major Tihāmī town, by al-Mahdī ᶜAbd Allāh because of 'a notice (*mulāḥaẓa*) by the Shaykh al-Islām in this regard'.[47] ᶜAbd al-Raḥmān b. Aḥmad al-Bahkalī (d. 1248/1832) was given the judgeship of Bayt al-Faqīh, in the Tihāma again, owing to the 'efforts (*saᶜy*) of the Shaykh al-Islām'.[48] Another Shawkānī student was Qāḍī Muḥammad b. Yaḥyā al-ᶜAnsī, who 'studied (*qaraʾa ᶜalā*) with Shaykh al-Islām some works of ḥadīth, grammar, Qurʾānic exegesis and some of his works'; then 'he [i.e., Shawkānī] permitted him (*adhina lahu*) to take up the judgeship in Dhamār'.[49] Qāḍī ᶜAbd Allāh b. ᶜAlī Suhayl (d. 1251/1835), who seems to have had a special penchant for Shawkānī's works, 'was selected (*jaᶜalahu*) by Shaykh al-Islām as one of the judges of Sanaa'.[50] Some of Shawkānī's students, such as Ṣāliḥ b. Muḥammad al-ᶜAnsī, who was also Shawkānī's son-in-law and was appointed judge in the town of Ibb after holding a judgeship in Sanaa, were to establish local scholarly families and networks in those areas in which they served, and which would last well after the Qāsimī imamate itself foundered and disappeared.[51]

What is notable in all the examples of Shawkānī's patronage is that they entailed nominating judges either in Sanaa or in areas south of the capital, mainly in Shāfiᶜī areas in Lower Yemen or the Tihāma. The only Zaydī areas in which appointments were made were those south of Sanaa, such as Dhamār, which remained throughout Shawkānī's life within the ambit of the imamate. The geographical distribution of these appointments in predominantly Shāfiᶜī areas is another indication of the extent to which these remained of paramount importance to the imamate, mainly as a source of revenue. The northern highlands north of Sanaa by contrast are described in the sources as falling juridically beyond the pale. Individual scholars in these regions are described as continuing to apply the Law in their regions.[52] But, on the whole, these areas are mentioned as a source of embarrassment, as it was from them that tribes descended, fomenting trouble and seeking subsidies, or rival claimants to the imamate rose to wrest control in the name of greater righteousness and generally with tribal backing.

[47] *al-Tiqṣār*, p. 367. Cf. *Badr*, I: 228–9. [48] *al-Tiqṣār*, p. 371. Cf. *Badr*, I: 318; *Nayl*, II: 23–5.
[49] *al-Tiqṣār*, p. 431. [50] *al-Tiqṣār*, p. 373. Also cf. *Nayl*, II: 84.
[51] Cf. Messick, *The Calligraphic State*, p. 45; also *Nayl*, II: 14. Another example of such a student was al-Ḥasan b. Aḥmad ᶜĀkish al-Ḍamadī (d. 1289/1872), cf. *Nayl*, I: 314–18.
[52] The regions of Kawkabān and Shibām are one such example where scholarly families, such as the Sharaf al-Dīn family, maintained an important centre of learning and presumably continued to run a court. Other *hijras*, which were self-sustaining religious enclaves, were also places where the Sharīᶜa continued to be applied regardless of the absence of centralized judicial structures.

The Imamate Loses Territory

We know from the account of Carsten Niebuhr that the imamate had lost effective control of most areas north and east of Sanaa by the 1760s.[53] Imamic influence in these territories, with the exception of a few pockets north and north-west of Sanaa like ᶜAmrān and Kawkabān, was to remain negligible, sometimes nonexistent, throughout Shawkānī's life. This state of affairs meant that the imamate's area of control was restricted to the highlands south of Sanaa and the coastal Tihāma as far north as Luḥayya. With the exception of Mocha, the imamate also lost much of the Tihāma from around 1803 till 1818, either to the Wahhābīs or to the Sharīfs of Abū ᶜArīsh.[54] Throughout this period, Wahhābī influence was important. It would be unrealistic, however, to reduce Shawkānī's intellectual positions either to answering Wahhābī theological and legal claims or to accommodating political pressure forced on the imamate by Wahhābī forces.

Wahhābī involvement in Yemen led to the imamate's effective loss of much of the Tihāma between 1803 and 1818, when the Wahhābīs were finally defeated by Muḥammad ᶜAlī's forces.[55] In 1801, the Wahhābīs were already active in the Hijaz: Mecca eventually fell into their hands in 1803 and Medina a year later – in both cities, they destroyed domes erected over the tombs of saints as well as other places of visitation.[56] In northern ᶜAsīr, the local ruler in the mountains of al-Sarāh, ᶜAbd al-Wahhāb b. ᶜĀmir al-Rufaydī, known as Abū Nuqṭa, answered the Wahhābī call after a visit paid to ᶜAbd al-ᶜAzīz b. Saᶜūd in his capital at al-Dirᶜiyya in 1802–3.[57] Ibn Saᶜūd proceeded to appoint Abū Nuqṭa as governor of Upper ᶜAsīr.

In southern ᶜAsīr, a ruler of the Sharīfs of Āl Khayrāt established himself an independent sovereign in 1802 in Abū ᶜArīsh. This was Sharīf Ḥamūd b. Muḥammad Abū Mismār, who until then had ruled in Abū ᶜArīsh in the name of Imam al-Manṣūr ᶜAlī, but was now to control much of the Tihāma from 1803 until his death 1818.[58] Fighting soon broke out between Abū Nuqṭa and Sharīf Ḥamūd, and the latter was soundly defeated in a battle in the middle of Ramaḍān 1217/January 1803. This led to Sharīf Ḥamūd's declaration of loyalty to Ibn Saᶜūd and to the Wahhābī cause, after which Ḥamūd was appointed emir of Lower ᶜAsīr, on behalf of Ibn Saᶜūd.[59] Sharīf Ḥamūd proceeded to strengthen his power base by conquering more of the Tihāma, taking al-Luḥayya, Hodeida, Zabīd, Bayt al-Faqīh and Ḥays.[60] He also attempted to take control of Ḥajja district in the high mountain

[53] Niebuhr, *Travels*, vol. II, pp. 45–7.

[54] ᶜAbd Allāh b. ᶜAbd al-Karīm al-Jirāfī, *al-Muqtaṭaf min tārīkh al-Yaman* (Beirut: Manshūrāt al-ᶜAṣr al-Ḥadīth, 1987), pp. 259, 262; Muḥammad b. Ismāᶜīl al-Kibsī, *al-Laṭāʾif al-saniyya fī akhbār al-mamālik al-Yamaniyya* (n.p.: Maṭbaᶜat al-Saᶜāda, n.d.), pp. 298–302.

[55] Cf. *Badr*, I: 240–1.

[56] Cf. H. St. J. B. Philby, *Arabia* (London: Ernest Benn, 1930), pp. 83, 87.

[57] ᶜAbd al-Raḥmān b. Aḥmad al-Bahkalī, *Nafḥ al-ᶜūd fī sīrat dawlat al-Sharīf Ḥamūd*, Muḥammad b. Aḥmad al-ᶜAqīlī (ed.) (Riyadh: Maṭbūᶜāt Dārat al-Malik ᶜAbd al-ᶜAzīz, 1982), pp. 128–9.

[58] *Badr*, II: 369. [59] al-Bahkalī, *Nafḥ al-ᶜūd*, p. 142.

[60] *Badr*, I: 240, 262; al-Bahkalī, *Nafḥ al-ᶜūd*, pp. 170–6.

region northwest of Sanaa, but was repulsed in 1220/1805 and the poet Qāḍī ᶜAbd al-Raḥmān al-Ānisī was reappointed governor of the district.[61]

Imam al-Manṣūr ᶜAlī tried on numerous occasions to regain control of the Tihāma, for the loss of the ports in particular must have resulted in a considerable decline in revenues and in the imam's ability to buy off the tribes.[62] However, because of the imamate's political and economic difficulties elsewhere in this period, the Tihāma could not be regained.[63] A telling example of this was the failure of an expeditionary force of one thousand warriors of Dhū Muḥammad and Dhū Ḥusayn with thirty cavalrymen from Sanaa sent by the imam to retake the Tihāma on 20 Rajab 1221/7 October 1806. They failed due to lack of reinforcements and provisions.[64]

The Āl al-ᶜAnsī *Qāḍīs* of Jabal Baraṭ

The rise in Sanaa of Traditionist scholars in the reign of Imam al-Mansūr Ḥusayn b. al-Qāsim (d. 1161/1748), and even more markedly during that of al-Mahdī al-ᶜAbbās, engendered a reaction by Hādawī scholars, namely the Āl al-ᶜAnsī *qāḍīs* from the peripheral region of Jabal Baraṭ. Little is known about these scholars, and the biographical dictionaries provide us with no entries on them, perhaps highlighting their peripheral status.[65] Both Ibn al-Amīr and Shawkānī speak of them with disdain as ignorant *fuqahāᵓ* who rallied the Bakīl tribes of Dhū Muḥammad and Dhū Ḥusayn in order to foment trouble and cause disorder. One of the first mentions of the Āl al-ᶜAnsī is in 1145/1732 when ᶜAbd al-Raḥmān b. Muḥammad al-ᶜAnsī led the tribes of Bakīl in a raid on the port of al-Luḥayya. Ibn al-Amīr reacted to this with a poem condemning them and Imam al-Manṣūr Ḥusayn for allowing this to take place.[66] At the time Ibn al-Amīr was supporting Muḥammad b. Isḥāq (d. 1167/1754), a rival contender for the imamate who rose against al-Manṣūr Ḥusayn but was soon defeated and retired to a life of learning in Sanaa.[67] In 1151/1738–9, Ibn al-Amīr was finally patronised by al-Manṣūr and given the post of preacher (*khaṭīb*) at the Great Mosque in Sanaa.

Ibn al-Amīr had to abandon the post in 1166/1753 when his failure to mention the name of Imam al-Qāsim b. Muḥammad in the Friday sermon caused riots. It is reported that because of this omission, a certain Sayyid Yūsuf al-ᶜAjamī al-Imāmī, a Persian who had come to live in Sanaa 'to spread Twelver Shīᶜite teachings', led a group of the common folk (*al-ᶜawāmm*) to the mosque with the intention of killing Ibn al-Amīr, accusing him of being a *nāṣibī* (a person who manifests

61 Ḥusayn ᶜAbdullāh al-ᶜAmrī, *The Yemen in the 18th & 19th Centuries* (London: Ithaca Press, 1985), p. 51.

62 Cf. Dresch, *Tribes*, p. 214; al-ᶜAmrī, *The Yemen*, pp. 30, 66, 92, also *Nashr*, I: 410.

63 Luṭf Allāh b. Aḥmad Jaḥḥāf in *Durar nuḥūr al-ḥūr al-ᶜīn* (the main chronicle of the period) gives us a good idea of the harm done by Ḥamūd's control over the Tihāma and the damaging effect this had on the imamate's monetary system, cf. al-ᶜAmrī, *The Yemen*, pp. 52, 56 fn. 75.

64 al-ᶜAmrī, *The Yemen*, p. 52.

65 Cf. Dresch, *Tribes*, pp. 134, 138, 199, 212–14.

66 al-Amīr, *Dīwān al-Amīr al-Ṣanᶜānī*, pp. 415–17.

67 Cf. *Badr*, II: 127–30.

hatred for ᶜAlī b. Abī Ṭālib and the Ahl al-Bayt).[68] Al-Mahdī al-ᶜAbbās intervened, banishing Sayyid Yūsuf from Yemen and imprisoning the other leaders of the riot, who were local Hādawī scholars and individual members of the House of Qāsim, all of whom objected to the Sunnī direction the imamate was taking. The imam also imprisonned Ibn al-Amīr for two months, but the terms of his imprisonment were light in comparison with the punishment meted out to his Hādawī opponents. Al-Mahdī al-ᶜAbbās continued with his policies of favouring the Traditionist scholars, as when he appointed Ḥusayn b. Mahdī al-Nuᶜmī the prayer leader of the Qubbat al-Mahdī mosque which he had built in Sanaa.[69]

Al-Mahdī's policies of allowing these Traditionist scholars to operate in Sanaa with impunity led ᶜAbd Allāh b. Yūsuf, a member of the House of Qāsim, to emigrate from Sanaa to Barāt in 1182/1768. Here he called on the Āl al-ᶜAnsī *qāḍīs* to react to the turn of events and to interfere directly in the affairs of Sanaa.[70] The Āl al-ᶜAnsī, who were led at this time by Qāḍī Ḥasan b. Aḥmad, wrote letters to the scholars of Ḥūth, Kawkabān and Dhamār, seeking their support against the imamate's Sunnī orientation, complaining of its unjust taxation policies and citing various topoi about the nature of its evil rule. Below is an example of what they had to say:

> It is incumbent on us to raise with you what we have seen happening in Sanaa in the form of innovations by Sayyid Muḥammad al-Amīr... who has defamed the *madhhab* of Ahl al-Bayt, and rendered the one who practises *taqlīd* a deviant and belittled the knowledge of Ahl al-Bayt... The condition of the state (*dawla*) has become clear to the elites as well as to the masses: they have usurped the wealth of God, the Exalted, from the people and have spent it on inappropriate things. They have used it to build palaces and gardens... They have appointed evil governors who have established uncanonical taxation practices (*maẓālim*), such as the *kharājāt* for which there is no proof in either the Book or the Sunna... If you know these matters, then it is incumbent on you, as it is on us, to unite your tribes and to ask of them what we have asked of ours, and to make them agree that all of us should meet in Sūq al-Ḥarf [i.e., Ḥarf Sufyān] in order to unite the word (*jamᶜ al-kalima*) on what is pleasing to God, the Exalted.[71]

The ulema of Ḥūth responded by defending Ibn al-Amīr, stating that as a *mujtahid* he had the right, indeed the obligation, to follow his own opinions. They also stated that the practices he advocated had been followed by many of the early imams of Ahl al-Bayt. Furthermore, they accused the Āl al-ᶜAnsī *qāḍīs* of seeking material benefit from all this and advised them instead to be just, to command their tribes of Bakīl to follow the canonical duties, and to abandon the tribal customary law

[68] *Hijar al-ᶜilm*, IV: 1833.

[69] Cf. *Hijar al-ᶜilm*, II: 639; *Nashr*, I: 617–18. Ḥusayn al-Nuᶜmī (d. 1187/1773) was a Tihāmī scholar who, like Ibn al-Amīr, advocated Sunnī teachings. He was famous for reading the Sunnī ḥadīth collections and for practising Sunnī ritual during prayer, such as the raising and clasping of hands (*al-rafᶜ wa ʾl-ḍamm*), and for saying *āmīn* after reciting the *Fātiḥa*, all of which were condemned by Hādawīs. Al-Nuᶜmī is also famous for a work in which he supported the Wahhābī practice of destroying tombs. Cf. Ḥusayn al-Nuᶜmī, *Maᶜārij al-albāb fī manāhij al-ḥaqq waʾl-ṣawāb* (Riyadh: Maktabat al-Maᶜārif, 1985).

[70] Cf. ᶜAbd Allāh al-Jirāfī, *al-Muqtaṭaf*, pp. 255–7; *Nashr*, III: 43–4.

[71] *Hijar al-ᶜilm*, IV: 1835–6.

(*ṭāghūt*), such as denying women their right to inherit and the practice of usury (*ribā*). They, however, agreed with the Āl al-ᶜAnsī that the state had usurped wealth in uncanonical ways, building with it palaces and 'decorating horses, slaves and slave girls'.[72] The rejoinder ends by saying that no one in Sanaa accepts the good counsel of the ulema in Ḥūth because

> they think us to be from the tribe of ᶜUṣaymāt and do not realise that we seek refuge in God from what they [i.e., ᶜUṣaymāt] do, and that there is as great a difference and distance between us and ᶜUṣaymāt as there is between Islam and infidelity.[73]

In other words, Sanaa viewed the people of northern highlands north of Sanaa in an undifferentiated manner as Godless tribesmen.

Obviously, the ulema in Ḥūth were not willing to engage Sanaa in war. The Āl al-ᶜAnsī sent them one final letter, accusing them of sharing Ibn al-Amīr's views, saying that they were disappointed because they had thought them to be Shīᶜites and did not realise that the influence of Sunnī thought had reached them too. They also stated that they needed Ḥūth's support in order to 'open a road' (i.e., they needed permission to pass through their tribal territory to attack Sanaa), since the Āl al-ᶜAnsī and their tribes had reached a consensus to fight the imam, for otherwise they would be considered supporters of evil and oppression. Finally, the Āl al-ᶜAnsī rejected the claim that they were seekers of material benefit (*ṭalab al-dunyā*); rather, they insisted that their aim was to have Ibn al-Amīr and his partisans expelled from Sanaa and to lift the uncanonical taxes which the government had established.[74] The argument was phrased in distinctly Hādawī terms.

In 1184/1770–1, the Dhū Muḥammad and Dhū Ḥusayn tribes of Jabal Baraṭ finally revolted under the leadership of Ḥasan b. Aḥmad al-ᶜAnsī in order, they said, to make Hādawism victorious (*li-nuṣrat al-madhhab*). The revolt was repulsed by Imam al-Mahdī and his son ᶜAlī (later to become Imam al-Manṣūr) at the gates of Sanaa.[75] Shawkānī suggests that, in fact, the Baraṭī tribes desisted only after the imam increased their stipend to 20,000 riyals per annum, the implication being that they already received regular payment.[76] The points of contention may not have been wholly doctrinal. But the Baraṭī attack indicates that Yemeni politics had acquired a doctrinal gloss by the latter half of the eighteenth century, since the official cause for the revolt was the imam's tolerance of Sunnī teachings. It is reported that Imam al-Mahdī sought to appease the Āl al-ᶜAnsī *qāḍī*s by issuing an order that worshippers in Sanaa, even Shāfiᶜīs and Ḥanafīs, should refrain from saying 'Amen' out loud during their prayers.[77]

Shawkānī explains Hādawī opposition to scholars like Ibn al-Amīr and himself as due to a combination of ignorance (*jahl*), fanaticism and the seeking of worldly benefit (*manāfiᶜ dunyawiyya*) by scholars like the Āl al-ᶜAnsī. These, he says, take advantage of the ignorant masses by deluding them into thinking that they are

[72] *Hijar al-ᶜilm*, IV: 1837–40. [73] *Hijar al-ᶜilm*, IV: 1840, also *Hijar al-ᶜilm*, I: 516–17.
[74] *Hijar al-ᶜilm*, IV: 1841–2.
[75] Serjeant, 'The post-medieval and modern history of Ṣanᶜāʾ and the Yemen', p. 86.
[76] *Badr*, II: 136; *Adab al-ṭalab*, pp. 161–2. [77] *Nashr*, I: 618.

defenders of the *madhhab*. His disdain for the northern highland tribesmen, who are used in this way, is evident in one of his statements. He says:

> It is one of the trials of this world that these evil ones come into Sanaa for their stipends every year, gathering in their thousands. If they see someone practise *ijtihād* in prayer, by lifting his hands or joining them on his chest or [tucking his feet beneath] his thighs, they condemn him for it, and violence has occurred on account of this. They [the tribesmen] get together and go to the mosques where one of the ulema is reading the books of Tradition [i.e., the Sunnī ḥadīth collections] and start fights there. And all this is the fault of devils among the learned men, whom we have mentioned [e.g., the Āl al-ᶜAnsī *qāḍīs*]. As for these brutish Arabs [i.e., tribesmen], most of them do not pray or fast or perform the duties of Islam, except for the *shahādatayn*, which they even pronounce incorrectly.[78]

Shawkānī places the dispute with the Āl al-ᶜAnsī *qāḍīs* within the then contemporary polemic of *ijtihād* versus *taqlīd*. In short, he says, the Hādawīs could not tolerate *mujtahids* whose opinions deviated from the established teachings of the school and insisted that everyone practise *taqlīd*. He then turns the argument against them by stating that the first thing a young student of Hādawī law is taught is that it is prohibited for a *mujtahid* to practise *taqlīd*. Hence, the claim that it is incumbent on all to practise *taqlīd* is in fact against the very Zaydī teachings these ignorant scholars are purporting to uphold.[79] Shawkānī's argument denies all political and social dimensions to the conflict between Hādawīs and Traditionists. Furthermore, it trades on an ambiguity, which is that his scholarship and that of Ibn al-Amīr, albeit the product of a process of *ijtihād*, in effect rejected the theological and legal teachings of the Hādawī *madhhab* in their entirety. And more to the point, the imams now supported their claims, adding political weight to their Traditionist opinions, something which had no precedent in Zaydī history. Hādawīs saw this conjunction of interests between the imams and the Traditionists as leading to the obliteration of their school. They must have realised that scholars who did not share in Traditionist ideas and methodologies would be excluded from posts of influence in Sanaa.

The loss of much of the Zaydī highlands meant the imamate ruled now over mainly Shāfiᶜī districts. The Shāfiᶜī ulema of these districts showed great enthusiasm for Shawkānī, largely because of his jurisprudential methodology which focused on Sunnī ḥadīth collections and resulted in opinions familiar to them. Shawkānī would issue his judicial opinions (*ijtihādāt*) in the form of short *fatwās*, longer treatises or as letters which were binding on the judges of the realm.[80] These *ijtihādāt* had a similar status to the *ikhtiyārāt* ('choices') of the twentieth-century Ḥamīd al-Dīn imams, which either abrogated or elaborated on the rulings of Hādawī law on specific issues. With his legal opinions superseding all others, as well as being enforceable in practice, Shawkānī became the ultimate legal

[78] *Badr*, II: 136. Cf. Dresch, *Tribes*, pp. 212–13. [79] *Badr*, II: 135.
[80] al-ᶜAmrānī, *Itḥāf al-nabīh*, fols. 44b–46a, 68b–70a, 82b–85a. Cf. Muḥammad b. Ismāᶜīl al-ᶜAmrānī, *Niẓām al-qaḍāʾ*, p. 245.

reference in the imamate. Since Shawkānī's opinions overturned many judgements of Hādawī law, which was applied throughout the imamate at the time[81] and perceived by Shāfiᶜīs as a northern highland imposition, it is not surprising that Shawkānī gained many Shāfiᶜī admirers.

Contacts between Shāfiᶜīs and Scholars from Upper Yemen

Despite all the political turmoil of the eighteenth and nineteenth centuries, contacts between Shāfiᶜīs and scholars from Upper Yemen remained intense, with scholars from both communities studying with and receiving licenses (*ijāza*) from each other. Shāfiᶜī scholars naturally felt great affinity towards the Traditionists among the Zaydīs, who seemed to them like Sunnīs in the emphasis they placed on Sunnī ḥadīth works. This affinity can be clearly seen from the lives of such men as Sayyid ᶜAbd al-Raḥmān b. Sulaymān al-Ahdal (d. 1250/1835) of Zabīd, whose scholarly wanderings included the Yemeni highlands as much as the Hijaz, where Mecca and Medina were at this juncture great centres of learning. Al-Ahdal studied with the main Sunnī scholars of his day in Zabīd and the Hijaz, and among his teachers was Muḥammad b. Murtaḍā al-Zabīdī (d. 1204/1790), author of the famous dictionary entitled *Tāj al-ᶜarūs*. But al-Ahdal also studied with the most notable Traditionist scholars of Sanaa such as ᶜAbd al-Qādir b. Aḥmad al-Kawkabānī (d. 1207/1792), who was regarded as the great *mujtahid* of his day and the scholarly link between Ibn al-Amīr and Shawkānī. Al-Ahdal also studied with all three of Ibn al-Amīr's sons. While formally remaining a Shāfiᶜī, al-Ahdal was a Traditionist by orientation, being inclined to the ḥadīth sciences, and is described in his biography as a *muḥaddith* (a scholar of ḥadīth).[82]

The presence of Traditionist scholars in Sanaa allowed for this interaction to take place, and in so doing reversed an educational trend whereby Sunnīs were now coming to the highlands seeking knowledge. Throughout the medieval period it had been Zaydī scholars who had left the northern highlands in search of knowledge from Sunnīs in centres like Taᶜizz, Zabīd and Mecca.[83] So intense was his association with the Traditionist scholars in the Yemeni highlands that al-Ahdal wrote *al-Nafas al-Yamānī*, a biographical work which was inspired by the licenses he gave Shawkānī's sons and brother, who had all come to Zabīd from the northern highlands to study with him. The regard in which Shawkānī was held by al-Ahdal is evident in his description of him in *al-Nafas*:

[81] Cf. Rashād al-ᶜAlīmī, *al-Taqlīdiyya wa'l-ḥadātha fī 'l-niẓām al-qānūnī al-Yamanī* (Cairo: Maṭābiᶜ al-Shurūq, n.d.), pp. 256–7.

[82] *Nayl*, II: 30–1.

[83] It can even be tentatively argued that it was contacts between Zaydīs and Sunnīs in eighth/fourteenth and ninth/fifteenth centuries, and in Mecca in particular, that exposed scholars such as Muḥammad b. Ibrāhīm al-Wazīr (d. 840/1434) to Traditionist ideas and teachings and hence bring these into the Zaydī highlands. Cf. Aḥmad b. ᶜAbd Allāh al-Wazīr, *Tārīkh Banī al-Wazīr*, ms. Milan, Ambrosiana, no. D 556, fols. 78b–79a; *Badr*, II: 90.

> ... the imam of our time in all the sciences, and the lecturer of our age in explaining the intricacies of the Truths ... [He is] the guardian, the guiding authority in elucidating the goal of the prophetic Traditions ...[84]

This mutual appeal and interaction between Sunnī scholars of Shāfiʿī Yemen and Traditionist scholars of the northern highlands could not have escaped the attention of the ruling imams. It is perhaps for this reason that imams saw the need to have Shawkānī accompany them on their various campaigns throughout the country. On these journeys, Shawkānī would teach in the towns at which the imams stopped, thereby expanding his scholarly network and undoubtedly also projecting his own scholarly standing as well as the religious authority of the state and the rule of the imams he served.[85] By contrast with earlier Zaydī campaigns which were led by imams of great scholarly stature, these campaigns, led by unscholarly imams in the company of learned scholars, bring into sharp relief the important shift in the nature of imamic authority and rule at this time. The recurrent image of the scholar-warrior imam, campaigning on horseback whilst writing works on such subjects as theology and law, is often invoked in the historical chronicles and biographical dictionaries as representing the ideal of Zaydī leadership. Such imams as al-Qāsim b. Muḥammad, and the much earlier al-Manṣūr ʿAbd Allāh b. Ḥamza among others, projected this ideal and to a great extent embodied it. All the imams of the eighteenth and nineteenth centuries by contrast are considered to have been merely worldly leaders (*aʾimmat dunyā*).[86] Indeed, the anonymous author of the chronicle *Ḥawliyyat Yamāniyya* is clear about the difference between the earlier period, i.e., the seventeenth century, and his own:

> The contemporary period is nothing when compared to the days of al-Mahdī Aḥmad b. al-Ḥasan and al-Mutawakkil ʿalā Allāh Ismāʿīl. The elite (*ghurra*) of this world are [now] the worldly people (*ahl al-dunyā*), not the people of religion (*ahl al-dīn*). As for the days of al-Mahdī ʿAbd Allāh [d. 1251/1835] and his brother al-Hādī Muḥammad b. al-Mutawakkil [d. 1259/1843], they are the best in terms of luxurious living for those who seek enjoyment and the accumulation of worldly goods, which are [ultimately] perishable.... Their epoch smiled upon them [i.e., the earlier imams] because the land of Yemen was entirely under government control (*fī yad al-dawla*): its ports, southern areas (*yamanihā*), Rayma and ʿUtma, and all areas. In the earlier period straw (*tibn*) was brought from the peripheries of the country, from Baraṭ! Recently, in the time of al-Mahdī, straw for the horses [could only be brought from as far as] ʿAmrān.[87]

The image of straw being brought to Sanaa from distant Baraṭ is a powerful one. Historically, Baraṭ was construed, and in fact continues to be seen by many Yemenis today, as the most unruly of tribal areas, the homeland of the Dhū Muḥammad and Dhū Ḥusayn tribes of Bakīl. For an imam to have controlled it would have meant

84 ʿAbd al-Raḥmān al-Ahdal, *al-Nafas al-Yamānī* (Sanaa: Markaz al-Dirāsāt waʾl-Abḥāth al-Yamaniyya, 1979), p. 176. The published edition does not provide the full title of this work which is *al-Nafas al-Yamānī waʾl-rawḥ al-rayḥānī fī ijāzat al-quḍāt Banī al-Shawkānī.*

85 For a description of Shawkānī's outings with the imams see *al-Tiqṣār*, pp. 75–95.

86 Cf. *Ḥawliyyāt Yamāniyya*, p. 282.

87 *Ḥawliyyāt Yamāniyya*, p. 278. Cf. Dresch, *Tribes*, pp. 208–9.

that he was powerful and wielded great influence: with even Baraṭ included in the economy and the whole of Yemen under central government control, seventeenth-century imams had allegedly been able to offer general prosperity and justice. Since the author of the *Ḥawliyyāt* was writing in the nineteenth century, the vision he presents of the seventeenth-century imamate is a backward projection by someone already intimately acquainted with a patrimonial system of rule in which the rulers no longer had the qualities of their predecessors. His vision of order in the early Qāsimī period is intimately connected with the personal qualities of rulers who had probity and more generally lived up to the Zaydī ideal.

The Coincidence of Power and Learning

By the end of the eighteenth century, the Qāsimī imamate was firmly on the side of the Traditionist ulema. Unlike his father al-Mahdī al-ᶜAbbās, al-Manṣūr ᶜAlī (r. 1775–1809) appeared little wary of the tribes and the conservative Hādawīs. He rallied to the side of these scholars in asking Shawkānī to accept the position of *qāḍī al-quḍāt*, which would allow him to supervise the imamate's judicial system, appointing and dismissing judges, as well as to head the imamic council (*dīwān*) on which sat a number of jurists and which effectively was the last court of appeal.[88] It is reported that Shawkānī accepted the position after setting a number of conditions. He insisted that his judgements be executed 'whatever they may be and whomever [they concern], even if the imam himself was implicated'. This the imam readily accepted. Shawkānī was kept on as chief judge by imams al-Mutawakkil Aḥmad (r. 1809–16) and al-Mahdī ᶜAbd Allāh (r. 1816–35), in whose reigns, it is said, Shawkānī's importance grew so that no order was promulgated without his advice being taken.[89]

The three Qāsimī imams who employed Shawkānī did not fulfil the rigorous conditions of the Zaydī doctrine of the imamate. As we have seen, this doctrine stipulated that the imam had to fulfil the rather stringent qualification of being a scholar-warrior who 'orders the good and prohibits the evil' (*al-amr biʾl-maᶜrūf waʾl-nahy ᶜan al-munkar*). Shawkānī, however, refuted this doctrine by basing his claims on Sunnī ḥadīths, which do not require the imam to be a *mujtahid* or even an ᶜAlawī-Fāṭimī, but simply a member of the Prophet's tribe, Quraysh. He also rejected the *daᶜwa* as the means to attaining the imamate, and stated that it is by receiving the allegiance (*bayᶜa*) of those 'who loose and bind' (*ahl al-ḥall waʾl-ᶜaqd*), i.e., the people of note, that one can become imam. Another way of attaining the imamate according to Shawkānī is by means of one imam designating another as his successor, as Abu Bakr did with ᶜUmar, a reference to the first and second caliphs of Islam. By acknowledging these two forms of accession to the imamate, Shawkānī placed himself squarely in the Sunnī tradition, seeing the accessions of Abū Bakr and ᶜUmar as the model for legitimate accession to

[88] Cf. Niebuhr, *Travels*, vol. II, pp. 83–4. [89] *al-Tiqṣār*, pp. 424–5.

the imamate. Furthermore, Muslims are forbidden to rise (*khurūj*) against an unjust imam (*ẓālim*) as long as he prays and commits no public act of unbelief (*lam yaẓhar minhum al-kufr al-bawwāḥ*).[90]

The Increasing Importance of the Ulema

In somewhat similar fashion to Cairene society in the Mamlūk period as described by Jonathan Berkey,[91] imamate society in the eighteenth century was increasingly characterised by a system of patronage tying the imam and his family to the ulema as a distinct group. In traditional Zaydī Islam the ulema played the crucial role of acknowledging the 'summons' (*daᶜwa*) of a given contender to the imamate through the *bayᶜa* (the act of allegiance) and thereby according legitimacy to his rule. This acknowledgement, however, could be withdrawn at any moment if the imam fell short of the qualifications or if a more suitable candidate emerged claiming the imamate for himself. Zaydī imams had to live under the constant threat of such challenges, and indeed much of Zaydī political history is taken up by struggles between contending claimants. In traditional Zaydism, however, the ulema, or more properly the *ahl al-ḥall waʾl-ᶜaqd* (the people who loose and bind) did not form a distinct cohort dependent on state patronage. Rather, they were largely learned men who were scattered in centres of learning throughout the highlands. With the establishment of the Qāsimī imamate the situation changed, particularly as state structures and institutions developed. By the eighteenth century, the ulema, at least those within the ambit of the state, behaved in a more traditionally 'Sunnī' manner. They legitimated the rule of the imams regardless of aptitude and probity, enjoined the people to obedience, collected taxes and provided other intangible services.[92] In return, they were offered posts throughout the realm through which they represented the imamic state.[93]

Imamic patronage took several forms: areas were allocated to the scholars for tax collection purposes; scholars were appointed as judges (*qāḍī* or *ḥākim*), scribes (*kātib*) and governors (*ᶜāmil*) of towns and entire districts; they were made guardians (*nāẓir*) over religious endowments (*awqāf*) and over testamentary dispositions (*waṣāyā*),[94] or appointed as preachers (*khaṭīb*) and prayer leaders

90 Muḥammad Shawkānī, *al-Sayl al-jarrār al-mutadaffiq ᶜalā ḥadāʾiq al-Azhār*, Maḥmūd Zāyid (ed.) (Beirut: Dār al-Kutub al-ᶜIlmiyya, 1985), vol. IV, pp. 505–15.

91 Cf. Jonathan Berkey, *The Transmission of Knowledge in Medieval Cairo* (Princeton: Princeton University Press, 1992).

92 This is clear from the personal role played by Shawkānī in ensuring the peaceful succession of rule from the sick and senile al-Manṣur ᶜAlī to his son al-Mutawakkil Aḥmad, and then from Aḥmad to his son al-Mahdī ᶜAbd Allāh. In each case Shawkānī was the first to offer the *bayᶜa* and then to take it on behalf of the imams from the other members of the Qāsimī family and the notables of the realm.

93 For a comparison with other contexts see Ira M. Lapidus, *Muslim Cities in the Later Middle Ages* (Cambridge University Press, 1984), pp. 130–41 and Berkey, *Transmission*, chapter 4.

94 For example the post of religious endowments secretary (*kātib al-awqāf*) was given to Qāḍī Aḥmad b. Ṣāliḥ b. Abī ʾl-Rijāl (d. 1191/1777) (not the author of the famous biographical work *Maṭlaᶜ al-budūr* but his namesake) by al-Mahdī al-ᶜAbbās and a member of this family still held this position in the year 1357/1938; cf. *Nashr*, I: 137–43; *Badr*, I: 61–2.

(*imām*) at designated mosques. In a discursion from the 'events' of his century, the anonymous chronicler of *Ḥawliyyāt Yamāniyya*[95] offers a picture of the political and administrative structures of the state as they had developed by the late eighteenth and early nineteenth centuries. At its apex, he says, the state was headed by the imam who, along with the *Shaykh al-Islām* (i.e., the chief judge), applied the Sharīᶜa according to the Book and the Sunna of the Prophet. Under these were the princes of the House of Qāsim, the Āl al-Imām, the first among whom was the crown prince (*sayf al-khilāfa*), who had 'fiefs' (*qiṭaᶜ*) and expense accounts (*maṣārīf*) and provided food for his retainers, all of whom came to him and were known to him. Under the imam, the *shaykh al-islām* and princes

> were the ministers (*wuzarāʾ*), who numbered five or six. One minister was appointed for each region: a minister for the Tihāma, a minister for Lower Yemen (*al-yaman*), a minister for Ānis, Rayma and ᶜUtma, a minister for the western regions (*al-bilād al-gharbiyya*), a minister for the north,[96] a minister of domanial estates (*wazīr al-ṣawāfī*), a minister of the imamic guards (*wazīr al-ᶜukfa*), a minister of seals (*wazīr al-khitām*), who in the eyes of the imam was above all the others [in importance]. Each minister would ladle from the world like the trowels of a yoke [i.e., steal a great deal], and their appointments would last only two or three years. When arrested immeasurable wealth would be found in their possession, as we have mentioned earlier in the book. Every minister would have countless retainers, and under each minister would be governors (sing. *ᶜāmil*) in the lands. For example, the minister of the Tihāma has under him three to four governors, in each port town and city; and similarly the minister of Lower Yemen has under him, in every city, a governor. Every governor eats and lives, and with them are many scribes (*kuttāb*), friends and servants living off the government, as do the gate keepers (*al-bawwābūn*)... Likewise are the military commanders (*al-umarāʾ*), [who are] five to six; their most senior is the commander of the palace (*amīr al-qaṣr*), and every commander has many learned men (*fuqahāʾ*) and retainers (*muᶜtāsẖūn*) [dependent on him]... So all the people [i.e., appointed officials and retainers] lived off the success of the House of Qāsim.[97]

It must be noted that the author's vision of a state takes for granted its patrimonial features; it is as a state should be, and he seems to have forgotten that earlier imamates did not have such elaborate structures. Moreover, the decline ensues not from the system itself, but from the nature of the men who man it. The imam and Shaykh al-Islām (here the reference is undoubtedly to Shawkānī who was the first to be given this title) are depicted in their idealised roles as applying rigorously the Sharīᶜa. Their government officials, however, are criticised for their corruption, and for retaining countless underlings all of whom lived off the state. The biographical dictionaries recount that many of these officials, especially the judges, were ulema. The reign of a given imam was often assessed by the extent of corruption in his administration, and among the markers of this was the debasement

95 Ḥusayn al-ᶜAmrī posits that the anonymous author of the *Ḥawliyyāt Yamāniyya* is Aḥmad b. ᶜAbd Allāh al-Zubayrī, who completed it relying on the work of Qāḍī Muḥsin b. Aḥmad al-Ḥarāzī (d. 1288/1871), cf. al-ᶜAmrī, *Miʾat ᶜām*, p. 296, fn. 2. The manuscript was edited by Ḥibshī who contends that the author is anonymous.

96 The edited text has *al-Jimāl wazīr*, which is probably a typographic error for *al-shimāl wazīr*.

97 *Ḥawliyyāt Yamāniyya*, pp. 279–82.

of currency through the diminution of the amount of silver in the coins.[98] The extent of corruption, obviously reflected the imam's personality and abilities, and it is on this basis that some were referred to as worldly imams (*a'immat al-dunyā*) whereas the more upright were called imams of religion (*a'immat dīn*).[99]

Unlike Mamlūk Egypt and Syria, Yemen under the Zaydī imamate never saw the endowment of professorships and formal teaching posts for the ulema. The educational system in Yemen remained informal. In the areas controlled by the imamate, scholars were dependent on the vicissitudes and whims of individual imams, who were effectively the sole patrons, and no separate interest group, like the Mamlūks in Egypt for example, could provide an independent source of patronage.[100] But in the *hijra*s – predominantly rural centres of learning – scholars continued to transmit knowledge, particularly Zaydī knowledge, outside the purview of the state. The transmission of knowledge remained a diffuse affair in Yemen and was never centralised; even today, different and differing centres of learning remain active in spreading their own version of 'proper Islamic' education, be it more Zaydī or more Sunnī in focus and stress. However, with the establishment of a strong nexus of interests between the 'state' and the Traditionist scholars in the eighteenth century, education and patronage became more focused than before.

The Qāsimī imams served by Shawkānī were not *mujtahids*.[101] To compensate for this lack, Shawkānī stipulates a condition which the non-*mujtahid* imam must fulfil:

> he must choose from among the notables, *mujtahid*s and accomplished ulema [who will] advise him in matters... He must render all disputes to the people of that stratum [the ulema], and whatever they judge he must execute and whatever they order he must do.[102]

With the institution of the *dīwān*, a sort of advisory council for the imams, and the seeking of advice from Shawkānī, the imams of this period were fulfilling this condition. The institutional structures set up by the Qāsimīs, therefore, seemed to reflect Shawkānī's theory of the imamate. The imam held council in the *dīwān*, where Shawkānī sat. When Shawkānī was absent he was represented in the *dīwān* by his son-in-law, Qāḍī Ṣāliḥ al-ᶜAnsī, who was also a jurist. The *dīwān* was a place in which the imam held audience, receiving foreign guests as well as his administrators from throughout Yemen, making decisions about state matters and appointments, and listening to petitions from far and wide.

Shawkānī played a central role in defining the imamate's policies against the Wahhābī threat in the early 1800s. He advised the imam to send an army to attack their vassal, Sharīf Ḥamūd b. Muḥammad (d. 1233/1818), in order to stop him from conquering the Tihāma.[103] The military efforts were unsuccessful and the Tihāma

98 Cf. al-ᶜAmrī, *Mi'at ᶜām*, pp. 150–1, 208–9. 99 *Ḥawliyyāt Yamāniyya*, p. 282.

100 The annals of the eighteenth and nineteenth centuries are filled with stories of scholars/administrators who were stripped of their possessions and imprisoned by the imams only to be later pardoned and, at times, re-instated to their former positions.

101 Cf. al-ᶜAmrī, *The Yemen*, p. 125. 102 Shawkānī, *al-Sayl al-Jarrār*, vol. IV, pp. 507–8.

103 *al-Tiqṣār*, pp. 38–40.

was lost to the Sharīf. This made the imam very anxious and it is reported that in 1222/1807 he sought Shawkānī's advice on how to proceed. Shawkānī advised that the best way to re-establish control would be to treat his subjects justly by not imposing the prevalent uncanonical taxes and to send a general edict to all districts informing them of this. He further explained that the Wahhābīs were welcomed only because the rights of his subjects had been infringed through corrupt taxation practices.[104]

Al-Manṣūr heeded his advice and Shawkānī drew up the edict, entitled *al-Marsūm al-Manṣūrī fī rafʿ al-maẓālim waʾl-musāwāt fī ʾl-ḥuqūq waʾl-wājibāt bayn abnāʾ al-Yaman* (The Manṣūrī Edict Regarding the Elimination of Unjust Acts and the Establishment of Equality of Rights and Obligations Among the Sons of Yemen), also called 'The Rising Sun' (*ṭulūʿ al-shams*) for the first two words of its text.[105] The terms of the edict illuminate Shawkānī's vision of an ordered state.

> Our Lord the Imam of the age . . . the Commander of the Faithful, al-Manṣūr, has come to the noble opinion . . . that all his subjects, in all the districts, and all who fall under his blessed government in the highlands and the lowlands have no obligation in all that they possess except what has been set by the noble law and to which God almighty has a right. They are not to be asked for anything other than this. Whoever demands any amount greater than what God – the Exalted – has set is not to be obeyed. It is incumbent on Muslims to disempower him and to refer his case to the local judge who will then make appeal to the imamic Presence (*al-ḥaḍra al-imāmiyya*) so that he is punished, making of him an example to others who proceed in like fashion. And if a judge colludes with an oppressor or favours a man who wants more than what God has commanded, then he deserves to be dismissed from his religious post for he is not deserving of it nor is he trustworthy in it. Let the subjects be pleased, satisfied, and secure that they will not be asked for a *jibāya*, a *qabāl*, a *siyāsa*, a *firqa*, or a *dafʿa* [the names of non-canonical taxes], nor anything which is innovated that God has not ordained.[106]

It is the judges, the upholders of religious law, who are the central players in his vision of a revamped fiscal order. Their judicial hierarchy, which is ultimately tied to Shawkānī himself, is the conduit that insures a just administration of the country. The centrality of their role is further highlighted by the following instructions in the edict:

> Every judge must assemble the subjects of his district and read this [edict] to them. He must [also] make copies of it in his own handwriting and place his mark on these and send one to each village in order that they may have it in perpetuity to ward off the evil of every evil doer and the injustice of every unjust person . . . Every judge must send his trustworthy and knowledgeable men to teach people the teachings of their religion and what their obligations are towards God almighty regarding prayer, fasting, pilgrimage and God's unicity (*tawḥīd*) . . .[107]

---

[104] *Adab al-ṭalab*, p. 37.   [105] Cf. al-ʿAmrī, *al-Imām al-Shawkānī*, pp. 118–27.
[106] Ibid., pp. 464–5.   [107] Ibid., pp. 465–6.

Shawkānī's efforts failed dismally, much to his dismay.[108] Al-Shijnī explains that the ministers undermined the new fiscal regulations by arguing that they would weaken the government because they resulted in lower revenues that were not sufficient to cover expenses, in particular the soldiers' salaries. In actual fact, al-Shijnī says, they were motivated by personal greed and corruption because the regulations spelt a cut in their own incomes, which were based on the non-canonical practices Shawkānī wished to abolish. Moreover, the ministers were abetted by certain leading scholars who were also corrupt.[109] The episode highlights a recurrent theme in Shawkānī's life, and that of Traditionist scholars before him, which is their attempts from Sanaa at reforming a world with its own moral order. These attempts were not readily accepted and resistance often ensued as we saw earlier in the instance of the Baraṭī tribal revolts.

The imams al-Manṣūr ^{c}Alī and al-Mutawakkil Aḥmad succeeded their fathers through nomination without regard to their learning or personal accomplishment. Their lack of knowledge in religious matters alone would have disqualified them according to the letter of Zaydī law. Both were appointed by their fathers to the post of commander of the troops (*amīr al-ajnād*).[110] Al-Mahdī ^{c}Abd Allāh became imam instead of his younger and more learned brother al-Qāsim, who had been designated by his father. Al-Qāsim was immediately sidelined by the elder and militarily more powerful ^{c}Abd Allāh and no one made an issue of this.[111] Each one became imam immediately after his father's death by receiving the *bay^{c}a* from the 'ulema, judges and the family of the Imam [i.e., descendants of al-Qāsim b. Muḥammad, the founder of the dynasty]'. Al-Mutawakkil Aḥmad and al-Mahdī ^{c}Abd Allāh first received the *bay^{c}a* from Shawkānī himself, who then accepted it on their behalf from all the important people of the realm.[112]

These imams were not models of Zaydī piety. Al-Wāsi^{c}ī says that al-Manṣūr ^{c}Alī 'followed the path of kings and nominated three ministers who looked after all matters and did not bother with any of the affairs of his kingdom . . .'. He also reports that 'his habit was to seclude himself (*al-iḥtijāb*) and to cavort with free and slave women'.[113] Al-Manṣūr never left Sanaa on a military campaign. Of al-Mutawakkil Aḥmad, al-Wāsi^{c}ī says that he 'filled a house with gold and silver and all kinds of clothes, precious stones . . . , weaponry . . . , medical instruments and vials, and trunks full of musk, amber and clocks'.[114] Al-Mahdī ^{c}Abd Allāh was more of a military man than his father and led a number of campaigns, most notably in Lower Yemen. Constant changes in ministerial appointments gave his rule an element of instability. Shawkānī, who is not normally terse in praising the imams, merely says that he was 'progressively improving, [had] a complete mind, noble traits, praiseworthy habits, outstanding horsemanship and remarkable aim [in shooting]'.[115] Al-Wāsi^{c}ī describes al-Mahdī ^{c}Abd Allāh as being in 'the habit

108 *al-Tiqṣār*, pp. 173–8; *Adab al-ṭalab*, pp. 162–3. 109 *al-Tiqṣār*, p. 173.
110 *Badr*, I: 77–8, 459. 111 *Ḥawliyyāt Yamāniyya*, pp. 25–6.
112 *Badr*, I: 77–9, 376–7, 461. 113 al-Wāsi^{c}ī, *Tārīkh al-Yaman*, p. 233.
114 Ibid., p. 234. 115 *Badr*, I: 376.

of secluding himself and indulging his desires and pleasures and listening to things pleasurable whilst ignoring his kingdom'.[116]

The imam had become very much a sultan on the Sunnī model. Some complained of this, and some in modern times have drawn attention to the change as an explanation of the decline of the House of al-Qāsim and the onset of political and social problems. Majd al-Dīn al-Muʾayyadī, a prominent contemporary scholar living in Ṣaʿda, considers Imam al-Muʾayyad Muḥammad to be the last imam to have fulfilled the conditions of the imamate. He quotes Ismāʿīl b. Ḥusayn Jaghmān as saying 'as far as I know, here ended the prophetic legacy (*wirāthat al-nubūwwa*), after which those who ruled did not attain the rank of the imamate, and they took it as kingship (*ittakhadhūhā mulkan*)'.[117] Al-Wāsiʿī says of al-Muʾayyad Muḥammad that he 'combined the conditions' (*kānā imāman jāmiʿan liʾl-shurūṭ*) and does not mention this phrase of another imam until Aḥmad b. ʿAlī al-Sirājī who led a failed attempt at claiming the imamate in 1249/1833 from al-Mahdī ʿAbd Allāh.[118] Yet another modern historian, Aḥmad Sharaf al-Dīn, says that for nearly two centuries after the reign of al-Muʾayyad Muḥammad the Yemen was overtaken with strife and disorder due to the internecine conflicts between the various contenders for the imamate amongst the House of al-Qāsim. Sharaf al-Dīn quotes the following from Aḥmad b. ʿAbd Allāh al-Jindārī's (d. 1337/1919) work entitled *al-Jāmiʿ al-wajīz fī wafāyāt al-ʿulamāʾ ulī ʾl-tabrīz*:

> After the death of al-Muʾayyad Muḥammad b. al-Mutawakkil Ismāʿīl the family of the Imam became divided into groups and filled each other with fright. All coveted the imamate until it seemed the Day of Reckoning would come. Al-Muʾayyad had designated the imamate to his son Yūsuf because he was the best amongst his brothers. Yūsuf therefore made the Summons (*duʿāʾ*) in Ḍūrān and Ḥusayn b. ʿAbd al-Qādir did the same in Kawkabān, as did al-Ḥasan b. Muḥammad in ʿAmrān, ʿAlī b. Aḥmad in Ṣaʿda and al-Ḥusayn b. al-Ḥasan in Radāʿ. The earth became corpse-like and every village had a caliph. Muḥammad b. Aḥmad made his summons in al-Manṣūra and was called *Ṣāḥib al-Mawāhib*. He defeated them and assaulted and pounced on them.[119]

Shawkānī, however, justified the rule of such imams as necessary for temporal and political order. As long as they remained Muslims and maintained the Sharīʿa it was incumbent on Muslims to be obedient. The alternative, according to him, was social disorder and chaos, which had to be avoided at all costs.

[116] al-Wāsiʿī, *Tārīkh al-Yaman*, p. 235.

[117] Majd al-Dīn b. Muḥammad al-Muʾayyādī, *Tuḥaf sharḥ al-zalaf* (n.p.: n.d.), p. 161.

[118] al-Wāsiʿī, *Tārīkh al-Yaman*, pp. 230, 235.

[119] Aḥmad Ḥusayn Sharaf al-Dīn, *al-Yaman ʿabr al-tārīkh* (Cairo: Maṭbaʿat al-Sunna al-Muḥammadiyya, 1964), pp. 245–7. Cf. Ḥusayn b. Aḥmad al-ʿArashī, *Kitāb Bulūgh al-marām fī sharḥ misk al-khitām* (Beirut: Dār Iḥyāʾ al-Turāth al-ʿArabī, n.d.), p. 68 where he says: 'the historians said: and from here on [i.e., with Ṣāḥib al-Mawāhib's accession] he [the imam] became king'.

CHAPTER 3

The Absolute Interpreter and '*Renewer*' of the Thirteenth Century AH

> O ignoramus of the religious sciences of the Prophet's family (*Āl Muṣṭafā*); whether of its earlier members or those more recent. Who amongst them closed the door of *ijtihād* on mankind? O stupid one, educate yourself; who made *taqlīd* obligatory for those who can practise *ijtihād*, and said the practice of *taqlīd* is a necessity? Who said abandon the Qur°ān and its sciences? Who said abandon the Sunna of Muḥammad? Who said the shaykh [who teaches] the canonical ḥadīth collections (*ummahāt*) leads one astray? Who said that those who study them transgress? Muḥammad b. °Alī al-Shawkānī[1]

The shift in political structure, which took place as the Qāsimī imamate became more dynastic and the imams less true to the Hādawī ideal, was accompanied by a corresponding shift in the legal structures and ideology of the state, away from Zaydī-Hādawī doctrines and legal opinions, and towards those espoused by the Traditionist Sunnīs. While the changing nature of the imamate and the expanded geography of the state created the possibility and impetus for new structures of rule, the Traditionist jurists who rose to the challenge emerged out of the same intellectual milieu as the Zaydīs. Thus, they had to formulate their differences with the Zaydīs in punctilious detail, and on a number of theoretical and practical levels. This new tendency, as exemplified in the oeuvre of Muḥammad b. °Alī al-Shawkānī, was radically ambitious in the context of Zaydī Yemen. Shawkānī's work was distinctive in several ways:

1) He reoriented the sources of law by insisting on the exclusive and direct use of the Qur°ān and of Sunnī ḥadīth collections without the mediation of the traditional legal manuals.
2) He developed a new, expanded methodology which any qualified jurist could employ to use these sources. This methodology was based principally on Shawkānī's understanding of *ijtihād*. It also enforced a measure of accountability by stipulating that the jurist must present the textual evidence for his judgement.
3) Shawkānī's legal methodology was coupled with a complete pedagogical theory and curriculum for the production of jurists trained in its use.

[1] Muḥammad al-Shawkānī, *Dīwān al-Shawkānī aslāk al-jawhar wa°l-ḥayāt al-fikriyya wa°l-sīyāsiyya fī °aṣrih*, Ḥusayn al-°Amrī (ed.), 2nd edn (Damascus: Dār al-Fikr, 1986), pp. 133–4.

4) Finally, Shawkānī conceived of a bureaucratic hierarchy that would employ the products of this epistemological and educational system to administer the state irrespective of the qualifications of the ruler.

Shawkānī arrived on the scene of the Qāsimī state at a time when the dual processes of dynastic patrimonialism and the gradual Sunnification of the intellectual and legal milieu were fully developed. In a sense, his work and ideas crystallise these two processes and offer a system for perpetuating them.

The following discussion will attempt to situate Shawkānī within the wider world of Islamic scholarship, arguing that he most appropriately fits into the Traditionist school (*Ahl al-Ḥadīth*), but that he also drew inspiration from the great Sunnī-Shāfiᶜī scholars of Egypt, such as Ibn Ḥajar al-ᶜAsqalānī and Jalāl al-Dīn al-Suyūṭī, as well as Ḥanbalī ones, like Taqī al-Dīn Aḥmad Ibn Taymiyya. This chapter will then offer a presentation of Shawkānī's views on the subject of *ijtihād*, since this was the cornerstone of his legal methodology, and discuss more generally his epistemology. Finally, it will go on to describe his pedagogical curriculum which was intended to produce and reproduce *mujtahids* like himself and perpetuate his vision of moral and juridical order.

Ijtihād in Modern Writings

In the writings of Western as well as Muslim authors in the modern period, *ijtihād* has been given an inordinately important place. In its technical sense, perhaps it is best defined as the 'expending of one's utmost effort in the inquiry into legal questions admitting of only probable answers'.[2] But in modernist works, it has often been associated with reason and the ability of Muslims (and thus of Islamic societies) to transcend the constraints of 'tradition'. These constraints in turn have been associated with *taqlīd*, the complement of *ijtihād*, whose technical sense is perhaps best conveyed as 'accepting someone else's opinion concerning a legal rule without knowledge of its bases'.[3] In a sense, *ijtihād* has come to be associated with liberal notions of progress, and *taqlīd* with the burden of tradition.[4] Jamāl al-Dīn al-Afghānī and Muḥammad ᶜAbduh argued very much along these lines, as do many authors and intellectuals in the West and the Middle East today.[5] There is a shared assumption that *ijtihād* will somehow allow for the liberation

[2] Aron Zysow, 'Ejtehād', *Encyclopaedia Iranica*, vol. VIII, p. 280.

[3] Cf. Rudolph Peters, 'Idjtihād and Taqlīd in 18th and 19th century Islam', *Die Welt des Islams* 20.3–4 (1980), 135.

[4] Albert Hourani, *Arabic Thought in the Liberal Age* (Cambridge University Press, 1983), pp. 127, 147–8, 235, 240, 243–4, 272; Fazlur Rahman, 'Revival and reform in Islam', in P. M. Holt *et al.* (eds.), 2 vols. in 4, *The Cambridge History of Islam* (Cambridge University Press, 1977), vol. II B, p. 638.

[5] Cf. Nikkie Keddie, *Sayyid Jamāl ad-Dīn "al-Afghānī"* (Berkeley: University of California Press, 1972), pp. 178–9, 396; Malcolm Kerr, *Islamic Reform* (Berkeley: University of California Press, 1966), p. 84; Hamid Enayat, *Modern Islamic Political Thought* (London: Macmillan Education, 1982), pp. 70–6.

of thought from backward ways and offer a brighter future for Muslim societies. This modernist literature, formed around ideas of rationality and progress, leaves aside a good many of the key questions. If intellectual liberty is not to be moral licence, one needs to know who can practise *ijtihād* and in what connection. The appeal of such modernist readings is widespread, although their arguments are often superficial.

Even state governments, like that in Yemen, share in these conceptions. The General People's Congress, the ruling party in Yemen since 1982, states in its political manifesto, the National Charter (*al-Mīthāq al-Waṭanī*):

> We reject any theory, whether about rule, economics, politics or social affairs, which contradicts our Islamic faith or our Sharīᶜa. However, we believe that it is the right of any individual or group to express or publish their opinions and ideas, as well as to participate in proper democratic activity to accomplish these – on condition that they not deviate from the Islamic framework, for *ijtihād* within this framework is one of the principles of Islam.[6]

Ijtihād and democratic freedoms, like freedom of expression, have become conflated. But again the conditions in which *ijtihād* is feasible ('the Islamic framework') are left unspecified. Any *ijtihād* which opposed some aspect of the framework to which the government is attached would not be welcome. Nor would the framework allow just anyone to practise *ijtihād* at the state's expense.

Despite modern 'liberal' assumptions about *ijtihād*, many recent Islamic thinkers and Islamist activists, such as Sayyid Quṭb and the Muslim Brotherhood, have used the term in quite different ways.[7] For them, *ijtihād* became the means by which Muslims are to liberate themselves intellectually as well as politically from the yoke of specifically modern regimes. Islamists share with 'liberals' the idea that *ijtihād* will offer a panacea to the dilemmas of the modern age although, beyond calling for a return to the 'True Sources', these Islamists are mute about the modalities of such reform. This is illustrated in a statement written by a Syrian Muslim Brother, Muḥammad Ḥallāq, who was living in exile in Yemen in the early 1990s:

> It is not concealed from you my brother the reader that it is necessary to have a *mujtahid* who manifests God's proofs in all ages (*qāʾim bi ḥujaj Allāh*) and that it is not legally permissible for an age not to have one (*lā yajūz sharᶜan khuluwwu al-ᶜaṣri minhu*). The Ḥāfiẓ Jalāl al-Dīn ᶜAbd al-Raḥmān b. Abī Bakr al-Suyūṭī wrote a treatise [on this matter which is entitled]: The Response to him who Makes Earth his Abode and is Ignorant that *Ijtihād* in all Ages is an Obligation (*al-Radd ᶜalā man akhlada ilā al-arḍ wa jahila anna*

6 *al-Mīthāq al-Waṭanī* (The National Charter), p. 41, quoted in Dresch and Haykel, 'Stereotypes and political styles', *IJMES* 27.4 (1995), 420. In the same vein, see the introduction by one of Yemen's leading judges, Muḥammad al-Ḥajjī, in al-Ḥusayn b. Badr al-Dīn, *Kitāb Shifāʾ al-uwām fī aḥādīth al-aḥkām* (n.p.: Jamᶜiyyat ᶜUlamāʾ al-Yaman, 1996), vol. I, pp. 15f.

7 Cf. Richard P. Mitchell, *The Society of the Muslim Brothers* (Oxford University Press, 1993), pp. 236–41; Aḥmad Mūṣallilī, *al-Uṣūliyya al-islāmiyya: dirāsa fī ʾl-khiṭāb al-īdiyūlūjī wa ʾl-siyāsī ᶜinda Sayyid Qutb* (Beirut: al-Nāshir, 1993), pp. 215f.; Emmanuel Sivan, *Radical Islam* (New Haven: Yale University Press, 1990), p. 69.

> *al-ijtihād fī kulli ʿaṣrin farḍ*). If *ijtihād* is a necessity in every age then our age is in dire need, more than any in the past. This is due to the changes in life's concerns in contrast to what these were in past times, and the overwhelming development of societies after the technological revolution which the world has witnessed.[8]

In his introduction to Ibn al-Amīr's treatise on *ijtihād* entitled *Irshād al-nuqqād ilā taysīr al-ijtihād*, Muḥammad Ḥallāq continues to enumerate the many areas in which *ijtihād* would prove of help to the Muslim community: the economic and financial spheres, because of the new and unprecedented kinds of companies and financial transactions, as well as the scientific and medical spheres among others. Ḥallāq points out that Islamic law has now to provide answers to the many new discoveries that modern science has developed, and especially discoveries in medical science, e.g., organ transplants (whether it is permissible to transplant organs from animals into humans), organ donation (both before and after death and from and to non-Muslims) and matters relating to pills which delay the menstrual cycle.[9] *Ijtihād*, as an interpretive methodology, is presumed to provide the answers to problems the modern age poses present-day Muslims. The discourse is not new. Muḥammad ʿAbduh was offering a similar answer to problems posed by modernity nearly a century ago. Wahhābīs also made a great issue of *ijtihād*, but Fazlur Rahman, lining up with the modernists, laments the fact that by rejecting intellectualism they rejected the actual tools of fresh thinking (read *ijtihād*). Rahman says of the Wahhābīs that they 'proved fruitless and *practically* [sic] have become 'followers' (*muqallidūn*) of the sum total of the Islamic legacy of the first two centuries and a half...'.[10] Obviously, there is a huge area of disagreement over the use of the term in both modern Muslim and Western writings.

A related aspect of the way in which *ijtihād* has been written about, especially in modern Yemeni works, is that it was the means used by the great Islamic reformers to initiate tolerance and unity among Muslims.[11] Here the rhetorics of pan-Islamism and Yemeni nationalism are conflated. Shawkānī, in this frame of reference, becomes not only the enemy of reprehensible innovations that had entered Islamic thought and practice, but also the one who called, through *ijtihād*, for transcending sectarian differences, for promoting the unity of Muslims and the unity of Yemen. In all these studies, the historical context is barely touched upon and, as with the 'liberals' who saw *ijtihād* as a means to their own ideal, it is largely considerations of the moment which determine how Shawkānī is depicted.

8 Muḥammad b. Ismāʿīl al-Amīr, *Irshād al-nuqqād ilā taysīr al-ijtihād*, Muḥammad Ṣubḥī Ḥallāq (ed.) (Beirut: Muʾassasat al-Rayyān liʾl-Ṭibāʿa, 1992), p. 8.

9 al-Amīr, *Irshād al-nuqqād*, pp. 8–9.

10 Rahman, 'Revival and reform in Islam', p. 638.

11 ʿAbd al-ʿAzīz al-Maqāliḥ, *Qirāʾa fī fikr al-Zaydiyya waʾl-Muʿtazila* (Beirut: Dār al-ʿAwda, 1982), p. 217; Ṣāliḥ Muḥammad Muqbil, *Muḥammad b. ʿAlī al-Shawkānī wa juhūduhu al-tarbawiyya* (Jeddah: Maktabat Jidda, 1989), p. 23; Ibrāhīm Hilāl, *al-Imām al-Shawkānī waʾl-ijtihād waʾl-taqlīd* (Cairo: Dār al-Nahḍa al-ʿArabiyya, 1979), pp. 9–12; Muḥammad al-Shawkānī, *Qaṭru al-walī ʿalā ḥadīth al-walī*, Ibrāhīm Hilāl (ed.) (Beirut: Dār Iḥyāʾal-Turāth al-ʿArabī, n.d.); Qāsim Ghālib Aḥmad, *Min aʿlām al-Yaman: shaykh al-islām al-mujtahid Muhammad b. ʿAlī al-Shawkānī* (Cairo: Maṭābiʿ al-Ahrām al-Tijāriyya, 1969); Ḥusayn al-ʿAmrī, *al-Imām al-Shawkānī*.

To anticipate briefly, the appeal of Shawkānī for modern nationalists does indeed reflect aspects of his work in the years around 1800. However, modern writers do not feel comfortable going into detail about who exactly can practise *ijtihād* and how its resulting opinions are put to effect in detail, since this draws attention to Shawkānī's practical position and the form of government he favoured.

The most sustained treatment of *ijtihād*, as a legal principle, was undertaken by Wael Hallaq who argued against Joseph Schacht's contention that the practice of *ijtihād* was discontinued among the jurists after the fourth/tenth century, a reference to the famous notion of the 'closure of the gate of *ijtihād*'.[12] Both Hallaq and Schacht's theses identify *ijtihād* with creative and innovative juristic thought and *taqlīd* with the lack of creativity, 'blind imitation' and decline. A number of scholars have commented on this debate, refining what is meant by *ijtihād* and especially *taqlīd*. Sherman Jackson, for instance, argues for a revamped understanding of *taqlīd*, seeing it as grounded in a search for established sources of authority rather than the ability, or inability, of jurists to arrive at novel opinions. On this basis, he demonstrates *taqlīd* to be a dynamic activity of a mature legal system best exemplified by the engagement of jurists with expanding or restricting the scope of existing laws.[13] Mohammad Fadel, another commentator, argues that there is a social logic for *taqlīd*, namely that it provides uniform rules, predictability of legal outcomes and judicial stability. By contrast, a legal system that is anchored purely in the subjective process of *ijtihād* and the concomitant ideal of judicial discretion remains inherently unstable.[14] The reason for this state of legal indeterminacy is that each *mujtahid* remains a reference unto himself, sometimes even changing his opinion on a given matter, and as a consequence, an interpretive community of jurists, bound to shared rules and doctrines, never forms. The importance of Jackson and Fadel's contributions lies in that in their discussion of *ijtihād* and *taqlīd* does not centre on the fraught issues of innovation and stagnation in Islamic law. Rather, their analysis is grounded in an understanding of legal process and the sociology of law. From this perspective, Shawkānī's endeavours can be seen as an attempt to create an authoritative position for himself in the legal system as a *mujtahid* and at the risk of legal indeterminacy. Whereas his opponents, the Zaydī-Hādawīs, sought to defend the doctrines of the established system which were centered on the authority of their imams. For the Zaydī-Hādawīs, the stability of their legal system and the preservation of their interpretive community were at stake.

12 Wael B. Hallaq, 'Was the Gate of Ijtihad Closed?', *IJMES* 16.1 (1984), 3–41; idem, 'On the Origins of the Controversy about the Existence of *Mujtahids* and the Gate of *Ijtihād*', *Studia Islamica* 63 (1986), 129–41; Joseph Schacht, *An Introduction to Islamic Law* (Oxford: The Clarendon Press, 1982), pp. 69–71; N. J. Coulson, *A History of Islamic Law* (Edinburgh University Press, 1978), p. 81.

13 Sherman Jackson, '*Taqlīd*, Legal Scaffolding and the Scope of Legal Injunctions in Post-Formative Theory', *Islamic Law and Society* 3 (1996), 165–92.

14 Mohammad Fadel, 'The social logic of *Taqlīd* and the rise of the *Mukhtaṣar*', *Islamic Law and Society* 3 (1996), pp. 193–233.

Shawkānī as *mujtahid* and *mujaddid*

In all of Shawkānī's works, a constant refrain is sounded: the absolute necessity of applying *ijtihād* as a means of combatting the sectarian and antagonistic tendencies amongst different schools of law, 'factionalism' (*madhhabiyya*), which has resulted from the practice of *taqlīd*, the blind imitation of past rulings and opinions. This, according to Shawkānī, has resulted in rulings being based on the mere opinion (*raʾy*) of scholars and lack of knowledge of the textual evidence (*dalīl*) for any given opinion. The practice of *taqlīd* was a reprehensible innovation which had been developed by the followers of the various schools of law, many of whom argued that *ijtihād* was no longer possible for later generations of Muslims – the door of *ijtihād* was closed.[15]

Shawkānī argued forcefully that the door of *ijtihād* never had been closed, and he tried to prove, through historical, juristic and theological arguments, that *mujtahid*s had lived and operated since the supposed closure took place. In explaining the reason for writing his only historical work, a biographical dictionary of some six hundred personalities, Shawkānī summarised his position in the preface:

> The opinion is widespread among some of the lowly folk (*jamāʿa min al-raʿāʿ*) that their predecessors alone had precedence in the sciences (*ʿulūm*), and not their successors; and it has been transmitted also that some people of the four schools (*madhāhib*) say it is impossible to find a *mujtahid* after the sixth century [AH, twelfth CE] or after the seventh century [AH, thirteenth CE] as yet others have claimed. It is easy for those of the lowest level of knowledge, of least perception and humblest understanding to see that this statement is based on ignorance because it would mean a restriction of the Divine grace and Lorldly abundance to some believers and not others, to the people of one era and not another and to those of one age and not another without evidence or textual proof. This forsaken and vile assertion would necessitate depriving the later eras of an upholder of God's proofs and an interpreter of His Book and the Sunna of His Prophet, and an elucidator of what He legislated for his worshippers. Without a doubt this would entail the loss of the Sharīʿa and the disappearance of religion. God, the Most High, has undertaken to preserve His religion, and the intention is not its preservation in the bodies of pages and registers but rather to have individuals who would present it at all times and in every necessity.
>
> This [has] spurred me to write this book which contains the biographies of the great ulema, about whom information has reached me, from the people of the eighth century [AH, fourteenth CE] and until our present age. This is to inform the adherent of the [aforementioned] statement that God, who is kind, was as bounteous with the successors as He was with the predecessors; it is even possible [to say] that there were ulema in the later ages whose all-round knowledge in the different sciences few of the people from the earlier generations would equal. And he who looks deeply in this book, and from whose neck the noose of *taqlīd* is unravelled, will see this.[16]

[15] Cf. Muḥammad al-Shawkānī, 'al-Qawl al-mufīd fī adillat al-ijtihād waʾl-taqlīd', in *al-Rasāʾil al-salafiyya fī iḥyāʾ sunnat khayr al-bariyya* (Beirut: Dār al-Kitāb al-ʿArabī, 1991), pp. 191f.

[16] *Badr*, I: 2–3.

Although *al-Badr al-ṭāliʿ bi-maḥāsin man baʿd al-qarn al-sābiʿ* (The Rising Moon Illuminating the Good Deeds of Those Who Came After the 7th Century) concentrates mainly on Yemeni figures, many of whom were contemporaries of Shawkānī, it seems to have been broadly intended as a continuation of Muḥammad al-Dhahabī's (d. 748/1348) *Siyar aʿlām al-nubalāʾ* since it takes up where the latter left off in the seventh century AH.[17] However, Shawkānī, as can be seen from the quote above, was interested in making a single point: that the gate of *ijtihād* had never been closed, and therefore many of the later ulema were indeed equal to those who preceded them, if only because more sources were available to them. This, he argues, makes the practice of *ijtihād* easier for the later generations than it was for those earlier.[18]

That Shawkānī considered himself to be a *mujtahid* is beyond doubt. His personal biography is included in *al-Badr al-ṭāliʿ*. Furthermore, in most of his works, he presents himself as an ultimate arbiter who illuminates the truth, provides the proofs and sweeps away all that is textually unfounded.[19] But more than a *mujtahid*, Shawkānī probably wanted to be considered a *mujaddid* ('renewer' of Islam), or at the very least a scholar of the highest calibre with a pan-Islamic reputation. He does not claim for himself the title of 'centennial renewer' (*mujaddid al-qarn*), but alludes to it when he asserts that although the proponents of *taqlīd* have brought about the abolition of the Book and Sunna and the refutation of sound Prophetic Traditions, 'a faction of this community remains pure in its righteouness' and that 'God sends to this community at the head of every century one who will renew its religion'.[20] The reference in the first ḥadīth is to the Traditionists, whereas in the second it was no doubt to himself; a position which was confirmed by his students and is adhered to by high ranking officials in the present Yemeni government who think of Shawkānī as the 'renewer of the thirteenth century AH.'.[21]

To bolster his claim to be a *mujtahid* of the first rank, Shawkānī wrote a work, similar to one written by Ibn Ḥajar,[22] entitled *Itḥāf al-akābir bi-isnād al-dafātir*.[23] In it he lists all the works he had either 'heard' (*samāʿ*) or received a license (*ijāza*) for,[24] and which he could transmit or teach. For each work he lists the chain(s)

[17] Cf. *Badr*, I: 4.

[18] Muḥammad al-Shawkānī, *Irshād al-fuḥūl ilā taḥqīq al-ḥaqq min ʿilm al-uṣūl* (Beirut: Dār al-Maʿrifa, n.d.), pp. 223–4, (hereinafter *Irshād al-fuḥūl*).

[19] Cf. Muḥammad al-Shawkānī, *Wabl al-ghamām ḥāshiya ʿalā Shifāʾ al-uwām*, *apud* al-Ḥusayn b. Badr al-Dīn, *Kitāb Shifāʾ al-uwām fī aḥādīth al-aḥkām* (n.p.: Jamʿiyyat ʿUlamāʾ al-Yaman, 1996), vol. I, pp. 20–1; *Irshād al-fuḥūl*, pp. 2–3.

[20] Cf. Shawkānī, *Qaṭru al-walī*, p. 353.

[21] Cf. *al-Tiqṣār*, pp. 33–5 where Muḥammad al-Akwaʿ asserts that Shawkānī is the renewer of the thirteenth century; also al-Ḥusayn b. Badr al-Dīn, *Shifāʾ al-uwām*, p. 16, where Muḥammad al-Ḥajjī, the vice-president of Yemen's supreme court (*majlis al-qaḍāʾ al-aʿlā*), makes the same assertion.

[22] Ibn Ḥajar's work is entitled *al-Majmaʿ al-muʾassas bil-muʿjam al-mufahras*, cf. Berkey, *Transmission*, p. 171.

[23] This work was published in Hyderabad by Maṭbaʿat Majlis Dāʾirat al-Maʿārif al-Niẓāmiyya in 1328/1910. Indian scholars are particularly interested in Shawkānī because he holds a prominent position in many of their own *isnād*s. Cf. Muḥammad Akram al-Nadwī, *Nafaḥāt al-Hind waʾl-Yaman bi-asānīd al-shaykh Abī ʾl-Ḥasan* (Riyadh: Maktabat al-Imām al-Shāfiʿī, 1998).

[24] Cf. Messick, *The Calligraphic State*, pp. 84f.

of transmitters back to the individual author. The list is impressive, for it includes over 450 works which range across the Islamic sciences and the various doctrinal and legal schools, Zaydī and Sunnī. In narrating his *isnād*s, Shawkānī gives the greatest detail when mentioning the canonical ḥadīth collections, providing numerous *isnād*s for these and underscoring the fact that he considered these works the most important on the list.[25] The idea behind providing these multiple *isnād*s is to show that he can transmit these works with certainty of their authenticity because they were transmitted to him by 'concurrence' (*tawātur*).[26]

The *Itḥāf* was intended to mark Shawkānī as a great scholar and to situate him temporally and historically as a purveyor of learning and knowledge. Indeed, he says that his main reason for writing the work was to benefit his students, who could read it to locate themselves exactly on the map of transmission chains sustaining the world of Islamic knowledge. However, Shawkānī's *mujaddid* status does not derive from any explicit assertion he made himself to this effect; rather, as in the case of *mujaddid*s before him, it was his disciples and students who bestowed on him the honour.[27] For his students, Shawkānī exhibited the qualifications of the *mujaddid*, and most noteworthy among these was that he was a *mujtahid* of the highest rank – *ijtihād* was the *conditio sine qua non.*

The Break with Zaydī Tradition

The break here with Zaydī intellectual tradition deserves noting. 'Renewers', in the Sunnī sense, are not a feature of Zaydī thought.[28] The imams are the focus both of intellectual truth and of the effort to have the world conform with this; and though there may be periods when no imam is evident, Zaydism had usually been content to extend the search for the righteous leader rather than accept *faute de mieux* a temporal lord. Imams who lacked the full range of conditions, restricted imams (*al-aʾimma al-muḥtasibūn*), were recognized in later Zaydī thought, but the character of the imamate was not compromised intellectually.[29] Shawkānī's interest

[25] Cf. Shawkānī, *Itḥāf al-akābir*, pp. 59f.

[26] *Tawātur* relates to the authentic quality of any transmitted report. A report that shares in this quality is understood to have been transmitted from a sufficient number of incongruent sources to exclude the possibility of collusion on its fabrication, and therefore its falsity.

[27] Shawkānī's students and disciples are not just those who studied with him directly, but also all those who claim to follow his methodology, and generally to belong to his school 'madhhab al-Shawkānī'. In many cases the so-called students are in fact generational students, i.e., students of students of Shawkānī (e.g., the contemporary Muḥammad b. Ismāʿīl al-ʿAmrānī).

[28] It is noteworthy that Ella Landau-Tasseron has tried to detail the use of the *mujaddid* tradition in Zaydism and discovered that the Sunnī model does not apply. Cf. Ella Landau-Tasseron, 'Zaydī imāms as restorers of religion: *Iḥyāʾ* and *Tajdīd* in Zaydī literature', *Journal of Near Eastern Studies*, 49 (1990), 247–63. In this regard, it must be pointed that the work *Itḥāf al-muhtadīn*, which led Landau-Tasseron to the topic of *tajdīd* among the Zaydīs, was written by Muḥammad b. Muḥammad Zabāra, a man who was highly influenced by Shawkānī's ideas on *ijtihād* and *tajdīd*. As such, he does not reflect earlier Zaydī-Hādawī opinion on the matter.

[29] In the commentary on the margins of *Sharḥ al-Azhār*, it is stated that some later Shīʿīs allowed for a *muqallid* to become imam – although he had to be a *mujtahid* in politics (*mujtahid fī abwāb*

in the role of the *mujaddid* or 'renewer', by contrast, fits with the theoretical acceptance of a *de facto* separation between truth and power. The imamate, as we shall see, becomes not simply the province of the *muḥtasibūn* but a source of temporal order identical with *mulk* or kingship;[30] righteousness, meanwhile, is the concern of a separate or distinct group of ulema, whose opinions must defer to the most learned among them. As a *mujtahid* and *mujaddid*, independent intellect and renewer of collective truth, Shawkānī would be the source to which scholars and rulers alike properly should resort. Shawkānī's insistence on *ijtihād* over *taqlīd* implies in fact, if paradoxically, that Muslims should follow his rulings and opinions, an important claim for a man who for most of his life was the 'judge of judges'.

For all his insistence on transcending the differences among the schools, Shawkānī's position fits into a tradition that is purely Sunnī. This is most evident in his criticism of the Zaydī-Hādawī doctrine of the imamate. He disputes the Hādawī claim that the path to becoming an imam is through 'making a call' (*daᶜwa*). Rather, he says that whenever a group of Muslims, which he specifies as the people 'who loose and bind' (*ahl al-ḥall waᶜl-ᶜaqd*, i.e., the notables), agree to give their allegiance (*bayᶜa*) to a pious man of the community (*min ṣāliḥī hadhihi al-umma*), then it becomes obligatory for them to obey him in 'the good he ordains and the evil he forbids'. Another way to become imam is by means of an incumbent delegating the imamate to a successor, as Abu Bakr did with ᶜUmar.

As for the strict Hādawī conditions, such as the imam being male, of mature age (*bāligh*), rational (*ᶜāqil*), free (*ḥurr*) etc., Shawkānī agrees with some and disputes others. For example, he agrees that the imam must be rational but disputes that he must be a Fāṭimī-ᶜAlawī, arguing that no proof exists for such specification because of the Tradition which states that 'imams are from Quraysh'.[31] Furthermore, obedience to a Sultan is mandatory even if he is a slave because of the Traditions which state, 'Obey and be obedient even if he is an Ethiopian slave whose head is like a raisin', and 'obedience is incumbent upon you even if he is an Ethiopian slave, because the believer is like a camel, if he is fettered, he is led'.[32] It may not

al-siyāsa) – because *ijtihād* according to them had become impossible in later times. Imam al-Muṭahhar (probably al-Wāthiq bi-Allāh al-Muṭahhar b. Muḥammad, d. 802 AH) was apparently one who claimed the imamate despite not having attained the rank of *ijtihād*. This commentary goes on to say that if a valid candidate for the imamate is not to be found then a *muḥtasib* (a restricted imam) can rule until a valid imam can assume the post. The *muḥtasib* need not be a *mujtahid* or a descendant of al-Ḥasan or al-Ḥusayn, or a member of Quraysh. His requirements are that he has enough reasoning ability, courage and perspicacity. The *muḥtasib* performs all the duties of the valid imam except the following: the four legal punishments (*al-ḥudūd al-arbaᶜa*), the Friday prayers (*jumuᶜāt*), conquest (*ghazw*) and collection of alms (*ṣadaqāt*), cf. *Sharḥ al-Azhār*, vol. IV, pp. 520–1; also al-Manṣūr al-Qāsim, *Kitāb al-Asās*, pp. 173–4; al-Sharafī, *Kitāb ᶜUddat al-akyās*, vol. II, pp. 223–6; Strothmann, *Das Staatsrecht*, pp. 94f.; Madelung, *Der Imam al-Qāsim*, p. 172.

30 Cf. al-Muʾayyadī, *al-Tuḥaf sharḥ al-zalaf*, p. 161.

31 Aḥmad b. Ḥanbal, *Musnad*, 3: 129.

32 Versions of these ḥadīths can be found in Bukhārī, *Ṣaḥīḥ*, *al-Adhān*, 4, 5, 156; *Aḥkām*, 4; Ibn Mājah, *Sunan*, *Jihād*, 29; Aḥmad, *Musnad*, 3: 114, 171. On the origins and use of this ḥadīth see Patricia Crone, '"Even an Ethiopian slave": the transformation of a Sunni tradition', *BSOAS* LVII (1994), 59–67.

have escaped Shawkānī's attention that the Qāsimī imams he served were indeed Ethiopian-looking, as Niebuhr pointed out.

The clearest elaboration of Shawkānī's vision of the separation between truth and order is when he discusses the Hādawī condition that the imam must be a *mujtahid*. In disputing this, he says instead that the ignorant sultan

> must employ a religious scholar who is a *mujtahid* and who will undertake to run the affairs of the pure Sharīᶜa, after determining that the latter is knowledgable, just and well informed in matters of religion ... For me [Shawkānī], the most important conditions and foundations which the imam or sultan must fulfil are: that he be able to safeguard the roads, bring justice to the oppressed, defend the Muslims in the event of a suprise attack by an infidel army or a rebel ... It does not harm an imam if he should fall short of a condition or more of those mentioned by the [Zaydī] author, so long as he fulfils what we have mentioned. Muslims do not need an imam who sits in his prayer chamber (*fī muṣallāh*), holding his prayer beads, devoting himself to reading religious books, teaching these to the students of his age, and commenting on the problems therein while ignoring the shedding of blood and property, Muslims plundering each other, and the strong oppressing the weak. In this case none of the [stipulations] of the imamate or the sultanate are being enforced because the more important matters, which I have already mentioned, are not being fulfilled [i.e., safety, justice and defence].[33]

The image Shawkānī portrays of a learned but inactive imam is hardly the model posited in Hādawī manuals of law or depicted in their historical sources. The early Qāsimīs had embodied the ideal of men of both sword and pen, and they were not beyond recent historical memory. Was this other model not sustainable or even relevant by Shawkānī's time? It is clear that the frame of reference had shifted away from the political doctrines and moral order envisioned in Hādawī teachings. This is further confirmed when Shawkānī asserts that Muslims are forbidden to rise (*khurūj*) against an unjust imam (*ẓālim*) so long as he prays and commits no public act of unbelief (*lam yaẓhar minhu al-kufr al-bawwāḥ*).[34]

Shawkānī's vision of a political order described the state of affairs in his day to a remarkable extent. The imams who ruled were not scholars or *mujtahids*. They were variously accused of imposing non-canonical taxes and their personal behaviour left them far from the ideal. Furthermore, Shawkānī was the *mujtahid* to whom the imams referred. A glimpse into the judicial system, its procedures and Shawkānī's role in it is offered in a story which is narrated in the chronicle of al-Manṣūr ᶜAlī's reign. It is said that on Sunday 13 Rajab 1210/24 January 1796 the following events took place.

> A group of the people of corruption in Bilād Ḥarāz sympathized with (*māla ilā*) the wife of Aḥmad al-Nashshād, and they agreed with her to murder her husband. This done, they were soon all arrested. The Qāḍī of Ḥarāz, Muḥammad b. Aḥmad al-Ghashm, discovered what they were up to and appealed [the case] to the imam [due to] the horrific nature of the event. [The Qāḍī] stated that he had imprisoned Yaḥyā b. Nāṣir

33 Shawkānī, *Wabl al-ghamām*, vol. III, pp. 500–1.
34 Shawkānī, *al-Sayl al-jarrār*, vol. IV, pp. 505–15.

> Jaḥḥāf, Sa^{c}d b. Ḥusayn Ḥamza, Aḥmad b. Ḥusayn Ḥamza, Ḥusayn b. ʿAbd Allāh ʿAbduh Nahshal and Sa^{c}d b. Ṣāliḥ al-^{c}Ajbalī and they had confessed (*aqarrū*) to killing Aḥmad al-Nashshād. The governor had them dispatched [to Sanaa]. The imam ordered his judge, al-Badr Muḥammad b. ^{c}Alī al-Shawkānī, to look into the case. [He did so] and issued a judgement that they should be executed. The imam had their heads cut off and the woman [i.e., al-Nashshād's wife] was brought to the place where they were executed, and each and every one of them was displayed to her. Then the imam had her lashed and ordered that she be paraded through the streets of the city, then she was sent to prison.[35]

Nothing more than this is said about the incident or the motives of the killers. The story reveals, however, the workings of a judicial system which, as we can see, runs along the theoretical lines set out by Shawkānī. The heinous nature of the crime leads the local judge to refer the case to the imam, after extracting a confession from the killers. The imam then refers the case to his *mujtahid*, Shawkānī, who issues his judgement, and the sentence is carried out. The wife's role as an accessory means she is whipped, whereas the practice of parading her through the streets, whose inhabitants were in the habit of pelting such prisoners with garbage, was more of a customary imamic punishment which was justified under the rubric of *ta^{c}zīr* (discretionary chastisement).

Situating Shawkānī Intellectually

Partly because Shawkānī was widely read and educated in both the Zaydī and Sunnī traditions, it is difficult to situate him entirely within one of the schools of Islam. Indeed, to do so would be in some sense to contravene the very claim he made to be a *mujtahid* who was above all schools. However, it can be said that he was a Traditionist; that is, his scholarly attention was directed at the canonical ḥadīth collections and the ḥadīth sciences, which he considered the most authoritative, and he therefore drew mostly on these in elaborating his opinions. In doing so, he was an heir to the tradition in the Zaydī highlands of Yemen which produced such scholars as Muḥammad b. Ibrāhīm al-Wazīr, al-Ḥasan b. Aḥmad al-Jalāl, Ṣāliḥ b. Mahdī al-Maqbalī, Muḥammad b. Ismā^{c}īl al-Amīr and the lesser known ^{c}Abd al-Qādir b. Aḥmad al-Kawkabānī, who was Shawkānī's most illustrious teacher. These Traditionists had rejected the practice of adhering to one school of law and condemned *taqlīd* while advocating *ijtihād*. They also rejected the rational sciences which were mainly associated with the Mu^{c}tazila among the Zaydīs in Yemen. The influence of the Shāfi^{c}ī scholars of Egypt, ḥadīth scholars and jurists, like Ibn Ḥajar (d. 852/1448) and al-Suyūṭī (d. 911/1505), and that of Ḥanbalī scholars like Ibn Taymiyya (d. 728/1328) and his disciple Ibn Qayyim al-Jawziyya (d. 751/1350), was also very important for Shawkānī. In fact, the argument can be made that Shawkānī modelled himself on them, seeking to emulate the polymathic nature

[35] Luṭf Allāh Jaḥḥāf, *Durar nuḥūr al-ḥūr al-^{c}īn*, ms. Sanaa, Garbiyya Library, tārīkh no. 86, fol. 171.

of their works, and perhaps wanted to be considered as having their stature as first-rank scholars and 'renovators'.

In Sunnī Islam there had developed a belief that every hundred years a scholar would emerge who would restore or renovate Islamic thought and practice. This tradition is best summarised in the Prophetic ḥadīth: 'God will send to this community at the turn of every century someone [or people] who will restore religion', (*inna Allāh yabᶜath li-hadhihi al-umma ᶜalā raʾs kull miʾat sana man yujaddid lahā amr dīnihā*).[36] The emergence of this ḥadīth and the 'renewer' tradition has been the subject of a study by Landau-Tasseron.[37] She argues that the 'renewer' ḥadīth originated in an attempt to legitimise and spread Shāfiᶜī's teachings, specifically that the Sunna, understood to be based on ḥadīth, was to have a principal role in Islamic jurisprudence. She also shows how this ḥadīth later played a role in the defence of the Sunna against innovation and heresy.[38] By appropriating the role of renewers, Shāfiᶜī scholars claimed that they were the upholders of Sharīᶜa. They could do this because of the belief in Islamic tradition that scholars were 'the successors to the Prophets'.[39]

Landau-Tasseron goes on to show that the concepts of *tajdīd* (renewal) and *ijtihād* became closely linked when al-Suyūṭī, who is considered to be the ninth *mujaddid* in the Shāfiᶜī chain, claimed the title on the basis of being a *mujtahid* himself.[40] With this, *ijtihād* became a condition for acquiring *mujaddid* status and the means by which one could make reference directly to the Sunna. But the title of *mujaddid* remained honorific, with no formal method of appointment being developed. In fact, many *mujaddids* were either self-appointed or, more commonly, they were recognized by a small circle of students and other jurists. The phenomenon was predominantly Shāfiᶜī since many of the transmitters of the ḥadīth, and the renewers themselves, were Shāfiᶜīs, and later mostly Egyptians.[41]

Shawkānī's identification with these Shāfiᶜī scholars can be gleaned from their biographical entries in his *al-Badr al-ṭāliᶜ*. In al-Suyūṭī's biography for instance, Shawkānī defends him against Muḥammad al-Sakhāwī's (d. 902 /1497) famous allegations in *al-Dawʾ al-lāmiᶜ*. He emphasizes that, in accordance with the sayings of the scholars of *isnād* criticism (*al-jarḥ waʾl-taᶜdīl*), the sayings of peers (*aqrān*) about each other should not be accepted once competition between them exists. The biographical entry ends with the following:

> The reason why he [al-Sakhāwī] has related the ulema's sayings which allow the denigration of al-Suyūṭī is the latter's claim to be a *mujtahid*. This remains the habit of people regarding those who attain this rank. However, as in the case of Ibn Taymiyya,

36 Abū Dāʾūd, *Sunan*, *Kitāb al-Malāḥim*, 1.

37 Ella Landau-Tasseron, 'The "cyclical reform": a study of the *Mujaddid* tradition', *Studia Islamica* 70 (1989), 79–117. See also Yohanan Friedmann, *Prophecy Continuous* (Berkeley: University of California Press, 1989), pp. 94–101.

38 Landau-Tasseron, 'The "cyclical reform" ', p. 113.

39 Ibid., p. 85.

40 Ibid., pp. 83, 87. Landau-Tasseron bases this on al-Suyūṭī's *al-Tanbiʾa bi-man yabᶜathuhu Allāh ᶜalā raʾs kull miʾa*, ms. Leiden, Or. 474, fols. 80–3b.

41 Ibid., pp. 84–96, 107.

> investigation shows that God Almighty raises the importance of the one who was shown enmity because of his knowledge and his uttering the truth. He also spreads his good deeds after death, makes him famous and allows people to benefit from his knowledge.[42]

Shawkānī is drawing here a parallel between himself, as *mujtahid*, and scholars like al-Suyūṭī and Ibn Taymiyya, because he too was attacked (by Hādawī scholars) for making claims about *ijtihād*.

The history of the *mujaddid* tradition highlights how *mujaddids* were associated with the defence of the Sunna against all who refused to derive the law exclusively from the Qurʾān and the Sunna, most notably the *ahl al-raʾy* and groups like the Shīʿa and the Muʿtazila. These opponents of the emergent Sunnī orthodoxy after al-Shāfiʿī's lifetime were branded heretics and innovators, and the understanding of Sunna developed to become the antithesis of *bidʿa* (reprehensible innovation).[43] The *mujaddid* became the one who renovates belief and practice by revivifying the Sunna (*iḥyāʾ al-sunna*) and eliminating whatever innovations had accrued to Islamic practice and belief in a given century. In order to do this, the scholar had to make reference directly to first sources, namely the Qurʾān and the Sunna, and therefore needed to be a *mujtahid*. The parallel between Shawkānī's situation, where the opponents of the Traditionist scholars were the Zaydī-Hādawīs, and that of the Sunnī *mujaddid*s, like al-Suyūṭī, who were combating *bidʿa* in the name of orthodoxy, did not escape the attention of Yemeni scholars on both sides of the divide. Shawkānī, and Ibn al-Amīr before him, wished to rid Yemen of the pervasive influence of the Hādawī teachings and all forms of *taqlīd*, of which Hādawism was a manifestation; the Hādawīs wished to protect their school, and consequently their identity, from the attacks of the Traditionist scholars. The attack that 'reformist' scholars like Shawkānī undertook against what they termed the opponents of the Sunna was two-fold. On the one hand, it entailed an elucidation and re-emphasis of certain sources of law – the field of *uṣūl al-fiqh* – and on the other, a purging of all normative rulings – the field of *furūʿ* – from opinions that were not consistent with their *uṣūl al-fiqh* methodology.

Shawkānī and *uṣūl al-fiqh*

Although several studies and articles have dealt with Shawkānī's views and opinions on the subject of *ijtihād*, and more broadly on his *uṣūl al-fiqh*, these have not sought to integrate his ideas into the historical, political and social contexts in which they developed.[44] Perhaps the best treatment so far of Shawkānī's *uṣūl al-fiqh* views is provided by Rudolph Peters in an article entitled '*Idjtihād* and *taqlīd*

42 *Badr*, I: 333–4; cf. Ibn Daqīq al-ʿĪd's, Ibn Ḥajar's and Ibn Taymiyya's biographical entries in *Badr*, II: 229–32, *Badr*, I: 87–92 and *Badr*, I: 63–72 respectively.

43 Landau-Tasseron, 'The "cyclical reform"', pp. 104–5; cf. Ignaz Golziher, *Muslim Studies*, trans. S. M. Stern (London: George Allen and Unwin, 1971), vol. II, pp. 31–7.

44 See for example Shaʿbān Muḥammad Ismāʿīl, *al-Imām al-Shawkānī wa manhajuhu fī uṣūl al-fiqh* (Manama: Qatar University, 1989).

in eighteenth and nineteenth century Islam' in which he compares four 'fundamentalist' authors.[45] In other studies, most notably by Yemeni and Egyptian authors, Shawkānī is depicted uncritically as a reformer fighting against the fanaticism of sectarians and imitators (*muqallidūn*) and as being 'the renewer of his century'.[46] These latter works seem to indicate that he is more often than not an object of study because his views reflect modern concerns. An Egyptian author for example describes Shawkānī as follows:

> He threw off the noose of *taqlīd* before reaching the age of thirty. Before that he followed the Zaydī school. He became one of the notables (*aᶜlām*) of *ijtihād* and the greatest exponent of abandoning *taqlīd*. He developed rulings through *ijtihād* from the Book and the Sunna. In doing this, he is considered among the vanguard of the renewers (*mujaddidūn*) and the *mujtahid*s in the modern period and among those who participated in awakening the Islamic and Arab nation (*umma*) in this epoch.[47]

Shawkānī has been slotted into the modern nationalist tradition which equates *ijtihād* with liberating thought, and which has in some unspecified sense had an instrumental role in Arab and Muslim renaissance. In our study of Shawkānī's own writings and the historical sources of the period, a more complex picture emerges. First, however, it must be pointed out that Shawkānī does not convey in any of his writings a concern about a European intellectual menace, despite having been aware of a European economic, political and military presence in the Islamic lands – notably Napoleon's invasion of Egypt.[48] His concerns lie with problems he regards as intrinsic to Islamic history and tradition, and which are summed up in the practice of *taqlīd*. This, he says, has divided Muslims into mutually opposing sects and has, more perniciously, led them away from the principal sources. Second, the solution he proposes makes appeal to the pristine past of the time of the Rightly Guided Caliphs, but also offers practical guidelines which can bring about a virtuous order similar to it. The solution lies in allowing jurists like himself to practise *ijtihād*, to reproduce themselves pedagogically and to administer the interpretation and application of the Sharīᶜa.

A Literalist Bent

A literalist bent permeates all of Shawkānī's writings. He constantly urges a return to the principal sources – the Qur᾿ān and the Sunna – which must be literally

[45] Peters, 'Idjtihād and Taqlīd in 18th and 19th century Islam'. Peters describes Shawkānī as being 'remotest from traditional doctrine . . . since he does not differentiate betweeen the various ranks of *ijtihād*, claims that anybody with minimal knowledge of jurisprudence can be a *mujtahid* and considers *taqlīd* absolutely forbidden', p. 143.

[46] Cf. ᶜAbd al-Ghanī al-Sharjī, *al-Imām al-Shawkānī ḥayātuh wa fikruh* (Beirut: Mu᾿assasat al-Risāla, 1988); al-ᶜAmrī, *al-Imām al-Shawkānī*; Ibrāhīm Hilāl, *al-Imām al-Shawkānī*; idem, *Min niqāṭ al-iltiqā᾿ bayna al-imāmayn Muḥammad ᶜAbduh wa᾿l-imām al-Shawkānī* (Cairo: Maktabat al-Nahḍa al-Miṣriyya, 1987).

[47] Ibrāhīm Hilāl in the preface of Shawkānī, *Qaṭru al-walī*, p. 17.

[48] Cf. Maḥmūd (ed.), *Dhikrayāt al-Shawkānī*, pp. 50–2, 55–6.

understood; any interpretation that draws one away from the texts is forbidden. The ethos in all his works is the undermining of the sciences which have created conceptual and methodological terminology that has drawn Muslims away from the original texts. On the level of *uṣūl* he aimed at more certainty than the standard model. With his insistence on the study of and almost exclusive dependence on ḥadīth works – notably the *Ṣaḥīḥayn* of Bukhārī and Muslim – this would add up to a legal system for which greater certainty could be claimed.

Shawkani's only comprehensive treatment of the science of *ūṣūl* is a work entitled *Irshād al-fuḥūl ilā taḥqīq al-ḥaqq min ᶜilm al-uṣūl* (Guidance for the Luminaries to Achieving the Truth in the Science of the Principles of Law). This work appears to draw mainly on Fakhr al-Dīn al-Rāzī's (d. 606/1209) *al-Maḥṣūl fī ᶜilm uṣūl al-fiqh* and Muḥammad b. Bahādur al-Zarkashī's (d. 794/1392) *al-Baḥr al-Muḥīṭ fī usūl al-fiqh*. Shawkānī says in his introduction that he wrote the *Irshād al-fuḥūl* in order to distinguish the sound from the unsound and the correct from the incorrect in the science of *uṣūl al-fiqh*, because it had acquired such prestige that no one dared criticize it any longer. No person, no matter how learned, would refute an argument that was made in *uṣūl al-fiqh* terms. And this, he argues, has led many people of knowledge to fall into the snare of *raᵓy* (mere 'opinion' or reasoning with no sound basis), thinking all the while that they are basing themselves on transmitted knowledge (*ᶜilm al-riwāya*). By referring to this science, he continues, many *mujtahid*s have reverted to *taqlīd* without realising it and many who cling to the evidence (*adilla*) have fallen into pure *raᵓy*, again without realising this.[49] In short, Shawkānī aims to show that the science of *uṣūl* had acquired methodological accretions that were textually baseless and were therefore unsound, and that most of the rules elaborated by *uṣūl* scholars were in fact presumptive (*ẓannī*) rather than definitive (*qaṭᶜī*) and should therefore be disregarded.

In elaborating his legal theory, Shawkānī's basic premise is that the Qurᵓān and the Sunna are sufficient and comprehensive sources for the elaboration of all legal rulings for all time. The *mujtahid* can find in these evidence or proof to substantiate his legal decisions without recourse to any other source, be it consensus (*ijmāᶜ*), most forms of analogical reasoning (*qiyās*), or independent reasoning (*raᵓy*). In order to bolster this argument, he makes claims for the indubitable authenticity of the ḥadīths in the canonical collections, in particular the *Ṣaḥīḥayn* of Bukhārī and Muslim. His main claim here is that the Muslim *umma* has universally accepted the *Ṣaḥīḥayn* as the soundest works after the Qurᵓān. This argument is based on a broad consensus (*ijmāᶜ*) and has a long pedigree, with various forms, in Islamic legal thought.[50] The *locus classicus* is Ibn al-Ṣalāḥ's *ᶜUlūm al-ḥadīth*, otherwise known as the 'Introduction to the Ḥadīth Sciences'.[51]

49 *Irshād al-fuḥūl*, pp. 2–3.

50 *Irshād al-fuḥūl*, p. 44; Muḥammad al-Shawkānī, *Tuḥfat al-dhākirīn bi-ᶜIddat al-ḥiṣn al-ḥaṣīn min kalām sayyid al-mursalīn* (Beirut: Dār al-Fikr, n.d.), p. 4. It is noteworthy that Ibn al-Amīr in his *Irshād al-nuqqād ilā taysīr al-ijtihād* does not concur with this view, but still grants the *Ṣaḥīḥayn* great authoritative status (see pp. 45–50).

51 Ibn al-Ṣalāḥ, *ᶜUlūm al-ḥadith*, Nūr al-Dīn ᶜItr (ed.) (Damascus: Dār al-Fikr, 1984), p. 18.

From the perspective of the Hādawīs, Shawkānī's claim is problematic because many of the Traditions contained in these works are isolated Traditions (*āḥād*).[52] The problem lies in the fact that the Hādawīs do not credit some of the Companions who had transmitted these Traditions with probity (*ᶜadāla*), because they had opposed ᶜAlī or the Ahl al-Bayt in some way and therefore are not considered trustworthy. The argument revolves around which of the Companions had probity. Shawkānī takes a maximal position that they all had *ᶜadāla*, whereas the Hādawīs are more selective on this issue, leading many of the stricter among them to reject the *Ṣaḥīḥayn* altogether.[53] Here is what one strict Hādawī has to say:

> If one of the People of Truth [*ahl al-ḥaqq*, i.e., a Zaydī] presents to them [i.e., the Sunnīs] a verse from the Book or a Sunna which accords with [Zaydī teachings], they cite in opposition a fabricated Tradition [*ḥadīth mawḍūᶜ*], and they say: 'We are the Ahl al-Sunna, we use the ḥadīths which we consider sound'. And in completion of their corrupt intentions, they [the Sunnīs] have committed themselves to declaring the probity of all the Companions, despite what is manifested in their *āḥād* Traditions [i.e., that which contradicts the Qurʾān and the teachings of Ahl al-Bayt].[54]

In ḥadīth terms, the classic retort that Shawkānī, and Yemeni Traditionists generally, made to the Zaydīs was that in elaborating judgements and rules the Zaydīs relied on Traditions of dubious authenticity, namely the *mursal* Traditions.[55] In other words, Zaydīs did not adhere to the strict methods of ḥadīth authentication, with the result that many of their opinions and views were based on weak or false Traditions and were therefore wrong. The *locus classicus* for this argument can be found in the works of Muḥammad b. Ibrāhim al-Wazīr. In his *al-Rawḍ al-bāsim*, an abridgement of his larger work *al-ᶜAwāṣim waʾl-qawāṣim*, he says:

> Zaydī imams do not have ḥadīth collections to satisfy the *mujtahid*... all their works have no transmission chains and do not refer to the imam who first reported the Tradition... To sum up, if Zaydīs do not accept 'unbelievers and sinners by interpretation' (*kuffār wa fussāq taʾwīl*), they accept *mursal* Traditions transmitted by their imams who had accepted these... none among them are known to be positively guarded against this. This indicates that their Traditions are of a category which only those who accept *mursal* Traditions, even *maqṭūᶜ* Traditions and those transmitted by unknown people (*majāhīl*)... would accept. Given this, how can it be said that it is better to refer to their [Zaydī] Traditions than to those of the [Sunnī] imams of ḥadīth, who spent

52 *Āḥād* traditions are those which fall short of the *tawātur* category because they have been transmitted by fewer reporters, and consequently their authenticity is not absolutely certain and their epistemological quality leads jurists to probable, not certain, judgements regarding God's will.

53 Cf. Ismāᶜīl al-Nuᶜmī, *Kitāb al-Sayf al-bātir*, ms. Sanaa, Gharbiyya Library, *majmūᶜ* no. 188, fols. 1–36 and *majmūᶜ* no. 91, fols. 55–77 (hereinafter *al-Sayf al-bātir*); Muḥammad b. Ṣāliḥ al-Samāwī, *al-Ghaṭamṭam al-zakhkhār al-muṭahhir li-riyāḍ al-Azhār min āthār al-Sayl al-Jarrār*, Muḥammad ᶜIzzān (ed.) (Amman: Maṭābiᶜ Sharikat al-Mawārid al-Ṣināᶜiyya al-Urduniyya, 1994), vol. I, pp. 3–157 (hereinafter *Ghaṭamṭam*); ᶜAbd Allāh al-ᶜIzzī, *ᶜUlūm al-ḥadīth ᶜinda al-Zaydiyya waʾl-muḥaddithīn*, Amman: Muʾassasat al-Imām Zayd b. ᶜAlī al-Thaqāfiyya, 2001.

54 *Ghaṭamṭam*, vol. I, p. 13.

55 *Mursal* ḥadīths are those that do not have full chains of transmission going back to the Prophet.

their years in the pursuit of finding the trustworthy (*thiqāt*), collecting the dispersed Traditions, distinguishing between the sound and the weak ...[56]

The Zaydī response to this attack is that the imams transmitted ḥadīths from their fathers and forefathers and that this chain of transmission is more elevated than any other. Moreover, a substantial portion of the teachings of the Hādawī imams is anchored in these ḥadīths, even though they do not furnish these with explicit chains of transmission.[57]

Shawkānī's views on *ijmāᶜ* and *qiyās*

Shawkānī's ideas on *uṣūl al-fiqh* cannot be dissociated from his attempts to empower himself as a *mujtahid*, an ultimate legal reference for his age, or from the Hādawī environment in which he operated and whose teachings he sought to disprove. It is in this light that his rejection of *ijmāᶜ* (the consensus of *mujtahid*s after the death of the Prophet in a given age on a given matter), the third principle in Islamic jurisprudence, is better understood. Shawkānī does not consider *ijmāᶜ* to be a source of law. For one thing, he says, there is no textual proof for it being a principle at all. Furthermore, it would be impossible to ascertain the opinion of all Muslims because of the vastness of the Islamic lands and the multitude of scholars who existed throughout the ages. He claims that few among them left written evidence of their opinions and even among those who did it remains an impossible task to adduce their opinions on a given matter. Finally, because of the dominance of the established schools of law, which were controlled by *muqallidūn*, many scholars did not dare express their true opinion for fear of retaliation.[58] Below is one of his statements on the matter:

Whoever claims to have the *ijmāᶜ* of the Muslim scholars of his age on a given religious issue has made a gross claim (*aᶜẓama al-daᶜwā*) and asserted its existence with something which does not obtain. The feasibility of this is impossible, even if one assumes that it is possible to have such agreement, without investigation and knowledge of the opinions of each man or group of men. The truth is that this is impossible (*mamnūᶜ*). This is because the consensus of all the scholars of all the regions on an issue is impossible given the [existence of] different schools, temperaments, differences in understanding, contradictory dispositions and the love of contradiction. This is the case with regard to a

[56] Muḥammad b. Ibrāhīm al-Wazīr, *al-Rawḍ al-bāsim fī ᵓl-dhabbi ᶜan sunnati Abī ᵓl-Qāsim*, 2nd ed. (Sanaa: al-Maktaba al-Yamaniyya liᵓl-Nashir waᵓl-Tawzīᶜ, 1985), pp. 94–6. For Shawkānī's views on the *mursal* Traditions see his *Irshād al-fuḥūl*, pp. 57–8. It should be noted that Ibn al-Wazīr's claims were refuted by Hādawīs such as Ṣārim al-Dīn Ibrāhīm b. Muḥammad al-Wazīr (d. 914/1508) in a work entitled *al-Falak al-dawwār*. This has recently been edited and published by contemporary Hādawīs in Ṣaᶜda and forms part of an ongoing refutation of the Traditionist claim that Zaydīs are not grounded in the ḥadīth sciences.

[57] Majd al-Dīn al-Muᵓayyadī, *Lawāmiᶜ al-anwār*, 3 vols. (Ṣaᶜda: Maktabat al-Turāth al-Islāmī, 1993), vol. II, pp. 124–8.

[58] *Adab al-ṭalab*, pp. 160–1; *Irshād al-fuḥūl*, p. 69. Ibn Ḥazm held similar views on *ijmāᶜ*, see his *al-Iḥkām fī uṣūl al-aḥkām*, 2 vols. (Beirut: Dār al-Kutub al-ᶜIlmiyya, n.d.), vol. I, pp. 546f.

> scholar speaking about the consensus of his generation. If he is claiming an *ijmāᶜ* about a generation which he did not know after the age of the Companions then the claim, too, is impossible.... The one who claims that *ijmāᶜ* constitutes proof is not correct, for such [a claim] constitutes mere conjecture (*ẓann*) on the part of an individual from the community of Muslims. No believer can worship God on the basis of this... In my works, when I report a consensus from others I do this in order to prove my point to the one who accepts that *ijmāᶜ* constitutes proof.[59]

There may appear to be a contradiction in Shawkānī's views on the matter of *ijmāᶜ*. As pointed out earlier, he bases his claim for the indubitable authenticity of the *Ṣaḥīḥayn* on the *ijmāᶜ* of the Muslim community throughout the ages, whilst also rejecting the possibility of ascertaining an *ijmāᶜ* on a given point. The contradiction disappears, however, if one sees these as two different types of *ijmāᶜ*: the former is a general Muslim consensus which concerns the *Ṣaḥīḥayn* only, and in that sense is unique; whereas the latter has to do with opinions on specific matters. The significance of Shawkānī's rejection of this latter type of *ijmāᶜ* comes out in his critique of Hādawī legal opinions. Hādawīs consider the *ijmāᶜ* of their imams, or the *ijmāᶜ* of Ahl al-Bayt or the *ᶜitra*, to constitute an authoritative source (*ḥujja*) for their legal opinions.[60] For example, Hādawīs insist on making the call to prayer in a twofold form (*al-adhān muthannā*), i.e., saying 'Allāhu Akbar' only twice, and saying 'Come to the best of works' (*ḥayya ᶜalā khayr al-ᶜamal*). They base these practices, in part, on the *ijmāᶜ al-ᶜitra* argument. In his works, Shawkānī refutes these claims by saying that the *ijmāᶜ* the Hādawīs are claiming has no validity and he proffers ḥadīths to prove that 'Allāhu Akbar' must be said four times. Furthermore, he says that *ḥayya ᶜalā khayr al-ᶜamal* has no basis in the Sunna, since it cannot be found in the canonical ḥadīth collections that the Prophet ever mentioned this phrase.[61] The same argument is made by Ibn al-Amīr against the Hādawīs, particularly when he argues against the specifically Hādawī teachings in ritual law. Ibn al-Amīr asserts that because members of the Ahl al-Bayt can be found in all the Islamic sects and schools of law, one cannot make a claim for an *ijmāᶜ* by basing oneself solely on the consensus of the Zaydī imams and scholars.[62]

As for *qiyās* (analogical reasoning), Shawkānī says that most forms of it, too, do not constitute a source for the derivation of legal opinions. Most *qiyās* is based on *raʾy*, and it is under this heading that *raʾy* was mostly applied in Islamic law. For Shawkānī, *qiyās* allowed for arguments and opinions deriving from unconstrained rationality which had no basis in either the Qurʾān or the Sunna.[63] One of the proofs adduced by the advocates of *qiyās* is the ḥadīth in which the Prophet asks the Companion Muᶜādh b. Jabal, upon sending him to Yemen: 'How will you judge

59 Shawkānī, *Wabl al-ghamām*, vol. I, pp. 26–9.
60 al-Ḥusayn b. al-Qāsim, *Kitāb Hidāyat al-ᶜuqūl*, vol. I, pp. 509f. The *ᶜitra* refers to the family of the Prophet, but it often specifically means the Zaydī imāms.
61 Shawkānī, *al-Sayl al-jarrār*, vol. I, pp. 202–5; idem, *Wabl al-ghamām*, vol. I, pp. 256–60; idem, *Nayl al-awṭār sharḥ muntaqā al-akhbār*, 9 sections in 4 vols. (Beirut: Dār al-Fikr, 1989), vol. I, part 2, pp. 16–20.
62 Cf. Muḥammad b. Ismāᶜīl al-Amīr, *Masāʾil ᶜilmiyya* (Sanaa: Maktabat al-Irshād, n.d.).
63 *Adab al-ṭalab*, pp. 163–5.

if a case is brought to you? Muʿādh said: I will judge in accordance with the Book of God. The Prophet [then] said: what if you do not find [proof] in the Book of God? Muʿādh answered: then in accordance with the Sunna of the Messenger of God. The Prophet then asked: and if you do not find [proof] in the Messenger's Sunna? Muʿādh said: I will perform an *ijtihād* (*ajtahid raʾyī*)'.[64] Amongst the arguments Shawkānī levels against interpreting this ḥadīth as allowing for *qiyās* is one which states that the practice of *qiyās* had stopped after the Prophet's death. Until then, the Sharīʿa was perhaps not complete and evidence could not always be found in the Qurʾān and Sunna. After the Prophet's lifetime, however, verses like: 'Today I have perfected your religion for you' (V: 3), 'We have neglected nothing in the Book' (VI: 38), 'not a thing, fresh or withered, but it is in a Book Manifest' (VI: 59) led Shawkānī to say:

> There is no meaning for the completion [of the message] except the fulfilment of the texts for the needs of jurists (*ahl al-sharʿ*), either in their stipulations about each and every individual or by finding whatever one needs under the comprehensively worded texts (*al-ʿumūmāt al-shāmila*).[65]

Further on in his discussion on *qiyās* in *Irshād al-fuḥūl*, Shawkānī appears to allow for some forms of *qiyās*. Here he says:

> Know that the *qiyās* which is considered valid is that in which the text comes with its cause (*ʿilla manṣūṣa*), and [also] that in which there is no reasonable cause to distinguish the case in the text from another case (*nafy al-fāriq*) and that which falls under *faḥwā al-khiṭāb* and *laḥn al-khiṭāb* ...[66]

Shawkani here is limiting himself to the least controversial (but not unimportant) forms of what some jurists have labelled *qiyās*. In fact, some would class all the types he mentions as *qiyās jalī*.[67] In this Shawkānī appears to adopt the methodology of the Ḥanbalīs, who similarly object to the use of *qiyās* unless one is obliged to do so out of necessity (*ḍarūra*).[68]

64 Tirmidhī, *Sunan*, *Aḥkām*, 3; Abū Dāwūd, *Sunan*, *Aqḍiya*, 11.

65 *Irshād al-fuḥūl*, p. 178.

66 Ibid. The *ʿilla manṣūṣa* covers the case where the text comes with its *ʿilla* more or less explicitly. The *nafy al-fāriq* is where there is no reasonable cause to distinguish the case in the text from another case. The classic example is treating a slave girl like a male slave in some rules. The *faḥwā* and *laḥn* cases are classified by some as *qiyās jalī*, but others, including Shawkānī, would treat them as being separate. They are commonly distinguished, *faḥwā* referring to a case that is more appropriately (*a fortiori*) subject to the rule than the textual case. The classic example is the prohibition of striking one's parents on the basis of the Qurʾānic prohibition of saying 'Fie' (*uffa*) to them (cf. XVII: 23). *Laḥn* is a case that falls under the textual rule with equal appropriateness; e.g., the Qurʾān prohibits consuming the property of orphans, destroying it by fire is equally prohibited (cf. Zakariyya b. Muḥammad al-Ansārī, *Ghayat al-wuṣūl* (Cairo: Maṭbaʿat Muṣṭafā al-Bābī al-Ḥalabī, 1360/1941), p. 37). Here, by contrast to the *nafy al-fāriq*, some reference to the purpose of the textual rule is involved.

67 Cf. ʿAbd al-Qādir b. Badrān, *al-Madkhal ilā madhhab al-imām Aḥmad* (Beirut: Dār al-Kutub al-ʿIlmiyya, 1996), p. 151.

68 It is to be noted that Shawkānī completely rejects the practice of 'preference' (*istiḥsān*), which can be broadly defined 'as the adoption of a rule of law recognised as a departure from analogy'. This is because it has not textual basis. Cf. *Adab al-ṭalab*, p. 165–6. On *istiḥsān* see Aron Zysow, 'The economy of certainty: an introduction to the typology of Islamic legal theory', Ph.D. dissertation, Harvard University (1984), pp. 399–402.

Shawkānī's rejection of most forms of *qiyās* has implications for Hādawī law as well as that of the other schools. When looking at his commentary on Hādawī law one gets the impression that he wanted to sweep away systematically all opinions which he felt were based on unsound methodology and had no basis in the textual sources. A good example of this, which also shows his strictness on *qiyās*, is his criticism of the Zaydī (and Ḥanafī) position on the cause (*ᶜilla*) of usury (*ribā*). Usury is deemed a major offence (*kabīra*) in Islam and its law entails that whenever an exchange takes place in certain substances, the quantities must be equal and the exchange simultaneous. One of the main Traditions relating to this is the one reported by Abū Saᶜīd al-Khudrī in which the Prophet says: 'Gold for gold, silver for silver, wheat for wheat, barley for barley, dates for dates, and salt for salt . . .'.[69] Basing himself on this Tradition, Shawkānī says that the law of *ribā* applies only when any of these six items is exchanged for another sample of the same substance. Another variation of this Tradition provides that when the good is not exchanged for a sample of the same substance but for something else, the rule of equality does not apply, but the exchange must still be simultaneous. Zaydīs, and Ḥanafīs, applied *qiyās* to this Tradition and saw the *ᶜilla* as the measurement of these goods by weight (*wazn*) or volume (*kayl*). Thus, they extended the rule to require simultaneous exchanges whenever the goods involved (assuming they were different) were both measured in the same way (the quantites could be different). By contrast, the Shāfiᶜīs and Mālikīs, with some differences, both see the *ᶜilla* (apart from the gold and silver cases) as being a foodstuff (*ṭuᶜm*). Shawkānī felt that this use of *qiyās* was objectionable, particularly when the issue involved a definite and major act of disobedience (*maᶜṣiya min al-kabāʾir wa min qaṭᶜiyyāt al-sharīᶜa*).[70] Here is what he says in this regard:

> We refuse [to accept] that legal judgements be established through such ways. Indeed, we refuse to consider what they have called *ᶜilla* in this matter to be anything of the kind. How much better it is to limit oneself to the texts of the Sharīᶜa and not to burden oneself by exceeding them, enlarging the scope of the believers' duties which is only increasing their burden. We are not among those who deny *qiyās*, but we forbid establishing rules by it, except when the text comes with its cause (*ᶜilla manṣūṣa*) or that which established the *ᶜilla* under *faḥwā al-khiṭāb*.[71]

Ẓāhirīs, as well as Ibn al-Amīr, shared Shawkānī's rejection of applying *qiyās* to the law of *ribā*; whereas all the other major Sunnī schools appear to have applied it.[72] An important implication of Shawkānī's position here is that if on a given matter there are no revealed texts, no *ijmāᶜ* of the Companions or of the *umma*

[69] Muslim, *Ṣaḥīḥ*, *Musāqāt*, 81–3, 85.

[70] Shawkānī, *al-Sayl al-jarrār*, vol. III, pp. 63f.; Muḥammad Ṣiddīq Ḥasan Khān, *al-Rawḍa al-nadiyya sharḥ al-Durar al-bahiyya*, Ḥasan Ḥallāq (ed.) (Beirut: Dār al-Nadā, 1993), vol. II, pp. 228–36; cf. *Sharḥ al-Azhār*, vol. III, pp. 69f.; Aḥmad b. Qāsim al-ᶜAnsī, *al-Tāj al-mudhhab li-aḥkām al-madhhab* (Sanaa: Maktabat al-Yaman al-Kubrā, n.d.), vol. II, pp. 376f.

[71] Shawkānī, *Wabl al-ghamām*, vol. II, p. 427.

[72] Cf. Ibn Ḥazm, *al-Muḥallā bil-āthār*, ᶜAbd al-Ghaffār al-Bindārī (ed.), 12 vols. (Beirut: Dār al-Kutub al-ᶜIlmiyya, 1988), vol. VII, p. 429; Muḥammad b. Ismāᶜīl al-Amīr, *Subul al-salām sharḥ Bulugh al-maram* (Beirut: Dār al-Kitāb al-ᶜArabī, 1987), vol. III, p. 73; idem, *al-Qawl al-mujtabā fī taḥqīq mā yaḥrum min al-ribā* (Sanaa: Maktabat Dār al-Quds, 1992).

and no *qiyās* is applicable then the rule is that of permissibility (*ibāḥa*) and not of interdiction (*ḥaẓr*). In other words, for him, the scope of law is restricted to those cases for which a text of revelation can be found to apply. And it is for this reason that one finds in the writings of Ibn al-Amīr and Shawkānī that the majority of their legal opinions are devoted to matters of ritual law, rather than transactional law, since many more ḥadīths are to be had for the former.

Other examples in Shawkānī's legal writings underscore his unambiguous commitment to bring to bear his ideas on *ūṣūl al-fiqh* to actual legal judgements. For instance, Shawkānī condemns the widely held opinion that specific statements have to be made in the process of the 'offer and acceptance' (*al-ījāb waʾl-qabūl*) to render a contract valid. He argues that there is no basis for such an opinion in the Qurʾān or the canonical ḥadīth collections and therefore it must be rejected. Instead, Shawkānī proposes that any customary practices which are construed to constitute an *ījāb* and *qabūl* render a contract valid.[73] In analysing Shawkānī's teachings the linkage between his *ūṣūl* and *furūᶜ* is either explicitly stated or assumed in each and every legal judgement. He could not envisage a sweeping reform of the substantive law without first revamping the *uṣūl*. The question of whether *uṣūl al-fiqh* is pertinent to the *furūᶜ* would have struck Shawkānī as absurd, not because many of the *furūᶜ* by his time were not anchored in the *uṣūl* (a fact he readily admitted and aggressively sought to remedy), but because his plan was to ground firmly the *furūᶜ* with his own chastened version of the *uṣūl*.

Shawkānī on *ijtihād*

The cornerstone of Shawkānī's epistemology and legal methodology comes out in his dicussions on *ijtihād*, the means by which a scholar independently derives his judgements. He argued that it provided a solution to the evils of sectarianism and fanaticism as well as a means of reforming misguided social practices. Shawkānī took most of his ideas on *ijtihād* from his predecessor Ibn al-Amīr and aimed to present a systematic method for producing *mujtahids*.[74] Both he and Ibn al-Amīr argued against those who claimed that *ijtihād* was no longer possible and that it was incumbent on Muslims to practise *taqlīd* of earlier *mujtahid*s, namely, the eponyms of the established schools. Ibn al-Amīr and Shawkānī's arguments are framed in universal Islamic terms but it is their opposition to the Hādawī *madhhab* which underpins many of their opinions on this matter. As such, their discourse has a strong social and personal element and is not presented in purely theoretical terms.

73 Shawkānī, *al-Sayl al-jarrār*, vol. III, p. 6; idem, *al-Darārī al-muḍiyya sharḥ al-Durar al-bahiyya* (Beirut: Dār al-Jīl, 1987), p. 297.

74 Cf. Muḥammad b. Ismāᶜīl al-Amīr, *Uṣūl al-fiqh al-musammā ijābat al-sāʾil sharḥ bughyat al-āmil* (Beirut: Muʾassasat al-Risāla, 1986), pp. 383f.; idem, *Irshād al-nuqqād ilā taysīr al-ijtihād*.

Later Hādawīs admitted the practice of *ijtihād* in their *uṣūl* works but in practice they expected adherence to al-Hādī's teachings as set forth in *Kitāb al-Azhār*.[75] Hādawīs consider the opinions of the early imams (primarily those of al-Hādī) and their consensus to be the main sources of authority in matters of law. Any opinion which contradicts their imams is invalid because they hold that the Ahl al-Bayt are the only group of Muslims who follow the righteous path and who will be saved in the hereafter.[76] In the sources they refer to themselves as 'the group which manifests the truth' (*al-firqa al-ẓāhira ᶜalā al-ḥaqq*) and 'the group that will attain salvation' (*al-firqa al-nājiya*); they also call the Hādawī school the 'Noble School' (*al-madhhab al-sharīf*). In making this claim, they interpret certain Qur'ānic verses and Traditions as referring to the special position of the Ahl al-Bayt. The most commonly cited Qur'ānic verses in this regard are:

> 'People of the House, God only desires to put away from you abomination and to cleanse you' (XXXIII: 33); 'Say: "I do not ask of you a wage for this, except love for the kinsfolk"' (XLII: 23); 'Then We bequeathed the Book on those of Our servants We chose . . .' (XXXV: 32); 'Question the people of the Remembrance, if it should be that you do not know' (XVI: 43 and XXI: 7).

From ḥadīth, Hādawīs quote the following traditions, amongst others, in which the Prophet says:

> 'I am leaving you with some things which, if you adhere to them, you will never stray into error after me. They are: the Book of God and my family, the people of my house. The kind informant has made it known to me that they will never be separated until the day of reckoning'; 'the example of the people of my house with regards to you is like that of Noah's ark: whoever got on it was saved and those who did not drowned and sank'; 'stars provide safety to the people of the sky; should the stars disappear, then the people of the sky will get what they were promised [i.e., perdition]. [Likewise], the people of my house provide safety to the people of earth, should they disappear, the people of earth will get what they were promised'; 'O ᶜAlī, whoever loves your child loves you; whoever loves you loves me; whoever loves me loves God; whoever loves God will be sent by Him to heaven. Whoever hates them [i.e., ᶜAlī's children] hates you; whoever hates you hates me; whoever hates me hates God; whoever hates God justly deserves to be sent to hell by Him'.[77]

In short, the Ahl al-Bayt, as the anointed leaders of the Muslim community, are to be followed and their legal opinions adhered to; *taqlīd* is permissible, indeed mandated. Al-Qāsim b. Muḥammad states that *mujtahid*s had to take account of the opinions of the imams of Ahl al-Bayt, and it is only when differences between the latter exist that they should look to the Qur'ān and Sunna for answers. Moreover,

[75] Cf. al-Ḥusayn b. al-Qāsim, *Ghāyat al-sūl fī ᶜilm al-uṣūl*, in *Majmūᶜ al-mutūn al-hāmma* (Sanaa: Maktabat al-Yaman al-Kubrā, 1990), p. 296; idem, *Kitāb Hidāyat al-ᶜuqūl*, vol. II, pp. 685–7; Muḥammad b. Yaḥyā b. Bahrān, *Matn al-kāfil*, in *Majmūᶜ al-mutūn al-hāmma*, pp. 326–8.
[76] al-Qāsim b. Muḥammad, *al-Irshād ilā sabīl al-rashād* (Sanaa: Dār al-Ḥikma al-Yamāniyya, 1996), p. 108.
[77] Ibid., pp. 60–8.

he states that if ᶜAlī b. Abī Ṭālib held an opinion in a matter upon which there was a conflict of views then his opinion was to be followed, because he is 'the interpreter of the Book of God and the Sunna of His messenger'.[78] Implicit in al-Qāsim's recommendations is that *ijtihād* is not easily attainable. He did not present a systematic method by which *mujtahid*s could be readily formed. *Ijtihād* was after all one of the conditions of the imamate and often in Zaydī history candidates were not found because there were no *mujtahid*s.

Another element in the Hādawī doctrine of *ijtihād* is their belief in the infallibility of *mujtahid*s, as expressed in the statement 'every *mujtahid* is correct' (*kull mujtahid muṣīb*) in legal matters which obtain probable answers (*masāʾil ẓanniyya ᶜamaliyya*). Al-Mahdī Aḥmad b. Yaḥyā al-Murtaḍā claims that the doctrine of infallibility was brought into Zaydism by Abū ᶜAbd Allāh b. al-Dāᶜī (d. 359/970) to resolve the ongoing disputes between the two Zaydī factions among the Caspians, the Nāṣiriyya and the Qāsimiyya.[79] One of its effects was to insert a degree of tolerance for a multiplicity of opinions among *mujtahid*s, and this may explain, in part, the relative tolerance shown to the Yemeni Traditionists.[80] Their legal opinions, even if considered valid, did not undermine Hādawī ones as these were correct too. It was only when Shawkānī, with the backing of the state, insisted on imposing his views that Hādawīs seriously reacted, accusing him of wanting to establish his own *madhhab*.[81]

Shawkānī's basic arguments are that *ijtihād* is a continuous and necessary process and that it is easier for *mujtahid*s to arise in later times. He begins by stating that no age may be devoid of a *mujtahid*, basing himself on the Prophetic Tradition: 'until the day of reckoning a group in my nation will remain manifesting the truth'.[82] In His fairness, God could not have been more bounteous to the earlier generations than to the later ones. Moreover, should *mujtahid*s no longer exist this would mean a severance between the later generations and the original sources – the Qurʾān and Sunna – because of the *muqallid*'s need for what amounts to an intermediary between himself and the texts. Hence, Shawkānī advocates a return to the sources, which, he argues, are comprehensive and sufficient for all situations. He says in this regard:

> As far as I am concerned, he who zealously follows the Qurʾānic verses and the Prophetic Traditions, and makes this his condition and directs his efforts at this and seeks God's aid, and draws from Him success, and if most of his concern and aim is to establish truth and to acquire what is correct without fanaticism to a school from among the schools,

78 Ibid., pp. 73–81.

79 Aḥmad b. Yaḥyā al-Murtaḍā, *al-Munya waʾl-amal fī sharḥ al-milal waʾl-niḥal*, Muḥammad Mashkūr (ed.) (Beirut: Dār al-Nadā, 1990), p. 99; idem, *Kitāb al-Baḥr al-zakhkhār*, 6 vols. (Sanaa: Dār al-Ḥikma al-Yamāniyya, 1988), vol. I (*muqaddima*), p. 40; Madelung, *Der Imam al-Qāsim*, p. 175.

80 Another broader effect, which was pointed out by Aron Zysow, was to diminish the importance of law while giving other sciences such as theology greater importance, cf. Zysow, 'The economy of certainty', pp. 459–83.

81 Cf. *Ghaṭamṭam*, vol. I, pp. 18–20.

82 Cf. Bukhārī, *Ṣaḥīḥ*, *Iᶜtiṣām*, 10; Muslim, *Ṣaḥīḥ*, *al-Imān*, 247.

> [he] will find in these two what he seeks... For these two contain much goodness and are the ocean that never dries up and the river to which all who go drink fresh cold water. They are the refuge of all who are afraid. So adhere to this, for if you accept it happily with a fortunate heart and a mind on which guidance has fallen then you will find in them all that you ask for in terms of proof for the rulings for which you have sought evidence whatever these may be. If you disqualify this contention, and consider it arrogant (*istaᶜẓamta hādhā al-kalām*), and you say what many have said that the proofs of the Book and the Sunna are insufficient for all contingencies, then you yourself have committed the sin, and due to your deficiencies you have committed injury...[83]

To prove that *mujtahids* have existed continually, even after the establishment of the *madhāhib*, Shawkānī says he has shown in *al-Badr al-ṭāliᶜ* that it is easier for later generations to practise *ijtihād* because the sources available to them are greater than those available in the time of the Companions. He then offers a list of *mujtahids* who lived in later periods:

> For those who have said that Shāfiᶜī *mujtahids* do not exist, we tell you here about those Shāfiᶜīs who lived after their age [i.e., the founders of the schools] and who combined in themselves many times the sciences of *ijtihād*. Among them are: Ibn ᶜAbd al-Salām, and his student Ibn Daqīq al-ᶜĪd, and his student Ibn Sayyid al-Nās, and his student Zayn al-Dīn al-ᶜIrāqī, and his student Ibn Ḥajar al-ᶜAsqalānī, and his student al-Suyūṭī... Each one of them is a great imam in the Book and the Sunna and comprehends the sciences of *ijtihād* many times more than a scholar in the sciences which are not related to these [i.e., the Book and the Sunna].[84]

All the scholars he mentions are Shāfiᶜīs belonging to the *mujaddid* circle, confirming the point made earlier about his identification with this tradition. His argument about the relative facility for later scholars to become *mujtahids* underscores his epistemological approach: authoritative knowledge is textual, and can only be derived textually. Given that generations of scholars from the time of the Prophet down to his had collected, classified and codified this textual legacy (i.e., the ḥadīth collections and affiliated works, dictionaries, grammars, etc.), and that these references were now literally at his fingertips in books, his ability to arrive at the authoritative legal decisions was greater than that of the earliest of generations.[85] At first sight this argument appears strange coming from a Traditionist, since Traditionists assert that the best generation was the Prophet's and the two following. The argument was that proximity to the period of revelation and the witnessing of the Prophet's actions and sayings assured the justice and authoritativeness of normative rulings, hence Shawkānī's continual insistence on the exemplary character of the Companions, who are the first links in the chains of ḥadīth transmission. Shawkānī obviously did not see the two arguments as incompatible. His assertion, however, that the later generations were better able to access the sources of revelation was a means of empowering himself, and by the same token refuting the

83 *Irshād al-fuḥūl*, p. 228. 84 Ibid., pp. 223–4.
85 The same argument is made by Ibn al-Amīr, cf. al-Amīr, *Irshād al-nuqqād*, pp. 36–7.

notion of irrevocable decline which underpinned the claim that the last *mujtahids* were the eponyms of the established schools.

In opposition to Hādawī views, Shawkānī rejected the doctrine of the infallibility of *mujtahids*, arguing for their fallibility and that there was only one correct judgement on a given issue. He bases this on the ḥadīth in which the Prophet says: 'If the judge judges by *ijtihād* and is correct, he receives two recompenses; if he judges by *ijtihād* and commits an error, he receives one recompense'.[86] He further condemns those who argue for the infallibility of *mujtahids* by saying:

> How odious is the saying of those who render God's judgement as numerous as the number of *mujtahids*...! Furthermore, this claim is not only contrary to the proper conduct towards God and His pure Sharīʿa, it is also based on pure opinion (*raʾy*) for which there is no proof...[87]

The test of a correct opinion according to Shawkānī lies in whether the *mujtahid* bases his opinion on textual proof and authority from the Qurʾān and Sunna. Shawkānī, however, offers no means for the ordinary Muslim of judging the soundness of one *mujtahid*'s opinion over that of another. Presumably, he envisaged a system in which *mujtahids* examined the arguments of two or more contending opinions, seeing which had greater textual evidence in order to ascertain the correct one. Another assumption about the *mujtahids* who would maintain this system of checks and balances was that they would share Shawkānī's educational training, mainly in the ḥadīth sciences, and his general outlook. Although he never explicitely stated it, Shawkānī probably thought of himself as the ultimate arbiter of the correctness of a given opinion. Furthermore, he did author a legal text in the *mukhtaṣar* tradition along with a commentary, and this was seen by some Zaydī-Hādawīs to be an attempt at establishing his own school.

Shawkānī's *mukhtaṣar* is *al-Durar al-bahiyya* and its commentary is *al-Darārī al-muḍiyya*. In presentational style and content, the *Darārī* exemplifies his Traditionist approach to law: he states his opinion on a given matter and then offers a great number of ḥadīths from the canonical collections to bolster it. The proof lies mainly in the copious citations. Zaydī legal commentaries differ markedly in that they are centered on the opinions of the imams who are referred to by a system of acronyms which is explained in the preface of a work such as the *Sharḥ al-Azhār*. Without knowledge of the imams, their relationship to one another and their respective authority within the school, the text is unusable and difficult to comprehend. While giving precedence to the opinion of al-Hādī, the Zaydī-Hādawī works proffer the views of different, and sometimes differing, imams on specific questions of law. Unlike Shawkānī's *Darārī*, they are not univocal, and in this they reflect the collective efforts of an interpretive community of scholars, not those of a single *mujtahid*.

86 Bukhārī, *Ṣaḥīḥ*, *Iʿtiṣām*, 21. 87 *Irshād al-fuḥūl*, p. 231.

Hādawīs objected to Shawkānī's scheme because they upheld the doctrine of the infallibility of *mujtahids*. Moreover, they suspected him of claiming infallibility for his own opinions partly because he upheld the doctrine of fallibility. It must be noted that Shawkānī never claimed infallibility (*ᶜiṣma*) with respect to his legal opinions; his opponents, however, attempted to attribute this claim to him or at least see it as the net result of his juristic endeavours. Muḥammad al-Samāwī (d. 1241/1825), otherwise known as Ibn Ḥarīwah, observes in this regard:

> The majority of *mujtahids* in legal matters either claim infallibility for all or fallibility without specification, since prefering an opinion (*tarjīḥ*) on the basis of probable evidence (*amāra ẓaniyya*) may contradict the [truth] in a given situation. However, the sum total of your claim is [your own] infallibility (*ᶜiṣma*), and because of this you have to assert that you have either joined the rank of the prophets... or admit that your *ijtihād* may contain error as in the case of other *mujtahids* given that the area here is one of probability. Then, there remains no argument favouring the acceptance of your opinions to the exclusion of others: your opinions are like those of other *mujtahids*, and the one practising *taqlīd* is free to choose from whichever he prefers. If this is so, what proof do you have that the one who accepts the opinion of someone other than yourself has gone astray while the one who accepts your opinion has become rightly guided?[88]

Shawkānī on *taqlīd*

Shawkānī is emphatic that the practice of *taqlīd*, which he defines as the following of someone else's opinion (*raʾy*) without knowing the textual proof (*ḥujja*) underpinning it, is absolutely prohibited.[89] He claims that the founders of the schools of law had prohibited *taqlīd* as well, and that it was only their followers who made it mandatory through an unprecedented and reprehensible innovation (*bidᶜa muḥdatha*).[90] Shawkānī explains that the Companions and the two following generations had not practised *taqlīd* and did not even know of it. If one of the Companions was unable to formulate an opinion for himself, he would ask someone who could provide the legal proof (*al-ḥujja al-sharᶜiyya*) on the given issue. In underpinning this assertion Shawkānī cites: 'If you should quarrel on anything, refer it to God and the Messenger' (IV: 59), as well as the famous Tradition of Muᶜādh to prove that Muslims were exhorted to refer to the Book and the Sunna.[91] In other words, use of textual proof is obligatory as is the requirement to refer to a living scholar who is able to present the supplicant with such proof (*dalīl*) which does not consist of a mere opinion, but is based on a textual transmission (*riwāya*). Hence, in the event of an issue arising, the lay person (*ᶜāmmī*) or the one who falls short (*muqaṣṣir*) must ask the ulema of his time who are knowledgeable in the Book and the Sunna. Shawkānī says:

[88] *Ghaṭamṭam*, vol. I, p. 65. [89] *Irshād al-fuḥūl*, pp. 237f.
[90] Shawkānī, *al-Qawl al-mufīd fī adillat al-ijtihād waʾl-taqlīd*, pp. 209f.
[91] Cf. Tirmidhī, *Sunan*, *Aḥkām*, 3; Abū Dāwūd, *Sunan*, *Aqḍiya*, 11.

> It is incumbent on him to ask about that which is determined by the Sharīʿa and the one who is asked must be from among those who are not ignorant of this. Then [the *muftī*] issues a *fatwā* which is Qurʾānic or Prophetic and discards the question about the schools of the people and suffices himself with the school of their first imam who is the Prophet of God.[92]

According to Shawkānī, these *mujtahid*s of the Book and the Sunna can be found in every town of the Islamic world so that the commoner need not search far for them. This matter, however, raises an important question which Shawkānī leaves unanswered: How is a commoner to make sense of the textual proof the *mujtahid* gives him? By definition, a commoner is ignorant of the Sharīʿa, and he therefore would not understand the import of the texts or be able to make comparative judgements with other plausible proofs. Because of this lack of comprehension, the commoner effectively would still be practising *taqlīd*, albeit under a new guise. Zaydī-Hādawīs were quick to point this out to Shawkānī and again accused him of wanting to make himself the ultimate authority so that every one would practise *taqlīd* of his decisions. Ibn Ḥarīwah argues against the assertion that *taqlīd* is prohibited by saying:

> Your [i.e., Shawkānī's] obstinate claim that providing the commoner with a text from the Book or ḥadīth, which he must then follow, does not constitute *taqlīd* is foolish. If the text which is provided to him is one over which there is no conflict, then the matter is not relevant here. [However], if [conflicting positions] (*ikhtilāf*) exist [with regards to the cited text] then the *muqallid* must choose between the various positions, and it is assumed that he cannot do this, so he must adhere to one of them which is pure *taqlīd* . . . In sum, you expect them [commoners] to adhere to your opinions and *ijtihād* in issues where differences of opinion exist (*masāʾil al-khilāf*) and you obligate them to practise *taqlīd* of yourself.[93]

The vision that Shawkānī posits where all Muslims would have access to the process and fruits of *ijtihād*, either by being *mujtahid*s themselves or consulting one and making sure that the opinion obtained is one based on textual evidence, raises interesting issues about how *mujtahid*s are to be formed and the difficulty or facility of the process.

Reproducing *mujtahid*s

Following on his claim that *mujtahid*s continued to exist in later times, Shawkānī provided a curriculum which, if followed systematically, would produce such scholars. He outlines this process in great detail in an unusual pedagogical work entitled *Adab al-ṭalab wa muntahā al-arab* (The Discipline of the Quest and the Ultimate Goal). Here, he enumerates the curriculum which a *mujtahid muṭlaq* (an absolute *mujtahid*) must follow to attain that rank, as well as the curricula for lesser

92 *Irshād al-fuḥūl*, p. 239.

93 *Ghaṭamṭam*, vol. I, p. 42–3.

scholars. The subjects that each category of scholar must study are listed and the degree of their mastery is mentioned, as are the books which ought to be studied in each of the different sciences. Another important aspect of this work is the implicit intentionality on the part of the student and the rationalisation which is built into the model of knowledge acquisition: the student sets out knowing which rank or level he wishes to attain and then follows the path outlined to achieve that goal. In short, scholars are formed according to a predetermined curriculum and goal. In describing the books to be studied, Shawkānī contextualises his advice by saying that the recommendations he is making are based on what is taught and found locally in Yemen; in other countries, the student must use what is available in his region.[94] Implicit in such a remark is his perception of his readership: it is any student anywhere in the Islamic world who wants to pursue one of the four paths outlined herein. His claims are not national or regional but universal. Because of its systematic and seemingly universal applicability, this programme contains intimations of a modern educational system. This, however, is illusory because Shawkānī did not intend it for just any Muslim.

Shawkānī lists four categories of students or seekers of knowledge:[95]

1. The one desiring to become 'an imam who is referred to' (*marji*ᶜ) and who teaches, produces *fatwā*s and writes books.
2. The one who desires to know independently what God has demanded of him (i.e., duties and obligations). A scholar of this category is considered to have attained the rank of *mujtahid* inasmuch as he can independently form opinions for himself. However, he is not an authority to which others can refer.
3. The one seeking to improve his Arabic in order to better understand whatever he seeks in the Sharīᶜa. Shawkānī makes clear that this category of student cannot act independently, but must rely on the questioning of ulema in cases where contradictions arise or in those which necessitate the giving of greater weight to one argument over another, a practice called *tarjīḥ*.
4. The one who seeks to learn a science or discipline for worldly ends, e.g., a poet or accountant.

In the section following the description of the four categories of knowledge-seekers, Shawkānī exhorts the student to try to belong to the first category for he says it is the highest possible rank, greater even than that of a king, because God has favoured the ulema.[96] He makes clear, however, that members of the lowly professions, e.g., weavers and butchers, should not be permitted into the scholarly ranks because of their base disposition, which is innate. Should a butcher, for instance, become a scholar, a vileness, which he has inherited, would inevitably manifest itself in his actions or words and thereby result in giving the ulema a bad reputation in the minds of the common folk.[97] For the modern supporters of Shawkānī, this argument has been a source of considerable embarrassment and

[94] *Adab al-ṭalab*, p. 108. [95] Ibid., pp. 97–8. [96] Ibid., pp. 99–101. [97] Ibid., pp. 129–31.

they are at pains to explain it away, while his antagonists, viz., contemporary Hādawīs, unceasingly refer to it.[98]

In enumerating the disciplines that a scholar of the first category must study, Shawkānī is consistent with his ideas on *ijtihād* in that he places the greatest emphasis and stress on knowledge of the Arabic language and the science of the Sunna (i.e., the study of the canonical ḥadīth collections and its attendant disciplines such as the science of *jarḥ* and *taᶜdīl*). However, he does stress that other disciplines, such as dogmatic theology (*kalām*) and even poetry, must also be studied, not so much for their own sake as for the *mujtahid*'s ability to defend himself against attacks from exponents of these disciplines. Shawkānī, as was mentioned already, was opposed to *kalām*, which he regarded as a science that led to more confusion than clarity for the believer. He admits that he felt confused by it (*lam azdad bihā illā ḥīratan*) and he found it to consist of idle talk (*khuzaᶜbalāt*).[99] From the few passages in which he mentions *kalām* in his legal works and short treatises, it seems inappropriate to label him an Ashᶜarite, though one might have expected him to be so, following in the mould of the Shāfiᶜī scholars who were mentioned earlier and whose works he tried to emulate. Rather, Shawkānī appears to fit more properly, though perhaps not entirely, in the Ḥanbalī tradition, which rejected outright many of the theological claims made by the various schools of *kalām*. Shawkānī, for example, insists that the scholar must follow in the path of the 'pious forefathers' (*al-salaf al-ṣāliḥ*) – the Companions and the two generations following them – relying on the proofs of the Book and the Sunna, accentuating (*ibrāz*) God's attributes (*al-ṣifāt*) as they have been depicted, and leaving to God that which is obscure (*al-mutashābih*).[100] Shawkānī admits that since he drew no personal benefit from *kalām*, and given that it left him confused and in obscurity, he 'threw these principles from above' and returned to the path where proofs are derived from the Book and the Sunna whose pillars are the Companions.[101] *Kalām* was, however, a science that had deeply influenced Zaydism, whose scholars had elaborated a set of credal tenets using its terms that became integral to the school's identity. The subtext of what Shawkānī was saying, in suggesting that the study of *kalām* was to primarily give the *mujtahid* conceptual means to refute those who use *kalām* in their argumentation, was that he rejected Zaydī methods. The context in which Shawkānī was living, where he was mainly arguing against Zaydī-Hādawīs, remained foremost in his mind even when elaborating a curriculum of study for the *mujtahid*. Let us now turn to the subjects or disciplines which needed to be mastered by students of each of the four categories enumerated above.

98 On the representation and appropriation of Shawkānī in the modern period, see chapter 7.
99 *Adab al-ṭalab*, pp. 115–16.
100 *Adab al-ṭalab*, p. 114; Muḥammad al-Shawkānī, *Fatḥ al-qadīr*, 5 vols. (Beirut: Dār al-Maᶜrifa, n.d.), vol. II, p. 211; idem, *Kashf al-shubuhāt ᶜan al-mushtabihāt*, in *al-Rasāʾil al-salafiyya*, pp. 1–12; idem, *al-Tuḥaf fī madhāhib al-salaf*, in *al-Rasāʾil al-salafiyya*, pp. 127–42.
101 *Adab al-ṭalab*, pp. 115–16.

The *mujtahid* of the first category, that is, someone whose intention was to become like Shawkānī himself, had to study the following subjects or disciplines:[102]

1. Grammar (*naḥw*).[103]
2. Logic (*manṭiq*).[104] Shawkānī says that the reason for studying logic is to understand terminology of Arabic grammarians.
3. Morphology (*ᶜilm al-ṣarf*).[105]
4. Rhetoric (*ᶜilm al-maᶜānī waʾl-bayān*).[106]
5. Semiology and argumentation (*fann al-waḍᶜ wa fann al-munāẓara*).[107]
6. The science of figures of speech (*ᶜilm al-badīᶜ*).
7. Dictionaries (*muʾallafat al-lugha*).[108]
8. The principles of jurisprudence (*uṣūl al-fiqh*).[109]
9. Dogmatic theology (*ᶜilm al-kalām*).[110]
10. Exegesis of the Qurʾān (*tafsīr*). Shawkānī says that to understand the Qurʾān one must rely first and foremost on Prophetic ḥadīth and then on the sayings of the Companions. For these, the student must look to the six canonical collections. In his estimation, the best *tafsīr* is Jalāl al-Dīn al-Suyūṭī's *al-Durr al-manthūr* and the best general work in the sciences of the Qurʾān is al-Suyūṭi's *al-Itqān fī ᶜulūm al-Qurʾān*. By ignoring most mainstream commentaries, he is again underscoring his ultra-Traditionist stance. Shawkānī finally makes the point that the whole of the Qurʾān is pertinent for judicial rulings and not just the verses which contain judgements (*āyāt al-aḥkām*).
11. The science of the Sunna (*ᶜilm al-sunna*). Shawkānī emphasises that of all the sciences that must be studied by the aspiring *mujtahid* this is the most important since it not only elucidates the Qurʾān but also contains innumerable rulings.

102 Ibid., pp. 113–24.

103 Among the works which must be studied in this discipline, are: al-Qāsim b. ᶜAlī al-Ḥarirī's *Mulḥat al-iᶜrāb*; ᶜUthmān b. ᶜUmar al-Ḥājib's *al-Kāfiya*; ᶜAbd Allāh b. Yūsuf's *Mughnī al-Labīb*.

104 The recommendation here is to study Athīr al-Dīn al-Abharī's *Īsāghūjī* (*eisagoge*); Saᶜd al-Dīn al-Taftazānī's *Tahdhīb al-manṭiq waʾl-kalām* and one of their commentaries.

105 To be studied are Ibn al-Ḥājib's *al-Shāfiya* and Ibn Mālik's *Lāmiyyat al-afᶜāl* along with a number of commentaries.

106 For this discipline, the recommendation is to study *Kitāb Talkhīṣ al-miftāḥ* by Jalāl al-Dīn Muḥammad al-Qazwīnī (the *Miftāḥ* is by Yūsuf al-Sakkākī) and its commentary (*sharḥ*) by Saᶜd al-Dīn al-Taftazānī and commentaries on the latter in turn.

107 For semiology, Shawkānī says that al-Sharīf al-Jurjānī's *Risālat al-waḍᶜ* and one of its commentaries would suffice, whereas for argumentation he says that ᶜAḍud al-Dīn ᶜAbd al-Raḥmān b. Aḥmad al-Ījī's *Ādāb al-baḥth al-ᶜAḍudiyya* and one of its commentaries would also be good to study.

108 Among the works to be studied in this science are: Ismāᶜīl al-Jawharī's *al-Ṣiḥāḥ*; al-Fayrūzābādī's *al-Qāmūs*; Nashwān al-Ḥimyarī's *Shams al-ᶜulūm*; and some works on the unusual words in the Qurʾān and ḥadīth.

109 Among the works Shawkānī mentions are Ibn al-Ḥājib's *Mukhtaṣar al-muntahā*; Tāj al-Dīn al-Subkī's *Jamᶜ al-jawāmiᶜ*; al-Ḥusayn b. al-Qāsim's *Ghāyat al-sūl* (the principal Zaydī-Hādawī work of this period) and a number of their commentaries.

110 Shawkānī advises the student to look at works by all the schools: the Muᶜtazilīs (Najm al-Dīn Mukhtār b. Muḥammad al-Zāhidī's *al-Mujtabā*), the Ashᶜarīs (ᶜAḍud al-Dīn ᶜAbd al-Raḥmān b. Aḥmad al-Ījī's *al-Mawāqif al-ᶜAḍudiyya* and Saᶜd al-Dīn al-Taftazānī's *al-Maqāṣid al-Saᶜdiyya*), the Māturīdīs, and the 'middle ground ones' (*al-mutawassiṭūn*) between these groups, the Zaydīs.

The science of the Sunna, he says, is a lantern unto all other sciences.[111] All the works and collections that are enumerated are Sunnī ones.[112]

12. The science of *isnād* criticism (*ᶜilm al-jarḥ waʾl-taᶜdīl*) and the technical terminology of the scholars of ḥadīth.[113]
13. Historical works. Shawkānī emphasises here the need for the scholar to know the history of the world, its different governments and events as well as the important people of every age, especially their birth and death dates.[114]
14. Law (*ᶜilm al-fiqh*). Here, Shawkānī says that the aspiring *mujtahid* must know an abridged legal manual (*mukhtaṣar*) of each of the main schools. The *mujtahid*, he says, needs to explain to the partisans (*al-mutamadhhibūn*) of the established schools the opinions of their respective imams as well as defend himself against attack from the fanatics of these schools. Shawkānī adds that it is also beneficial for the *mujtahid* to read works reporting the debates between the partisans of the various schools, such as those by Ibn Mundhir al-Naysābūrī, Ibn Qudāma, Ibn Ḥazm and finally Ibn Taymiyya.
15. Poetry. It is important for the *mujtahid* to know poetry in order to respond to a question sent to him in verse and to conduct debates with other scholars in this form. He should also have a good prose style. Shawkānī says that both aspects are crucial in order to avoid the situation in which a person with sound knowledge of poetry and prose but little knowledge of the religious sciences is able to make fun of a more learned *mujtahid* who cannot defend himself as eloquently using these forms.[115]
16. The study of mathematics, physics, geometry, natural science and medicine. Shawkānī says that the study of these disciplines is recommended for the *mujtahid* in order to get what might be termed a well-rounded education. A *mujtahid* of the first rank has to come to his own conclusions by mastering a given discipline and cannot rely on the opinion of others, regardless of subject matter, for this would only lead back to *taqlīd*. He adds that as long as a scholar is well grounded in the sciences of the Book and Sunna he has nothing to fear from any discipline.

The list is impressive and is intended as a guide, which if followed, will lead to the formation of a *mujtahid* like Shawkānī himself; references to Shawkānī's own education pepper the work and are intended to make the process tangible. More than a manual of how one becomes a *mujtahid*, *Adab al-ṭalab* is a personal manifesto which presents the illnesses afflicting the Muslim community – viz.,

111 *Adab al-ṭalab*, p. 119.

112 Amongst these are: Ibn al-Athīr's *Jāmiᶜ al-uṣūl min aḥādīth al-rasūl*; al-Muttaqī al-Hindī's *Kanz al-ᶜummāl*; ᶜAbd al-Salām b. Taymiyya's *al-Muntaqā*; Ibn Ḥajar's *Bulūgh al-marām*; ᶜAbd al-Ghanī al-Maqdisī's *ᶜUmdat al-aḥkām*; the six canonical collections; Aḥmad b. Ḥanbal's *Musnad*.

113 Among the works mentioned here are: al-Dhahabī's *Aᶜlām al-nubalāʾ*, *Tārīkh al-Islām*, *Mīzān al-iᶜtidāl* and *Tadhkirat al-ḥuffāẓ*; Ibn Ḥajar's *Nukhbat al-fikr fī muṣṭalaḥ ahl al-athar*; Ibn Ṣalāḥ's *Muqaddima*; Zayn al-Dīn al-ᶜIrāqī's *al-Alfiyya*.

114 The histories that he recommends are al-Ṭabarī's *Taʾrīkh* and Ibn al-Athīr's *al-Kāmil*.

115 Shawkānī recommends for this discipline Aḥmad b. Muḥammad al-Jazzāz's *al-Manẓūma*, and Naṣr Allāh b. al-Athīr's *al-Mathal al-sāʾir fī adab al-kātib waʾl-shāᶜir*.

madhhabiyya which is a result of *taqlīd* – and the remedy which would provide the cure: *ijtihād* in the guise of a return to the principal sources, the Qur'ān and Sunna, and the formation of *mujtahid*s.

The aim of becoming a *mujtahid* for Shawkānī, therefore, is to be able to deduce (*istikhrāj*) judgements whenever one wishes and not have to look at who gave a certain judgement, but rather to look at the content of what was said and be able to judge it critically in the light of one's knowledge of the Qur'ān and Sunna. A *mujtahid* according to Shawkānī

> is one who extracts the legal proofs from their sources and imagines himself present at the time of the Prophecy (*fī zaman al-nubuwwa*) and the coming of revelation, even though he is in fact living at the end of time. [He must imagine that] no scholar has preceded him or any *mujtahid* taken precedence over him. The legal provisions (*al-khiṭābāt al-sharᶜiyya*) relate to him as they did to the Companions, without any difference.[116]

Shawkānī emphasises the study of the non-Sharīᶜa disciplines (e.g., logic, *kalām*) because it allows the *mujtahid* to attack and refute the claims of the practitioners of these disciplines, especially those whom he calls the fanatics (*mutaᶜaṣṣibūn*) and liars (*mubṭilūn*).[117]

Shawkānī accords the description of curricula for the second, third and fourth categories of student much less space in *Adab al-ṭalab*. The second type of student is a *mujtahid* but only with regards to himself and must use direct evidence from the Qur'ān and Sunna and not act as a person to be referred to by others.[118] The curriculum he must study is the following:

1. Grammar (*naḥw*).
2. Morphology (*ᶜilm al-ṣarf*).
3. Rhetoric (*ᶜilm al-maᶜānī wa'l-bayān*).
4. Principles of jurisprudence (*uṣūl al-fiqh*).
5. Qur'ānic exegesis (*tafsīr*).
6. Ḥadīth (the six canonical collections).

The third category of student is the one who wishes to improve his Arabic and therefore must always ask a scholar for the evidence on which an opinion is based; and in the case of a ḥadīth, for the transmission (*riwāya*) not the opinion (*ra'y*).[119] Shawkānī sees most of the Companions of the Prophet as having belonged to this third category. The disciplines or sciences that a student in this category must study are the following:

1. The science of desinential inflection or the proper vocalisation of words in sentences (*ᶜilm al-iᶜrāb*).
2. The terminology of the science of ḥadīth.
3. Qur'ānic exegesis (*tafsīr*).

[116] *Adab al-ṭalab*, p. 122. [117] Ibid., p. 124. [118] Ibid., pp. 136–7. [119] Ibid., pp. 138–9.

What Shawkānī was advocating was in fact not new in Yemen. The fifteenth-century scholar Muḥammad b. Ibrāhīm al-Wazīr, is seen by many, including Shawkānī, to have been the first to call for the exclusive use of the Sunnī collections and he wrote in their defence against Zaydīs who saw in their use an attack on the Zaydī-Hādawī school. The systematised guidelines for reproducing like-minded scholars which Shawkānī established was new, however, as were his forceful vision and political influence. This led to an intensification of a long-standing debate between Zaydīs and Traditionists in the eighteenth century. The terms of this debate revolved around whether one should read and refer to the *fiqh* manuals or, instead, the canonical ḥadīth collections. In other words, was one to consider the Zaydī and other legal manuals (*kutub al-furūᶜ*) as authoritative in and of themselves or admit the need to either abrogate or at least complement them by referring directly and/or exclusively to the Sunnī canonical ḥadīth collections in the elaboration of legal rulings. The crux of the matter here was that by using the Sunnī collections, a jurist might elaborate judicial and theological opinions that would invariably be at odds with those of the Zaydī-Hādawī school. The debate was not simply about postures of prayer and ablution rituals; it centred around fundamental questions of authority, belief and identity. The community of scholars split into several factions over the issues raised by this controversy – roughly, the Traditionists, the Hādawīs and those who took a neutral position and avoided taking sides. Identifying scholars, or coalitions of scholars, in these terms seems appropriate while realising that allegiances changed and that Zaydī scholars, at least since Imam al-Mutawakkil Aḥmad b. Sulaymān (d. 566/1171) did refer to Sunnī ḥadīth works and based some of their opinions on these while remaining in every sense Zaydī.

Shawkānī was calling for something qualitatively different from what 'traditional' Zaydī scholars had espoused; many rightly saw that he had abandoned traditional Zaydism for what amounted to little less than Sunnism. For these Zaydīs, Shawkānī's only concession to Zaydism was his continued call for *ijtihād* and his refusal to declare himself openly as belonging to one of the established Sunnī schools. This, however, amounted to little; for, in effect, Shawkānī's opinions, whether legal or theological, were often indistinguishable from Sunnism, and in particular in its Traditionist guise as seen in the works of the likes of Ibn Taymiyya. Having established here in fine detail the nature of Shawkānī's ideas and his vision of an Islamic order centered on himself, I will explore next the implementation of his teachings and his attempt at reforming Yemeni society.

CHAPTER 4

The Triumph of Sunnī Traditionism and the Re-Ordering of Yemeni Society

Let us now turn in detail to the dramatic change in the religious orientation of the imamic state in favour of Traditionist scholars. These scholars rejected the historic Zaydī concern with *kalām* matters as well as Zaydī theological doctrines; their concern and focus lay in the ḥadīth sciences and the elaboration of normative legal rulings based principally on the Prophetic Traditions, which they understood to be the Prophetic Sunna. The change in the religious orientation of the imamate became especially marked after the accession of al-Mahdī al-ᶜAbbās (d. 1189/1775). This did not mean that the imams rejected outright Hādawī law, since this was the school in which most judges were trained and to replace these posed insuperable problems and might have led to a situation of severe legal indeterminacy.[1] The shift to Traditionism was primarily effected in Sanaa and its influence spread only gradually, and at times haltingly, to the rest of the country. Al-Mahdī al-ᶜAbbās, more than his predecessors, favoured the Traditionist scholars and placed them at the apex of the judicial and religious hierarchies of the state. Their ascendance can be traced back further, since al-Manṣūr al-Ḥusayn b. al-Qāsim (d. 1161/1748) – al-Mahdī al-ᶜAbbās's father – was already appointing such scholars to high administrative positions as will be shown below. However, the general impression conveyed by the biographical dictionaries of the period is that until the reign of al-Mahdī al-ᶜAbbās the most influential scholars in the imamate's circles of power remained Hādawī in allegiance and orientation.

The most notable example of this in the seventeenth century was Qāḍī Aḥmad b. Saᶜd al-Dīn al-Maswarī (d. 1079/1668), who was held in great esteem in the imamates of al-Muᵓayyad Muḥammad and al-Mutawakkil Ismāᶜīl, having been a student of their father al-Qāsim b. Muḥammad.[2] Al-Maswarī issued many *fatwā*s and treatises and would probably have been treated in his time rather like a chief judge, although he never had an official title or held an official post. By all accounts, al-Maswarī was a strict Hādawī, who had condemned the use of the six

[1] We know that al-Mahdī al-ᶜAbbās sent a letter to his judges (dated 1188/1775) in which he insists on adherence to the Hādawī *madhhab*, cf. Rashād Muḥammad al-ᶜAlīmī, *al-Taqlīdiyya waᵓl-ḥadātha fī ᵓl-niẓām al-qānūnī al-Yamanī* (Cairo: Maṭābiᶜal-Shurūq, n.d.), p. 256.

[2] Al-Maswarī's fortunes waned somewhat during the reign of al-Mutawakkil Ismāᶜīl because he had initially sided with Ismāᶜīl's rival, Aḥmad, during the struggle for al-Muᵓayyad's succession.

Sunnī canonical ḥadīth collections (*al-ummahāt al-sitt*), declared that many of the Companions would not be saved in the hereafter and refused to bless them in his Friday sermons at the Great Mosque in Sanaa. Instead, he was the first to list the names of the Zaydī imams, commencing with Zayd b. ᶜAlī and ending with the name of the reigning imam, in the invocations he made during his Friday sermons. He was attacked, by Ṣāliḥ al-Maqbalī for his extremism, as well as by the famous Yemeni chronicler, Yaḥyā b. al-Ḥusayn b. al-Qāsim, for his ignorance in claiming that the contents of the *ummahāt al-sitt* could not be used as proof since it consisted of lies.[3]

In *al-Badr al-ṭāliᶜ*, Shawkānī says that al-Maswarī had a great reputation which continued down to his own day, and then comments on this by saying, 'This is probably due to his close association (*mutākhamat*) with the imams and his good fortune in their government'.[4] Of course, much the same could be said about Shawkānī's reputation today, having been the chief judge of the state through the reigns of three successive imams. Contemporary Yemeni intellectuals are at odds about al-Maswari, much as they are about Shawkānī. Qāḍī Ismāᶜīl al-Akwaᶜ, for example, describes al-Maswarī as one of the extremist Jārūdī Shīᶜites; whereas Zayd al-Wazīr considers him to have been a great scholar, though he qualifies this by saying that al-Maswarī's support and legitimation of the Qāsimī imams makes him the 'Māwardī of the Zaydīs'. By this he means that al-Maswarī provided in his writings the doctrinal underpinnings for the transformation of the Qāsimī imamate into a dynastic kingdom.[5]

Another example of a seventeenth-century scholar who was a strict Hādawī and played an important role in the imamates of al-Mutawakkil Ismāᶜīl and al-Mahdī Aḥmad b. al-Ḥasan was Qāḍī Aḥmad b. Ṣāliḥ, otherwise known as Ibn Abī ʾl-Rijāl (d. 1092/1681).[6] Ibn Abī ʾl-Rijāl was noted for writing letters on behalf of the imams. He also wrote treatises in defence of the Hādawī school. In one of these, entitled *Tafsīr al-sharīᶜa li-wurrād al-sharīᶜa*, he argued that the only school that is to be followed is that of Ahl al-Bayt as established by the teachings of al-Hādī Yaḥyā b. al-Ḥusayn because, he says, this is where the truth is to be found.[7] Furthermore, he boasts to his reader:

[3] Cf. Ṣāliḥ b. Mahdī al-Maqbalī, *al-ᶜAlam al-shāmikh* (Sanaa: al-Maktaba al-Yamaniyya liʾl-Nashr waʾl-Tawzīᶜ, 1985), pp. 21–2 and Yaḥyā b. al-Ḥusayn, *Yawmiyyāt Ṣanᶜāʾ*, ᶜAbd Allāh al-Ḥibshī (ed.) (Abu Dhabi: Manshūrāt al-Majmaᶜal-Thaqāfī, 1996), p. 48. This is an abridgement of his *Bahjat al-zaman*. Yaḥyā b. al-Ḥusayn says that he refuted al-Maswarī's treatise, *al-Risāla al-munqidha min ʾl-ghiwāya fī turuq ahl al-riwāya*, with his treatise entitled *Ṣawārim al-yaqīn al-qāṭiᶜa li-shukūk al-qāḍī Aḥmad b. Saᶜd al-Dīn*, ms. Sanaa, Sharqiyya Library, *majmūᶜ* no. 499, and *majmūᶜ* no. 108.

[4] *Badr*, I: 59; cf. *Maṭlaᶜ al-budūr*, I: 111–18; *Hijar al-ᶜilm*, II: 1081–3.

[5] Cf. *Hijar al-ᶜilm*, II: 1081. Zayd al-Wazīr's opinions are based on a personal interview. ᶜAlī b. Muḥammad al-Māwardī (d. 450/1058) is seen to have crystallised mediaeval Sunnī political doctrine in his *al-Aḥkām al-ṣulṭāniyya*, in which he calls for accepting the rule of unjust rulers while forbidding rebellion.

[6] Cf. *Badr*, I: 61–2; *Nashr*, I: 137–42; *Hijar al-ᶜilm*, I: 560–3.

[7] Aḥmad b. Ṣāliḥ b. Abī ʾl-Rijāl, *Tafsīr al-sharīᶜa li-wurrād al-sharīᶜa*, ms. London, British Library, no. OR 3852, fol. 24.

> If you consider matters carefully you will see that what predominates in the majority of regions is that celebrity and fame belong to the sultans. The seeker of knowledge will not know the *madhhab* of the people of a region except by asking after the accession of a given sultan. As for the *madhhab* of Ahl al-Bayt, their sultan is only mentioned in conjunction with the mention of the *madhhab*. It is as if they have no sultanate other than truth and religion. Take heed of this.[8]

An eighteenth-century scholar who was in the same mould of the Hādawī scholars mentioned above was Sayyid ᶜAbd Allāh b. ᶜAlī al-Wazīr (d. 1147/1735). Al-Wazīr was a staunch Hādawī and among the most influential scholars in the reigns of al-Mutawakkil al-Qāsim b. al-Ḥusayn (d. 1139/1727) and his son al-Manṣūr al-Ḥusayn. It is not recorded, however, that he ever accepted an official post.[9]

Al-Mutawakkil al-Qāsim b. al-Ḥusayn, al-Mahdī al-ᶜAbbās's grandfather, was it seems the first imam who attempted to patronise Traditionist scholars. He offered Ibn al-Amīr, for example, the post of governor of Mocha, which must have been extremely enticing given the large revenues accruing from taxation of coffee exports. Ibn al-Amīr refused, perhaps in fear of retribution from the imam, and he remained in self-imposed exile away from Sanaa. The fear was due to an alleged association Ibn al-Amīr had with a rival claimant to the imamate. In a further attempt to entice Ibn al-Amīr, al-Mutawakkil offered him the post of chief judge of the imamate, but he again declined. It seems that al-Mutawakkil was politically motivated in trying to enlist the backing of Ibn al-Amīr, who appears to have offered his support to al-Mutawakkil's rival, al-Nāṣir Muḥammad b. Isḥāq (d. 1167/1754). Al-Nāṣir was allegedly more learned and hence more qualified than al-Mutawakkil, which in Zaydī doctrinal terms posed a significant challenge. In attempting to enlist Ibn al-Amīr, al-Mutawakkil was doubtless trying to render the scholar dependent on him and extract recognition for his rule.[10]

The mere support of a scholar such as Ibn al-Amīr now seemed to matter and to confer legitimacy on the rule of an imam who, by all accounts, did not fulfil the qualifications of the post. This did not escape the attention of al-Mahdī al-ᶜAbbās, and it was only with the latter's accession to power that Ibn al-Amīr finally accepted an official post: that of preacher at the Great Mosque of Sanaa. No scholar has yet elaborated on al-Mahdī al-ᶜAbbās's policies except to say, as Serjeant does, that he pursued a 'general Islamisation policy'; others attribute al-Mahdī's policies to the fact that he was a scholar in his own right and was personally inclined to the Traditionist position.[11] In his biography of al-Mahdī al-ᶜAbbās, Shawkānī certainly

[8] Ibid., fol. 24b. [9] Cf. *Badr*, I: 388–90; *Nashr*, II: 112–15; *Nashr*, III: 37.

[10] Cf. *Nashr*, III: 31; *Hijar al-ᶜilm*, IV: 1830–2.

[11] Cf. A. Shivtiel *et al.*, 'The Jews of Ṣanᶜāʾ', in R. B. Serjeant and R. Lewcock (eds.), *Ṣanᶜāʾ: An Arabian Islamic City* (London: World of Islam Festival Trust, 1983), p. 418. Also see al-ᶜAmrī, *The Yemen*, pp. 7–9. The lack of knowledge we have about al-Mahdī al-ᶜAbbās's policies is due largely to the fact that no historical chronicle of his reign has survived. Shawkānī mentions that ᶜAlī b. Qāsim Ḥanash (d. 1219/1804) wrote a work on the reign of al-Mahdī al-ᶜAbbās and that of his son al-Manṣūr ᶜAlī, but this is apparently not extant, cf. *Badr*, I: 310–13, 472; *Nayl*, II: 154; *Nashr*, II: 25.

implies that al-Mahdī had a scholarly bent and was close to the people of knowledge (*ahl al-ʿilm*).[12] Whatever motivations underlay these policies, however, they show that a nexus of interests had developed between those in power and scholars such as Ibn al-Amīr and later Shawkānī. By accepting positions in the imamate, these ulema now wielded great influence and used this to perpetuate a system which rewarded like-minded scholars. The legacy of this influence has marked the legal and intellectual history of the last two centuries in Yemen.

The Office of *qāḍī al-quḍāt*

The creation of the post of chief judge (*al-qāḍī al-akbar*, later called *qāḍī al-quḍāt*) in the eighteenth century illustrates how the Traditionist scholars came to predominate in the administrative and legal structures of the imamate. The Qāsimī imams always had individual scholars who acted as special advisors. None, however, was made a supreme legal authority or source of formal reference until the eighteenth century. This was due to the fact that the loci of judicial authority and legal opinions were the imams themselves, as in the example of al-Mutawakkil Ismāʿīl (d. 1087/1676), who was regarded as a *mujtahid*. One of the first scholars who is mentioned in the biographical dictionaries as being given the 'highest judicial position' (*al-qaḍāʾal-akbar*) was Sayyid Aḥmad b. ʿAbd al-Raḥmān al-Shāmī (d. 1172/1759).[13] The history of the rise of al-Shāmī within the imamate's patronage system deserves relating here in order to elucidate how the post of *qāḍī al-quḍāt* was institutionalised.

Shawkānī describes al-Shāmī in *al-Badr al-ṭāliʿ* as having been one of the greatest ulema of Sanaa who excelled in the basic 'instrumental' disciplines (*al-ālāt*)[14] as well as in jurisprudence and ḥadīth. His education is outlined in Zabarā's biographical dictionary *Nashr al-ʿarf*, and is noteworthy for the fact that his studies centred on the transmitted sciences (*ʿilm al-riwāya*, i.e., the ḥadīth sciences), and that many of his teachers were Sunnī and from beyond the Zaydī highlands. Among these were ʿAbd al-Khāliq b. al-Zayn al-Mizjājī (d. 1152/1739),

[12] *Badr*, I: 310–11.

[13] *Badr*, I: 75–6; *Nashr*, I: 148–54. His paternal uncle, and later his father (ʿAbd al-Raḥmān b. al-Ḥusayn), managed the endowments of Sanaa. Sayyid Muḥsin b. al-Muʾayyad al-Ṣaghīr (d. 1141/1728) is also one who is mentioned as being *qāḍī al-quḍāt* during the imamates of al-Mutawakkil al-Qāsim b. al-Ḥusayn and his son al-Manṣūr al-Ḥusayn b. al-Qāsim. It would appear, however, that Sayyid Muḥsin replaced al-Shāmī on the occasions when the latter fell out of favour with the imams. Cf. *Badr*, supplement to II: 192; *Nashr*, II: 377–8; *Nashr*, III: 38.

[14] The *ālāt* refer to such disciplines or sciences as Arabic grammar, morphology, rhetoric, logic, and the principles of law and religion: the basic educational skills whose mastery is necessary for becoming a scholar. For a list of *ʿulūm al-ālāt*, see *al-Tiqṣār*, p. 395. In the published Yemeni biographical literature, which is predominantly Traditionist in orientation, the *ʿulūm al-ālāt* are distinguished from the *ʿulūm al-ijtihād*. It seems that *ijtihād* sciences entailed a study of the ḥadīth sciences while the *ālāt* sciences did not necessarily do so. This makes sense in that being a *mujtahid* for Shawkānī, for example, entailed first and foremost a deep knowledge of the ḥadīth sciences and collections, since it was in these that most of the proof-texts (*adilla*) on which to base rulings (*aḥkām*) were to be found, cf. *Adab al-ṭalab*, pp. 118–19.

Yaḥyā b. ᶜUmar al-Ahdal (d. 1147/1734), both from Zabīd, and Ṭāhā b. ᶜAbd Allāh al-Sāda (d. 1141/1729) of Dhū Jibla. Al-Shāmī also studied the *ummahāt al-sitt*, amongst other works, with a number of scholars in Mecca during his pilgrimage there, and his most notable teacher in Mecca was Muḥammad Ḥayāt al-Sindī (d. 1163/1750).[15] The educational world to which al-Shāmī belonged was hardly constrained by, or restricted to, Zaydī circles; rather, he appears as a scholar well versed in, and acquainted with, the Sunnī tradition and evidently was Traditionist in bent.

Al-Shāmī's professional career in the service of the imamate began when al-Mutawakkil al-Qāsim b. al-Ḥusayn (d. 1139/1727), al-Mahdī al-ᶜAbbās's grandfather, appointed him as supervisor over the poor visitors who came up to Sanaa from the Tihāma. Recognising his abilities, al-Mutawakkil then appointed him as chief judge on the imamic council in Sanaa (*wallāhu al-qaḍāʾ al-akbar bi-ḥaḍratihi fī Ṣanᶜāʾ*). Shawkānī explains that in the reign of al-Manṣūr al-Ḥusayn (d. 1161/1748), al-Mutawakkil's successor,

> al-Shāmī's rank rose to great heights so that his word was accepted in both important and small matters, and all judicial matters in the regions of Yemen depended on him. He ruled justly and acted well in ordaining the good and forbidding the reprehensible. His reputation was great as was his influence in the Yemeni kingdom (*mamlakat al-Yaman*)...[16]

Among al-Shāmī's responsibilities was to appoint judges, to give general counsel to the imam,[17] to vet and respond to any correspondence which came to the imam as well as act as intermediary between the imam and the ulema and other outsiders.[18] By the middle of al-Mahdī al-ᶜAbbās's reign (circa 1166/1753), al-Shāmī was too old to continue with his duties as chief judge. He had been superseded in the *dīwān* by a more intelligent and dynamic judge, Qāḍī Yaḥyā b. Ṣāliḥ al-Saḥūlī (d. 1209/1795), and is described as taking up the post of preacher (*khaṭīb*) at the Great Mosque in Sanaa.[19] Soon after, however, al-Shāmī endeavoured to have his brother-in-law, Yūsuf b. al-Ḥusayn Zabāra, appointed preacher, since he himself had no male issue.[20] The mantle of the chief judgeship had to be passed on, and it was given to Yaḥyā al-Saḥūlī, who is considered by many to have been the most technically accomplished judge of the Qāsimī period.

Qāḍī Yaḥyā b. Ṣāliḥ al-Saḥūlī's professional career begins with his appointment as judge in Sanaa by al-Manṣūr al-Ḥusayn b. al-Qāsim at the age of about seventeen. Before this, he was a student. He appears to have excelled at his office, and, because

[15] Cf. *Nashr*, III: 145–8. [16] Cf. *Badr*, I: 76.

[17] Zabāra states that al-Shāmī would often ask Ibn al-Amīr to counsel the imam about certain reprehensible matters (presumably matters regarding official corruption) which he could not broach himself, cf. *Nashr*, I: 153.

[18] *Nashr*, I: 153.

[19] Al-Shāmī took up the post of preacher (*khaṭīb*) at the Great Mosque in 1166/1753 after Ibn al-Amīr was forced to relinquish the post because of Hādawī opposition to his Sunnī teachings.

[20] Cf. *Nashr*, I: 154. It was common at this time in the imamate, as it was at other times and in other places of the Islamic world, to have sons succeeding fathers to the post of judge or any other official post for that matter.

of this, he sat in the most privileged place in the imam's *dīwān* (*taṣaddara fī ʾl-dīwān*), while Aḥmad al-Shāmī still acted as chief judge. Al-Saḥūlī appears to have eclipsed al-Shamī, and al-Manṣūr initially delegated most judicial matters to him, later making him chief judge in 1153/1740. Al-Mahdī al-ᶜAbbās is reported to have praised al-Saḥūlī highly and to have given him both ministerial and judicial duties (*ḍamma ilayhi al-wizāra ilā ʾal-qaḍāʾ*), so that most matters of government now revolved around him. However, in 1172/1759 al-Mahdī confiscated all his wealth and imprisoned him.[21] After al-Mahdī's death in 1189/1775, al-Saḥūlī was rehabilitated and reappointed chief judge by al-Manṣūr ᶜAlī (d. 1224/1809), al-Mahdī al-ᶜAbbās's son and successor.

Shawkānī's description of al-Saḥūlī's job and all the powers associated with the position of chief judge shows the extent to which the imam's religious and legal authority had now shifted to his chief judge:

> al-Manṣūr ᶜAlī returned the subject of this biography [i.e., al-Saḥūlī] to the chief judgeship (*al-qaḍāʾal-akbar*) and delegated to him all that pertains to this. He became [therefore] the authority which was referred to (*al-marjiᶜ*) among all the judges of the Yemeni lands... and he sat in the most privileged place in the *dīwān*. No judge could refute him; whatever he ruled upon was not criticised; whatever he rendered false could not be made sound by others. The caliph (*al-khalīfa*)[22] – may God preserve him – would consult with him in all important matters, especially those relating to matters of rule. Indeed, all the ministers would consult with him and perform whatever he advised... It was said in his lifetime that if he were to die the order of the kingdom would be impaired, not to mention the judicial system.[23]

Unlike Shawkānī, however, al-Saḥūlī appears to have clung to Zaydī-Hādawī teachings in his legal opinions, though like al-Shāmī before him he was educated by Zaydīs as well as by Sunnīs.[24] He cannot be described as a strict Hādawī and one of his Sunnī teachers was ᶜAbd al-Khāliq b. ᶜAli al-Mizjājī of Zabīd. In fact, Shawkānī mentions that al-Saḥūlī was fully acquainted with the 'books of the [Zaydī] imams and all the Zaydī ulema, and occupied himself much with these, but also with other works since he taught Muslim's *Ṣaḥīḥ* to a number of the ulema

21 Cf. *Nashr*, II: 378 where the same is reported to have happened to Aḥmad b. ᶜAbd al-Raḥmān al-Shāmī. This was a common practice among the imams of Yemen in the eighteenth and nineteenth centuries, further highlighting the patrimonial nature of their rule. That Shawkānī escaped this fate throughout his long tenure as chief judge, probably reflects the power he wielded or perhaps his skill at navigating the turbulent vicissitudes of imamate politics.

22 It is noteworthy that the term *khalīfa* is used here when referring to the imam. This is an uncommon appelation for the imams in earlier Zaydī sources, and its use here is perhaps another indication of the changed nature of the later Zaydī imamate. The usage of the term *khalīfa*, which denotes the exalted status of vice-regent of God on earth, can be understood here as sycophantic praise of the ruler.

23 *Badr*, II: 334–5; also *Nayl*, II: 384–91.

24 I have recently discovered a copy of al-Saḥūlī's collected *fatwā*s in Firestone Library at Princeton University, ms. 3181 (Yahuda Section). In it, al-Saḥūlī declares a preference for the teachings of the Zaydī *madhhab* but maintains that the Sunnī ḥadīth collections are sound sources on which to base one's opinion, cf. fols. 67a f. I intend to publish a study of this work as it seems to be the only extant copy and reveals much about the workings of the Qāsimi judicial system.

of Sanaa'.[25] Zabāra also says that al-Saḥūlī would often read the *Ṣaḥīḥayn* of Muslim and Bukhārī as well as the *Sunan* of Abū Dāwūd.[26] In Yemeni biographical dictionaries, such statements signal that the scholar in question was not a fanatical adherent of the Zaydī school, but a 'moderate' (*mu*ᶜ*tadil*) person with respect to religious and juridical affiliation.

A figure similar to al-Saḥūlī and al-Shāmī, and one who played a central role in the government of al-Mahdī al-ᶜAbbās, probably taking over the role of chief judge while al-Saḥūlī was in prison, was Qāḍī Aḥmad b. Muḥammad Qāṭin (d. 1199/1785). Qāṭin is described by Shawkānī in terms which clearly indicate his Sunnī orientation.

> He had an abiding interest in the Sunna sciences (ᶜ*ulūm al-sunna*) and a strong hand in their memorization (*yadun qawīya fī ḥifẓihā*). He practised *ijtihād* himself and did not imitate anyone.[27]

The important roles that scholars like Aḥmad al-Shāmī, Aḥmad Qāṭin and Yaḥyā al-Saḥūlī played in the government of al-Mahdī al-ᶜAbbās is indicative of the orientation that the imamate had now chosen. The extent to which the imam identified with these scholars can be gleaned from the positions he accorded them in his government and from the way he protected them. The imam sometimes punished his officials by confiscating their property, such punitive actions were motivated by political intrigue and court politics, not ideology.

The scholars who rose to power in the latter half of the eighteenth century posited a vision of social order that challenged the one in existence in Yemen. They used their influence with the imams, intervening with tribal and social structures and practices whenever they felt these contradicted the teachings of the Sharīᶜa. There are two notable instances in this period which will be described here.

Traditionists, Jews and Banias

As we have already seen, the influence of Sunnism on Zaydī scholars increased progressively through the end of the seventeenth century and throughout the eighteenth century, culminating in the identification of the imams with the Traditionist scholars, such as Ibn al-Amīr and Shawkānī, from al-Mahdī al-ᶜAbbās's reign onward. The imamate's changing treatment of its non-Muslim subjects, namely Jews and Hindu Banias (known in Arabian sources as Bāniyān), nicely illustrates this doctrinal shift. The history of the Jews and Banias also highlights the constraints placed upon these rulers, who, while wanting to enforce the letter of the law (as understood by the Traditionists) on their non-Muslim subjects, by expelling them from Yemen, did not or could not do so, for practical reasons. The non-Muslim subjects

[25] *Badr*, II: 335. [26] *Nayl*, II: 385.

[27] *Badr*, I: 114. Qaṭin was Sayyid Aḥmad b. ᶜAbd al-Raḥmān al-Shāmī's brightest student. His fortunes, however, were not good as he was imprisoned on at least two occasions by al-Mahdī al-ᶜAbbās, and had all his property expropriated or destroyed, cf. *Badr*, I: 115–16.

performed services which rendered them indispensable to Yemeni society, were a source of direct revenue through the poll-tax (*jizya*) they paid, and resided in areas that were not under direct government control.

From its creation in the late third/ninth century until the latter half of the seventeenth century, the Zaydī imamate tolerated the presence in Yemen of Jews and later, in the Qāsimī period, of Banias. The famous treaty which al-Hādī Yaḥyā b. al-Ḥusayn drew up with the *dhimmīs* of Najrān in 284/897 provides proof that this was the case with the founder.[28] In the early Qāsimī period, the point is well illustrated in a story narrated by Qāḍī al-Ḥaymī, the imam's emissary to the Negus, about when he was on his mission in Ethiopia. Here a Coptic priest called Khāṭirūs mentioned to al-Ḥaymī his wish to return to Yemen with him on the condition that he could keep his religion. Al-Ḥaymī responded by saying: 'Many are the Jews and Christians who, like you, ask the Muslims for protection and come to our regions in safety and security. Some remain while paying the *jizya* fixed per head, and some stay for a short time and then return to their country'.[29] Zaydī imams, and the *sayyids* more generally, did not make an issue of non-Muslims living in Yemen, in part because the poll-tax (*jizya*) could be used to defray their own personal expenses, whereas all other canonical taxes, like the *zakāt*, belonged properly to the public treasury (*bayt al-māl*) and legally could not be handled by *sayyids*. Al-Mutawakkil Ismāᶜīl, for example, was adamant that the Ahl al-Bayt were not to take the *zakāt*.[30] Receipt of the *jizya* may also explain why the imams tolerated the presence of Bania merchants, who were regarded as infidels, but were nonetheless recognized for their key role as traders, supplying Yemen with Indian, Turkish and Persian goods, and were a source of revenue.[31]

Several ḥadīths are pertinent to the issue of whether non-Muslims, in particular Jews, are allowed to reside in the Arabian Peninsula. In the first, reported on the authority of Ibn ᶜAbbās, the Prophet, whilst on his deathbed, gave three testamentary commands (*waṣāyā*), one of which was to expel the polytheists (*mushrikūn*) from the Arabian Peninsula.[32] Another Tradition, reported by Abū ᶜUbayda b. al-Jarrāḥ, says that the Prophet's last words were: 'Expel the Jews of the people of Hijaz… from the Peninsula of the Arabs'.[33] In their legal commentaries, Hādawīs consider the second ḥadīth as specifying (*mukhaṣṣiṣ*) the first more general command, and have therefore held that Jews are allowed to live in Yemen.[34] They consider the

[28] Cf. al-Hādī Yaḥyā b. al-Ḥusayn, *Kitāb al-Funūn*, which follows upon his *Kitāb al-Muntakhab* (Sanaa: Dār al-Ḥikma al-Yamāniyya, 1993), pp. 505–7; al-ᶜAlawī, *Sīrat al-Hādī ilā al-Ḥaqq*, pp. 47–8, 62, 76–9; C. van Arendonk, *Les Débuts de l'Imāmat Zaidite au Yémen* (Leiden: E. J. Brill, 1960), pp. 142–4, 322–9.

[29] E. J. van Donzel, *A Yemenite embassy*, pp. 186–7.

[30] *Ṭabaq al-ḥalwā*, p. 325.

[31] Cf. R. B. Serjeant, 'The Hindu, Baniyān, merchants and traders', in R. B. Serjeant and R. Lewcock (eds.), *Ṣanᶜāʾ: an Arabian Islamic City* (London: World of Islam Festival Trust, 1983), pp. 432f.; Frank Mermier, *Le Cheikh de la Nuit* (Paris: Sindbad, 1997), pp. 25–6.

[32] Bukhari, *Ṣaḥīḥ*, *Jizya*, 6.

[33] Aḥmad b. Ḥanbal, *Musnad*, I:196.

[34] Cf. al-Ḥusayn b. Badr al-Dīn, *Kitāb Shifāʾal-uwām*, vol. III, pp. 569–70; *Sharḥ al-Azhār*, vol. IV, p. 568; Ibn al-Murtaḍā, *al-Baḥr al-zakhkhār*, vol. V, pp. 459–60; Yaḥyā b. al-Ḥusayn, *Ghāyat al-amānī fī akhbār al-quṭr al-Yamānī*, Saᶜīd ᶜĀshūr (ed.) (Cairo: Dār al-Kātib al-ᶜArabī, 1968), vol. II, p. 685.

actions of the caliphs Abū Bakr and ᶜUmar, who did not expel the *dhimmī*s from the Yemen, as proof that only the Hijaz and not the entirety of the Peninsula was intended by the Prophet. Moreover, Jews formed an integral part of Yemeni society. In tribal areas, they were accorded the status of 'protected clients' (*jīrān*) and thus were protected by the tribes. They were allowed to farm and were otherwise associated with such crafts as silver-working and leather-working.[35]

Problems arose, however, in the seventeenth century, when the Jews of Yemen became involved in activities relating to Sabbatai Sevi.[36] Two messianic waves took place, starting in Rajab 1077/December 1666 – January 1667, at which time Jews began selling their moveable property and real estate and were perceived by Muslims to behave oddly and arrogantly. This culminated in a dramatic event: a Sanaa rabbi named Sulaymān Jamāl, known as al-Aqṭāᶜ, went to the governor of Sanaa, Muḥammad b. al-Mutawakkil Ismāᶜīl (d. 1097/1686, later Imam al-Muᵓayyad), and said to him in Hebrew: 'Stand up from this place of yours, for your days are numbered and your rule has come to an end! Power is ours now!'[37] The governor had this translated, interrogated him to see if he was insane and wrote to Imam al-Mutawakkil Ismāᶜīl about the matter. A few days later, after it was decided he was not in fact mad, Sulaymān was executed.

During and immediately after these events a series of punitive measures and decrees against the Jews were taken by al-Mutawakkil Ismāᶜīl. These included the arrest, torture and imprisonment of Jewish leaders, a ban on Jews wearing turbans, the imposition of a tax of fifty percent on their crops and the confiscation of Jewish property. The imam justified his action by declaring that the messianic activities of the Jews had led to the nullification of the covenant of protection (*ᶜaqd al-dhimma*), which had hitherto allowed them to profess their faith while they paid the poll-tax (*jizya*). They were no longer *dhimmī*s but slaves. In the following years, al-Mutawakkil gradually repealed these measures and eased the burden on the Jews, restoring their traditional status. However, on his death bed, the imam inexplicably ordered the expulsion of all Jews from Yemen. The reasons for this testamentary order (*waṣiyya*) remain puzzling: al-Mutawakkil had repealed the punitive decrees; and, more importantly perhaps, the testamentary order contravened the explicit opinion of the Hādawī school on the matter. Al-Mutawakkil's extended biography, his *sīra*, ends in 1663, three years before the Sabbatian movement begins in Yemen and thirteen years before his death in 1676. His *sīra*, therefore, offers no clues as to why he ordered the expulsion. A conjecture might be that al-Mutawakkil had accepted Ibn ᶜAbbās's ḥadīth as probative and by issuing this testament he was attempting to emulate the Prophet on his own deathbed. Whatever the case, it was left for his successor, al-Mahdī Aḥmad b. al-Ḥasan (r. 1676–1681), to carry it out.

35 Dresch, *Tribes*, pp. 61, 118.

36 Cf. P. S. van Koningsveld *et al.*, *Yemenite Authorities and Jewish Messianism* (Leiden: Leiden University, 1990); *Ṭabaq al-ḥalwā*, pp. 222–3, 304, 352–3, 361; A. Shivtiel *et al.*, 'The Jews of Ṣanᶜāᵓ', pp. 398–400; Yosef Tobi, 'The Sabbatean activity in Yemen', in *The Jews of Yemen: Studies in their History and Culture* (Leiden: Brill, 1999), pp. 48–84.

37 van Koningsveld *et al.*, *Yemenite Authorities*, p. 16.

The Jews are Expelled

In Sha^cbān 1088/September 1677, al-Mahdī Aḥmad gave the governor of Sanaa, Muḥammad b. al-Mutawakkil, the order to expel the Jews and destroy their synagogues. It is not clear whether there were any reasons for this other than his predecessor's wish that it should be done, and it is paradoxical that al-Mahdī Aḥmad, who was the strictest Hādawī of the early Qāsimī imams, should have followed through with this order, since it ran directly counter to his school's teachings. This last fact was obvious to the governor, who before carrying it out, sought the opinion of the scholars on the matter. Ibn al-Wazīr, in *Ṭabaq al-ḥalwā*, tells us that the jurists were divided. The prominent ones in the imam's court, most notably Qāḍī Aḥmad b. Ṣāliḥ Ibn Abī ʾl-Rijāl (d. 1092/1681), supported the expulsion, claiming to base their opinion of the Shāfiʿī scholar Zakariyya al-Anṣārī (d. 926/1520). Al-Anṣārī's opinion stipulated a literal application (*ʿalā ẓāhirih*) of Ibn ʿAbbās's ḥadīth: 'Expel the polytheists from the Arabian Peninsula'. Others, more committed to traditional Hādawī views, demurred, arguing on the basis of Abū ʿUbayda's ḥadīth that only the Hijaz was intended.[38]

It took over one-and-a-half years before the order was finally put into effect. In 1090/1679, the main remaining Jewish synagogue was broken into, its books destroyed, its wine poured out and the building demolished.[39] Again reflecting traditional Hādawī views, Muḥammad b. al-Mutawakkil, the governor of Sanaa, tried to intercede with the imam, arguing against the destruction of the synagogue given its 'antiquity' (it reportedly was built before the coming of Islam to Yemen). The imam, however, was adamant that it be demolished and in its stead erected a mosque called Masjid al-Jalā' (Mosque of the Expulsion).[40] Thereafter, the Jews were given a choice between expulsion or conversion to Islam. After refusing conversion, they were expelled from Sanaa and other places to Mawzaʿ, an area not far from the port of Mocha.

Mawzaʿ was most probably intended as a temporary staging post until such time as the imam could find the safe means to expedite the Jews by sea from Mocha to India. The safe passage never materialised, possibly because of the logistical difficulties involved. Many of the Jews perished in what amounted ultimately to an internal Yemeni exile. In the following years, they were allowed to return to Sanaa and their villages. Different reasons have been posited for their return. Some,

[38] *Ṭabaq al-ḥalwā*, p. 352–3; cf. ʿAbd al-Hādī al-Tāzī, 'al-Nuṣūṣ al-ẓāhira fī ijlāʾal-Yahūd al-fājira li-Aḥmad Abī ʾl-Rijāl', *al-Baḥth al-ʿilmī* (Rabat: al-Maʿhad al-Jāmiʿī liʾl-Baḥth al-ʿIlmi, Jāmiʿat Muḥammad al-Khāmis), 32 (1981), 15–35; Muḥammad Ḥusayn al-Zabīdī, 'Makhṭūṭatān min al-Yaman', *al-Mawrid* (Baghdad: Ministry of Information), 3.4 (1974), 187–96; Muḥammad al-Ḥarīrī, 'Fatḥ al-malik al-maʿbūd fī dhikr ijlāʾal-Yahūd li-Ṣāliḥ b. Dāʾūd al-Ānisī', in *Dirāsāt wa buḥūth fī tārīkh al-Yaman al-islāmī* (Beirut: ʿĀlam al-Kutub, 1998), pp. 137–78.

[39] *Ṭabaq al-ḥalwā*, p. 361.

[40] Cf. Muḥammad b. Aḥmad al-Ḥajrī, *Masājid Ṣanʿāʾ*, 2nd edn (Beirut: Dār Iḥyāʾal-Turāth al-ʿArabī, 1398/1978), p. 42. Inscribed in the wall of the mosque is a poem by Muḥammad b. Ibrāhīm al-Saḥūlī praising the imam for expelling the Jews and turning their synagogue into a mosque.

Inscription in Masjid al-Jalā’ about the expulsion of the Jews (author)

like Goitein and Ratzaby, have argued that the authorities recalled them because they realised that the Jews were indispensable as artisans and craftsmen.[41] Al-Jirāfī, on the other hand, says that it was because the imam could not dispatch them to a place of safety.[42] This is borne out by a report from one of the leading Traditionist jurists of the period, Ṣāliḥ b. Mahdī al-Maqbalī (d. 1108/1696), which also underscores the important role Traditionist scholars now had in determining the course of events.

Al-Maqbalī was a scholar from Thulā, a town which lies north-west of Sanaa. Like Ibn al-Amīr and Shawkānī he was a determined anti-Hādawī with strong Traditionist views. By the time of the expulsion, he had had several altercations with Hādawīs which may have led him to leave Yemen and settle in Mecca.[43] From here al-Maqbalī reports on the Sabbatian events in Yemen and on how Imam al-Mahdī Aḥmad sought his opinion about what to do with the Jews. His role may have been decisive in determining why the Jews were sent to Mawzaᶜ. He writes:

> In our age the devil has bewitched them [the Jews] in Yemen and enticed them [into believing] that their time to rule has come. It was as if they desired the rule of the Deceiver (*al-dajjāl*; False Messiah), because they used to say: 'the Messiah has come!' [They] began manifesting a disregard for Islam and Muslims until one of them came up to the governor of Sanaa and said to him: 'Rise from this seat! Your rule has ended!' The Imam adopted a position of neutrality (*tawaqqafa*), to await the final outcome (*al-maʾāl*) and out of respect for the covenant of protection (*iḥtirāman liʾl-dhimma*). The jurists were very critical of him for this. So God humiliated them [Jews] because the commoners assaulted them at once after the Friday prayers in many different places outside Sanaa and its dependencies. They were brought back to their humiliated and humble origins. Then Imam al-Mahdī Aḥmad b. al-Ḥasan – may God have mercy on him – sought to expel them from Yemen. I do not know whether this was based on ḥadīth or in order to ward off their evil. The commander of the [Yemeni] pilgrimage (*amīr al-ḥajj*) relayed to me a message from the Imam in which he says: 'I wish to expel the Jews, but where must they be sent to?' It is as if he wanted to see whether I would agree with the jurists (*fuqahāʾ*) in prohibiting their expulsion. So I answered him: 'God has granted you correct guidance regarding their expulsion. India would be the [best] destination, after you correspond with them [India's rulers] about this. They would like it because of the poll-tax. All other directions consist of deserts that would kill them off [the Jews], and because of their numbers they would need armies to secure their safe arrival. As for India, they would only be a droplet in a downpour, because of all the infidels already there'. So he expelled them to the sea coast in the governorates of Mocha and Aden, and kept them at a distance awaiting the response [from India's rulers], or so I think. He died before this [i.e., the response arrived] – may God have mercy on him – so they returned to the country in any which way. They were greatly humiliated and

[41] S. D. Goitein, *Jews and Arabs*, 3rd edn (New York: Schocken Books, 1974), p. 74; cf. Yehuda Ratzaby, 'Galūt Mawzaᶜ', *Sefunot* 5 (1961), 337–95; idem, 'Gerūsh Mawzaᶜle-Or Meqōrōt Ḥadashīm', *Zion* 37 (1972), 197–215.

[42] al-Jirāfī, *al-Muqtaṭaf*, p. 236.

[43] Cf. *Badr*, I: 288–92; *Nashr*, I: 781–7; *Hijar al-ᶜilm*, I: 270–8.

> humbled and some of them pretended to be Muslims – may God fight them. [Do not be fooled,] none among them is truly a believing Muslim because they are pure Jews (*li-annahum yahūdun baḥt*), and [because] none of them is a Christian. This happened in the final years of the eleventh century of the Prophetic Hijra.[44]

Hādawī jurists wanted the imam to punish the Jews for their rebellious actions, but stopped short of calling for their expulsion, except those who were the imam's closest advisors. For the Hādawīs, it seems, the school's teachings outweighed the arguments presented by the Traditionist jurists and the imam himself. However, the imam wanted them expelled and in order to substantiate the expulsion he had to resort to non-Hādawī juridical authority. The imam's request for al-Maqbalī's counsel on the matter should be understood in this light.

All the other principal Traditionist scholars (al-Jalāl, Ibn al-Amīr and Shawkānī) held in their legal writings that Jews must be expelled from the Arabian Peninsula, and otherwise insisted on the strictest enforcement of the stipulations of the Pact of ᶜUmar, which the Caliph ᶜUmar b. al-Khaṭṭāb allegedly had concluded with the non-Muslim subject populations.[45] This Pact imposed on *dhimmī*s regulations whose aims were to abase and humiliate them as well as to distinguish them from Muslims. Based on the Qur'ānic verse 'until they pay the tribute out of hand and have been humiliated' (IX: 29), *dhimmī*s were, for example, expected to ride their beasts in a fashion different from Muslims; they could not build houses taller than those of Muslims; they could only wear clothes of a certain colour and were restricted in constructing or repairing houses of worship. These restrictions were not always enforced in Yemen. Some imams were more tolerant and ignored them, whereas the authority of others simply did not extend to all the areas in which Jews resided for which reason they could not enforce the stipulations even had they wanted to. It is clear, for example, that, until the Sabbatian events, Jews were allowed to wear turbans since one of the punitive decrees explicitly prohibited this.

After their return from the Mawzaᶜ exile, the situation of the Jews improved considerably, especially during the reign of al-Mahdī Muḥammad b. Aḥmad, otherwise known as Ṣāḥib al-Mawāhib (r. 1098–1130/1687–1718), who returned to them their previous status. In this more tolerant atmosphere a number of new synagogues were built, apparently without official authorisation, thereby contravening another stipulation of the Covenant of Protection. Moreover, both Ṣāḥib al-Mawāhib and his successor al-Mutawakkil al-Qāsim b. al-Ḥusayn (r. 1128–1139/1716–1727) developed strong relations with members of the Jewish al-ᶜIrāqī family, who were given the task of overseeing the mint and whose members, like Sālim al-ᶜIrāqī,

[44] al-Maqbalī, *al-Manār*, vol. II, pp. 503–4.

[45] Cf. al-Ḥasan b. Aḥmad al-Jalāl, *Ḍaw'u al-nahār al-mushriq ᶜalā ṣafaḥāt al-Azhār*, 4 vols. (Sanaa: Majlis al-Qaḍā'al-Aᶜlā, n.d.), vol. IV, pp. 2569–76 and Ibn al-Amīr's commentary *Minḥat al-ghaffar* on the same pages; Shawkānī, *Nayl al-awṭār*, vol. IV, part 8, pp. 222–5; idem, *al-Sayl al-jarrār*, vol. IV, pp. 569–75; Seth Ward, 'A fragment from an unknown work by al-Ṭabarī on the tradition "expel the Jews and Christians from the Arabian Peninsula (and the lands of Islam)" ', *BSOAS* 53 (1990), 407–20; Mark Cohen, 'What was the pact of ᶜUmar? A literary-historical study', *JSAI* 23 (1999), 100–57.

held the official posts of minister of finance and tax-collector of the Jewish community as well as chief rabbi (*Nasī* in the Jewish sources and *Shaykh* or *Kabīr al-Yahūd* in the Arabic sources).[46] Some Jews, therefore, were integrated, albeit in a subservient position, into the institutional fabric of the state, at a time when the imams were also developing other institutions, such as the standing army. These developments, however, conflicted with the rising influence of the Traditionist scholars in Sanaa and elsewhere.

Matters came to a head in 1137/1725, when an inebriated Muslim man sexually assaulted a Muslim boy in the lavatory of one of Sanaa's mosques. One of the stipulations of the Covenant of Protection was the prohibition on *dhimmīs* selling alcoholic beverages to Muslims. Thus, the incident constituted a flagrant breach of the Covenant. Upon hearing of this, Imam al-Mutawakkil al-Qāsim became angry and summoned Ṣālim al-ᶜIrāqī and accused him of contravening the terms of the Covenant. Jewish sources say that the imam commanded the chief rabbi to present a register of all those who sell wine to gentiles, stipulating a deadline of three days for compliance. But al-ᶜIrāqī did not divulge any names; instead, he placated the imam with a bribe of money, after which the incident apparently was forgotten.[47]

Zabāra, in *Nashr al-ᶜarf*, offers us a more detailed account that sheds light on the court intrigues of the period and the factional strife between Hādawī and Traditionist scholars.[48] When confronted with the imam's anger, Zabāra says, al-ᶜIrāqī justified the sale of alcohol by stating that Ibn al-Amīr and al-Ḥasan b. Isḥāq (d. 1160/1747) had issued him a *fatwā* permitting the sale. Zabāra explains that it was Ibn al-Amīr's enemies who had told al-ᶜIrāqī to say this. At the time the Āl Isḥāq were closely allied with Ibn al-Amīr and were rivals of the ruling branch of Qāsimī imams.[49] Al-ᶜIrāqī seems, therefore, to have wanted to place the blame on them, thereby hoping to absolve the Jewish community and safeguard it from punishment.

Upon hearing of al-ᶜIraqī's allegation, Ibn al-Amīr went to al-Mutawakkil to deny that he had issued such a *fatwā* and demanded that the chief rabbi be summoned 'so that you [the imam] may know the truth about his lie and also what the Jews have done in contravention of their abasement (*ṣaghār*) and humiliation (*dhilla*), by building many synagogues and jostling Muslims on the roads'.[50] Al-ᶜIrāqī was summoned and asked how many synagogues were in his village. After listing these, Ibn al-Amīr pointedly remarked their great number and interrogated

[46] Cf. Yosef Tobi, *ᶜIyyūnīm Bi-Mgīlat Teyman* (Jerusalem: Hebrew University, 1986), pp. 151f.; Niebuhr, *Travels*, vol. I, p. 378.

[47] Tobi, 'ha-Nisyōnōt', p. 461. Here quoting Rabbi Saᶜīd Ṣaᶜdī's book *The Chastisements of Time*, cf. Yōsef Qāfiḥ, 'Sefer "Dōfi ha-Zeman" le-Rabbī Saᶜīd Ṣaᶜdī', *Sefunot* 1 (1957), 185–242; cf. Yosef Tobi, 'The attempts to expel the Jews from Yemen in the 18th century', in Ephraim Isaac and Yosef Tobi (eds.), *Judeo-Yemenite Studies* (Princeton: Institute of Semitic Studies, 1999), pp. 41–64; idem (ed.), *Toldot Yehudey Teyman mi-Kitveyhem*, (Jerusalem: The Zalman Shazar Center and The Dinur Center, 1979), pp. 86–7, 90.

[48] *Nashr*, III: 36–7. This source does not mention whether the Muslim assailant was punished for drunkenness and assault.

[49] *Badr*, I: 194, II: 127–30; *Nashr*, III: 39–40; *Hijar al-ᶜilm*, IV: 1830–3.

[50] *Nashr*, III: 36.

him about the issuance of the *fatwā*. Al-ᶜIraqī could not adequately respond and was therefore put in prison, and Ibn al-Amīr recommended he be thrown in chains (*yuqayyad*). Ibn al-Amīr then advised the imam that the Jews must be expelled from the Peninsula on the basis of the Prophet's last will and testament, and if this was not possible, he said, then they must be abased and all the synagogues they had built without permission must be demolished. Al-Mutawakkil gave the order for the demolitions, but Ibn al-Amīr warned publicly that al-ᶜIrāqī would bribe the officials so that this would not be carried out. This is effectively what happened, because no sooner had Ibn al-Amīr departed than the imam had the demolition order lifted, no sanctions were imposed or enforced on the Jewish community and al-ᶜIrāqī was released probably that same day.[51] The imam's leniency was sustained by some of the leading Hādawī scholars of the day, including the *sayyid*s Yūsuf b. al-Mutawakkil Ismāᶜīl (d. 1140/1727–28) and ᶜAbd Allāh b. ᶜAlī al-Wazīr (d. 1144/1732); the latter wrote a treatise in which he adduced proofs and argued for allowing the Jews to remain.[52]

Ibn al-Amīr's efforts to have the Jews expelled and their synagogues demolished did not end here. In the reign of al-Mahdī al-ᶜAbbās, he and ᶜAbd Allāh b. Luṭf al-Bāriʾal-Kibsī and Aḥmad b. ᶜAbd al-Raḥmān al-Shāmī, prevailed on the imam to have some synagogues destroyed, Jewish houses in Sanaa levelled and certain Jewish leaders imprisoned.[53] Niebuhr, who visited al-Mahdī's court in 1763, reports on these events.

> Two years before our arrival here, he [al-ᶜIrāqī] had fallen into disgrace, and was not only imprisoned but obliged to pay a fine of 50,000 crowns. Fifteen days before we arrived at Sanaa, the Imam had let him at liberty... The disgrace of Oroeki [sic] had drawn a degree of persecution upon the rest of the Jews. At that period, the government ordered fourteen synagogues, which the Jews had at Sanaa, to be demolished. In their village are as handsome houses as the best in Sanaa. Of those houses likewise all above the height of fourteen fathoms was demolished, and the Jews were forbidden to raise any of their buildings above this height in future. All the stone pitchers in which the inhabitants of the village had used to keep their wines were broken.[54]

Imam al-Mahdī had been educated by Traditionist scholars, such as ᶜAbd Allāh al-Kibsī (d. 1173/1759–60), and was in favour of implementing their rulings as much as possible.[55] For example, he sent teachers, who could instruct people in matters of prayer and religion, into Sanaa and the countryside at Ibn al-Amīr's instigation and paid their wages out of the public treasury.[56] In commenting on the events relating to the Jews and the Banias, Zabāra says:

51 In a reference to these events Ibn al-Amīr says that his efforts in fact led to the demolition of seven newly built synagogues (*kanāʾis muḥdatha*) but that the expulsion failed because the 'jurists confused the reigning imam'; cf. Ibn al-Amīr, *Minḥat al-ghaffār* on the margins of al-Jalāl's *Ḍawʾ al-nahār*, vol. IV, p. 2574.

52 *Nashr*, III: 37. 53 *Nashr*, II: 136. 54 Niebuhr, *Travels*, vol. I, pp. 378–9.

55 Cf. *Nashr*, II: 19–28, 135, *Nashr*, III: 41.

56 *Nashr*, II: 19–28; cf. Muḥammad b. Ismāᶜīl al-Amīr, *Jawāb fīmā yustaḥsan min tawẓīf al-khārijīn ilā al-bawādī li-taᶜlīm al-ṣalāt*, ms. Sanaa, Gharbiyya Library, *majmūᶜ* no. 39.

> He [ᶜAbd Allāh al-Kibsī] tried to convince al-Mahdī to expel the Jews and Bāniyān from the Peninsula of the Arabs and wrote a question [regarding this]. Al-Badr Muḥammad b. Ismāᶜīl al-Amīr and Sayyid Aḥmad b. ᶜAbd al-Raḥmān al-Shāmī and others responded to it. Al-Mahdī [then] imprisoned a group of their leaders and wanted to expel whomever of them was in the land and to carry out the last will and testament of the Messenger of God – may His peace and blessings be upon him and upon his house – but the matter was not carried out.[57]

It is worth noting that the process by which scholars were able to influence government policy is outlined here. Al-Kibsī raised a question with the aim of eliciting response-treatises, in which arguments and proofs are adduced by scholars, favouring the expulsion. In such situations, some responses can argue the opposite. In this case, it seems the overwhelming number of responses were written by scholars who had influence on the imam, all of whom were in favour of the expulsion and the humiliation of the Jews and Banias. This led to some of the prescriptions being carried out, but the expulsion never took place. Yosef Sadan has argued that the fact that expulsion could be contemplated at all by the imams had to do with the fact that the Jews after the Sabbatian messianic waves and the Mawzaᶜ exile were deemed worthless as a source of fiscal revenue. This, he claims, is because many Jews had abandoned their land in favour of artisan work (therefore paying less tax), and because the Mawzaᶜ exile set a precedent of a Yemen without the active presence of Jews.[58] Yosef Tobi, by contrast, has argued that it was 'doubtless due to practical economic considerations' that Imam al-Mahdī finally refrained from carrying out the expulsion.[59] Tobi's assessment is more plausible, in particular since the imams appeared to contemplate the expulsion only as a symbolic gesture to the increasingly more dominant group of Traditionist scholars in Sanaa. This, in addition to pressures exerted by Zaydī-Hādawī scholars and *sayyids*, who held opposite views on the matter, logistical problems (as seen in the earlier expulsion attempt) and probably bribes from Jews, would have doomed any serious undertaking at expelling them. Indeed, it was Jewish bribes thirty years after the al-Kibsī affair which prevailed on al-Mahdī's successor, Imam al-Manṣūr ᶜAlī to allow the synagogues to be re-opened and some rebuilt.[60] The constraints of rule rendered the Traditionist opinion impracticable for the ruler to implement, despite its theological and juridical claims. The issue itself continued to animate scholarly debate well after the incidents here, and, despite their ongoing failure to achieve this through the imams, Traditionists continued to devise new ways for accomplishing what they saw as a clear Prophetic injunction.[61]

57 *Nashr*, II: 136.
58 Yosef Sadan, 'Beyn ha-Gzerōt ᶜal Yahadūt Teyman be-Sōf ha-Meᵓa ha-17 li-"Gzerat ha-Mqammeṣīm" ba-Meᵓot ha-18 ve-ha-19', in Ezra Fleischer *et al.* (eds.), *Masᵓat Moshe*, (Jerusalem: The Bialik Institute, 1998), pp. 212–15.
59 Tobi, 'ha-Nisyōnōt', pp. 468, 470.
60 Ibid., p. 468; cf. ᶜAmram Qoraḥ, *Saᶜarat Teyman*, Shimᶜōn Greydī (ed.) (Jerusalem: Kook, 1954), p. 22.
61 For example, Ibrāhīm b. ᶜAbd al-Qādir al-Kawkabānī (d. 1223/1808) wrote *al-Tanbīh ᶜalā mā wajaba min ikhrāj al-Yahūd min Jazīrat al-ᶜArab* in 1219/1804 in favour of the expulsion;

The Banias

The Hindu merchant community, or the Banias, were also targeted by Traditionist scholars, and in particular by Ibn al-Amīr. From his perspective, their residence in Arabia was a more flagrant violation of the Sharīᶜa than that of the Jews. Already in the seventeenth century, al-Jalāl had written a treatise in favour of their expulsion from Yemen.[62] A riot broke out against them in Sanaa in Ramaḍān 1066/June–July 1656, largely because of their commercial ascendancy in the market. The reigning Imam al-Mutawakkil Ismāᶜīl, however, defended them, arguing that since they paid the *jizya*, they were protected and could not be molested.[63] By comparing the Banias with the *Ahl al-Kitāb*, al-Mutawakkil was perhaps reflecting the relative tolerance of Hādawī law regarding the presence of non-Muslims in Yemen. By contrast, Ibn al-Amīr insisted on the implementation of the letter of the law: they should be expelled.[64] Zabāra says:

> He [Ibn al-Amīr] advised al-Mahdī al-ᶜAbbās to destroy the Bāniyān idols which were in the port of Mocha, and he wrote a valuable treatise about this. So al-Mahdī ordered that they be destroyed, their temples demolished and all the monies therein seized. These contained great wealth which was estimated at around fifty thousand *riyāls*. One of the idols was taken and brought before the imam, whilst al-Badr [Ibn al-Amīr] was with him. So al-Badr ordered it to be broken up – it had the form of a female – and it was trampled on with sandals.[65]

The Banias, however, were not expelled but continued to trade in Yemen, though al-Mahdī appears to have imposed on them a sumptuary decree, forcing them to wear a red turban.[66] Niebuhr reports seeing Banias throughout his travels in Yemen, even running a bills-of-exchange system, and estimated their number in Sanaa at 125 in 1763.[67]

With Shawkānī's assumption of the chief judgeship, the discrimination against the Jews, and probably the Banias, increased significantly. He conducted a vigorous exchange of treatises with other scholars, arguing for the enforcement of the decree which obliged Jews to collect human and animal excrement from Sanaa's houses and public places. This humiliating practice was initiated sometime in the early 1790s, when Shawkānī first wrote about this issue, and continued well into the

cf. al-Zabīdī, 'Makhṭūṭatān minᵓal-Yaman', pp. 193–6. Whereas, ᶜAbd Allāh b. ᶜĪsā al-Kawkabānī (d. 1224/1809), a more traditional Hādawī and a critic of Shawkānī's anti-Jewish policies and opinions, wrote *al-Salwā waᵓl-mann fī ᶜadam ikhrāj al-Yahūd min ᵓl-Yaman*, arguing against their expulsion; cf. *Nayl*, II: 94; *Badr*, I: 391–2.

62 This treatise ('Risāla fī ᶜadam taqrīr al-Bāniyān (al-Hunūd) wa Ahl al-Dhimma fī ᵓl-Yaman') has been edited (by Ḥusayn b. ᶜAbd Allāh al-ᶜAmrī) and published recently. In it, Jalāl argues for the expulsion of all non-Muslims – the *Ahl al-Kitāb* and the Banias included – from Arabia; cf. al-ᶜAmrī and al-Jirāfī, *al-ᶜAllāma waᵓl-mujtahid*, pp. 469–76.

63 *Ṭabaq al-ḥalwā*, p. 143; Serjeant, 'The Hindu, Bāniyān, Merchants and Traders', pp. 432–3.

64 al-Amīr, *Dīwān al-Amīr al-Ṣanᶜānī*, pp. 135–8.

65 *Nashr*, III: 41. The idol was possibly Lakshmi, the goddess of wealth, traditionally worshipped by trading casts in India.

66 *Nashr*, II: 196.

67 Niebuhr, *Travels*, vol. I, pp. 329–30, 379.

twentieth century.[68] In his treatises on the matter, Shawkānī asserted that such treatment of *dhimmīs* was consistent with the legal stipulations that they be abased and humiliated, and he adduces numerous legal arguments and textual sources to prove his point.[69] Here is some of what he has to say on the matter.

> The Lord, may He be lofty and exalted, has reported in His Book that humiliation is permanently affixed to the Jews, adhering to them permanently as long as they exist, encompassing all persons at all times, in all conditions. By this [humiliation] is not meant some innate or essential characteristic, rather what is intended is to have mastery over them... Indeed what is meant is the abasement which results from any reason which God has not prohibited. Obliging them to collect excrement results in the abasement that is pitched upon them, and everything that results in the abasement that is pitched upon them is permissible, therefore obliging them to collect it is permissible.[70]

Shawkānī also saw to the enforcement of the decree which forcibly converted Jewish orphans to Islam, and wrote a treatise on this subject entitled *Risāla fī ḥukm ṣibyān al-dhimmiyyīn idhā māta abawāhum*. These punitive judgements were probably a consequence of the persistent frustration of the Traditionist scholars at not being able to expel the Jews from Yemen. Their ultimate aim was in likelihood to convince the Jews either to convert to Islam or quit the country of their own accord. Most Jews refused to take up either option, and the decrees of humiliation remained in force until their mass exodus to Israel in the late 1940s.

Shawkānī's View of the Periphery

As pointed out in chapter two, Shawkānī managed to convince al-Manṣūr ᶜAlī to issue a decree aiming at reforming the imamate's taxation policies. This was part of a larger attempt to stave off the Wahhābīs who were threatening the imamate. His efforts, however, failed to effect fiscal reform and this led him to write a treatise describing the ills of Yemeni society in which he also provided the imam with further advice on how to resolve these. He entitled the treatise *al-Dawāʾal-ᶜājil fī dafᶜ al-ᶜaduw al-ṣāʾil* (The Quick Cure Warding off the Assaulting Enemy). In it, Shawkānī offers a typology of Yemenis whom he divides into three distinct groups:

> First there are those subjects (*raᶜāyā*) who come under the absolute control of the state (*dawla*) and submit to its orders. The majority of them cannot pray, or pray

[68] Cf. Shalom Gamliel, *ha-Yehūdīm we-ha-Melekh be-Teyman*, 2 vols. (Jerusalem: The Shalom Research Center, 1986–7), vol. II, pp. 152–4.

[69] Cf. *Nayl*, II: 94; Joseph Sadan, 'The "Latrines Decree" in the Yemen versus the Dhimma principles', in Jan Platvoet and Karel van der Toorn (eds.), *Pluralism and Identity: studies in ritual behaviour* (Leiden: E. J. Brill, 1995), pp. 167–85. These treatises are on microfilm in Cairo at al-Hayʾa al-Miṣriyya Library, no. 2216. I have edited the first of these by Shawkānī and will be publishing it with a study providing the context of this debate.

[70] Muḥammad al-Shawkānī, *Ḥall al-ishkāl fī ijbār al-Yahūd ᶜalā iltiqāṭ al-azbāl* (Cairo: Dar al-Kutub, microfilm no. 2216), fol. 45b.

> incorrectly... He who does not practise prayer properly is a mere infidel (*kāfir*)... The second group consists of those of the far north and east (*bilād al-qibla wa'l-mashriq*) who have not come under the control of the *dawla*. They are... even worse, since they cannot read or write and they submit to the customary laws of their predecessors (*aḥkām al-ṭāghūt*), instead of to the Sharīʿa... Those who do so... are unbelievers.
>
> The third group consists of the townspeople... As a result of their ignorance and indulgence, they neglect many of their duties towards God... However, they are the closest to goodness and readier than others to learn and receive an education, if one persists with educating them.[71]

Shawkānī's patrician disdain for those on the periphery is evident here as is his belief that only those who have yielded to the authority of the state can be good Muslims. He directs his criticism mainly at the governors, court notaries and judges, all of whom he sees as being corrupt and ignorant. He describes a 'typical' rural judge as follows:

> The *qāḍi* [in the outlying areas] is a man who is ignorant of the Sharīʿa... He does not know [the difference] between justice and injustice... However, he desires to be called a *qāḍī* and that his name be widely known among the people... He also desires to wear elegant clothes so he has placed on his head a turban as tall as a tower and lengthened his sleeves so that they resemble saddlebags and has adopted a posture of dignity and tranquillity, always saying: 'yes' and 'maybe'. He also fiddles with long prayer beads and has amassed a fortune.[72]

The underlying message of Shawkānī's treatise is that whenever he can the imam should remove the judges who are not as well trained and educated as Shawkānī and his students. It is only by empowering scholars like himself and by giving them posts that the Sharīʿa can be applied and therefore remedy the problems facing the realm.

Wahhābīs and the Issue of Visiting Graves (*ziyārat al-qubūr*)

The destruction of the graves of Sufi saints in September 1994 in Aden by Salafi activists is not the first time that the matter of graves and their visitation has been a contentious issue in Yemen. At the beginning of the nineteenth century, this issue was as explosive as it is today. The Wahhābīs were then active in spreading their message throughout Arabia, destroying tombs wherever they went in their drive to stop the practices associated with the cult of saints. Threatened both ideologically and militarily by the Wahhābīs, the imamate offered its own answers to these controversial issues and responded vigorously to the Wahhābī attacks. The text which forms the subject of this section was probably the principal statement by the imamate on the issue of visiting graves and the practices associated with the

[71] Muḥammad b. ʿAlī al-Shawkānī, *al-Dawāʾ al-ʿājil fī dafʿ al-ʿaduw al-ṣāʾil*, in *al-Rasāʾil al-salafiyya* (Beirut: Dār al-Kutub alʿIlmiyya, 1930), pp. 29, 33, 37; cf. al-ʿAmrī, *al-Imām al-Shawkānī*, p. 128–38; Dresch, *Tribes*, p. 214.

[72] Shawkānī, *al-Dawāʾal-ʿājil*, p. 31.

cult of saints. Its author, Shawkānī, uses lines of argument similar to those of the Wahhābīs. He condemned the cult of saints but allowed for the visitation of graves as long as *taqlīd* did not take place there. In so doing, Shawkānī responded to the Wahhābīs by employing their discourse but arrived at more lenient prescriptions: tombs did not have to be destroyed and grave visitation could take place under certain restrictions.

The Wahhābī movement was initiated in 1744 with a pact between the scholar Muḥammad b. ʿAbd al-Wahhāb (d. 1206/1792) and the emir of the town of al-Dirʿiyya, Muḥammad b. Saʿūd (d. 1179/1766). By the turn of the nineteenth century, the Wahhābīs constituted a formidable military force promoting a powerful renovative message which had to be reckoned with. Drawing on Ḥanbalī doctrine as interpreted by Taqī al-Dīn Aḥmad Ibn Taymiyya (d. 728/1328) and Ibn Qayyim al-Jawziyya (d. 751/1350), the Wahhābī message exalted the doctrine of God's unicity (*tawḥīd*) and attacked all whom they felt were derogating from it. The two principal requirements for *tawḥīd* were the affirmation of God's uniqueness as omnipotent lord of creation (*tawḥīd al-rubūbiyya*) and His uniqueness in deserving worship and the absolute devotion of His servants (*tawḥīd al-ulūhiyya*).[73] The Wahhābīs found their principal opponents in the partisans of the cult of saints and tombs whom they accused of unbelief (*kufr*). This was because many of their practices were considered to constitute *bidaʿ* (reprehensible innovations) which led to *shirk* because they associated persons or things with God, and as such contradicted *tawḥīd*. Wahhābism sought to purge from the Islamic community these innovations and polytheistic practices, which they claimed were later accretions to the Sunna of the Prophet and the first generations of pious Muslims (*al-salaf al-ṣāliḥ*).

By following the school of Aḥmad b. Ḥanbal (d. 241/855), the Wahhābī movement found itself in accord with the Traditionist school which had developed within Yemen, particularly in the emphasis that both placed on literal understanding of the Qurʾān and ḥadīth. The influence of both Ibn Taymiyya and Ibn al-Qayyim on the Wahhābīs and Shawkānī is extensive. Another point of agreement was the disdain both tendencies had for popular Sufism, as represented in the cult of saints. Despite these similarities, a doctrinal polemic raged between the Wahhābīs and the Yemeni Traditionists, in which the latter accused the Wahhābīs of extremism and compared them to the *Khawārij*.[74]

The ulema of Sanaa were aware of the Wahhābī *daʿwa* from early on, since Ibn al-Amīr composed and sent a poem in praise of them as early as 1755.[75]

[73] Henri Laoust, *Essai sur les Doctrines Sociales et Politiques de Taki-D-Din Ahmad b. Taimiya* (Cairo: Imprimerie de l'Institut Français d'Archéologie Orientale, 1939), p. 531. For an excellent examination of the early history of the Wahhābī movement see Esther Peskes, *Muḥammad b. ʿAbdalwahhāb im Widerstreit* (Beirut: Orient-Institut, 1993).

[74] Cf. Shawkānī, *Dīwān al-Shawkānī*, pp. 160–4.

[75] Cf. Michael Cook, 'On the Origins of Wahhābism', *Journal of the Royal Asiatic Society* 2.2 (1992), 200–1; Ḥamad al-Jāsir, 'al-Ṣilāt bayn Ṣanʿāʾwaʾl-Dirʿiyya', *al-ʿArab* 22 (1987), 433–5; Muḥammad Ṣiddīq Ḥasan Khān, *Abjad al-ʿulūm*, 3 vols. (Damascus: Dār al-Kutub al-ʿIlmiyya, 1978), vol. III, pp. 196f.

He retracted the poem a year later, however, upon receiving news of the systematic Wahhābī excommunication (*takfīr*) of fellow Muslims, including the Zaydīs, and the brutality the Wahhābīs inflicted during their expansionist attacks.[76] Shawkānī, at first, also praised the Wahhābīs and was seemingly impressed by the works of its founder, Muḥammad b. ᶜAbd al-Wahhāb. Upon the latter's death in 1206/1792 Shawkānī eulogised him in a poem, praising him for calling for a return to the Qurᵓān and Sunna.[77] However, like Ibn al-Amīr before him, Shawkānī changed his mind about the Wahhābīs, especially after they had entered Yemen. In one of his poems, Shawkānī explicitly criticised the Wahhābīs for their extremism:

> Do you not know that we [i.e., Traditionists of Yemen] and you [i.e.,Wahhābīs] // have recourse to the correct path . . .
> We both refer to the Book [Qurᵓān] if we differ // in our respective doctrines, we cannot deny this
> And to the purest of our Prophet's sayings [ḥadīth] // we also refer, for the Book attests to such . . .
> How is it said that people [i.e., visitors] are unbelievers // if one sees stones and sticks by their graves
> For if they [i.e., Wahhabīs] say that a sound order was given [in ḥadīth] // to level graves, I would not deny this
> But this [i.e., the actions of the visitors of graves] is a misdeed (*dhanb*) and not unbelief (*kufr*), // nor is it sinfulness (*fisq*), is there in this any refutation?
> For if there is, it would entail calling the person who disobeys through a misdeed // an unbeliever, and such an assertion is deviant
> And the *Khawārij* went toward this [i.e., excommunication], // and why would one partake in the conduct of the *Khawārij*?
> By doing this they [i.e., the *Khawārij*] had truly violated the *ijmā*ᶜ, // and all who have knowledge are witnesses to this
> For if you [i.e., Wahhābīs] say they have believed in the graves, // our land [Yemen] knows it not [i.e., this belief]
> And whosoever comes to a lowly worshipper // and claims to be the Lord of creation
> This is *kufr* which cannot be disguised, // nor can there be a defence or denial of this
> I am not against the destruction of a grave // if monkeys [i.e., believers in the dead] play beside it
> And they say the Lord of the grave accomplishes // for us needs, so delegations begin streaming to it [i.e., the grave] . . .
> Benefit us [O Wahhābīs], or else benefit [from us] // and revert back to us in what can be reverted to
> I [Shawkānī] have a book (*kitāb*) in this matter in which I said // something of worth which even the jealous wouldn't deny . . .
> The book of God is our model as are // the words of the Prophet, for they are both the pillar

76 Cf. Muḥammad b. Ismāᶜīl al-Amīr, *Risāla ḥawl madhhab Ibn ᶜAbd al-Wahhāb*, ms. Sanaa, Sharqiyya Library, *majmū*ᶜ no. 1; idem, *Irshād dhawī al-albāb ila ḥaqīqat aqwāl Muḥammad b. ᶜAbd al-Wahhāb*, ms. Sanaa, Gharbiyya Library, *majmū*ᶜ no. 107, fols. 131–42.

77 For the complete text of the poem, see Shawkānī, *Dīwān al-Shawkānī*, pp. 160–1, fn. 1.

> The guidance of the Companions is the best of all guidance // and the most distinguished, even if it is denied by him who denies
> So will you [Wahhābīs] turn back to this [the Qur'ān and Sunna]; // for if you do, we will thus return[78]

Shawkānī's Treatise

Shawkānī's treatise (*risāla*) on the issues of grave visitation and the unicity of God is entitled *Kitāb al-Durr al-naḍīd fī ikhlāṣ kalimat al-tawḥīd* (The Book of Well-Strung Pearls Rendering the Word on God's Unicity Exclusively to Him).[79] It was written in response to a question addressed to Shawkānī on 7 Rajab 1216/14 November 1801 by a fellow jurist and student, Qāḍī Muḥammad b. Aḥmad Mashḥam (d. 1223/1808),[80] who was then the imamate's judge in Hodeida, a port town on Yemen's Red Sea coast. The treatise takes the form of an extended *fatwā* that was intended to give the imamate's definitive position on the issue of grave visitation and its associated practices. The date of the treatise, as well as the contentious nature of the issues dealt therein, confirm that it was Wahhābī activity in the Tihāma which formed the setting against which this treatise was written. That Qāḍī Mashḥam should have queried the imamate's chief judge on the subjects of intercession and tomb visitation during his tenure in Hodeida illustrates that these were issues he, and the imamate, had to deal with at this juncture. Mashḥam was the imamate's judge in an important Shāfiᶜī town, where the veneration of saints and the practice of visiting the graves of pious people and saints thrived. This was a period of menacing Wahhābī influence, which fiercely contested such practices and sought to expand in ᶜAsīr and the Tihāma at the expense of the imamate. As such, this *fatwā*-treatise can be seen as a manifestation of the Qāsimī-Wahhābī polemic and competition over these regions during this period.

The *risāla*, as the title indicates, is dominated by the theme of *tawḥīd* (God's oneness or unicity) and the condemnation of all acts and beliefs which detract from this. These beliefs and practices, described in detail in the text, are invariably characterised as falling in the category of *shirk* (associating someone or something with God, or simply polytheism), the antithesis of *tawḥīd*. The subjects of Shawkānī's condemnation are a group of people whom he calls the *qubūriyyūn*, i.e., believers in the dead (*ahl al-qubūr*), who venerate dead saints by visiting their tombs and pursuing reprehensible acts while there. In condemning the *qubūriyyūn*, Shawkānī, like the Wahhābīs, repeatedly emphasises the dual nature of the condemnation: on

78 Shawkānī, *Dīwān al-Shawkānī*, pp. 161–4; cf. Nayl, II: 300–1. For a view that seeks to reconcile the differences between Shawkānī and the Wahhābī movement, see Ḥamad al-Jāsir, 'al-Imām Muḥammad b. ᶜAlī al-Shawkānī wa mawqifuhu min al-daᶜwa al-salafiyya al-iṣlāḥiyya', *al-Dirᶜiyya* 8 and 10 (2000), 9–16 and 13–19.

79 Muḥammad al-Shawkānī, 'Kitāb al-Durr al-naḍīd fī ikhlāṣ kalimat al-tawḥīd', in *al-Rasāʾil al-salafiyya* (Beirut: Dār al-Kutub al-ᶜIlmiyya, 1930), (hereinafter *al-Durr al-naḍīd*).

80 For Mashḥam's biography, see *Badr*, II: 116; *Nayl*, II: 235.

the one hand, he condemns their beliefs (*iʿtiqādāt*), and on the other their practices (*afʿāl*).

The question that Qādī Mashḥam addresses to Shawkānī is:

> [The query] is about using the dead and the living who are famous for excellence as a means of approaching God (*tawassul*), and the appeal to them for aid (*istighātha*) when needs arise; the query is also about the glorification (*taʿẓīm*) of their tombs and the belief (*iʿtiqād*) that they [the dead] have the power (*qudra*) to accomplish the needs (*ḥawāʾij*) and demands (*ṭalabāt*) of the needy. Furthermore, how is one to judge someone involved in such doings? And is it permissible to go to a tomb for the purposes of visiting (*ziyāra*) and invoking (*duʿāʾ*) God without appealing for aid (*istighātha*) from the dead, but only to use the dead as a means (*tawassul*) to God?[81]

Shawkānī begins by defining the terms *istighātha, istiʿāna, tashaffuʿ* and *tawassul*. These, he states, are all permissible practices in relation to the living in whatever humans are capable of accomplishing. The dead, however, may not be asked for aid or intercession. One can only beseech God by citing the good acts of the dead. In the next section of the treatise, Shawkānī asserts that the *umma* includes people who believe that the dead have powers, which in fact are reserved for God alone.

> The calamity of all calamities and the trial of all trials... is what many among the laymen (*ʿawāmm*) and some among the elite (*khawāṣṣ*) have come to believe about the dead (*ahl al-qubūr*) and about the living who are known for righteousness. A belief that the latter have the capacity to accomplish, and do accomplish, what is uniquely in God's prerogative. So that these folk begin to express with their tongues what their hearts have inclined to: at times they invoke them [the dead] with God and sometimes independently [without God]; they shout their names; they glorify them as if they had power over harm and benefit; and they submit (*khuḍūʿ*) to them more than they would to God when praying or invoking Him. If such is not *shirk* then we know not what is, and if this is not unbelief (*kufr*) then this world knows it not.[82]

Shawkānī goes on to say:

> ... the *qubūriyyūn* have made of some mortals associates and partners with God. They have asked from these mortals what can only be asked of God, and have sought aid in matters over which only God has sovereignty.[83]

According to Shawkānī the beliefs of the *qubūriyyūn* are the result of *taqlīd*. Shawkānī gives an account of how tomb visitation can become institutionalised as a result of 'the devil and a few charlatans' who deceive the common people into believing that the dead person can accomplish their needs. With the passing of centuries an unquestioned acceptance of such practices prevails, so that many in the *umma* can no longer recognise as valid the legitimate arguments, based on the Qurʾān and Sunna, which are conveyed in this treatise.[84] Hence, Shawkānī says, the *shirk* of the *qubūriyyūn* has gone unnoticed.

[81] *al-Durr al-naḍīd*, p. 2. [82] Ibid., pp. 7–8. [83] Ibid., p. 16. [84] Ibid., pp. 27–8.

Shawkānī recounts a contemporary story about a group of people from the north (*ahl jihāt al-qibla*) who, upon arriving at the dome over the tomb of Imam Aḥmad b. al-Ḥusayn[85] (d. 665/1267) in the town of Dhī Bīn, and seeing it all lit with candles and incense and draped with precious drapes, addressed the dead imam with the salutation: 'Good evening, O most merciful of all!'[86] The heinous nature of this salutation lies in the fact that the attribute 'most merciful of all' (*arḥam al-rāḥimīn*) is reserved exclusively for God. This story again illustrates Shawkānī's patrician disdain for the impiety of those outside the confines of the imamate's cities. In the same vein, he reports another contemporary account criticising the vows that rural people make to the dead:

> And we have heard that many from among a group of *ahl al-bādiya* who live in contiguity to Sanaa pledge an amount of money to the dead in whom they believe if a child is born to them. And he [i.e., a member of *ahl al-bādiya*] says that he has bought the child from that dead person for the pledged amount. If the child lives to the age of maturity (*sinn al-istiqlāl*), [then the father] pays the pledged amount to the swindler who has withdrawn to the grave of that dead man [i.e., the grave keeper] and who is concerned with gathering money.[87]

Shawkānī also criticises the cults surrounding the Sufi figures of Ibn ᶜAlwān (d. 665/1267, a famous saint buried in Yafrus near Taᶜizz), of Ibn ᶜUjayl (d. 690/1290, the saint of Bayt al-Faqīh) and of Aḥmad b. ᶜUmar al-Zaylaᶜī (d. 704/1305, a saint from al-Luḥayya). He asks rhetorically:

> And how much one hears in Yemen [as invocations and appeals to dead saints] with such calls as: O Ibn ᶜUjayl! O Zaylaᶜī! O Ibn ᶜAlwān![88]

Shawkānī, however, hastens to add that

> outside the Yemen it is even worse: every village has acquired for itself a dead saint who is invoked and appealed to, and even in the Holy sanctuary [in Mecca] one hears calls to Ibn ᶜAbbās.[89]

As for the judgement of the *qubūriyyūn*, Shawkānī states explicitly that the *qubūriyyūn* are in the same category as idolaters (*wathaniyyūn*). They are outlaws who have no right to life and wealth unless they accept the legal arguments (*al-ḥujja al-sharᶜiyya*) presented in this treatise; otherwise their fate is the sword

85 More information on this imam can be found in Muḥammad b. Aḥmad al-Ḥajrī, *Majmūᶜ buldān al-Yaman wa qabāʾiluhā* (Sanaa: Wizārat al-Iᶜlām waʾl-Thaqāfa, 1984), vol. I, p. 353. Also see the study of the inscriptions in this tomb-complex by Nahida Coussonnet and Solange Ory, *Inscriptions de la mosquée Dhi Bin au Yémen* (Sanaa: Centre Français d'Études Yéménites, 1996).

86 *al-Durr al-naḍīd*, p. 12. 87 Ibid., p. 36.

88 Ibid., p. 20. The biographies of Aḥmad b. ᶜAlwān, Aḥmad b. ᶜUjayl and Aḥmad al-Zaylaᶜī can be found in Aḥmad b. Aḥmad al-Sharjī, *Ṭabaqāt al-khawāṣ ahl al-ṣidq waʾl-ikhlāṣ* (Sanaa: Dār al-Yamaniyya liʾl-Nashr waʾl-Tawzīᶜ, 1986), pp. 69–71, 57–64, 74–7 respectively. For a study of Sufism in Yemen see Alxander Knysh, *Ibn ᶜArabi in the Later Islamic Tradition* (Albany: State University of New York Press, 1999), pp. 225–69 and ᶜAbd Allāh al-Ḥibshī, *al-Ṣūfiyya waʾl-fuqahāʾ fiʾl-Yaman* (Sanaa: Maktabat al-Jīl al-Jadīd, 1976).

89 *al-Durr al-naḍīd*, p. 20.

(*al-sayf*).[90] To reach this judgement, however, Shawkānī presents a long argument in which he attempts to show that the *qubūriyyūn* have failed to realise the principal purpose for which God sent the prophets and scriptures: 'To render exclusively to God His unicity (*ikhlāṣ al-tawḥīd*), and to render all worship exclusive to God (*ifrādihi biʾl-ʿibāda*)'.[91]

Although condemning grave visitation and all the practices associated with the cult of saints, Shawkānī concludes the treatise with an important injunction, allowing for the visitation of graves as long as a bad example is not set for the ignorant masses. The basic idea here is that a knowledgeable person knows when visiting a grave not to ask the dead person for favours; he visits in order to pray to God for the soul of the dead person or to beseech God through the good works of the dead. An ignorant person, on the other hand, might not realise the substance of what is taking place and, seeing only the form, he might think that one can pray to the dead rather than to God. In a concluding paragraph to the treatise, Shawkānī summarises his judgement of the three types of visitors who invoke God at grave sites:

> ... he who goes [to a tomb] only to visit (*ziyāra*), and while at the tomb invokes without setting a bad example for others to follow (*taghrīr*); this type of visitation is licit... He who goes to the tomb only with the intention of invoking, or to visit as well, while sharing the belief which we have presented [i.e., the belief of the *qubūriyyūn*] is in danger of falling into *shirk*, aside from already being disobedient. And if he does not share any belief in the dead [but still visits by following the example of others]... then he is a disobedient sinner (*'āṣin āthim*) and this is the least of his conditions...[92]

Although Shawkānī still considers the beliefs and practices of the *qubūriyyūn* reprehensible because they lead one into *shirk*, it is the incitement to *taqlīd* or its actual practice, which are deserving of the worst castigation. Tempering the central content of the text, which is a condemnation of all the beliefs and practices associated with the cult of saints, Shawkānī allows for the actual practice of visiting grave sites and invoking there, on condition that no incitement to imitation takes place, i.e., no *taqlīd*.

The Condemnation of the Cult of Saints: *tawḥīd* versus *shirk*

The condemnation of the cult of saints is a long standing feature of Wahhābī polemic taken up by Shawkānī in this *risāla*. In this polemic, the *qubūriyyūn* are said to represent all that is reprehensible in the cult of saints because their beliefs and practices with regard to the dead saint or his grave derogate from God's unicity, and as such the *qubūriyyūn* have become practising polytheists. The Wahhābī attack against the cult of saints also includes an attack on those who make the Prophet or any living person the object of a cult.[93] Both of these

[90] Ibid., p. 24. [91] Ibid., p. 17. [92] Ibid., p. 47.
[93] Cf. Laoust, *Essai sur les Doctrines*, p. 529.

are issues Shawkānī is concerned with, but they take a subsidiary role to the main issue which is a condemnation of those who visit the tombs of saints or people famous for righteousness. As the leading scholar of the imamate, it is noteworthy that Shawkānī should partake so fully in this Wahhābī discourse. The similar forms of argumentation which he uses in this *risāla* and his sources of inspiration show the degree to which he could use sources external to the Zaydī tradition – here the Ḥanbalī writings of Ibn Taymiyya. It is also noteworthy that Shawkānī, as chief judge of the imamate, could share many identical theological and jurisprudential sources and arguments with the Wahhābīs, when it is evident that the latter denigrated the Zaydī rite for never having been conclusively set or defined with enough rigour, as well as for containing heresies.[94]

In his attack on the cult of saints Muḥammad b. ᶜAbd al-Wahhāb incorporated Ibn Taymiyya's most characteristic ideas.[95] Ibn Taymiyya's influence on Shawkānī is far from negligible on this issue, as can be seen from the first pages of the *risāla* in which he defines the terms *tawassul*, *istighātha* and *istiᶜāna* using Ibn Taymiyya's *fatwās*. The content and conclusions of this first section are almost identical with what can be found in Ibn Taymiyya's works. For example, the polemic against Shaykh ᶜIzz al-Dīn b. ᶜAbd al-Salām (d. 660/1262) on whether *tawassul* through other than the Prophet is licit is included in Ibn Taymiyya's work to prove the same point: that *tawassul* through the good works of a saint or a scholar is licit since the invocation or demand is made through the good works (*aᶜmāl al-ṣāliha*) of that person and not directly to him.[96] To prove this Shawkānī uses the same ḥadīths as Ibn Taymiyya, e.g., the case when ᶜUmar sought the provision of rain (*istisqāʾ*) through al-ᶜAbbās. Furthermore, the definitions of *istighātha* and *istiᶜāna* as well as the conditions under which their practice is acceptable are similar in both works. Shawkānī also takes citations from Ibn Taymiyya's *fatwās* when quoting from Abū Yazīd al-Biṣṭāmī (d. 261/875) and Abū ᶜAbd Allāh al-Qarashī (d. 599/1203), both celebrated Islamic mystics who condemned the practice of *istighātha*.[97]

It is obvious from the *risāla* that Shawkānī shares the Wahhābī conception of *shirk*. This is most noticeable in the section in which the various forms of *shirk*

94 Cf. Laoust, *Essai sur les Doctrines*, p. 522 and Annexe 14, pp. 91–9; idem, *EI*², art. 'Ibn ᶜAbd al-Wahhāb', vol. III: 678, where Laoust mentions that the son of Muḥammad b. ᶜAbd al-Wahhāb, ᶜAbd Allāh, accompanied Saᶜūd b. ᶜAbd al-ᶜAzīz on his conquest of the Hijaz in 1803–5 CE, and wrote an important refutation of the doctrines of the Twelver Shīᶜites as well as those of the Zaydīs. This refutation was published in the *Majmūᶜat al-rasāʾil waʾl-masāʾil al-Najdiyya*, 4 vols. (Cairo: al-Manār Press, 1346/1928), vol. IV, pp. 47–222. Also see Sulaymān b. Saḥmān (ed.), *al-Hadiyya al-saniyya waʾl-tuḥfa al-Wahhābīyya al-Najdiyya* (Cairo: al-Manār Press, 1342/1923), p. 44.

95 Laoust, *Essai sur les Doctrines*, p. 519.

96 Aḥmad Ibn Taymiyya, *Majmūᶜ fatāwā Shaykh al-Islām Aḥmad b. Taymiyya*, ᶜAbd al-Rahman b. Muḥammad b. Qāsim (ed.), 27 vols. (Rabat: al-Maktab al-Taᶜlīmī al-Saᶜūdī biʾ-l-Maghrib, n.d.), vol. I, pp. 102–7, 309, 347; also ibid., *Iqtiḍāʾ al-ṣirāṭ al-mustaqīm mukhālafat aṣḥāb al-jaḥīm*, Aḥmad Ḥamadī (ed.) (Jedda: Maktabat al-Madanī, n.d.), pp. 408–12. Shawkānī cites this last work extensively in his treatise since Ibn Taymiyya treats the issue of the visitation of graves and the cult of saints in it, see especially pp. 328–413.

97 Cf. Ibn Taymiyya, *Majmūᶜ fatāwā*, vol. I, p. 106; *al-Durr al-naḍīd*, p. 4. It is interesting that Shawkānī, like Ibn Taymiyya, uses famous Sufis to condemn a popular Sufi practice like *istighātha*.

are enumerated and contrasted with the beliefs and practices of the *qubūriyyūn*. When, for example, Shawkānī explains that the *kufr* of the *qubūriyyūn* lies in their belief that a being can be an associate with God in the knowledge of the invisible or transcendental world (*ᶜālam al-ghayb*), he is in fact referring to what Wahhābī theorists have called *shirk al-ᶜilm*.[98] Another form of *shirk* which both Shawkānī and the Wahhābīs condemn is the dissimulation of piety (*riyāʾ*) in order to gain the plaudits or admiration of fellow Muslims, as 'it associates consideration for men with the thought of God'.[99] Other shared conceptions of *shirk* include: *shirk al-taṣarruf*, i.e., the assumption that anyone except God has power, e.g. intercession; *shirk al-ᶜibāda*, i.e., the revering of any created thing such as the tomb of a saint through circumambulation, offering sacrifices or money, vows, prayer at the grave; *shirk al-ᶜāda*, i.e., pre-Islamic beliefs which have persisted in Islam such as the belief in omens or the reliance on astrology, amulets and lithomancy; and finally, *shirk fi ʾal-adab*, i.e., swearing in the name of other than God, e.g. the Prophet, ᶜAlī or the saint.[100]

The concept of *tawḥīd* is central to Wahhābī doctrine. Members of the Wahhābī movement refer to themselves as *muwaḥḥidūn* (unitarians) not as Wahhābīs, an appellation given to them by their opponents that has become widely used in western scholarship.[101] The Wahhābī understanding of *tawḥīd* is derived from Ibn Taymiyya's thought and consists of two inseparable aspects relating to God's unicity: the unity of divine omnipotence (*tawḥīd al-rubūbiyya*), and the unity of the moral conscience of the believer who is concerned to serve God uniquely in the ways that God Himself has ordained through the medium of His Prophet (*tawḥīd al-ulūhiyya*). It is particularly because of the latter concept in Wahhābī doctrine that Wahhābism saw as its duty not only the restoration of the dogma of divine unity but also adopted a missionary zeal to accomplish God's Oneness in the realm of practice.[102]

In order to accomplish *tawḥīd al-rubūbiyya*, the Wahhābīs demand that one affirm God's omnipotence in such matters as 'creation (*khalq*), sustenance (*rizq*), giving life (*iḥyāʾ*) and death (*imāta*), provision of rain (*inzāl al-maṭar*), growth of vegetation (*inbāt al-nabāt*) and in the direction of all affairs (*tadbīr al-umūr*)'.[103] Ibn Taymiyya adds to this list that one must also affirm 'that God . . . is the provider (*al-muᶜṭi*) and the withholder (*al-māniᶜ*), the harmful (*al-ḍārr*) and the beneficent (*al-nāfiᶜ*) . . . '.[104] According to the Wahhābīs, however, to assert *tawḥīd al-rubūbiyya* on its own is not enough to make one a *muwaḥḥid* (i.e., a Muslim who

98 Cf. *EI*[1] art. 'Shirk' (Walther Bjorkman), vol. II, p. 380.

99 *al-Durr al-naḍīd*, p. 14 and Muḥammad b. ᶜAbd al-Wahhāb, *Kitāb al-Tawḥīd* (Beirut: al-Maktab al-Islāmī, 1408/1988), pp. 80–1.

100 For a discussion of these various types of *shirk* as understood by the Wahhābīs, see Ibn ᶜAbd al-Wahhāb, *Kitāb al-Tawḥīd*, pp. 32–46, 62–71.

101 *EI*[1], art. 'Wahhābīya' (D. S. Margoliouth), vol. IV, p. 1086.

102 Laoust, *Essai sur les Doctrines*, pp. 531–2; cf. Rentz, 'The Wahhābīs', pp. 270–2 .

103 Anonymous Wahhābī, *Anwāᶜ al-tawḥīd al-thalātha*, in ᶜAlī al-Rathānī (sponsor), *Majmūᶜat al-tawḥīd* (Damascus: al-Maktab al-Islāmī, 1381/1962), p. 79.

104 Ibn Taymiyya, *Majmūᶜ fatāwā*, vol. I, p. 92.

exclusively renders to God His unicity), for one also has to accomplish *tawḥīd al-ulūhiyya*. By this the Wahhābīs mean that worship (*ᶜibāda*), in all its forms, has to be directed to God, e.g., 'invocation (*duᶜāʾ*), fear (*khawf*), hope (*rajāʾ*), trust (*tawakkul*), repentance (*ināba*), wish (*raghba*), awe (*rahba*), vows (*nudhūr*) and seeking aid (*istiᶜāna*)'.[105] Failure to accomplish either of the two aspects of *tawḥīd*, by either giving potency or directing worship to other than God, would imply that one was taking partners with God (*andād*), and therefore partaking in *shirk*. This, of course, was the accusation the Wahhābīs leveled against the *qubūriyyūn*.

Shawkānī shares the Wahhābī conception of *tawḥīd*. Although he does not mention the terms *tawḥīd al-rubūbiyya* and *tawḥīd al-ulūhiyya* in the *risāla* except when quoting Ibn al-Amīr, it is evident that he means the same thing when he condemns the *qubūriyyūn* for failing to render God's unicity exclusively to Him (*ikhlāṣ al-tawḥīd*) and to render all worship exclusively to Him (*ifrādihi biʾl-ᶜibāda*). Shawkānī describes the failure to accomplish these two aspects of *tawḥīd* in the same terms that the Wahhābīs and Ibn Taymiyya use. For example, he states that in order to affirm *ikhlāṣ al-tawḥīd* and render all worship exclusive to God

> all invocation (*duᶜāʾ*), all cries (*nidāʾ*), all appeals for aid (*istighātha*), all hope (*rajāʾ*) and all summons for the good and the warding off of evil have to be directed to God and no one else.[106]

Furthermore, Shawkānī says that despite any verbal or outward confession by the *qubūriyyūn* that God is the sole creator (*khāliq*), sustainer (*rāziq*), giver of life (*muḥyi*) or death (*mumīt*), i.e., the accomplishment of *tawḥīd al-rubūbiyya*, they still partake in *shirk* by believing 'that God may have associates who have the power to benefit (*nafᶜ*), to harm (*ḍarr*), to bring one closer to God and to intercede on their behalf with Him'.[107] In short, *tawḥīd* for Shawkānī is not accomplished unless God's omnipotence is affirmed and all worship is rendered exclusively to Him. It was for these reasons, Shawkānī says, that the prophets and scriptures were sent to man. For him, as for the Wahhābīs, religion in its entirety belonged to God who had created man only to be served by him.[108]

The zeal with which the Wahhābīs attacked the practice of visiting the tombs of saints seems to have exceeded that of Ibn Taymiyya as well as that of Shawkānī. This is reflected in the intensity with which the Wahhābīs razed burial mounds, steles and domes over the graves of saints.[109] Ibn Taymiyya, for his part, did not consider the visitation of tombs to contradict the Sharīᶜa, and despite his

[105] *Anwāᶜ al-tawḥīd al-thalātha*, p. 79. For Ibn Taymīya's definition of the necessary requirement for fulfilling *tawḥīd al-ulūhiyya* and *tawḥīd al-rubūbiyya*, see Ibn Taymiyya, *Majmūᶜ fatāwā*, vol. I, p. 91.

[106] *al-Durr al-naḍīd*, p. 17. [107] Ibid., p. 17.

[108] Cf. Laoust, *Essai sur les Doctrines*, p. 532; *al-Durr al-naḍīd*, p. 17.

[109] Laoust, *Essai sur les Doctrines*, pp. 529–30.

attack on the cult of saints and the dead, he considered it highly recommendable when in proximity to a tomb to address God in favour of the dead person therein, as well as to visit the tombs of the Companions or those of the martyrs of the battle of Uḥud.[110] In this, and by contrast with the Wahhābīs, Shawkānī views are closer to those of Ibn Taymiyya. Shawkānī considered visitation, and even the practice of *tawassul* through the dead person's good works and virtuous characteristics, to be licit, on condition that no simple-minded person follow suit in imitation not knowing that it is through the dead person's works and virtues, not the person himself, that *tawassul* takes place.[111] Unlike Shawkānī, the Wahhābīs rejected *tawassul* and *istighātha* as ruses through which the practice of visiting tombs and an accompanying spirit of exaggeration (*ghulūw*) could persist, leading to polytheism.[112] A Wahhābī polemicist has this to say about *tawassul*:

> Whosoever invokes other than God, be [that invoked person] dead or absent, and implores his aid, is a polytheist and an infidel, even though all he seeks is to get nearer God, to demand the intercession [of the invoked person] with God. It is like this that many of the believers of this community have slid towards polytheism and were led to solicit other than God. They [who are in error] call this practice . . . *tawassul* and *tashaffuᶜ*. The change in the names [of the practice] makes no difference in the matter and does not change its legal status or its reality.[113]

Despite the similarities between Shawkānī's discourse against the cult of saints and that of the Wahhābīs, it appears the latter had a more simplistic view of the matters at hand. They did not share Shawkānī's more nuanced views. By allowing a person to visit a tomb, to invoke God at the grave site and to practise *tawassul* through the dead person's works and virtues, Shawkānī seems to have differed with Wahhābī doctrine and practice while still attacking the cult of saints in very similar terms. In so doing, Shawkānī was defending the imamate by showing that its position was similar to that of the Wahhābīs.

Soon after this treatise was written the imamate lost control over the Tihāma to the Sharīfs of Abū ᶜArīsh who ruled in the name of Ibn Saᶜūd. It therefore appears that Shawkānī's treatise resulted in no practical measures being taken on the basis of its rulings, except the destruction of some domes and raised tombs in and around Sanaa and Dhamār.[114] However, it provides an example of the leading judge of the Zaydī imamate partaking in a discourse which would normally be categorised as falling in the Ḥanbalī tradition. One can see how easily Shawkānī could respond to the Wahhābī doctrinal polemic by using their terms without compromising himself. When Shawkānī encountered the Wahhābīs espousing the

[110] Ibn Taymiyya, *Iqtiḍāʾ al-ṣirāṭ al-mustaqīm*, pp. 335–6; Laoust, *Essai sur les Doctrines*, pp. 334–5, 353.
[111] *al-Durr al-naḍīd*, p. 47. [112] Cf. Sulaymān b. Saḥmān (ed.), *al-Hadiyya al-saniyya*, pp. 47–8.
[113] Sulaymān b. Saḥmān (ed.), *al-Hadiyya al-saniyya*, p. 93; cf. *Majmūᶜat al-rasāʾil waʾl-masāʾil al-Najdiyya*, 4 vols. (Cairo: al-Manār Press, 1346/1928), vol. II, section III, p. 63.
[114] *Badr*, I: 262–3.

ideas and drawing on the works of Ḥanbalī scholars, it was not alien concepts and sources he was encountering, but ones he felt were already part of his own tradition. By contrast, the polemics he waged against the strict Zaydīs involved a clash with a tradition he had rejected. The debate regarding the status of the Prophet's Companions brings this out in sharp relief, and it is to this question that we turn next.

CHAPTER 5

Clashing with the Zaydīs: the Question of Cursing the Prophet's Companions (*sabb al-ṣaḥāba*)[1]

> Shīᶜism in the people of our generation is confined to these reprehensible innovations: enmity to the Sunna, defaming the ancestors, combining [prayers] and abandoning the Friday congregational prayers. Muḥammad b. ᶜAlī al-Shawkānī
>
> Curse Abū Bakr the tyrant, his second and the filthy third, ᶜUthmān b. ᶜAffān; All three have a place in hell below that of Pharaoh and Hāmān; O God, curse them and those who favour them and do not accord them any reward on judgement day; they superseded the brother of the best of Messengers and unjustly and aggressively usurped what belonged to his daughter. al-Ḥasan b. ᶜAlī al-Habal[2]

No issue raises the spectre of the Sunnī–Shīᶜī divide, and more specifically the Zaydī–Traditionist one, more than that of the cursing the Companions of the Prophet. It continues to occupy Yemenis today. A contemporary request for a *fatwā* in Yemen, for example, asked 'What is the position of the scholars of Islam about those who curse the Companions of the Messenger of God – may His blessings and Peace be upon him – and the Rightly Guided Caliphs? Inform us'.[3] Predictably, as religious discourse in republican Yemen is dominated by Shawkānī's Traditionist views, the answer was a resounding denunciation, and went on to say that all the Companions had to be respected and accepted for their high moral worth; were cursing to be allowed, the *muftī* says, the whole edifice of the Sharīᶜa

[1] A number of studies in European languages on attitudes to the Companions are worthy of note and are listed here. For the Imāmī position, see Etan Kohlberg, 'The Attitude of the Imāmī-Shīᶜīs to the Companions of the Prophet', D.Phil. thesis, University of Oxford (1971). Chapter one deals with the Sunnī position whereas chapter two discusses that of the Muᶜtazila. Also see Kohlberg, 'Some Imāmī Shīᶜī views on the Ṣaḥābā', *JSAI* 5 (1984), 143–75. For the Sunnī position, see Albert Arazi, 'Ilqām al-ḥajar li-man zakkā sābb abī bakr wa-ᶜumar dʾal-suyūṭī', *JSAI* 10 (1987), 211–87; and Lutz Wiederhold, 'Blasphemy against the Prophet Muḥammad and his Companions (*Sabb al-Rasūl, Sabb al-Ṣaḥābah*): the introduction of the topic into Shāfiᶜī legal literature and its relevance for legal practice under Mamluk rule', *Journal of Semitic Studies* 42.1 (1997), 39–70. For the Zaydī position, see Etan Kohlberg, 'Some Zaydī views on the Companions of the Prophet', *BSOAS* 39.1 (1976), 91–8.

[2] The first poem is by Shawkānī and can be found in *Adab al-ṭalab*, p. 62. The second poem is by al-Ḥasan al-Habal (d. 1079/1668), a strict Zaydī of the seventeenth century, and is quoted in *Hijar al-ᶜilm*, I: 239.

[3] ᶜIzz al-Dīn Ḥasan Taqī (ed.), *Kitāb al-Fatāwā al-sharᶜiyya waʾl-ᶜilmiyya waʾl-dīniyya li-ᶜulamāʾ al-diyār al-Yamaniyya* (Sanaa: Maktabat al-Irshād, n.d.), pp. 406–9.

would collapse. It is not surprising that the next question (*istiftā*ʾ) in the book cited was whether the Zaydī *madhhab* was to be considered the most correct when compared to the four Sunnī schools, or were the latter better and more complete. Again, the answer is consistent with prevailing 1990s views: the Zaydī school is, on the whole, identical with the Sunnī schools, and in particular the Ḥanafī; unlike the others, it kept the 'door of *ijtihād*' open, allowing 'freedom of opinion from the [constraints] of *taqlīd* and the use of proof texts'. The *muftī* then lists the greatest Yemeni scholars who exemplified this: Ibn al-Wazīr (the renewer of the ninth century AH), al-Maqbalī (the renewer of the eleventh century AH), Ibn al-Amīr (the renewer of the twelfth century AH) and finally Shawkānī (the renewer of the thirteenth century AH).[4] The *muftī* makes several conscious oversights in both *fatwās*. The Hādawī tradition, which differed considerably from the Sunnī schools on points of theology and law, is completely ignored despite being dominant in Yemeni Zaydism. Rather, Shawkānī and his Traditionist forebears are taken to represent 'true' Zaydism, when in fact they had levelled the most severe criticism at the school in their writings. For the *muftī*, Zaydism is on a par with Sunnism and, as in it, all Companions are to be honoured. The traditional teaching, however, on the status of the Companions in Zaydism is more complicated and problematic than the *muftī* would admit.

Traditionists forbid the belittling of the Companions of the Prophet and insist on the principle that all Companions were righteous persons of moral probity (*ᶜudūl*). In the same vein, Shawkānī insisted in all his works on the probity (*ᶜadāla*) of all the Companions, who were the first transmitters of the ḥadīths of the Prophet. Any derogation from their status would lead, in his estimation, to undermining the canonical corpus of ḥadīths, hence the Sunna, and ultimately the Sharīᶜa.

The attitude one adopted towards the Companions, especially in the charged atmosphere of Yemen in the late eighteenth and early nineteenth century, when Traditionists vied with Zaydī-Hādawīs over proper belief and legal practice, raised a series of related issues. The first and perhaps most important has to do with their *ᶜadāla*. Are they to be regarded as having all shared in this quality, or is the probity of some of them to be questioned and therefore also their standing as upright Muslims? Underlying this first question is the thorny issue of the right of succession to the Prophet. Zaydīs universally claimed ᶜAlī's superiority over the other Companions and his right to succeed on the basis of the Prophet's implied designation, but were not agreed about the probity of those who had sided against him. Traditionists, like Sunnīs generally, ranked ᶜAlī fourth, reflecting the historical order of his rule as Caliph, and refrained from discussing the conflicts which arose amongst the Companions. The stance one took on the disputes between ᶜAlī and the other Companions was crucial to the issue at hand. The centrality and importance of ᶜAlī, and consequently the position accorded to Abū Bakr, ᶜUmar and ᶜUthmān, who had at first taken ᶜAlī's place, in all the debates described here cannot be overstated. Second is the question of which Companions are to be considered

[4] Taqī, *Kitāb al-Fatāwā al-sharᶜiyya*, pp. 409–12.

valid transmitters of the Prophet's sayings, since without probity, a Companion may not be considered a reliable transmitter, just as a witness lacking this quality may not provide testimony in court. Third is the question of whether the Companions are to be considered legal authorities in their own right. Finally, there is the issue of the proper attitude and etiquette one should have towards the Companions, both collectively and individually. What formula of blessing should one utter after a Companion's name? Is it ever allowed to curse a Companion? And what is the punishment for a person wrongfully cursing the Companions or a Companion?

This chapter will present the various opinions Zaydīs adopted on the issues pertaining to the Companions as well as Shawkānī's views on these matters. Shawkānī wrote an important treatise about this question of cursing which will be analysed here as well. As in his other writings, Shawkānī was attempting to place the stamp of orthodoxy on his views while condemning as heretics those with whom he disagreed. This led to dramatic political and doctrinal reactions, which will be presented in the following chapter.

Shawkānī and the Companions

Differences exist among Muslim jurists over the definition of a Companion of the Prophet. Some, like Shawkānī, adopted a very broad and inclusive definition whilst others insisted on restrictive conditions, e.g., a certain length of time spent in the Prophet's company, that they actually saw him, and that they were of mature age while in his company. Shawkānī cites approvingly what he considers to be the majority opinion (*al-jumhūr*), which defines a Companion as anyone who as a believer met the Prophet at least once even for a short time.[5] Shawkānī also sees the Companions, much as the Ḥanbalīs did, as all sharing in the quality of excellence, and he insists that one should refrain from mentioning derogatory statements about them and from delving into their disagreements. He held that both God and the Prophet had accorded all the Companions the status of *ᶜadāla*, relying on Qurʾānic verses such as 'you are the best nation ever brought forth to men' (III: 110); 'Thus we appointed you a midmost nation' (II: 143); and 'and those who are with him are hard against the unbelievers, merciful one to another' (XLVIII: 29).[6] From the ḥadīth, he cites the most oft quoted ones in praise of the Companions and which are found in the canonical Sunnī collections, e.g., 'the most excellent [persons] are my generation, then the following [generation], then the following [generation]'; 'do not defame my Companions; for even if one of you were to spend [an amount of] gold equal in size to Mount Uḥud, this would not bring him the reward they

5 *Irshād al-fuḥūl*, pp. 62–3; cf. Goldziher, *Muslim Studies*, vol. II, p. 222.

6 Muḥammad al-Shawkānī, *al-ᶜAdhb al-namīr fī jawāb masāʾil ᶜālim bilād ᶜAsīr*, in *Kitāb al-Fatḥ al-rabbānī min fatāwā al-imām al-Shawkānī* (Sanaa: al-Maᶜhad al-ᶜĀlī liʾl-Qaḍāʾ, n.d.), pp. 82–3. Shawkānī also quotes the following Qurʾānic verses: II: 143 and XLVIII: 18. Also see *Irshād al-fuḥūl*, pp. 61–2 and Muḥammad al-Shawkānī, *al-Qawl al-maqbūl fī radd khabar al-majhūl min ghayr ṣaḥābat al-rasul*, ms. photocopy Maᶜhad al-ᶜĀlī liʾl-Qaḍāʾin Sanaa, fols. 27a–29a.

are given for spending the price of a bushel of wheat – or even their reward for spending the price of half a bushel'; 'I commend to you my Companions, then those who follow them and those who follow them, after which lying will spread'; and 'My Companions are like lodestars; by imitating anyone among them you will find the right path'.[7]

By adopting the broadest definition of Companionship and insisting on the universal probity of the Companions, Shawkānī was trying to bolster the claim of authority for the Sunnī ḥadīth collections, on which his epistemology and legal/theological views were primarily based. Shawkānī thus asserted that accepting the probity of all the Companions required acceptance of their transmission (*riwāya*) and abstention from probing into their status. This acceptance is based on their truthful speech and their being safeguarded against lying. On the basis of the aforementioned Traditions, he says that the Companions and the two generations of Muslims after them did not lie, and the least they deserve is the status of *ᶜadāla* in view of their numerous virtues attested in sound proof-texts.[8] Their own role as purveyors and preservers of the Prophetic Traditions was important.

> For me [i.e., Shawkānī], and for any just person, the truth lies in accepting and using the transmission (*riwāya*) from anyone who has been proven to be a Companion. The Prophet of God – may God's peace and blessings be upon him – has accorded them probity (*ᶜaddalahum*) when he said: 'The most excellent [persons] are my generation'.[9] [Regarding] the conflicts which arose between them, even if it is possible to know the correct party through proof-texts (*adilla*), the incorrect party is still bestowed with the merit of Companionship (*ṣuḥba*). Taken generally, the explicit proof-texts (*ᶜumūm al-adilla al-nāṭiqa*) protect them (*yadfaᶜ ᶜanhum*) from the errors [they may have] committed. . . . Extolling them, acknowledging their importance and the loftiness of their rank over all other generations is the concern of every Muslim who glorifies the Sharīᶜa and prophethood. To endeavour [in highlighting] their defects and faults, which attach to them through lies and slander, is the concern of every forsaken person.[10]

Shawkānī admits here that some of the Companions may have committed errors and were not infallible, and that it was possible, in some cases, to know which Companion's opinion was correct by examining the proof-texts for that opinion. This conforms with his textualist approach, which posits the texts of the Qurʾān and the canonical ḥadīth collections as the ultimate references for truth which any *mujtahid* can consult and verify. But Shawkānī also insists that it is wrong to delve into the Companions' differences for this would lead to undermining the Sharīᶜa. This implied that a Muslim must not discuss the matter of ᶜAlī's alleged superiority over the other Companions or his right to succeed the Prophet

7 For the last ḥadīth, see Khaṭīb al-Tibrīzī, *Mishkāt al-maṣābīḥ*, Muḥammad al-Albānī (ed.), 3 vols. (Damascus: al-Maktab al-Islāmī, 1961), vol. III, p. 219.
8 Shawkānī, *al-ᶜAdhb al-namīr*, p. 83.
9 Implicit in this Tradition is the notion that decline will set in with time and that the most pristine period was that of the Prophet's lifetime. Whilst admitting to this, Shawkānī also posits a countervailing argument, claiming that *mujtahids* can have the status of Companions in that they can interpret the core texts of the Qurʾān and Sunna in an unmediated fashion, as was pointed out in chapter three.
10 Shawkānī, *Wabl al-ghamām*, vol. I, p. 26.

in leading the community, both central tenets of Zaydī dogma. Thus, he says about the question of the succession:

> Each of the Rightly Guided Caliphs did his utmost for the benefit of Muslims . . . and if one of them committed what appears to be a mistake then his noble status demands that he be considered in the best possible light. God – the exalted – has generally accorded the people of that generation the highest moral status and so has the Messenger . . . We worship God according to the obligations in the Sharīᶜa . . . and it is not incumbent on us to know that a person was the Caliph at time x or that y was not the Caliph at time z. All will be judged by God Who will show who was right and who was wrong. We must not delve into the matters of those who are long gone.[11]

According to Shawkānī, not even the conflict that arose between ᶜAlī and Muᶜāwiya should be discussed by a believing Muslim. In this regard, a slight distinction must be drawn between Shawkānī's early opinion and the one he adopted in later life. In his early writings, he took the position that ᶜAlī had been designated by the Prophet as a legatee (*waṣī*), and that Muᶜāwiya had been at fault in his conflict with ᶜAlī. His later writings do not accord ᶜAlī a pre-eminent place amongst the Companions, and, in this regard, he becomes indistinguishable from Sunnī authors. The difference between his two views reflects Shawkānī's development from a Zaydī-educated scholar acting in a Zaydī environment to a mature scholar with wider claims and an awareness of the larger Sunnī world. It also shows how Shawkānī's opinions, as he became an established figure in the state structures of the imamate, grew more distinctly Traditionist and anti-Hādawī.

The Early and Mature Shawkānī on ᶜAlī and Muᶜāwiya

On the 3 May 1791, when Shawkānī was slightly over thirty years old and recognised to have become a *mujtahid*, he completed a treatise entitled *al-ᶜIqd al-thamīn fī ithbāt wiṣāyat amīr al-muʾminīn* (The Precious Necklace Proving the Legateeship of the Commander of the Faithful).[12] The treatise is a response to a question put to him by *sayyid*s of the Tihāmī town of Zabīd, about the Tradition in which ᶜĀʾisha, the Prophet's wife, denies that the Prophet had designated ᶜAlī as his *waṣī*.[13] The *sayyid*s in question are not mentioned by name. They were certainly Sunnīs, given their home town, and most likely were members of the Ahdal family with whom Shawkānī maintained a lively correspondence. Coming from Sunnī *sayyid*s, the question was probably not unmotivated, since it goes to the heart of the Zaydī, and more generally Shīᶜī, claim about ᶜAlī's right to succeed the Prophet. At the time, Shawkānī was the rising scholarly star in Sanaa, and the question was

[11] Ibid., vol. III, p. 496.

[12] This work was published in 1990 in Sanaa by Maktabat Dār al-Turāth, a pro-Zaydī publishing house.

[13] Cf. Muslim, *Ṣaḥīḥ*, *Waṣiyya*, 19: 'They mentioned to ᶜĀʾisha that ᶜĀlī – may God be pleased with them – was the legatee. She said: "when did he designate him as such? I was holding him against my chest – or she said my lap – and he asked for the washbowl and went limp in my lap and I did not feel him pass away. So when did he designate him?" '

perhaps intended as a test of his adherence to Zaydī teachings, and, more generally, an attempt to gauge the pro-Sunnī scholarly climate in Sanaa. The Zabīdī *sayyids* were not to be disappointed with the answer they received.

Shawkānī's response, in three parts, avoids the thorny issue of ᶜAlī's succession right. In the first section he disputes ᶜĀʾisha's denial on both jurisprudential and personal grounds. He argues that the saying of Companions, of whom she was one, does not constitute legal proof (*ḥujja*), that according to *uṣūl al-fiqh* an affirmative statement (*muthabbit*) takes precedence over a negating one (*al-nāfy*), and that ᶜĀʾisha was known to be hasty in rejecting whatever contradicted her own opinion.[14] To this point, Shawkānī would seem to be defending the Zaydī position. In the second section, Shawkānī quotes an impressive number of Traditions proving that the Prophet had made a number of unconditional testamentary recommendations (*waṣāyā muṭlaqa*) to his community, such as the 'offering of *zakāt* after prayers', and 'that no two religions should remain in the Arabian Peninsula'. In the last section, Shawkānī cites Traditions in which the Prophet makes specific mention of ᶜAlī as his legatee. For example, he cites a Tradition, which he claims is in Aḥmad b. Ḥanbal's *Musnad*, in which the Prophet says: 'my legatee (*waṣiyyī*), my heir and the one who will accomplish my promise is ᶜAlī b. Abī Ṭālib'. This Tradition is not to be found in Aḥmad's collection. In fact many of the Traditions quoted by Shawkānī here are among those which in his later work – particularly in his *al-Fawāʾid al-majmūᶜa fī ʾal-aḥādīth al-mawḍūᶜa* (The Sum of Beneficial Things about the False Traditions) – he claimed were false and did not constitute valid proof-texts.[15]

In concluding the treatise Shawkānī explains that

> it is incumbent upon us to believe that [ᶜAlī] – peace be upon him – is the legatee of the Prophet – may God's peace and blessings be upon him and his family – [but] it is not necessary for us to engage in the details of the legateeship . . . we do not engage in giving preference (*tafḍīl*) [to one Companion over another], but the Prophet said that he was his legatee, so we say that he is his legatee . . .[16]

[14] Muḥammad al-Shawkānī, *al-ᶜIqd al-thamīn fī ithbāt wiṣāyat amīr al-muʾminīn* (Sanaa: Maktabat Dār al-Turāth, 1990), pp. 8–9. For the sake of brevity, some of Shawkānī's arguments are omitted here.

[15] Cf. Muḥammad al-Shawkānī, *al-Fawāʾid al-majmūᶜa fī ʾl-aḥādīth al-mawḍūᶜa* (Beirut: Dār al-Kitāb al-ᶜArabī, 1986), pp. 367–402.

[16] Shawkānī, *al-ᶜIqd al-thamīn*, pp. 18–19. Shawkānī's intellectual forebear, Ibn al-Amīr, wrote a work in praise of ᶜAlī, entitled *al-Rawḍa al-nadiyya fī sharḥ al-tuḥfa al-ᶜalawiyya*, in which he discusses the same ḥadīth and reaches the same conclusion as Shawkānī, namely that one should not delve into the details of ᶜAlī's legateeship; cf. Muḥammad b. Ismāᶜīl al-Amīr, *al-Rawḍa al-nadiyya* (n.p.: al-Maktaba al-Islāmiyya, n.d.), pp. 96–7. This work was originally published in Sanaa in 1371/1952 by the Ministry of Education (*Wizārat al-Maᶜārif*), during the reign of Imam Aḥmad Ḥamīd al-Dīn. The intention behind its publication was probably to show the love that Traditionist scholars like Ibn al-Amīr had for ᶜAlī and the Prophet's family and to affirm the special status the latter enjoyed in Islamic history. A *fatwā* is appended to the edition of the *Rawḍa* (quoted above, p. 264), which explains the Yemeni practice of referring to the descendants of al-Ḥasan and al-Ḥusayn as *sayyids*. This practice, the *fatwā* explains, is followed merely as a sign of love and respect for the Prophet.

Shawkānī thus avoided the issue of whether or not ᶜAlī was designated by the Prophet as his successor by taking the term *waṣī* to mean testamentary legatee in a specific matter, like his command to ᶜAlī to fight the 'violators, the unjust and the heretics', or that ᶜAlī should bathe him after he died. However, it is important to note that Shawkānī accepted ᶜAlī to be a *waṣī* on the basis of weak Traditions. Also notable is his dismissal (considered sound by Sunnīs because it is reported in the *Ṣaḥīḥayn* of Bukhārī and Muslim of ᶜĀʾisha's ḥadīth).

Concerning the conflict between Muᶜāwiya and ᶜAlī, only one reference in Shawkānī's works can be found in which he explicitly takes the side of ᶜAlī. Again this is from one of his earlier works, the well known compendium of ḥadīth-based legal rulings entitled *Nayl al-awṭār*, written at his teachers' behest and completed in 1210/1795.[17] Shawkānī there quotes the Tradition found in Muslim's *Ṣaḥīḥ* in which the Prophet states: 'My community will consist of two factions; a heretical faction will emerge out of one of these, after which they will be killed, and the first of the two is just'.[18] Shawkānī observes:

> The statement 'the first of the two is just' contains an indication that ᶜAlī and his partisans were in the right (*al-muḥiqqūn*), and that Muᶜāwiya and his partisans were in the wrong (*al-mubṭilūn*). This is a matter that no fair person would doubt and only a presumptuous deviant would reject. There is sufficient evidence of this in this Tradition.[19]

In his later works, Shawkānī departed from this opinion and adopted a position of neutrality (*imsāk*, lit. refraining from taking sides) in regard to the conflict between Muᶜāwiya and ᶜAlī, and he accorded ᶜAlī the same rank of precedence as given to him by Sunnīs, namely, the fourth in chronological order of succession to the caliphate. Ibn Ḥanbal, and Ḥanbalīs generally, adopted the position of *imsāk* regarding the conflicts between Companions, and specifically the one between ᶜAlī and Muᶜāwiya.[20] In a *fatwā*-treatise written in Shawwāl 1222/December 1807, Shawkānī responded to a set of questions posed to him by a pro-Wahhābī scholar, Shaykh Muḥammad b. Aḥmad al-Ḥafẓī of ᶜAsīr,[21] one of which was about the conflict between ᶜAlī and Muᶜāwiya. Shawkānī responded as follows:

> Refraining from discussion of this matter (*al-imsāk ᶜan al-kalām*) is best... the sayings of the factions in this matter are known, 'each party rejoicing in what they believe'... (XXIII: 53). Those who gave allegiance to ᶜAlī were the same as those who had given it to Abū Bakr and ᶜUmar, [whereas] those who did not give it to him did so without legal proof (*ḥujja sharᶜiyya*)... and it has been attested in the *Ṣaḥīḥ* [of Bukhārī] that the Prophet – may God's peace and mercy be upon him – said about al-Ḥasan [his grandson from ᶜAlī]: 'My son here is a lord (*sayyid*) and through him God will make peace between two great Muslim factions'. To sum up, no benefit can result from prolixity in this matter. Each [side] has presented what they had to say, and God does not oblige us

[17] Cf. *Badr*, II: 214. [18] Muslim, *Ṣaḥīḥ*, *Zakāt*, 151.

[19] Shawkānī, *Nayl al-awṭār*, vol. IV, section 7, p. 348. Ibn al-Amīr adopts the same opinion in his *al-Rawḍa al-nadiyya*, see p. 76.

[20] Cf. Kohlberg, 'The Attitude of the Imāmī-Shīᶜīs', p. 8.

[21] For his biography see *Nayl*, II: 225–6.

> to accept any of it; rather, he has advised us by what he said in his great Book: 'And as for those who came after them, they say, "Our Lord, forgive us and our brothers, who preceded us in belief, and put Thou not into our hearts any rancour towards those who believe" ' (LIX: 10). God forgives a man who says good things and [then] falls silent.[22]

In yet another *fatwā*-treatise, in which he was asked about the Tradition in which the Prophet says: 'I am the city of knowledge and ᶜAlī is its door', Shawkānī denies that ᶜAlī is the sole transmitter of religious knowledge to the exclusion of the other Companions; rather, he says, they are all transmitters. He then specifies that the 'knowledge' to which the Prophet referred to was ᶜAlī's ability to predict future events, as attested by numerous Traditions, some of which he then quotes. In the final lines of the treatise Shawkānī states that he did not probe into the issue of the soundness of the Tradition although he doubts its authenticity and considers it to be weak (*ḍaᶜīf*).[23] In one of his later works entitled *Darr al-saḥabā fī manāqib al-qarāba waʾl-ṣaḥāba* (The Copious Flow of the Cloud Regarding the Virtues of the Prophet's Relatives and Companions, completed on 13 Jumādā al-Ūlā 1241/23 December 1825), Shawkānī ranks the Companions according to precedence and enumerates the Traditions in praise of each one under his or her name. His ranking is consistent with Sunnī doctrine, which ranks the caliphs according to the historical order in which they ruled. As the title of the work suggests, however, Shawkānī was attempting to appease the Ahl al-Bayt by according them in his classification a place second only to that of the ten Companions who were promised by the Prophet a place in paradise (*al-ᶜashara al-mubashsharūn*), and also by not giving Muᶜāwiya any place at all in the work. Ultimately, however, this did not bridge the gap between the two sides because the Shīᶜite position is based squarely on ᶜAlī's and his family's excellence.

The Companions as *mujtahid*s

A final point about Shawkānī's views on the Companions must be raised before examining the possible reasons for the difference between his young and mature views. In order to exonerate the Companions from the guilt of error (e.g., not choosing ᶜAlī over Abū Bakr), Ashᶜarīs, among others, held that the Companions were *mujtahid*s. The basis for this claim was the Tradition, 'If a *mujtahid* arrives at a correct opinion he will receive two rewards in the world to come whereas if he

22 Shawkānī, *al-ᶜAdhb al-namīr*, p. 82. For similar statements by Shawkānī, see his other treatise in the same collection entitled *Irshād al-sāʾil ilā dalīl al-masāʾil* where he reiterates that it is best not to probe into the disputes of the Companions. He maintains, however, that those who fought ᶜAlī were to be considered rebels (*bughāt*), and that he was in the right and they were in the wrong. Muᶜāwiya is not mentioned here, and Shawkānī explicitly states that 'only an inquisitive person, who has no concern for his religion, would go beyond this limit'. Cf. Shawkānī, *Kitāb al-Fatḥ al-rabbānī*, pp. 322–3.

23 Muḥammad al-Shawkānī, *Baḥth fī ḥadīth anā madīnat al-ᶜilm wa ᶜAlī bābuhā* in *Kitāb al-Fatḥ al-rabbānī*, pp. 207–13. For his criticism of this Tradition, see his *Darr al-ṣaḥāba*, p. 203 and his *al-Fawāʾid al-majmūᶜa fī ʾal-aḥādīth al-mawḍūᶜa*, pp. 373–4.

errs he will receive one reward'.[24] Shawkānī upholds this position. In a passage in his *Irshād al-fuḥūl*, he cites approvingly the opinion that some of the Companions were *mujtahids* and that this exonerated them from any guilt for the wars among them.[25] It must be noted, however, that he did not believe that each and every one of the Companions was a *mujtahid*, because he states that the less learned ones asked those who were *mujtahids* and knew the texts for an opinion on a given matter.[26] On this hinges, in part at least, his argument that the opinion of a Companion was not necessarily authoritative and that it was necessary to consult the proof-texts in order to ascertain its validity.

Accounting for the Difference in Shawkānī's works regarding ᶜAlī and Muᶜāwiya

ᶜAbd Allāh Nūmsūk, an Indonesian-born graduate of the Islamic University in Medina who has written a voluminous work on Shawkānī's credal thought, claims that his increased knowledge of the ḥadīth sciences in later life led him to realise the error of his earlier opinions in the matter of ᶜAlī versus Muᶜāwiya, as these were based on weak Traditions in favour of ᶜAlī.[27] Nūmsūk, like a number of recent Saudi graduates who have worked on Shawkānī, has tried to graft him onto the Salafī-Wahhābī tradition and finds it embarrassing whenever one of his opinions does not conform with the latter.

Whilst the argument that Shawkānī's knowledge increased with age cannot be denied, he was none the less thirty years old in 1205 AH when he wrote *al-ᶜIqd al-thamīn*, and thirty-five when he finished *Nayl al-awṭār* in 1210 AH, and by his own admission had attained the rank of *mujtahid* before thirty. To argue, therefore, that he did not know the difference between various degrees of ḥadīths is unfounded. Rather, it might appear that the Zaydī imprint left by his early education was more evident in his youth than in his mature years. This explanation finds support in a cursory reading of *Nayl al-awṭār*, where Shawkānī regularly presents the legal opinions of Zaydī imams on nearly all the issues covered in the work. In *Nayl al-awṭār*, Zaydī opinions still mattered; but this may be because he was requested to write it by his teachers, who were mainly Zaydī. It was also intended as an educational work, which had to be comprehensive and attest to his having become a full-fledged *mujtahid* with knowledge of all the schools. There is yet another answer, which may provide a better explanation: As Shawkānī became a powerful figure in the state – after his appointment as *qāḍī al-quḍāt* – he became bolder and more forthright in his anti-Hādawī opinions. From his earliest days, Shawkānī displayed pro-Sunnī and Traditionist tendencies, but it was not until he felt safe

24 Cf. Kohlberg, 'The Attitude of the Imāmī-Shīᶜīs', pp. 10–11; Joseph Schacht, *The Origins of Muhammadan Jurisprudence*, (Oxford University Press, 1950), p. 96.

25 *Irshad al-fuḥūl*, p. 61.

26 Ibid., p. 237.

27 'Abd Allāh Nūmsūk, *Manhaj al-imām al-Shawkānī fī 'l-ᶜaqīda*, (Riyadh: Maktabat Dār al-Qalam, 1994), pp. 129, 855.

from attack by the Hādawīs that he conspicuously did so. This would explain his initial manipulation of the issue of ᶜAlī and the *waṣiyya* as well as his condemnation of Muᶜāwiya; these can be seen in light of his efforts to stave off Hādawīs from attacking him. His assumption of the chief judgeship was a watershed in that it accorded him the protection he needed.

Shawkānī's Condemnation of the *Rāfiḍa*

In *Adab al-ṭalab* and *al-Badr al-ṭāliᶜ* Shawkānī presents himself as a victim of attack and persecution by strict Hādawīs, those he calls the *Rāfiḍa*.[28] These were people whose love for ᶜAlī and the Ahl al-Bayt was in his view so excessive that they rejected the caliphates of Abū Bakr and ᶜUmar and cursed them and all those Companions who had sided against ᶜAlī. As we shall see, the Zaydīs in Yemen held a variety of opinions on the subject of the Companions who had opposed ᶜAlī: some were generally approving whilst others maintained a rejectionist attitude; all claimed, however, to represent 'true' Zaydism. In the seventeenth century, the most notable examples of the rejectionist Hādawīs were Imam al-Mahdī Aḥmad b. al-Ḥasan (d. 1096/1685) and a number of his retainers, among them al-Ḥasan b. ᶜAlī al-Habal (d. 1079/1668). In Shawkānī's time, men with a similar attitude included (suprisingly) the minister ᶜAlī b. Ḥasan al-Akwaᶜ (d. 1206/1791), and, most notably, Ismāᶜīl b. ᶜIzz al-Dīn al-Nuᶜmī (d. 1220/1805) and Muḥammad b. Ṣāliḥ al-Samāwī (d. 1241/1825). The main difference between al-Mahdī Aḥmad's time in the seventeenth century and that of the late eighteenth century was that the imams now sided unequivocally with the Traditionist scholars, protecting them and punishing the stricter Hādawīs.

Although all Zaydīs, and in particular Hādawīs, would in principle have raised questions about the probity of some of the Companions, it was the more rejectionist type who was most villified by Shawkānī. He and many who have followed in his tradition tried to argue that true Zaydism is represented in the moderate wing of the school and that the rejectionists were not representative of the school's teachings; rather, these were beyond the pale, belonging to the more extreme Shīᶜite sect of the Imāmiyya.[29] The two leitmotivs in condemnation of the latter group were their alleged practice of the cursing the Companions and their refusal to refer to the Sunnī canonical ḥadīth collections.[30] It must be borne in mind that few Zaydī-Hādawīs openly cursed the Companions (other than Muᶜāwiya who is consistently cursed), but many voiced disapproval of actions taken by Abū Bakr and ᶜUmar

28 The name was said to have been given initially to those who had forsaken Zayd b. ᶜAlī when he refused to declare Abū Bakr and ᶜUmar unbelievers; cf. Kohlberg, 'The Term "Rāfiḍa" in Imami Shiᶜi Usage', *JAOS* 99 (1979), 677–9; idem, ᶜSome Imāmī Shīᶜī views on the Ṣaḥāba', p. 146. In eighteenth-century Yemen, this was a label given by the pro-Sunnī scholars to anyone who questioned the probity of the Companions or rejected the Caliphates of Abū Bakr or ᶜUmar and even to those who condemned the use of the Sunnī canonical ḥadīth collections.

29 See, for example, al-ᶜAmrī, *al-Imām al-Shawkānī*, pp. 95f.

30 For a contemporary attack of this sort, see *Hijar al-ᶜilm*, I: 238f. and *Hijar al-ᶜilm*, IV: 2106f.

and condemned them without cursing them. The lines quoted in the epigram at the opening of this chapter by al-Habal are therefore not representative of the entire school, but of a vociferous minority within it. Shawkānī tends to give the mistaken impression that those who condemn also curse, and in so doing he places all Zaydī-Hādawīs into the Rāfiḍī camp.

For Shawkānī, those who cursed the Companions were Rāfiḍīs and their action was tantamount to atheism (*ilḥād*) and heresy (*zandaqa*). They were enemies of Islam who used the issue of love for the Prophet's family to engender hatred for the Companions, and ultimately were out to undermine and negate the Sharīᶜa. He says of them:

> It is no wonder that the origin of the Rāfiḍī manifestation is one of atheism (*ilḥād*) and heresy (*zandaqa*). It is performed by one who secretly desires to undermine Islam, so he manifests love and allegiance to the House of the Prophet of God – may God's peace and blessings be upon him and his family – in order to attract the hearts of people . . . and then he explains to the people that the rights of the [Prophet's] kin (*qarāba*) cannot be had except by forgoing the rights of the Companions . . . All he wishes is to undermine and negate the Sharīᶜa because the Companions – may God be pleased with them – are the ones who related to the Muslims the knowledge of the Sharīᶜa from the Book and the Sunna. Were this concealed heretic and openly declared Rāfiḍī to accomplish slandering the Companions, declaring them to be infidels and judging them as apostates, the Sharīᶜa in its entirety would be nullified because they [the Companions] are its transmitters and narrators from the Prophet . . .[31]

This accusation is commonly made by Sunnīs against Shīᶜites, in particular against the Ismāᶜīlīs and the Imāmīs. Indeed, Shawkānī goes on to mention the Ismāᶜīlīs in the passage cited. From his perspective, even to tolerate the cursing of the Companions, who were the first transmitters of the ḥadīth, would lead to undermining the whole ḥadīth corpus. Hence, like most Sunnī jurists, he considered the cursing of a Companion a major offence (*kabīra*) which rendered the curser (*sābb*) a grave sinner (*fāsiq*). Generally, Sunnī jurists considered the *sābb* a *fāsiq* and as a result denied him the right to be a witness. Few went so far as to declare the *sābb* an outright infidel (*kāfir*), for the repercussions of this were severe, possibly implicating the one who practises the *takfīr* with *kufr* himself.[32] Shawkānī expected a Muslim to have a good opinion (*ḥusn al-ẓann*) of his fellow Muslims, and he explicitly forbad any defamatory statement (*ghība*), in whatever situation, by one Muslim about another.[33]

31 *Adab al-ṭalab*, pp. 71–2.

32 Cf. Arazi, ᶜIlqām al-ḥajar, pp. 222f.; Kohlberg, 'Some Zaydī views', p. 96, fn. 37; Wiederhold, 'Blasphemy against the Prophet Muḥammad', pp. 39–70. The last reference is a study of a treatise on the *sābb* of the Prophet and the Companions by the Shāfiᶜī jurist Taqī al-Dīn al-Subkī. In it, Subkī appears to break ranks with the majority Sunnī opinion on the judgement of a curser of the Companions by advocating that such a person be declared a *kāfir* and be executed. Subkī's opinion was perhaps meant to be *an ex post facto* justification for a judgement of *takfīr*, which had been passed in his time after a Shīᶜite cursed Abū Bakr, ᶜUmar and ᶜUthmān in the Umayyad mosque in Damascus.

33 Cf. Muḥammad al-Shawkānī, *Rafᶜ al-rība fīmā yajūz wa mā lā yajūz min al-ghība*, ᶜAqīl al-Maqṭarī (ed.) (Beirut: Dār Ibn Ḥazm, 1992); Shawkānī, *al-Sayl al-jarrār*, vol. IV, pp. 584–5. It is interesting

Zaydī views on the succession to the Prophet and on the Companions

The early Zaydīs in Kufa were broadly divided into two groups, the Batriyya and the Jārūdiyya. Reflecting a moderate Shīᶜism, the Batriyya were those who claimed that ᶜAlī was the most excellent of men after the Prophet but who nonetheless accepted the caliphates of Abū Bakr, ᶜUmar and the first six years of ᶜUthmān's. They accepted the leadership of the less excellent (*al-mafḍūl*) despite the presence of the more excellent (*al-afḍal*). By contrast, the Jārūdiyya reflected the more radical views of the later Imāmiyya and rejected outright the caliphates of Abū Bakr, ᶜUmar and ᶜUthmān, claiming that the Prophet had invested ᶜAlī as his legatee by designation. They asserted that the designation did not mention ᶜAlī explicitly by name but did describe him (*biʾl-waṣf*), and declared all those who did not accept this to be grave sinners (*fussāq*). The Jārūdiyya also rejected the Traditions and legal opinions transmitted by such Companions, whereas the Batriyya would accept these.[34]

Jārūdī tenets, as Madelung has shown, came to dominate in Zaydī circles from the third/ninth century onwards and influenced such imams as al-Qāsim b. Ibrāhīm and his grandson al-Hādī Yaḥyā b. al-Ḥusayn. In a departure from al-Qāsim's opinions, however, al-Hādī held that Abū Bakr and ᶜUmar were apostates (*murtaddūn*) deserving the death penalty.[35] The Zaydīs in Yemen have had to contend with this uncompromising position adopted by the founder of their imamate, and throughout their history individuals would remind others of this and call for the application of the principle in practice. In the fourth/tenth century Zaydīs appear to have softened their position with regards to the opponents of ᶜAlī. They continued to hold that ᶜAlī and his two sons by Fāṭima, al-Ḥasan and al-Ḥusayn, had been invested by the Prophet through designation, but that this designation was obscure (*khafī*) and needed investigation (*naẓar*) to be discovered. This allowed them to lessen the sin of the early Companions, and in particular that of the caliphs Abū Bakr and ᶜUmar.[36]

Perhaps owing to the increasing influence of the Muᶜtazila, many of whom were Sunnīs and whose teachings came to predominate in Yemen from the sixth/twelfth

to note that some scholars who opposed the Traditionists, and Shawkānī specifically, used the *ḥusn al-ẓann* argument, or some version thereof, to claim that Muslims are permitted to practise *taqlīd*. The claim made is that the ordinary Muslims should have a good opinion of the *madhhab* scholars inasmuch as they must assume that their judgements are not based on pure whim, but on the sound principles of the Sharīᶜa. Cf. Isḥāq b. Yūsuf, *al-Tafkīk li-ᶜuqūd al-tashkīk*, ms. Sanaa, Gharbiyya Library, *ᶜilm kalām* no. 33, fols. 2a–2b and Yūsuf al-Dijwī, 'al-Ḥukm ᶜalā al-Muslimīn biʾl-kufr', *Nūr al-Islām* 4.3 (Cairo 1352/1933), 179.

34 For a thorough discussion of the Batriyya and the Jārūdiyya, see Madelung, *Der Imam al-Qāsim*, pp. 44f.; al-Murtaḍā, *al-Munya waʾl-amal fī sharḥ al-milal waʾl-niḥal*, pp. 96–9; al-Ḥasan b. Mūsā al-Nawbakhtī, *Kitāb Firaq al-Shīᶜa*, Helmut Ritter (ed.) (Istanbul: Maṭbaᶜat al-Dawla, 1931), pp. 8–9, 12, 18–19, 48–51.

35 Madelung, *Der Imam al-Qāsim*, pp. 45, 167; cf. van Arendonck, *Les Débuts de l'Imāmat Zaidite*, pp. 276f.; al-Sharafī, *Kitāb ᶜUddat al-akyās*, vol. II, pp. 111f.

36 *EI*², art. 'Imāma', vol. III, p. 1166.

century onwards, Zaydīs adopted an even more moderate stance towards the Companions and many advocated the practice of stating the formula 'may God be pleased with him' (*tarḍiya*) after mentioning a Companion's name.[37] But this practice remained controversial, and many Zaydī imams preferred to abstain from adopting it, favouring instead the neutral stance reflected in the practice of *tawaqquf* (lit. remaining silent after the mention of a Companion's name). The motive behind this was the suspension of views on what God's judgement would be of the Companion who had defied ᶜAlī.

The basic problem confronting the Zaydīs with regard to those Companions who had opposed ᶜAlī was the legal status of their act of insubordination against the legitimate successor of the Prophet. A distinction was made between Companions such as Abū Bakr and ᶜUmar who usurped the Caliphate after the Prophet's death and other Companions, like Muᶜāwiya, who opposed ᶜAlī's becoming Caliph after ᶜUthmān's death. It appears that Zaydīs unequivocally considered Muᶜāwiya to be an apostate and most would systematically curse him. But with regard to Abū Bakr and ᶜUmar the question arose for later Zaydīs as to whether they were to be declared apostates in accordance with al-Hādī's practice. Or were they to be deemed grave sinners (*fussāq*) since their action of usurping power constituted a major offence (*kabīra*). Or was one to suspend judgement about them and remain silent about their status. Or were they to be exonerated by declaring that they had committed a pardonable error (*khaṭaʾ*). Different Zaydīs appear to have adopted all four of these positions. Some stated that Abū Bakr and ᶜUmar committed an error (*khaṭaʾ*) or an odious deed (*qabīḥ*) and an act of rebellion (*maᶜṣiya*), but not *fisq*.[38] These generally adopted the practice of *tarḍiya*. Others refused to state their opinion on the matter and practised *tawaqquf*. And yet others continued to uphold the Jārūdī and Hādawī positions or some variation thereof. This last group of strict Hādawīs condoned the cursing, but did not systematically practise it, believing that it was not generally appropriate for believers to practise cursing (*laᶜn, sabb*).[39]

The use of the Sunnī canonical ḥadīth collections was closely entwined with the position a Zaydī adopted on these matters. Those who were more accepting of the Companions inclined to using them and considered them authoritative. Stricter Hādawīs either rejected them outright or, if they cited them, did so selectively, reflecting the dubious nature of their authenticity. In the Yemeni highlands, it was only the Traditionists, like Ibn al-Wazīr and Shawkānī, who advocated their exclusive use and considered them the most authoritative sources after the Qurʾān. For this reason, the degree to which a scholar used and gave these sources primacy determined where he fit along the spectrum running from strict Hādawī to Traditionist.

37 Cf. Kohlberg, 'Some Zaydī views', pp. 91–8.

38 An example of someone who adopted this position is al-Ḥusayn b. Badr al-Dīn, *Kitāb Shifāʾ al-uwām*, vol. III, pp. 495–7. See also Shawkānī's commentary in the margins.

39 *al-Sayf al-bātir*, fol. 3a–b; Muḥammad b. Muḥammad al-Manṣūr, *al-Kalima al-shāfiya fī ḥukm mā kāna bayn al-imām ᶜAlī wa Muᶜāwiya* (n.p.: Dār al-Ḥaḍāra, 1992), p. 83.

Al-Muʾayyad Yaḥyā b. Ḥamza: an example of the moderate Zaydī scholar

Reflecting the early position of the Batriyya, a number of Zaydī scholars in the eighth/fourteenth and ninth/fifteenth centuries, ones who were greatly influenced by the Muʿtazilī school, adopted a moderate attitude to the Companions by practising *tarḍiya.* A key figure in this moderate tendency was Imam al-Muʾayyad Yaḥyā b. Ḥamza (d. 749/1348), whose treatise on the question of cursing the Companions, entitled *al-Risāla al-wāziʿa liʾl-muʿtadīn ʿan sabb ṣaḥābat sayyid al-mursalīn* (The Missive which Restrains the Aggressors from Cursing the Companions of the Lord of the Messengers) has recently been edited and published.[40] The treatise consists of a set of answers to questions posed by ʿAbd Allāh b. Masʿūd al-Dhubyānī[41] about the imamate of ʿAlī, the judgement of the Caliphs who had opposed him and whether they would enter paradise, and finally the question of who are the Zaydīs.

In this work Yaḥyā affirms that ʿAlī was the best of men after the Prophet because of the explicit virtues (*faḍāʾil ẓāhira*) God had bestowed on him and that his imamate, as well as that of his two sons, was determined through designation (*naṣṣ*). He then enumerates twenty of ʿAlī's virtues among which are that he was the first to believe (*al-sabq biʾl-īmān*) and his closeness in kinship to the Prophet (*al-qarāba*).[42]

Having established ʿAlī's excellence, Yaḥyā turns to the judgement of Abū Bakr and ʿUmar. After summarising five different positions[43] adopted by various Shīʿite groups on the issue, he states unequivocally

> that what we see as being the Law (*al-sharʿ*)... and what we command those who read this book to follow is the road of soundness for the fair-minded. This is that their [the Companions'] contravention of the textual designations [in favour of ʿAlī], even if these are apodictic (*qāṭiʿa*), does not entail their infidelity (*kufr*), grave sinfulness (*fisq*), apostasy (*khurūj ʿan al-dīn*) and does not necessitate severing [one's] loyalty (*muwālāt*) to them. For their belief is sound... it is the path chosen by the most eminent among the Ahl al-Bayt and the [most] accomplished among their followers...[44]

40 al-Muʾayyad Yaḥyā b. Ḥamza, *al-Risāla al-wāziʿa liʾl-muʿtadīn ʿan sabb ṣaḥābat sayyid al-mursalīn* (Sanaa: Maktabat Dār al-Turāth, 1990) (hereinafter *al-Risāla al-wāziʿa*).

41 I could not find his biography, but the name indicates that he belonged to the Bakīlī tribe of Dhubyān, which bordered Arḥab in the northern Yemeni highlands.

42 *al-Risāla al-wāziʿa*, pp. 19–26.

43 The five groups mentioned are first the Imāmiyya and Rāfiḍīs who declare those who opposed ʿAlī to be infidels because they contravened the Prophet's intention (*qaṣd*), which is obligatorily known (*maʿlūm biʾl-ḍarūra*). The second group are the Jārūdiyya who declare the proof of 'Alī's designation to be apodictic (*qāṭiʿa*) and that therefore anyone who opposes it is a grave sinner (*fāsiq*). The third group are the Ṣāliḥiyya (= Batriyya) who accept the caliphates of Abū Bakr and ʿUmar but not that of ʿUthmān. The fourth group, who are unnamed, accept Abū Bakr and ʿUmar but declare ʿUthmān to be an infidel. The fifth group are the Ṣabbāḥiyya (= Nizārī Ismāʿīlīs) who declare Abu Bakr and ʿUmar to be infidels, cf. ibid., p. 26.

44 *al-Risāla al-wāziʿa*, p. 27.

The imamate is for the Zaydīs a principle of religion (*aṣl dīn*), like God's unicity (*tawḥīd*) and justice (*ᶜadl*). According to Zaydī theology, every Muslim must believe in these principles after undertaking a process of personal investigation (*naẓar*), which leads to certain knowledge (*ᶜilm*) of these tenets of faith.[45] This did not, however, imply giving total freedom to the investigator to arrive at any conclusion; the Muslim was expected to acknowledge the doctrines established by the school, and in practice the process of investigation was expected to be perfunctory since a majority of Muslims were not sufficiently learned to navigate the conceptual field of *uṣūl al-dīn*. For the Zaydīs, to reject any one of these principles meant renouncing the faith. This posed a problem with regards to those Companions who opposed the imamate of ᶜAlī. This was to be the argument levelled by the strict Hādawīs against the Traditionists, who not only accepted the imamates of Abū Bakr and ᶜUmar but also held that the Companions, even those who had fought against ᶜAlī, had moral probity (*ᶜadāla*) and were the best generation of Muslims and worthy of emulation. The moderate Zaydī position was not so extreme in its veneration of the Companions, but it nonetheless tried to exonerate most of the Companions from the sin of opposing ᶜAlī, with the exception of Muᶜāwiya and some whose bitter enmity to ᶜAlī was explicit.

In his treatise, al-Muʾayyad Yaḥyā adduces statements of the early Zaydī imams, starting with ᶜAlī b. Abī Ṭālib, in favour of the Companions, focusing in particular on Abū Bakr and ᶜUmar. The gist of Yaḥyā's argument is that none of the early Zaydī imams had declared any of the Companions to be infidels (*kuffār*) or grave sinners (*fussāq*) despite Abū Bakr's and ᶜUmar's contravention of apodictic texts (*nuṣūṣ qāṭiᶜa*) about ᶜAlī's precedence and right of succession.[46] *Ijmāᶜ* requires the existence of apodictic proof (*dalāla qaṭᶜiyya*) before declaring a Muslim to be an infidel or a grave sinner, and this is not present here. The legal proof indicates only that a mistake was committed by the Companions in the process of examining (*khaṭaʾ fī ʾal-naẓar*) the designation texts (*nuṣūṣ*).[47] Yaḥyā argues that while the indication for ᶜAlī's imamate is absolutely certain and the truth in it is one and is not a matter open to reasoning (*ijtihād*), one must still have a good opinion of the Companions who committed an error when contravening these apodictic texts. This is because the indication (*dalāla*) of these texts is open to reasoning and entails obscurities and subtleties and one cannot, therefore, consider the Companions infidels or grave sinners.[48] ᶜAlī himself had given the first caliphs his allegiance and did not treat them the way he treated Muᶜāwiya, ᶜAmr b. al-ᶜĀṣ, Abū ʾal-Aᶜwar al-Sulamī and Abū Mūsā al-Ashᶜarī, whom he cursed and from whom he dissociated himself (*tabarraʾa*).[49] With the exception of these latter, ᶜAlī had treated all the Companions with love, friendship, assistance and support. Yaḥyā then claims that no statement has been transmitted from either of ᶜAlī's two sons, al-Ḥasan and al-Ḥusayn, in which Abū Bakr or ᶜUmar are cursed, impugned, or declared infidels or grave sinners. There follows the well-known story about Zayd

[45] al-Sharafī, *Kitāb ᶜUddat al-akyās*, vol. II, p. 168. [46] *al-Risāla al-wāziᶜa*, pp. 38–9.
[47] Ibid., p. 27. [48] Ibid., p. 44. [49] Ibid., p. 29.

b. ᶜAlī refusing to dissociate himself from the two Shaykhs (*al-shaykhayn*), i.e., Abū Bakr and ᶜUmar, for which refusal most of the people of Kūfa rejected his leadership and for which reason they came to be known as the Rāfiḍīs.[50] Moderate Zaydīs and Traditionists, like Shawkānī, often use this report about Zayd to claim that the early Zaydī spirit was tolerant and worthy of emulation.[51]

After narrating additional reports about the positive attitude of early imams towards Abū Bakr and ᶜUmar, Yaḥyā reaches the more intransigent position taken by al-Qāsim b. Ibrāhīm, al-Hādī's grandfather. When al-Qāsim reportedly was asked about the two Shaykhs, he responded by citing the Qurᵓānic verse: 'That is a nation that has passed away; there awaits them what they have earned, and there awaits you what you have earned' (II: 134). Yaḥyā sees this as an indication of al-Qāsim's refusal to defame them and relegating their fate to God. Another indication for Yaḥyā of al-Qāsim's refusal to insult and curse Abū Bakr and ᶜUmar is a report that al-Qāsim had disavowed their action of preceding ᶜAlī to the Caliphate and had become angry. Yaḥyā stresses that al-Qāsim only became angry and did not exceed this to curse them as the Rāfiḍīs do.[52] It is notable that al-Hādī's opinion is not mentioned anywhere in Yaḥyā's treatise, but is placed together with that of his grandfather, and the only later imams mentioned are the Caspian imams al-Nāṣir al-Uṭrūsh and al-Muᵓayyad Aḥmad b. al-Ḥusayn. Al-Nāṣir is reported to have said the *tarḍiya*, whereas al-Muᵓayyad practised *tawaqquf* in his youth but later in life said the *taraḥḥum* (i.e., saying 'may God have mercy on them') after the names of Abū Bakr and ᶜUmar.[53]

After establishing that none of the early Zaydī imams had declared the Companions infidels or grave sinners, Yaḥyā asserts that there are two groups amongst the Zaydīs regarding the Companions. The first and preponderant group is the one which practises the *tarḍiya* and *taraḥḥum* and includes among its members ᶜAlī, Zayd b. ᶜAlī, al-Nāṣir al-Uṭrūsh, and al-Muᵓayyad Aḥmad. Their practice, Yaḥyā says, is what he chooses to follow. The basis for this group's position is that the Companions' belief is certain and that their contravention of the textual evidence constitutes a mere error (*khaṭaᵓ*) that cannot be construed as constituting either a major or a minor act of disobedience. The second group practises *tawaqquf*, i.e., abstains from saying the *tarḍiya* or the *taraḥḥum*, and includes al-Qāsim, al-Hādī, his children and al-Manṣūr ᶜAbd Allāh b. Ḥamza. Yaḥyā says the reason for this is that they are not sure whether the error committed by some of the Companions was major or minor, although they did forbid the practice of declaring them infidels or grave sinners. He criticises the second group by saying that it would have been better for them to have asserted the certainty of the Companions' belief and that the error did not constitute a major sin.[54] In the last section of his treatise, before providing the questioner with a definition of Zaydism, Yaḥyā asserts that the Companions, even those who opposed ᶜAlī's initial succession, would enter

50 Ibid., pp. 33–4.
51 Ibid., pp. 41–2 and Shawkānī, *Irshād al-ghabī ilā madhhab Ahl al-Bayt fī ṣaḥb al-nabī*, ms. photocopy from the library of Muḥammad b. Ismāᶜīl al-ᶜAmrānī, pp. 7–8 (hereinafter *Irshād al-ghabī*).
52 Ibid., p. 35. 53 Ibid., pp. 36–7. 54 Ibid., pp. 40–1.

paradise on the basis of their deeds, which excel those of other Muslims, and he cites the Tradition that they are the best generation. He finally condemns those who refuse to pray behind those who believe this to be the case.[55]

Al-Mahdī Aḥmad b. Yaḥyā al-Murtaḍā (d. 840/1436) is another representative of the moderate Zaydīs on this issue. He also held that those who had preceded ᶜAlī to the caliphate had committed a definite error because they had contravened an explicit text. In his opinion, however, they are not grave sinners because they acted not out of rebellion but rather because of a doubt (*shubha*). He insists that saying the *tarḍiya* for them is permissible because their faith is certain.[56]

Strict Hādawī views of the Companions

Yaḥyā b. Ḥamza's division of Zaydīs into those who practise *tarḍiya* and those who practise *tawaqquf* reflects their major disagreement over the Companions who had opposed ᶜAlī – with the exception of Muᶜāwiya and his associates whom Zaydīs unanimously condemn as having been grave sinners. The group which practised *tawaqquf* included many of the great figures of Yemeni Zaydism and can be said to represent the majority opinion down to the Qāsimī period. An early example of such a scholar is Ḥumaydān b. Yaḥyā (fl. seventh/thirteenth century) who called for a return to the earlier Zaydī doctrines of al-Qāsim b. Ibrāhīm and al-Hādī whilst rejecting the preponderant influence the Baṣran Muᶜtazilī school had acquired in Yemen at his time, especially the highly scholastic discussions it engendered. Like al-Hādī, Ḥumaydān held radical Shīᶜite views regarding the Companions: he rejected the argument that as *mujtahid*s their sins were forgiven and he allowed the cursing of those whose sinfulness had been established, namely Muᶜāwiya and his followers.[57] Other examples of scholars who held this position on the Companions, although not necessarily agreeing with Ḥumaydān's anti-scholastic stance, were al-Mutawakkil Aḥmad b. Sulaymān (d. 566/1171), al-Manṣūr ᶜAbd Allāh b. Ḥamza (d. 614/1217) and al-Qāsim b. Muḥammad (d. 1029/1620), the founder of the Qāsimī dynasty, amongst others.

The founder of the Qāsimī dynasty upheld the doctrine of *tawaqquf* and criticized the position which called for accepting the probity (*ᶜadāla*) of the Companions without exception.[58] In his *Kitāb al-Asās*, al-Qāsim states that those Companions who did not realise (*lam yaᶜlamū*) that ᶜAlī was more deserving of the caliphate, even after investigation, had not committed a sin (*ithm*). Whereas, he

[55] Ibid., pp. 44–50.

[56] al-Murtaḍā, *Kitāb al-Baḥr al-zakhkhār*, vol. I (*muqaddima*), p. 95; cf. Muḥammad Kamālī, *al-Imām Aḥmad b. Yaḥyā al-Murtaḍā* (Sanaa: Dār al-Ḥikma al-Yamāniyya, 1991), pp. 474f.

[57] Ḥumaydān b. al-Qāsim b. Yaḥyā, *Kitāb Tanbīh al-ghāfilīn ᶜalā maghāliṭ al-mutawahhimīn*, in *Majmūᶜ al-sayyid Ḥūmaydān*, ms. British Library, no. OR. 3959, fols. 113a f.; cf. Kohlberg, 'Some Zaydī views', pp. 92, fn. 16, 97; Madelung, *Der Imam al-Qāsim*, pp. 218f.

[58] al-Manṣūr al-Qāsim b. Muḥammad, *al-Iᶜtiṣām bi-ḥabl Allāh al-matīn*, 5 vols. (Sanaa: Maktabat al-Yaman al-Kubrā, 1987), vol. I, pp. 44f.

maintains, those who did realise this and did not side with him committed a major sin (*kabīra*), because of the consensus (*ijmā*ᶜ) that whoever opposes the righteous imam transgresses against him (*baghā* ᶜ*alayh*), and this constitutes *fisq*. The difficulty lies in knowing who among the Companions had realised this. Since this was not easily discernible, many of the Zaydī imams chose to practise *tawaqquf*.[59] Al-Qāsim, however, cursed Muᶜāwiya.[60] He also rejected the argument made by the moderate Zaydīs that the presumption of their faith requires their acceptance as faithful Muslims (*al-aṣl al-īmān faʾl-natawallahum*) because, according to al-Qāsim, the ambiguity (*iltibās*) of their sin (*ma*ᶜ*ṣiya*) abrogates the knowledge of their apparent belief (*ḥuṣūl al-iltibās nasakha al-*ᶜ*ilm bi-īmānihim fī ʾl-ẓāhir*).[61] Al-Qāsim's son, al-Mutawakkil Ismāᶜīl, was perhaps more moderate. He says in his creed, *al-*ᶜ*Aqīda al-ṣaḥīḥa waʾl-dīn al-naṣīḥa*, that 'it is necessary to be devoted to the Companions – may God be pleased with them all – and [to uphold the position] that none of them were hypocrites (*munāfiqūn*) or grave sinners (*fussāq*)', and that according to 'the sound Tradition they [i.e., the *munāfiqūn* and the *fussāq*] are not considered Companions for the mischief they have caused' (*wa fī ʾl-ḥadīth al-ṣaḥīḥ annahum laysū bi-aṣḥāb limā aḥdathūh*).[62] Were Abū Bakr and ᶜUmar to be stripped of Companion status according to al-Mutawakkil? He seems to leave the door open for that possiblity.[63] It is reported that he did prevent the Ḥaḍramīs from saying the *tarḍiya* on the Shaykhayn when Ḥaḍramawt came under his control.[64]

In the Qāsimī period scholarly conflicts over the issue of the status of the Companions took place on various occasions, and treatises were written on the subject by both those who advocated accepting their probity and those who rejected it. Yaḥyā b. al-Ḥusayn b. al-Qāsim (d. 1100/1688–9), the famous historian and author of *Anbāʾal-zaman*, was known for his pro-Companion stance. He wrote a treatise against the strict Hādawī Aḥmad b. Saᶜd al-Dīn al-Maswarī, a retainer and court official of the early Qāsimī imams, in which he defended the scholars of ḥadīth, and also another treatise entitled *al-Īḍāḥ limā khafiya min al-ittifāq*ᶜ*alā ta*ᶜ*ẓīm ṣaḥābat al-Muṣṭafā* (Clarifying the Concealed Consensus about the Veneration of

59 al-Qāsim b. Muḥammad, *Kitāb al-Asās*, pp. 162–3 (Nadir's edition, pp. 168–9); cf. al-Sharafī, *Kitāb* ᶜ*Uddat al-akyās*, vol. II, pp. 168f. and al-Ḥusayn b. al-Qāsim, *Kitāb Hidāyat al-*ᶜ*uqūl*, vol. II. pp. 73f.

60 al-Qāsim b. Muḥammad, *Kitāb al-Asās*, p. 156. 61 Ibid., p. 164.

62 al-Mutawakkil Ismāᶜīl b. al-Qāsim, *Kitāb al-*ᶜ*Aqīda al-ṣaḥīḥa* (Sanaa: Maktabat Dār al-Turāth, 1990), p. 14.

63 One of the leading jurists in al-Mutawakkil's court, Aḥmad b. Ṣāliḥ b. Abī ʾl-Rijāl (d. 1092/1681) wrote a treatise on this issue as well entitled *I*ᶜ*lām al-muwālī bi-kalām sādatihi al-a*ᶜ*lām al-mawālī*, ms. British Library, no. OR. 3852, fols. 36–59. In this work Ibn Abī ʾl-Rijāl argues against cursing because, he says, it is not becoming for Zaydīs to do so, but he also argues that all Zaydīs are Jārūdīs and that there is no doubt that those Companions who did not side with ᶜAlī have committed a sin. He criticises Yaḥyā b. Ḥamza's assertion that a consensus exists among Zaydī imams against declaring the Companions sinners. However, he appears to leave open the choice of whether one should practise the *tawaqquf* and *tabriʾa* or the *tarḍiya* of the Companions. One can probably assume that Ibn Abī ʾl-Rijāl's views here reflected those of al-Mutawakkil Ismāᶜīl.

64 Muḥammad al-Muḥibbī, *Khulāṣat al-athar fī a*ᶜ*yān al-qarn al-ḥādī* ᶜ*ashar*, 4 vols. (n.p.: n.d.), vol. I, p. 412.

the Companions of the Prophet).[65] Shawkānī claims that because of his pro-Sunnī opinions Yaḥyā b. al-Ḥusayn faced many trials and tribulations at the hands of the Hādawīs of his age. A cousin once-removed of his, who confusingly is also called Yaḥyā b. al-Ḥusayn (d. 1090/1679), held the opposite view on the Companions, allowing them to be cursed.[66]

In a slightly later period, the same issue arose and again treatises on the subject were written. The defender of the Companions this time was a *sayyid* named Ṣalāḥ b. al-Ḥusayn al-Akhfash (d. 1142/1730), the prayer leader at the Dāʾūd mosque in Sanaa, who wrote a treatise entitled *Risāla fī masʾalat tanzīh al-ṣaḥāba* (A Treatise on the Matter of the Exculpation of the Companions). ᶜAbd Allāh b. ᶜAlī al-Wazīr, a close advisor of the reigning imams and a strict Hādawī, wrote a rebuttal to al-Akhfash's treatise entitled *Irsāl al-dhuʾāba bayn janbay masʾalat al-ṣaḥāba* (Loosening the Lock of Hair from Within the Question of the Companions).[67]

These clashes involved larger issues than the probity of any particular Companion. They were about what it meant to be a Zaydī, the role and special standing of the Ahl al-Bayt as religious and political leaders of the Muslim community and what constituted an authoritative source of law and belief. A strict Hādawī opponent of Shawkānī states:

> They [Shawkānī and his peers] say: we are the *Ahl al-Sunna*, we follow those ḥadīths we consider to be sound. To accomplish their evil intention they have promoted the *ᶜadāla* of all the Companions, even if one of them manifests an evil, and they follow a ḥadīth which has been transmitted by a single one of them even if it is contrary to the Qurʾān ... The *Ahl al-Sunna* adhere to this evil belief, that of the *ᶜadāla* of all of them, because of what we have pointed out, namely the realisation of their intention to cling to the ḥadīths which they [i.e., the Umayyads and ᶜAbbāsids] have fabricated for them. Such as the ḥadīths about the *visio beatifica* (*al-ruʾya*), predestination (*jabr*), anthropomorphism (*tashbīh*), that believers will not remain eternally in hell and other false beliefs. Were they to relinquish this belief in their probity, most of them [i.e., the Companions] would be found to be unreliable...[68]

One point must be borne in mind when considering these late Hādawī attacks on those who argued for the *ᶜadāla* of the Companions and the practice of *tarḍiya*. The debate was not confined to various constituents within the Zaydī camp, as it had been during al-Muʾayyad Yaḥyā b. Ḥamza's time; now, the argument was

[65] This treatise is also known by the title *Muntahā al-iṣāba fīmā yajibu min riᶜāyat ḥuqūq al-ṣaḥāba*, ms. Gharbiyya Library Sanaa, *majmūᶜ* no. 106. See al-Ḥibshī, *Maṣādir al-fikr*, p. 131 and *Badr*, II: 328–9.

[66] *Badr*, II: 330.

[67] See al-Ḥibshī, *Maṣādir al-fikr*, pp. 134–5. Al-Akhfash's treatise can be found in ms. Sanaa, Gharbiyya Library, *majmūᶜ* no. 124, fols. 28–35 and al-Wazīr's response is in the margin. Mr. Zayd al-Wazīr graciously provided me with a copy of both treatises. Cf. *Badr*, I: 295–6; *Nashr*, I: 789. Akhfash also wrote a treatise entitled *ᶜIjālat al-jawāb fī al-radd ᶜalā shīᶜat Muᶜāwiya al-kilāb* (ms. Sanaa, Gharbiyya Library, *majmūᶜ* no. 91), which indicates that he may have later changed his views.

[68] *Ghaṭamṭam*, vol. I, pp. 13, 15. For a theological defence of Zaydī-Muᶜtazilī beliefs against those of the Sunnīs, see Muḥammad al-Samāwī's, *al-ᶜIqd al-munaẓẓam fī jawāb al-suʾāl al-wārid min al-ḥaram al-muḥarram* (Sanaa: n.p., 1992).

between Sunnī Traditionists, like Shawkānī, and strict Hādawīs. The Hādawīs in this engagement saw their own opinions as consistent with the true teachings of Zaydism, those opinions of the early Qāsimī imams and those of earlier scholars like Ḥumaydān. By contrast, the Traditionists argued that true Zaydism is represented by the moderates in the school and attempted to negate most of the Shīcī specificities of its teachings.

Shawkānī's *Irshād al-ghabī*

The issue of the proper attitude towards the Companions brings into sharp relief the way in which the Traditionist scholars were now defining proper religious belief and practice, and the alliance they had struck with the state, which brought to bear its coercive powers on these matters. The scholarly debates over the status of the Companions in late eighteenth-century Sanaa give a much fuller picture of the tensions between the strict Hādawīs and the Traditionist scholars as well as the issues at stake: What constituted being a Hādawī and what role should the state play in promulgating and defending the Hādawī cause? In their specific arguments about the Companions Shawkānī and his Traditionist peers asserted that true Zaydism is represented by its moderate scholars – an argument already seen in the work of Yaḥyā b. Ḥamza – and that no Zaydī imam had ever cursed or allowed the cursing of the Companions. The Traditionists ignored the opinions of stricter Zaydī-Hādawī imams, like those of al-Hādī and the early Qāsimīs, who did not adopt a moderate stance. They also traded on an ambiguity by treating the Companions as a homogeneous group, including the more problematic ones like Mucāwiya, Abū Bakr, and cUmar, whom the Zaydīs had treated in more nuanced terms. The strict Hādawīs, on the other hand, invoked the more hard-line position of al-Hādī and other Yemeni imams, such as al-Manṣūr cAbd Allāh b. Ḥamza and the early Qāsimī imams, as being representative of true Zaydism. Cursing, they said, was not the habit of the followers of the Ahl al-Bayt as it was not becoming, except in the case of Mucāwiya and his followers. However, they also went on to condemn Abū Bakr and cUmar for their disregard of the rights of the Prophet's family, without outrightly cursing them. They accused the Traditionists of wanting to undermine the Zaydī *dacwa* altogether and complained bitterly about the Sunnī direction the state had taken, seeing Shawkānī, whom they described as a Nāṣibī (an opponent of cAlī and the Ahl al-Bayt), as the sower of the destruction of Zaydism.

In the year 1208/1793–4, Shawkānī received a question from scholars about the cursing of the Companions. His answer took the form of a treatise entitled *Irshād al-ghabī ilā madhhab Ahl al-Bayt fī ṣaḥb al-nabī* (Guidance to the Ignorant about the Doctrine of Ahl al-Bayt Concerning the Companions of the Prophet). The questioner's name is not known, and the treatise is in the form of a long argument addressed to an imagined strict Hādawī interlocutor with the aim of convincing him that there is a consensus (*ijmāc*) among the Zaydī imams against cursing the Companions, and that indeed doing so constitutes infidelity.

Shawkānī's main sources in the *Irshād al-ghabī* are Yaḥyā b. Ḥamza's *al-Risāla al-wāziᶜa* and Yaḥyā b. al-Ḥusayn's *al-Iḍāḥ*. He goes beyond Yaḥyā b. Ḥamza, however, in adducing statements positive in their appraisal of the Companions by Zaydī imams who came after Yaḥyā b. Ḥamza's time. In the introductory remarks, Shawkānī claims that in his day Zaydism and its literary sources were no longer known by those who purported to be its followers, who would now study only a single abridged text (*mukhtaṣar*). As a result, much confusion had ensued and false opinions were attributed to their imams. The situation had become such that many were now attacking the Companions' honour and claiming that this was in accordance with the teachings of the Ahl al-Bayt.[69] Shawkānī proposes to show the truth of the matter by relying exclusively on Zaydī sources and to prove that the noble Zaydī centres of learning had indeed disintegrated (*indirās maᶜāhid ᶜulūmihim al-sharīfa fī hādhihi al-azmina*).[70] The tenor and content of his answer is provocative and patronising.

The crux of Shawkānī's argument is, as noted, his claim that an established consensus exists among the imams of the Ahl al-Bayt which prohibits the cursing (*sabb*) of the Companions as well as declaring them to be infidels (*takfīr*) or grave sinners (*tafsīq*). He then sets out to cite thirteen Zaydī authorities to prove that this consensus exists. The first authority is the Caspian imam al-Muʾayyad Aḥmad b. al-Ḥusayn al-Hārūnī (d. 411/1020), who is quoted as reporting that all his forefathers had forbidden the cursing of the Companions.

The second authority is al-Manṣūr ᶜAbd Allāh b. Ḥamza (d. 614/1217), a more important imam for the Zaydīs of Yemen and a more problematic figure concerning the Companions for he appears to have expressed two different opinions in his works. Al-Manṣūr advocated *tawaqquf* in his major work *Kitāb al-Shāfī*, whereas he adopted the more lenient practice of *tarḍiya* in his treatise *Jawāb al-masāʾil al-Tihāmiyya*.[71] This ambiguity in al-Manṣūr's opinion was pointed out by Yaḥyā b. Ḥamza in his *al-Risāla al-wāziᶜa*, in which the latter criticized those who claimed that al-Manṣūr had held that true Zaydīs were Jārūdīs, and that he had stated: 'Do not pray behind the one who says the *tarḍiya* for them [i.e., Abū Bakr and ᶜUmar], and ask the one who curses them for his evidence [allowing such a practice]'. Yaḥyā b. Ḥamza retorts by saying that al-Manṣūr had meant that Zaydīs had adopted the Jārūdī claim that the imamate of ᶜAlī was valid through designation (*thābita biʾl-naṣṣ*), not that they took on the Jārūdī practice of declaring the Companions grave sinners. Moreover, he adds that al-Manṣūr had not made the above statement but the following one: 'Do not pray behind the one who curses them and ask the one who says the *tarḍiya* for his evidence'.[72] Shawkānī pursues this line of argumentation, quoting passages from al-Manṣūr's writings to the effect that the Zaydī imams had not cursed Abū Bakr and ᶜUmar, rather they had considered them the best people after the Prophet, ᶜAlī and Fāṭima. They had committed an error (*khaṭaʾ*) and an act

[69] *Irshād al-ghabī*, p. 1. [70] Ibid., p. 2.

[71] Cf. al-Manṣūr ᶜAbd Allāh b. Ḥamza, *Kitāb al-Shāfī*, 4 vols. in 2 (Sanaa: Maktabat al-Yaman al-Kubrā, 1986), vol. III, pp. 271–2. It is perhaps no accident that al-Manṣūr upheld the *tarḍiya* position in responding to questions from the Tihāma, as these would have been posed by Sunnīs.

[72] *al-Risāla al-wāziᶜa*, pp. 41–3.

of disobedience (*ma*ᶜ*ṣiya*) in acceding to the caliphate before ᶜAlī which only God can judge, yet deserved to be pardoned because of all their previous good deeds.[73] Shawkānī goes on to cite passages from the works of Yaḥyā b. Ḥamza to argue that the majority of Zaydī imams practised *tarḍiya*. He then cites other authors such as al-Hādī b. Ibrāhīm al-Wazīr and Yaḥyā b. al-Ḥusayn b. al-Qāsim (d. 1100/1688–9), followed by a list of the names and works of the remaining thirteen authorities. All the citations present the Zaydī imams as having prohibited or condemned the practice of cursing the Companions. Shawkānī seeks to argue that the moderate Zaydī position on the Companions, as espoused by Yaḥyā b. Ḥamza and Aḥmad b. Yaḥyā al-Murtaḍā, was representative of the school's teachings, and in so doing he ignores the fact that the early Qāsimī imams were not in that tradition since they had adopted a more uncompromising position on the issue of the Companions.

In the next section of the *Irshād al-ghabī*, Shawkānī begins a debate with the imaginary strict Hādawī interlocutor who is a curser of the Companions. He argues with the curser that he cannot base his practice of cursing on the Qurʾān, the Sunna, the writings of Zaydī imams, those of the ulema of the ḥadīth or the four Sunnī schools since in none of these can a statement be found allowing this practice; rather, the Companions are unequivocally praised in all these sources and considered to be 'the best generation' and 'the people of paradise'. As to the scholars of ḥadīth and the Sunnī schools, Shawkānī approvingly says that they all considered the curser a reprehensible innovator (*mubtadi*ᶜ), with some declaring him a grave sinner whilst others outrightly condemned him as an infidel.[74] The only source upon which a curser can base his practice, Shawkānī says, is that of the extremist Imāmīs (*ghulāt al-Imāmiyya*; the Twelver Shīᶜites), who are the *Rāfiḍa*, and who are condemned by all Muslim scholars, including the Zaydīs. By taking the case of the curser and labelling him an Imāmī, Shawkānī has adopted the most uncompromising position on the question of the status of the Companions, which does not allow for any middle ground or subtlety in the matter.

Shawkānī now quotes from Zaydī imams who condemn the *Rāfiḍa* and later delves into the definition of this appellation. He first cites Aḥmad b. Yaḥyā al-Murtaḍā, who declares that the *Rāfiḍa* are those who curse the 'two shaykhs' and are to be considered grave sinners.[75] This is followed by a quotation from al-Hādī Yaḥyā b. al-Ḥusayn's *Kitāb al-Aḥkām* in which al-Hādī condemns the Imāmiyya and cites the ḥadīth 'O ᶜAlī, at the end of time there will be a group who have a sobriquet by which they are known. They are called the *Rāfiḍa*. Kill them should you chance upon them, God has killed them for they are polytheists'.[76] To bolster his argument, Shawkānī emphasises that this ḥadīth is the only one in al-Hādī's work which has a full chain of transmission (*isnād*) back to the Prophet, implying

[73] *Irshād al-ghabī*, pp. 2–3.
[74] Shawkānī's source here is the Shāfiᶜī Egyptian scholar Ibn Ḥajar al-Haytamī (d. 974/1567) whom he quotes as saying that 'many imams have declared those who curse the Companions to be infidels', cf. *Irshād al-ghabī*, pp. 6–7.
[75] *Irshād al-ghabī*, p. 7. Cf. al-Murtaḍā, *Kitāb al-Baḥr al-zakhkhār*, vol. V, p. 25.
[76] Cf. al-Hādī Yaḥyā b. al-Ḥusayn, *Kitāb al-Aḥkām*, vol. I, p. 455.

that if there is an opinion of al-Hādī's which is truly founded on indubitable authority then this is it. To prove that the *Rāfiḍa* are those who curse the Companions, Shawkānī now narrates the story which gave rise to the name '*Rāfiḍa*', relying on Fayrūzābādī's dictionary, the *Qāmūs*, where they are described as those who rejected the imamate of Zayd b. ᶜAlī because he refused to dissociate himself from Abū Bakr and ᶜUmar (*abā an yatabarraʾa min al-shaykhayn*). Zayd's refusal is interpreted by Shawkānī to mean that he refused to curse them. The Imāmiyya, Shawkānī asserts, not only curse the 'two shaykhs' and the majority of the Companions (*jumhūr al-ṣaḥāba*) but also all Muslims including Zayd b. ᶜAlī. This is in fact not true; moreover, the Imāmiyya's rejection of Zayd can be seen in less polemical terms as their having recognised Jaᶜfar al-Ṣādiq as imam instead of Zayd after Muḥammad al-Bāqir's death.

The *Irshād al-ghabī* continues in this polemical style, making the point that ᶜAlī had not cursed but had practised the *tarḍiya*, and he quotes Ṣārim al-Dīn Ibrāhim b. Muḥammad al-Wazīr's (d. 914/1508) historical poem about the Zaydī imams, *al-Bassāma*, in which the author says:

> say the *tarḍiya* for them [Abū Bakr and ᶜUmar] as Abū Ḥasan [ᶜAlī] had done // abstain from cursing if you want to be cautious[77]

The poem reflects the compromise position of some Zaydīs, like Ṣārim al-Dīn Ibn al-Wazīr, who believed that imam ᶜAlī had been accepting of Abū Bakr and ᶜUmar because of their earlier merits in the cause of Islam (*sawābiq*). Such moderates neglected al-Hādī's opinion which had been more severe. Indeed, both the *tawaqquf* and *tarḍiya* positions deviated from al-Hādī's more severe position, the former less so than the latter. Because of these differences amongst Zaydīs, Shawkānī could highlight the opinion of the moderate Zaydīs while neglecting that of the stricter ones and conveniently ignore the fact that all approved the cursing of Muᶜāwiya. His focus also turned to some of the issues of early Islamic history which had long been the subject of polemics between Sunnīs and Shīᶜites. One such matter was Fadak, an oasis which Shīᶜites believe was left by the Prophet as an inheritance to his daughter Fāṭima and which was denied her by Abū Bakr. According to the standard accounts, Abū Bakr, when approached by Fāṭima for her inheritance, claimed that he had heard the Prophet say: 'We [the prophets] do not have heirs. Whatever we leave is alms (*ṣadaqa*). The Family of Muḥammad can eat from that property'. Upon realising that she had been disinherited, Fāṭima is reported to have become angry and henceforth kept away from Abū Bakr, not speaking to him until she died six months later.[78]

[77] Cf. *Badr*, I: 31–2. The *Bassāma* has been edited by Zayd al-Wazīr and will be published soon; I am grateful to him for providing me with a copy. Its author, Ṣārim al-Dīn Ibn al-Wazīr, exemplifies a moderate Zaydī trend, advising the practice of *tarḍiya* for Abū Bakr and ᶜUmar though he is explicit about the need to curse Muᶜāwiya and his companions whom he considers Nāṣibīs.

[78] Cf. Madelung, *The Succession to Muḥammad* (Cambridge University Press, 1997), pp. 50–1; Goldziher, *Muslim Studies*, vol. II, pp. 102–3.

Fadak is a shibboleth for the strict Hādawīs. Where one stands vis-à-vis Abū Bakr's judgement determines for them whether one is a Hādawī or whether one has crossed over to the other side. Shawkānī would, however, highlight the fact that the moderate Zaydīs had indeed approved of Abū Bakr's ruling.[79] In his *Kitāb al-Qalā'id*, Ibn al-Murtaḍā says that 'Abū Bakr's ruling on Fadak was sound, against the [opinion] of the Imāmiyya and some of the Zaydī Muᶜtazilīs. According to me, had the ruling been false ᶜAlī would have refuted it, and had it been unjust the Banū Hāshim and the Muslims would have disavowed it'.[80] Shawkānī also points out that, in his *Kitāb al-Shāmil*, Yaḥyā b. Ḥamza endorsed the same view when he said:

> He [Abū Bakr] asked her [Fāṭima] to present the evidence for her claim [of ownership of Fadak], upon which she proffered ᶜAlī and Umm Ayman [as witnesses]. He [then] said: 'A woman with the woman or a man with the man'. She got angry because of this; justice made her angry (*al-ḥaqq aghḍabahā*).[81]

The idea here is that Fāṭima did not adhere to the Islamic rules of evidence, which would necessitate that she bring forward one additional female or male witness to satisfy the requirement of either two male or one male and two female witnesses. As a result, Abū Bakr rejected her evidence and presented his own in the form of the ḥadīth mentioned above. The approval by these scholars of Abū Bakr's ruling, Shawkānī says, proves they believed he had the probity (*ᶜadl*) required for his acting as a judge in this matter.

Shawkānī fails to mention that al-Qāsim b. Muḥammad, the founder of the Qāsimī dynasty and a figure of great prestige in late Zaydism, held the opposite view. Al-Qāsim stated that as one of the disputants Abū Bakr could not rule as judge in the matter, and moreover, since ᶜAlī was the legitimate imam at the time and had not acquiesced in Abū Bakr's reign (*wilāya*), the latter's judgement could in no way be accepted. Furthermore, Fāṭima was already in possession of the property and therefore could not be asked to provide evidence of ownership.[82] Al-Hādī makes the same arguments in his *Tathbīt al-imāma* and outrightly condemns Abū Bakr as a detestable apostate for his ruling on Fadak. Al-Manṣūr thus was indeed closer to al-Hādī's teachings than either Yaḥyā b. Ḥamza or Ibn al-Murtaḍā.[83] Concealing this fact, Shawkānī in the next section of the *Irshād al-ghabī* quotes al-Hādī as upholding the very opposite views. In a letter al-Hādī had written to the people of Sanaa:

[79] This is in fact not true since not all moderate Zaydīs approved of Abū Bakr's ruling as can be gleaned from the Ibn al-Wazīr's *Bassāma* where he says: 'they [i.e., Abū Bakr and ᶜUmar] preceded Haydar [i.e., ᶜAlī] in rule and usurped by force the inheritance of the meritorious and shy [i.e., Fāṭima]'.

[80] Aḥmad b. Yāḥyā al-Murtaḍā, *Kitāb al-Qalā'id fī taṣḥīḥ al-ᶜaqā'id*, Albert Nader (ed.) (Beirut: Dār al-Mashriq, 1985), p. 144; *Irshād al-ghabī*, p. 9.

[81] *Irshād al-ghabī*, p. 9.

[82] al-Manṣūr al-Qāsim b. Muḥammad, *Kitāb al-Asās*, pp. 165–7; al-Sharafī, *Kitāb ᶜUddat al-akyās*, pp. 174–83. For another concurring view on the matter see al-Manṣūr ᶜAbd Allāh b. Ḥamza, *Kitāb al-Shāfī*, vol. IV, pp. 210–13.

[83] Cf. van Arendonk, *Les Débuts de l'Imāmat Zaidite*, pp. 279f.

> I do not hate any of the Companions – may God be pleased with them – the sincere [amongst them] (*al-ṣādiqīn*) or their succeeding generation (*al-tābiᶜīn*), because of the good deeds of the believing men and women among them. I support all those who emigrated and those who provided refuge and support. For me anyone who curses a believer, holding it to be licit, has committed infidelity; and anyone who curses, holding it to be prohibited, has strayed and committed a grave sin. I only curse those who have broken the pledge (*naqaḍa al-ᶜahd*). These will always be defeated. [I curse] the ones who have ventured into heresy and who time and again rebelled against the Messenger and boldly defamed his family.[84]

The statement cuts both ways. The last few sentences indicate that al-Hādī *did* curse those who showed enmity to the the Prophet's family and whom he would not consider to be Companions. Abū Bakr and ᶜUmar fall into this category in al-Hādī's estimation, and Shawkānī here is deliberately obfuscating in order to make the point that al-Hādī considers the curser an infidel or a grave sinner.

After citing some more moderate Zaydīs on the matter, Shawkānī continues his argument by enumerating ḥadīths from the Sunnī canonical ḥadīth collections which warn against cursing fellow Muslims, declaring them infidels and grave sinners or making defamatory statements (*ghība*) about them.[85] In one of his concluding arguments, Shawkānī maintains that according to the Zaydī school the question of cursing and declaring others to be infidels or grave sinners is not a matter in which *taqlīd* is permitted; rather, one must attain the rank of *mujtahid* before expressing an opinion, since the issues at hand are not derivative (*masāʾil farᶜiyya*), but ones in which certain knowledge (*ᶜilm*) is required. Therefore, even if an opinion from a Hādawī authority can be found approving of the cursing, it would not be permissible to follow it. In stressing the need for *ijtihād*, Shawkānī displays his disdain for his Hādawī opponents whom he considers ignoramuses.

In his conclusion, Shawkānī laments the situation in his day in which strict Hādawīs label as Nāṣibīs all those who do not curse the Companions, those who read the Sunnī canonical ḥadīth collections and study the ḥadīth sciences as well as the scholars of ḥadīth and the Sunnīs generally. This, Shawkānī says, means declaring all Muslims to be infidels, since to be a Nāṣibī is to hate and show enmity to ᶜAlī, which constitutes infidelity according to many ḥadīths. Yet to declare a single Muslim to be an infidel is an act of infidelity in itself. The Hādawīs who have called others Nāṣibīs thus have in fact unwittingly declared themselves to be infidels and have joined the ranks of the Khārijīs. Finally, Shawkānī gives thanks to God for

> relieving [the believers] from the Nāṣibīs and the Khārijīs and those who tread their path, for only a small group of them is left in Oman and a minuscule one on the edges of India who are called the *Ibāḍīs*.[86]

[84] *Irshād al-ghabī*, p. 10; cf. ᶜAlī Aḥmad al-Rāziḥī (ed.), *al-Majmūᶜa al-fākhira* (Sanaa: Dār al-Ḥikma al-Yamāniyya, 2000), p. 146.

[85] *Irshād al-ghabī*, pp. 11–12.

[86] Ibid., p. 14.

With respect to the labelling of the scholars of ḥadīth and the readers of the canonical collections as Nāṣibīs by the strict Hādawīs, Shawkānī says:

> this is a calamity which leads to the unbelief of the one who is lax in these matters; and it is only one of two people who would do this: either one who is ignorant and does not know the meaning of *naṣb* or what a Nāṣibī is, or one who takes no heed of unbelief.[87]

Clearly, therefore, for Shawkānī, the Khārijīs were the true Nāsibīs, and no scholar of the Sunna could be labelled as such.

Shawkānī's *Irshād al-ghabī* polarised in a radical fashion the community of scholars in and around Sanaa. Earlier voices of moderation between the extremes of Traditionism and strict Hādawism, as reflected for instance in the writings of Isḥāq b. Yūsuf (d. 1173/1760), were no longer to be heard.[88] Enraged, strict Hādawīs responded vituperatively to Shawkānī and led riots in the streets. The question of whether one could or should curse certain Companions became a symbol of all that differentiated one group from the other, and strict Hādawism became an ideology of resistance to the state. More importantly, the manner in which the government resolved the religious clash would crystallise the transformations in favour of Sunnism that had taken place in the second half of the eighteenth century. The following chapter will describe the Hādawī reactions to this new order and their attempts to counter it by all means at their disposal.

87 Ibid., p. 14.

88 *Badr*, I: 135–7. In two treatises Isḥāq b. Yūsuf adopts a mediating position: he encourages the Traditionist to consult the legal works of the Hādawī school and advises Hādawīs to refer to the Sunnī ḥadīth collections; cf. Isḥāq b. Yusuf, *al-Wajh al-ḥasan al-mudhhib liʾl-ḥazan* (Sanaa: Maktabat Dār al-Turāth, 1990); idem, *al-Tafkīk li-ʿuqūd al-tashkīk*.

CHAPTER 6

Riots in Sanaa: the Response of the Strict Hādawīs

> O who wants confirmation for himself and certainty of his belief in God; tread the path of the Āl Muḥammad and ask us, the ships of salvation, if you're about to ask Yāqūt; don't substitute the Āl Muḥammad for others, for can pebbles be compared to sapphire?
>
> al-Manṣūr al-Qāsim b. Muḥammad[1]

Shawkānī's efforts in appointing his students and spreading his views throughout the realm engendered much resistance from Hādawīs who saw in these an attack on their school's teachings. Others took exception to him for less ideological reasons; he had simply become too influential. But whatever the case, Shawkānī was perceived by many, especially those who were not in power, to be an enemy of Zaydism. Consequently, Zaydī-Hādawism became an ideology of resistance to the state and the twin issues of cursing the Companions and whether one could study and read the Sunnī canonical ḥadīth collections became the focal points around which opposition coalesced. This chapter will describe some of the Hādawī reactions to Shawkānī and to the state's shift towards Sunnism. The resulting disputes went beyond the theoretical aspects of Islamic law and took on important political and social dimensions.

Reactions to Shawkānī's *Irshād al-ghabī*

Over twenty responses were written against the *Irshād al-ghabī*.[2] In describing the events, Shawkānī states that his enemies tried to persuade government ministers as well as the Imam al-Manṣūr ᶜAlī to imprison or exile him, and some even advocated entering his home and confiscating all books containing legal opinions which were against the Hādawī school. They argued that he sought to replace and nullify the school of the Ahl al-Bayt; however, the imam, Shawkānī says, 'remained silent

[1] This poem by Imam al-Manṣūr al-Qāsim b. Muḥammad is directed against the sufis. Yāqūt is apparently an Ethiopian sufi shaykh who is buried in Aden, and al-Manṣūr does a word play on his name to bolster the claim of the Ahl al-Bayt to the religious leadership of the Muslim community; cf. *Badr*, II: 50; Ḍiyāʾal-Dīn Yūsuf b. Yaḥyā, *Nasmat al-saḥar bi-dhikr man tashayyaᶜa wa shaᶜar*, 3 vols. (Beirut: Dār al-Muʾarrikh al-ᶜArabī, 1999), vol. II, pp. 514–15.

[2] Cf. *Badr*, I: 232f.; *Adab al-ṭalab*, pp. 30f.

and impartial, fearing God, wishing to protect the ulema and to defend those who proffer proof to the faithful'.[3] The imam's decision to take Shawkānī's side at this juncture reflects his pro-Sunnī stance and his willingness to forgo the Hādawī teachings which formed part of the imamate's foundations.

Shawkānī goes on to report that after he had written *Irshād al-ghabī* the general atmosphere in Sanaa was filled with danger for him and that he was advised not to continue teaching in the Great Mosque. He insisted on doing so, however, because of his students' ardent desire to learn. Some strict Hādawīs now came to the mosque to intimidate him: one evening, they stood along his route as he was going home from the mosque and just stared at him. At a later date, an unnamed Rāfiḍī minister sent slave troops into the mosque to cause strife (*fitna*). In his account, Shawkānī presents the conflict as one between himself, a victimised upholder of the Sunna, and fanatics who were opposed to his teaching the Sunnī sources.

> They arrived when the last evening prayers were still being held. They entered the mosque in a disguised manner [but] I saw them arrive. After the prayers were over, a group of my acquaintances mentioned that it would be best if I did not teach *Bukhārī* this evening [but] I was not convinced. Asking God's aid and relying on Him, I sat in my usual place and some of my students attended whilst others absconded, seeing the troops there. Once I began the lesson and started reading I saw them circling the study circle from side to side making noise with their weapons and striking their swords against one another. Then they left and nothing happened thanks to God's help, bounty and protection.[4]

Very little is known about the events described here from sources other than those of the official chroniclers of the period and Shawkānī himself and his devoted students. In these, his Hādawī opponents are invariably described as fanatics and extremists, and the view has been accepted by most contemporary authors writing on the period.[5] The irony that a Zaydī-Hādawī state would persecute Hādawīs and that its imam would take the side of Traditionists is either presented in an unproblematic fashion or explained away as reflecting the obvious righteousness of Shawkānī's claims, which were recognised by the imams. Be that as it may, the responses to *Irshād al-ghabī* sought to inflame the pro-Zaydī sentiments of the masses against its author and the Traditionist scholars who were depicted as destroying Zaydism with the collusion of the rulers. Several of these treatises have been compiled into one volume, entitled *Iẓhār al-khabī fī ʾal-radd ʿalā Irshād al-ghabī* (Exposing the Hidden Deceipt in Answer to the Guidance to the Ignorant), which throws light on the other side of the controversy.[6]

[3] *Adab al-ṭalab*, p. 31. [4] Ibid., p. 32.

[5] Cf. al-ʿAmrī, *al-Imām al-Shawkānī*, pp. 95f.; al-Sharjī, *al-Imām al-Shawkānī*, pp. 79–80; Ṣāliḥ Muḥammad Muqbil, *Muḥammad b. ʿAlī al-Shawkānī* (Jeddah: Maktabat Jidda, 1989), pp. 137–8.

[6] Al-Ḥibshī in his *Maṣādir al-fikr*, p. 141 states that a copy of the *Iẓhār al-khabī* is in the Ambrosiana library. However, the only printed reference to it I could find is in the catalogue of the Sharqiyya Library of the Great Mosque in Sanaa under *majmūʿ* no. 90 (see *Fihrist Makhṭūṭāt Maktabat al-Jāmiʿal-Kabīr*, vol. 2, p. 532) and I was not permitted to consult it.

Amongst those who responded was Sayyid al-Ḥusayn b. Yaḥyā al-Daylamī (d. 1149/1834) who wrote *Durr al-laʾālī fī ḥujjat daʿwat al-Batūl li-Fadak waʾl-ʿAwālī* (The Glittering Pearls proving Fāṭima's claim to Fadak and the ʿĀliya lands [of Medina]).[7] Al-Daylamī was a close friend of Shawkānī's, sharing his Sunnī Traditionist outlook and was an important figure in Dhamār at this time. His refutation of the *Irshād* must have come as a surprise. Shawkānī, however, explains that al-Daylamī was impelled to respond because of the pressure which was brought to bear on him by the strict Hādawīs of Dhamār to show his enmity to his friend. He also asserts that, upon closer reading, al-Daylamī's treatise is in fact supportive of his claims and that the Hādawīs were fooled by believing otherwise. In his only response to his critics, Shawkānī wrote a rebuttal to al-Daylamī's work, which he entitled *al-Durr al-munaḍḍad fī manāqib Āl Muḥammad wa mathālib man ṭaghā ʿalayhim wa tamarrad* (The Well Strung Pearls Regarding the Virtues of Āl Muḥammad and the Defects of Those who Oppose and Rebel Against Them).[8] Another responder was ʿAbd Allāh b. Ismāʿīl al-Nihmī (d. 1228/1813), who had been one of Shawkānī's teachers, and Shawkānī explains that al-Nihmī did this because of the prompting of some government ministers.[9] Clearly, the issue of the cursing of the Companions was a source of great controversy among scholars, but more importantly, it now defined the terms around which political rivalry was conducted.

The Sanaa Riots of 1210/1796

In the month of Shawwāl 1210/April 1796 an anti-Sunnī riot took place in Sanaa. The immediate occasion was that a slave called Sindraws al-Ḥabashī, who was owned by the Imam al-Manṣūr ʿAlī's son ʿAbd Allāh (d. 1229/1814), would curse Muʿāwiya whenever he met another slave called Sulṭān al-Ḥabashī, who was owned by al-Manṣūr ʿAlī. Some slaves, like Sindraws and Sulṭān, were official functionaries of the state, either with the army or in the administration, and their political and religious views often reflected those of their masters. The latter commonly used these slaves to advance their interests in court politics.[10]

One evening, Sindraws met Sulṭān at the door of the Taqwā mosque and again cursed Muʿāwiya. This time Sulṭān did not hold back, as was his habit, but fought with Sindraws and injured the latter's upper arm. When news of this altercation became public, a riot ensued:

> the reason [for the fight] spread among the commoners, and the mob (*ghawghāʾ*) and scoundrels (*al-awghād*) rioted. At night they shouted curses against Muʿāwiya and the *tarḍiya* for ʿAlī b. Abī Ṭālib – may God be pleased with him. They headed for the mosque

[7] A copy of al-Daylamī's treatise, which I have not seen, is in the Gharbiyya Library of the Great Mosque in Sanaa, ms. *majmūʿ* no. 140, fols. 25–32.

[8] *Adab ṭalab*, p. 34; *Badr*, I: 234. This work is not extant.

[9] *Badr*, I: 235, 380.

[10] Cf. al-ʿAmrī, *al-Umarāʾal-ʿabīd*, pp. 53–65.

> of Qubbat al-Mahdī al-ᶜAbbās in lower Sanaa, because here Hāshimites [i.e., *sayyids*] were praying the late evening prayer. They continued cursing Muᶜāwiya and headed for Bustān al-Sulṭān where Sindraws al-Ḥabashī was. Here they implored [God] that he recover quickly and went on. Every time they passed in front of a house belonging to those who follow the Sunna they would stone it. They also stoned the houses of the Qurayshites who were ministers of the imam. All this took place at night for fear that the government would know who they were. Sayf al-Islām Aḥmad, the son of the Commander of the Faithful, sent some of his troops who imprisoned the two slaves. The fervour of the rioters did not abate, [however], and people continued to curse Muᶜāwiya and his partisans. They also cursed Sulaymān, the commander of the troops sent out, and his companions. The clamour increased, so Sayf al-Islam placed Sulaymān and his companions in prison [too] in order to quell the riot. . . .[11]

As a result of the riot, a number of *sayyids* from the Āl al-Maswarī and the Āl Luṭf al-Bāriᵓ families lost the religious posts to which they had been appointed by al-Mahdī al-ᶜAbbās, al-Manṣūr ᶜAlī's father. Soon, the properties of the minister Muḥammad b. Aḥmad Khalīl were expropriated by the imam because he was thought to have had a hand in the troubles.[12] The exact involvement of these people in the riot is not clear from the chronicle whose author, Jaḥḥāf, was an official court historian of the period, but the houses of people of Quraysh, people of Umayyad descent, were targeted by the rioters. Al-Manṣūr ᶜAlī had appointed as minister al-Ḥasan b. ᶜUthmān al-ᶜUlufī (d. 1216/1802), who is described as an Umayyad in the sources. This was resented by some members of the ruling house as well as by a *sayyid* minister, Aḥmad b. Ismāᶜīl Fāyiʻ (d. 1219/1804), who had been demoted whilst al-ᶜUlufī's star rose in government.[13] However, it is not clear whether ᶜAbd Allāh, the imam's son and Sindraws' master, had incited his slave because of a grudge against his father or, as seems more likely, against Shawkānī. ᶜAbd Allāh had been appointed by his father as a supervisor over the affairs of the court (*dīwān*), stood in for his father on the council of judges, which met twice weekly, and acted as the last court of appeal for cases from all over Yemen. As chief judge, Shawkānī was performing much the same functions, and this may have led to friction between the two men.[14]

While personal rivalries between ministers may have played a role in the events described here, this was a period of intense Sunnī–Shīᶜī friction in Sanaa, with the imam unequivocally taking the side of the Sunnīs against opposition both from within the ruling house and from outside it. As the account of the incident indicates, the Qubbat al-Mahdī mosque was a centre of Hādawī influence at this time. It is

[11] Jaḥḥāf, *Durar nuḥūr*, fols. 170b–171a. The Hāshimites mentioned here are *sayyids* (i.e., descendants of al-Ḥasan and al-Ḥusayn), whereas the Qurayshites are people of Umayyad descent, and more specifically descendants of ᶜAbd al-Malik b. Marwān (d. 86/705). Even today, one finds Yemenis who claim to know the descent of different families, tracing them back in some instances to pre-Islamic times. The persistence of the genealogical imagination is one of the enduring features of Yemeni society, although this has come under attack in the republican period, and it has become impolite to discuss publicly such matters.

[12] See his biography in *Badr*, II: 124–6.

[13] Cf. al-ᶜUlufī's biography in *Nayl*, I: 342–3.

[14] Cf. *Badr*, I: 462; *Nayl*, II: 84–5.

telling that a later Hādawī Imam, al-Nāṣir ᶜAbd Allāh b. al-Ḥasan (d. 1256/1840) rose from the teaching circles of this mosque. The zeal of the commoners also indicates that Shīᶜite sentiments could be whipped up easily and constituted a form of protest against the rulers, whose commitment to the Zaydī tradition was seen as nominal. Let us now turn to the teachings that the strict-Hādawīs were advocating and the texts they were reading in the mosques and which had led to the riots against the Traditionists and the Qāsimī state.

Ismāᶜīl al-Nuᶜmī's *al-Sayf al-bātir*

The most important rebuttal to Shawkānī's *Irshād al-ghabī* was a treatise written by Ismāᶜīl b. ᶜIzz al-Dīn al-Nuᶜmī (d. 1220/1805). It is entitled *al-Sayf al-bātir al-muḍīʾ li-kashf al-īhām waʾl-tamwīh fī Irshād al-ghabī* (The Luminous Sharp Sword which Reveals the Deception and Distortion in the Guidance to the Ignorant).[15] This is a lengthy and vituperative Shīᶜite response to Shawkānī, in which the latter is called a Nāṣibī and is accused of hating the Ahl al-Bayt and of wanting to destroy Zaydism by spreading false theological beliefs, mainly by teaching Sunnī texts in Zaydī mosques. The attack is highly personal and refutes the *Irshād al-ghabī* point by point, quoting Hādawī authors, such as Ḥumaydān b. Yaḥyā, who had advocated a very strict stance against certain Companions. The quotations, as in the case of the *Irshād*, are selective: whereas Shawkānī chose to highlight the opinions of moderate Muᶜtazilī-influenced scholars like Yaḥyā b. Ḥamza and Ibn al-Murtaḍā, al-Nuᶜmī chooses to dispute these by quoting those who maintained a commitment to al-Hādī's strict opinions. Al-Nuᶜmī even refuses to accept the veracity of Shawkānī's quotations and implies that he is a liar. In effect, the argument and counterargument proceed by marshalling as many opinions of previous imams and scholars as possible in order to bolster opposing claims about what 'true' Zaydī beliefs are.

The Arabic in the *Sayf al-bātir* is weak and belies al-Nuᶜmī's scholarly competence. It is evident that he did not have a good grasp of grammar because the autograph text is replete with errors such as incorrect gender and case endings. In places, the textual corruptions make it impossible to understand the author's intent. The work is an exhortatory pamphlet by a 'low-grade' scholar that was intended to be read out loud, as it had been in the Great Mosque prior to a second set of riots, to which we will turn to shortly. It consists of emotive and largely rhyming prose, as well as poetry, which was aimed at moving listeners into lamenting the fate of Zaydism and evoking hatred for Shawkānī as an enemy of the Āl Muḥammad and their cause. It harps extensively, for example, on emotionally charged Shīᶜite accounts, such as the usurpation of Fadak by Abū Bakr, by which he disinherited Fāṭima and left her angry until her death. It also provides an example of the way in

[15] Ismāᶜīl b. ᶜIzz al-Dīn al-Nuᶜmī, *Kitāb al-Sayf al-bātir*, ms. Sanaa, Gharbiyya Library, *majmūᶜ* no. 188, fols. 1–36 and *majmūᶜ* no. 91, fols. 55–77.

which the Hādawīs articulated their doctrines, what they understood Zaydism to be, and what they saw as the proper role of a Zaydī state in defending these doctrines. Al-Nu^cmī's argument is circumlocutory and difficult to summarise. Indeed, the text was not written in the form of a scholarly argument, but more as an *ad hominem* attack on Shawkānī intended to stir Shī^cite sentiments and spur the listeners to some sort of action.

As the full title of *al-Sayf al-bātir* suggests, al-Nu^cmī accuses Shawkānī of deceiving (*īhām*) and distorting (*tamwīh*) the teachings of the Ahl al-Bayt. He accuses him of 'maligning the *Ahl al-ʿAdl waʾl-Tawḥīd* [= Zaydīs] with falsehood (*zūr*) and slander (*buhtān*), of [claiming] that the followers of the Family (*qarāba*) curse the rightly guided (*rāshidūn*) among the Companions... of attributing to them religious ignorance (*ghabāwa fīʾl-dīn*)... and of instilling the belief that the Āl Muḥammad and their partisans are Rāfiḍīs and people of sin and error'.[16] All this, al-Nu^cmī says, indicates Shawkānī's unbelief (*kufr*).

A constant refrain repeated throughout the work is that the Ahl al-Bayt and their followers do not curse,

> for cursing is not in their character, which [instead] lies in the pursuit of knowledge, being patient and chivalrous, and their habit is to persevere... and be patient if something befalls them.[17]

This does not mean that they do not consider the likes of Abū Bakr and ʿUmar, not to mention Muʿāwiya and his partisans, to be grave sinners and even infidels. Here, al-Nuʿmī comes to his second major point, which is to reject Shawkānī's claim that a consensus exists amongst the Zaydīs against declaring the Companions to be grave sinners or infidels. To prove this, al-Nuʿmī cites the works of Ḥumaydān and Sayyid Muḥammad b. Idrīs (d. 736/1335) to the effect that one who shows enmity or rejects ʿAlī is to be considered an infidel. He also quotes al-Manṣūr al-Ḥasan b. Badr al-dīn (d. 668/1270) and Abū ʾl-Jārūd (fl. second/eighth century) according to whom Zayd b. ʿAlī stated, 'The imamate and the consultation (*shūrā*) are only valid for us [i.e., the Ahl al-Bayt]', and 'every banner which was raised in Islam for other than us is a banner of error'. Then he quotes, to the same effect, Aḥmad b. ʿAbd al-Ḥaqq al-Mikhlāfī and Yāḥyā b. al-Ḥusayn b. al-Muʾayyad Muḥammad (d. 1090/1679).[18] The latter belonged to a group of strict Hādawīs who coalesced around Imam al-Mahdī Aḥmad b. al-Ḥasan in the seventeenth century, and represented thereafter for people like al-Nuʿmī the true ideals of Zaydism out of which the Qāsimī 'summons' was created and which it was meant to propagate. After citing these authorities, al-Nuʿmī asks rhetorically about the consensus Shawkānī claims to exist, and states that if the latter rejects the proof provided here he will consider him a heretical Nāṣibī on a par with the ḥadīth scholars Shams al-Dīn al-Dhahabī (d. 748/1347) and Yaḥyā b. Maʿīn (d. 233/848). No doubt is left about al-Nuʿmī's stance vis-à-vis the caliphs preceding ʿAlī when he says:

[16] *al-Sayf al-bātir*, fols. 1b–2b. [17] Ibid., fol. 9b.
[18] For Yaḥyā b. al-Ḥusayn's biography see *Badr*, II: 329–30.

> Notice how Abū Bakr, ᶜUmar and ᶜUthmān all superseded him, [despite] his being designated textually by God and His Messenger. They tried to kill him,... they took Fadak from the daughter of God's Messenger...[19]

They were to be considered *fussāq* and *infidels*; cursing them, however, was another matter, but only because it is not becoming for Zaydīs to do so.

In the following section al-Nuᶜmī attacks Shawkānī for dividing the Zaydī imams into two camps – those who practise *tarḍiya* and *taraḥḥum* versus those who practise *tawaqquf* – and says that doing so is like dividing the Prophets. The Ahl al-Bayt are as 'one body in their beliefs and are agreed that Abū Bakr was not the caliph after the Messenger of God; he was not appointed by the Imam [i.e., ᶜAlī] and was not suitable'.[20] He then quotes a major Hādawī scholar of the Qāsimī period, Sayyid Dāwūd b. al-Hādī (d. 1035/1625), who had taught many of the central figures in the early Qāsimī state (e.g., Saᶜd al-Dīn al-Maswarī). Sayyid Dāwūd blamed the Muᶜtazila for promoting the *tarḍiya* doctrine.

> The people of *tarḍiya* have weak proofs and narrations which do not accord with those of the elders of the Ahl al-Bayt. They were taken from the writings of the Muᶜtazila about the *tarḍiya* which have no basis or soundness with the elders. Rather, what is known from [the early Zaydī imams] is their grave accusation and condemnation of the crime committed by the Shaykhs [Abū Bakr, ᶜUmar and ᶜUthmān].[21]

Although al-Nuᶜmī does not acknowledge it, passages like these highlight the difference of opinion which existed among Zaydīs over these issues. The more Muᶜtazilī-influenced scholars inclined to a moderate stance, whereas the early Qāsimī scholars, including all the imams of the seventeenth century, had taken the stricter position of *tawaqquf*. A few – such as al-Mahdī Aḥmad b. al-Ḥasan and al-Ḥasan al-Habal – went as far as al-Nuᶜmī by going beyond *tawaqquf* and accusing the Companions of outright infidelity. The latter group were closer to the spirit of the early and stricter Qāsimīs than the imams of the second half of the eighteenth century, under whom Shawkānī served, and who in fact had abandoned the doctrines of their forebears on this issue and others.

Occasionally, al-Nuᶜmī employs technical legal rules in his argument, as when he notes that the specific (*al-khāṣṣ*) always specifies (*yukhaṣṣiṣ*) the general (*al-ᶜāmm*). He argues then that the Shīᶜite proof-texts regarding the offences perpetrated by Abū Bakr and ᶜUmar specify, and thus partially negate any ḥadīths about practising *tarḍiya* of the Companions in general. Another technical argument he posits is that ᶜAlī's sayings constitute a proof (*ḥujja*), which supersedes all other opinions. In this, al-Nuᶜmī is being faithful to the view posited by al-Qāsim b. Muḥammad about the privileged role accorded to ᶜAlī in matters over which there is a difference of opinion.[22] So, for example, ᶜAlī's corroboration of Fāṭima's story that Fadak had been given to her is testimony enough for her ownership and invalidates any other claims or rulings on the matter.

19 *al-Sayf al-bātir*, fol. 2b. 20 Ibid., fol. 4b. 21 Ibid., fol. 4b.
22 Ibid., fol. 5b; cf. al-Manṣūr al-Qāsim b. Muḥammad, *al-Irshād ilā sabīl al-rashād*, pp. 78–81.

Such arguments, however, remain marginal to the main content which consists of emotive stories about the special role accorded to the Ahl al-Bayt by God and the Prophet and about the injustices perpetrated against them. Al-Nuᶜmī, thus, narrates the story of *ḥadīth al-thaqalayn* and that of Saqīfat Banī Sāᶜida; the first is seen by Shīᶜites as a key instance of the designation of the Ahl al-Bayt, and more specifically ᶜAlī, to succeed the Prophet; the second is the story of Abū Bakr's usurpation and the collusion which took place stripping ᶜAlī of his right while he was busy attending to the Prophet's funeral. However, the largest space, about a third of the treatise, is occupied by the story of Fadak.

Highlighting his attachment to the opinions of the early Rassid imams, al-Nuᶜmī states that the only legitimate stance on Fadak is the one taken by al-Qāsim b. Ibrāhīm, who said: 'We have a mother who was Righteous, the daughter of the Righteous one, and who died feeling angry, and we are angry because of her anger'.[23] Al-Nuᶜmī then accuses Shawkānī of vilifying Fāṭima and of hating the Ahl al-Bayt in approving of Abū Bakr's judgement about Fadak, and disputes his claim that Zayd b. ᶜAlī, Yaḥyā b. Ḥamza and Ibn al-Murtaḍā had also approved it. Abū Bakr's judgement on Fadak is discussed in great detail and al-Nuᶜmī presents quotations refuting it. Amongst these is one which adduces proof from the Qurʾān and the Sunna that Prophets do leave inheritances, and that Abū Bakr had based his judgement on an isolated Tradition (*āḥād*).[24] This type of ḥadīth, al-Nuᶜmī says, cannot invalidate judgements based on the Qurʾān because of the consensus of the Companions and the Ahl al-Bayt disallowing this.[25] Al-Nuᶜmī then adduces an extensive quotation from al-Hādī's *Tathbīt al-imāma* on the issue of Fadak to prove his point that Abū Bakr's ruling was unjust and cruel, and more importantly that neither Abū Bakr nor ᶜUmar were fit to rule as they were not the legitimate successors of the Prophet. He emotively criticises Shawkānī for quoting imams like Yaḥyā b. Ḥamza on Fadak.

> How dishonourable and horrible is this deception! Or, is this *faqīh's* [Shawkānī] highlighting the errors of the [Zaydī] imams – God's peace be upon them – like the fly which hovers around garbage or the crow which pecks at wounds?... Take heed, O believers in God, of this grave matter, and of this serious claim that Fāṭima, the daughter of Muḥammad, the lord of mankind – God's blessing and peace be on him and his family – died feeling angry and was denied justice. Has any Muslim ever made the claim [that she was treated justly]? He [Shawkānī] has rebelled against his Lord, violated His commands, and harmed his Prophet by attacking his daughter – the *Batūl*, mistress of the worlds' women. What a calamity it is to violate the lord of Messengers. Did you know, O faqīh, that God gets angry when she is angry? It is not an exaggeration to say that you do not believe in her, or her children or the Traditions relating her virtues and theirs. This you do in imitation of al-Dhahabī and Ibn Maᶜīn. For according to you the sound [Traditions] are those which they have claimed to be sound, and the unsound are those they have said were unsound. This is what constitutes blindness, forsakenness, falsehood and slander. God is the grantor of all assistance.[26]

[23] *al-Sayf al-bātir*, fol. 9b.
[24] Cf. chapter 3, f.n. 52.
[25] *al-Sayf al-bātir*, fol. 14b.
[26] Ibid., fol. 14b.

The last third of *al-Sayf al-bātir* consists of an extensive critique of the Sunnī canonical ḥadīth collections, the science of *isnād* criticism, and the scholars of ḥadīth. Al-Nuᶜmī argues for prohibiting the reading and teaching of these sources in Zaydī mosques. The debate over which sources were to be considered authoritative is central to the polemic which raged between the Traditionists and the Hādawīs. The Sunnī sources were brought into Yemen and were used selectively by the Zaydīs from the twelfth century on, with imams such as al-Mutawakkil Aḥmad b. Sulaymān being amongst the first to use them. The effect of this on Hādawī Zaydism was in the long-term destructive: once their use became legitimate, Sunnī doctrines and opinions were adopted by individual scholars, who then criticised the inherited tradition, threatening the integrity of the school's teachings. From the perspective of the strict Hādawīs, Shawkānī came to symbolise the culmination of the process of accepting these sources, because he rejected the Zaydī sources altogether, relying exclusively on the Sunnī ones. He came to be considered, even by today's Hādawīs, to be a Ḥashwī: an anthropomorphist Traditionist, but among Hādawīs also one who narrates ḥadīths on the authority of transmitters who are considered to be heretics (*zanādiqa*), and who interprets them literally; hence, he is accused of anthropomorphising God, claiming that the Qurᶜān was not created, and believing in determinism among other matters.[27] This explains the vehemence of al-Nuᶜmī's attacks on the use of these sources.

After criticising the Sunnī ḥadīth scholars for excluding Shīᶜites from their chains of transmission, al-Nuᶜmī explains the pernicious effect of using the Sunnī ḥadīth sources.

> According to the Āl Muḥammad, whoever reads these books and believes in them has strayed into error. Amongst their beliefs are predestination (*jabr*) and anthropomorphism (*tashbīh*). They also believe and prove in their books that Abū Bakr is better than ᶜAlī b. Abī Ṭālib: the spirit (*nafs*) of the Messenger – God's peace and blessing be upon him. They also prove the *visio beatifica* above which God is highly exalted. They affirm determinism (*khalq al-afᶜāl*), and claim that the wrongdoing Muslims (*al-muwaḥḥidūn al-ẓālimūn*) will come out of hell on Judgement Day ... the collections of ḥadīth contain what al-Tirmidhī transmitted ... that the Prophet said to Muᶜāwiya, the rebel, 'God make him a rightly guided leader'. They fabricated Traditions from the Prophet, they have led others astray and have strayed themselves [from the right path]. God have mercy on the ignoramus who has such ḥadīths read to him without knowing their significance (*dalāla*). He will think well of Muᶜāwiya b. Abī Sufyān, the rebel ... O the error and blindness! For whoever believes Muᶜāwiya to be a rightly guided leader is truly a Nāṣibī without a doubt. The claim, [therefore], which is made by the majority of Zaydīs that whoever reads the works of ḥadīth is a Nāṣibī is indeed true.[28]

In the last section of *al-Sayf al-bātir* we find al-Nuᶜmī lamenting the state of affairs in his day with the Qāsimī imams allowing the reading of these sources, thus betraying the cause of their forefathers. He asks the question: 'How is it that

[27] On the Zaydī view of the Ḥashwīs see al-Murtaḍā, *Munya waʾl-amal*, pp. 121f.
[28] *al-Sayf al-bātir*, fol. 23b.

the rulers of the Āl Muḥammad are not condemning the readers of these works in the Zaydī mosques?'[29] Elsewhere he writes:

> But oh, but oh where are the rulers who defend the honour of their fathers, the pure imams? Here is Fāṭima, the daughter of Muḥammad the beloved of God, who has been dishonoured by him [Shawkānī] and nothing has happened to him. Only recently, he was made one of the rulers' judges, adjudicating over the small and the great. He is [even] rewarded for what he has done to Fāṭima and the imams of the Prophet's house. This has become the custom of today's imams... [who] facilitate and do not rebuke this grave error, so that now many of the religious students in the Great Mosque in Sanaa and other mosques are devoted to reading these books, believing what is in them. They have neglected the books of the Ahl al-Bayt, the pure, and they have strayed and become amongst the forsaken... If a student is seen to study the books of the Ahl al-Bayt or often mentions ᶜAlī b. Abī Ṭālib – God's blessings be upon him – his rights are trespassed upon and enmity is shown to him. Their great Shaykh [Shawkānī] is the author of this false treatise, who has caused pain to the heart and prevented sleep. Where are the defenders and the people of religion? Where are the fortunate Zaydīs? By God, should the reins be loosened for this jurist (*faqīh*) he would surely issue a *fatwā* like that of al-Daybaᶜ which made licit the blood of the Āl al-Ḥasan.[30]

Al-Nuᶜmī then provides examples of previous imams who prohibited the use of these works in mosques in order to prove this was common Zaydī practice. The earliest imam he cites is a pre-Qāsimī imam called al-Mahdī ᶜAlī b. Muḥammad b. ᶜAlī (d. 773/1371) who is reported to have ordered that 'whoever sits in Zaydī mosques teaching from their enemies' books and refuting the sayings of the Family (*ᶜitra*) will be stopped, and restrained should he continue to pursue this'.[31] More significantly, al-Nuᶜmī claims that this was also the practice of the seventeenth-century Qāsimī imams al-Muʾayyad Muḥammad and al-Mutawakkil Ismāᶜīl. The latter had apparently prevented the Sunnī collections from being taught in Sanaa's Great Mosque. Al-Muʾayyad Muḥammad, the second Qāsimī imam, appears to have included in his letter calling on people to accept his imamate (*risāla ilā ahl Allāh*) the decree which was issued by the Caspian al-Dāᶜī al-Ḥasan b. Zayd in 252/866 to his governors. Exemplifying the Zaydī spirit of these early Qāsimīs, the decree says:

> We command you to rule over the people in your domain in accordance with the Book of God, the Sunna of his Messenger – God's blessings and peace be upon him – and those Traditions which are sound from the Commander of the Faithful ᶜAlī b. Abī Ṭālib – God's blessing be upon him – in matters of the principles of religion and the law. [You must] show that he is better than all other imams. Prevent them, in the strictest possible way, from believing in predestination, anthropomorphism, from antagonising the believers

[29] Ibid., fol. 26b.
[30] Ibid., fols. 28b–29b. Nuᶜmī is probably referring to the famous Yemeni historian of Zabīd, ᶜAbd al-Raḥmān b. ᶜAlī al-Shaybānī (d. 944/1536), who is known as Ibn al-Daybaᶜ. I could not find a reference to the above-mentioned *fatwā*; cf. Ayman Fuʾād Sayyid, *Maṣādir tārīkh al-Yaman*, pp. 200–5.
[31] *al-Sayf al-bātir*, fol. 30b.

who uphold God's justice and unicity, from picking fights with Shīʿites, from transmitting stories that give preference to the enemies of God and the Commander of the Faithful – God's peace and blessings be upon him. Command them to say in prayer '*bism Allāh al-raḥmān al-raḥīm*'; to perform the *qunūt* [i.e., an invocation] in the daybreak prayer; to say the *witr* [an invocation] from the Qurʾān; to perform five *takbīr*s over the dead; to stop wiping their shoes (*masḥ ʿalā al-khuffayn*) [during ablution]; to say '*ḥayya ʿalā khayr al-ʿamal*' in the call to prayer; to say the call to prayer and the announcement of its commencement and repeating them (*al-adhān waʾl-iqāma muthannā*). Warn those who disobey our commands for their punishment will be death . . .[32]

For al-Nuʿmī, the use of the Sunnī collections entailed forgoing certain Hādawī legal opinions (e.g., ritual practices) in addition to credal beliefs. It was the entirety of the Hādawī *madhhab* which was at stake here. By pointing out that the early Qāsimīs had been stricter Zaydīs, he was drawing a contrast between them and the imams of his day. The early imams had embodied Zaydī doctrines about the righteous rule of the Ahl al-Bayt and defended their doctrines while sustaining an ever expanding state; those of the late eighteenth century had not only given up on Zaydism in al-Nuʿmī's estimation but sponsored and protected those who, like Shawkānī, were striving for its demise. In one of his final statements al-Nuʿmī refers to Shawkānī by making allusion to a much earlier foe of the Hādawīs, Nashwān b. Saʿīd al-Ḥimyarī (d. 573/1178), and says 'truly every age must have its Nashwān'.[33] The historical continuities of this conflict were very long-term indeed and its repercussions were to manifest themselves in yet another riot.

The Sanaa Riots of 1216/1802

On 12 Ramaḍān 1216/11 January 1802, another anti-Sunnī riot took place in Sanaa; this time, however, the events took a more violent turn than in the previous riot and the consequences for the Hādawīs were much more serious. Shawkānī reports that in Ramaḍān of this year he was teaching Bukhārī's *Ṣaḥīḥ* in Sanaa's Great Mosque after the evening prayers and many learned scholars and ordinary people were attending his lectures.[34] This, he says, aroused the ire of an unnamed Rāfiḍī minister, who then requested Sayyid Yaḥyā b. Muḥammad al-Ḥūthī, one of Shawkānī's former teachers, to teach a pro-ʿAlī Zaydī work. A chair was installed for al-Ḥūthī in the Ṣalāḥ al-Dīn mosque with numerous candles lit around it. From it, al-Ḥūthī read out a work entitled *Tafrīj al-kurūb* by Isḥāq b. Yūsuf b. al-Mutawakkil Ismāʿīl,

[32] Ibid., fol. 29b; cf. Ignaz Goldziher, *Introduction to Islamic Theology and Law*, trans. Andras and Ruth Hamori (Princeton University Press, 1981), pp. 205–6; Madelung, *Der Imam al-Qāsim*, pp. 154–9.

[33] *al-Sayf al-bātir*, fol. 31b.

[34] Shawkānī was trying to establish the practice of reading and teaching the Sunnī canonical ḥadīth collections in mosques during the month of Ramaḍān, with special emphasis being given to the *Ṣaḥīḥayn* of Bukhārī and Muslim. It seems that since his time this has indeed become a common practice for scholars in Yemen to do.

which extolled the virtues of ᶜAlī.[35] Shawkānī adds that al-Ḥūthī went beyond what was contained in the work by cursing some of the Companions, at the behest of the Rāfiḍī minister who wanted to irritate the 'Umayyad' government officials of the time. It appears that many commoners came to see and listen to al-Ḥūthī and they would shout out with him curses against the Companions.[36]

The situation became grave when al-Ḥūthī started reading the work in Sanaa's Great Mosque, the major centre of teaching where the Traditionist scholars appear to have held sway at the time. Upon hearing of this, Imam al-Manṣūr ᶜAlī sent word to his minister of religious endowments (*awqāf*), Sayyid Ismā'īl b. al-Ḥasan al-Shāmī, to order al-Ḥūthī back to the Ṣalāḥ al-Dīn mosque. Al-Shāmī in turn asked Aḥmad b. Muḥsin Ḥātim, the head muezzin at the Great Mosque (*ra'īs al-ma'dhana*), to inform al-Ḥuthī. When those who had been listening to al-Ḥūthī arrived at the Great Mosque that evening and discovered that al-Ḥūthī had not come because of the imam's order, they rioted 'raising their voices, cursing and preventing the evening prayer from being performed'. Soon 'those who were suspicious of the government and those who had been concealing their *rafḍ* [i.e., their Shīᶜite sentiments]' joined them and all left the mosque shouting.[37] A detailed description of what happened next is provided in Jaḥḥāf's chronicle:

> In the year 1216, in Ramaḍān, the common people rioted in gang-like fashion and the Shīᶜites revealed their hatred. The mob shouted in the streets and markets curses against Muᶜāwiya and blessings on ᶜAlī – may God be pleased with him. This took place on Monday evening the 12th of Ramaḍān in the first third of the night. They left the Great Mosque of Sanaa after ignorantly and stupidly preventing the prayer leader from approaching the *miḥrāb*. They went to the house of Ḥasan b. ᶜUthmān, the Umayyad, and threw stones at his windows... They did this until he [Ḥasan] ordered his slaves and companions to shoot at them with rifles. Fear of the bullets and of death forced them to leave and they went to the house of the minister al-Ḥasan b. ᶜAlī Ḥanash, which was close by. [The latter's] companions threw stones at them which hit the rioters and they returned to Ibn ᶜUthmān's, shouting curses against him and Muᶜāwiya. The imam was in his palace perplexed about the commoners' revolt. A faction of the rioters then went to the house of the minister of endowments, Ismāᶜīl b. Ḥasan al-Shāmī – the Hāshimī – and threw stones at it, striking fear in the hearts of the women of the Prophet's family inside. [The women] screamed about their distress and destruction whilst the rioters threw stones and shouted curses at Muᶜāwiya.... Some of the rioters heard the women screaming, whereupon they told them that they would not stop throwing stones until they, too, cursed Muᶜāwiya. This they did and then the rioters ceased throwing... The rioters then headed for the Imam Sharaf al-Dīn school because the minister of endowments

[35] Isḥāq b. Yūsuf also wrote a book entitled *Ijābat al-dāᶜī ilā nafy al-ijmāᶜ fī anna Abā Bakr afḍal min amīr al-mu'minīn ᶜAlī*, ms. Sanaa, Gharbiyya Library, *majmūᶜ* nos. 22 and 37. Cf. *Badr*, I: 135–7 where Shawkānī says that he inclined to justice (*inṣāf*) in the matter of the Sunna versus the Hādawī school and was not fanatical in favour of the latter, but that he did not show this out of fear of retribution from the strict Hādawīs (*al-jāmidūn min'l-fuqahā'*).

[36] The sources for the events described here are: *Badr*, II: 344–8; *Adab al-ṭalab*, pp. 30–4; Jaḥḥāf, *Durar nuḥūr*, fols. 222b–224a; al-ᶜAmrānī, *Itḥāf al-nabīh*, fols. 34b–35a; al-ᶜAmrī, *al-Imām al-Shawkānī*, pp. 106–16.

[37] *Badr*, II: 345.

> (*nāẓir al-awqāf*) was [hiding] there. He was [truly] from among the best of ᶜAlī b. Abī Ṭālib's descendants... They wanted to kill him, but he locked its doors and fled through its eastern gate. They broke down the western door and entered but did not find him. Then the rioters massed and went to the imam's palace screaming curses against Muᶜāwiya, and many people also massed around the house of the Umayyad minister. This led the imam to dispatch his son Muḥammad with his troops to save the minister Ibn ᶜUthmān, and when the people saw him coming, they dispersed...[38]

Unlike Shawkānī who presents the Rāfiḍī minister as playing a key role in these events, Jaḥḥāf blames the riot on the actions taken by the muezzin Aḥmad Ḥātim, who, he claims, was envious of ᶜAlī b. Ibrāhīm al-Amīr's success with the public. The latter, a grandson of Ibn al-Amīr, was one of Sanaa's leading preachers at this time. He held Traditionist views and his house was also stoned in the events described above.[39] Jaḥḥāf says that the muezzin, Ḥātim, was trying to reduce al-Amīr's popularity by getting al-Ḥūthī to preach in the Great Mosque. Later, however, Ḥātim was forced to obey the imam's orders. Whatever the case, Shawkānī, who comments on the events, says that ᶜAlī al-Amīr's house was attacked because 'he was not an ever-cursing Rāfiḍī (*lam yakun rāfiḍiyyan laᶜᶜānan*)', and in al-ᶜUlufī's case it was because 'he was of Umayyad descent (*Umawī al-nasab*)', whereas in that of Ḥanash it was due to his 'manifesting the Sunna and dissociating from *rafḍ* (*mutaẓāhiran biʾl-sunna mutabarriʾan min al-rafḍ*)'.[40]

One can only guess who the unnamed Rāfiḍī minister was. The most likely candidate is Sayyid Aḥmad b. Ismāᶜīl Fāyiᶜ, who had been a minister in al-Manṣūr's government overseeing the revenues from Hodeida, Ḥayma, Bilād Ḥarāz and most of Lower Yemen. In 1196/1782 the imam was informed by the governor of Hodeida that Fāyiᶜ was asking for more than the customary monthly revenue of 3,000 riyals from the port. The common practice for the Tihāmī port towns was similar to that in Hodeida which supplied Sanaa with 3,000 riyals per month and the remaining tax revenues – anywhere from 4,000 to 12,000 riyals – would remain in savings at the port.[41] The imam could then draw on these savings in case of an emergency elsewhere. As a result of this information about Fāyiᶜ's doings the imam took away his supervision rights over Hodeida, and, for reasons unknown, in 1206/1791–2 took away Fāyiᶜ's supervision rights over the Ḥarāz regions, giving these to al-ᶜUlufī, the Umayyad.[42] Perhaps jealousy or resentment led Fāyiᶜ to incite al-Ḥūthī to recite a Hādawī work in the Great Mosque, which was a factor in instigating the riots during which al-ᶜUlufī's house was stoned. However, the riots cannot be blamed solely on the actions of a single individual, as Shawkānī implies. They must be seen in the context of the religious tensions in Sanaa at this time as reflected in the scholarly debates. Only so can the draconian measures taken by the state

[38] Jaḥḥāf, *Durar nuḥūr*, fols. 222b–224a.
[39] Cf. *Badr*, I: 420–2. ᶜAlī b. Ibrāhīm al-Amīr died in 1219/1805.
[40] *Badr*, II: 346. [41] Cf. *Nayl*, I: 73.
[42] *Nayl*, I: 71–3. Ismāᶜīl al-Akwaᶜ also suspects that it was Fāyiᶜ who was behind the specific events here, cf. *Hijar al-ᶜilm*, IV: 2252–3; also al-ᶜAmrī, *Miʾat ᶜām*, pp. 74–7.

against the strict Hādawīs, many of whom were not involved directly in the riots, be explained.

The evening after the riot the imam summoned his ministers, military commanders and Shawkānī, his chief judge, for counsel and decided to put everyone in prison: al-Ḥūthī, ᶜAlī al-Amīr, al-Shāmī, Ḥātim and Ismāᶜīl b. ᶜIzz al-Dīn al-Nuᶜmī, author of the *Sayf al-bātir*. The last had not been involved in the incidents but was imprisoned, by Shawkānī's own admission, for his strict Hādawī beliefs.[43] Shawkānī's role was decisive. He advised the imam not only that all strict Hādawīs be imprisoned, but that an investigation be undertaken to discover all those who played a part in the riots. The rest of the month of Ramaḍān was taken up with this. Shawkānī's justification for al-Nuᶜmī's arrest reveals his perception of the threat posed by the strict Hādawīs.

> Amongst the most extreme was Ismāᶜīl b. ᶜIzz al-Dīn al-Nuᶜmī who was a committed Rāfiḍī in addition to being a great ignoramus. His extremism led to a kind of madness. He started collecting passages from the books of the Rāfiḍa, which he would read in the mosque to those who were even more ignorant than he was. He sought to divide the Muslims and to delude them [into believing] that the great ulema were Nāṣibīs, who hated ᶜAlī – may God honour him. In fact, he compiled a work in which he mentions the greatest ulema and tries to make people hate them. At times he refers to them as Sunnīs, and at others he calls them Nāṣibīs. Despite this, he does not know grammar, morphology, the principles of jurisprudence and theology, law, Qurʾānic exegesis and ḥadīth... He does not know anything except what he has read in the works of the Imāmī Rāfiḍīs. Like [al-Nuᶜmī], but more ignorant, was Dirghām, a slave belonging to our lord the Imam – may God preserve him. His greatest interest lay in reading some of the works of the Rāfiḍīs in which the caliphs are cursed along with others among the great Companions. He would sit in the mosque and teach the cursing of the caliphs to those who were more ignorant than him. These matters are the reason for what we just mentioned [i.e., the riots].[44]

Shawkānī presents the strict Hādawī as being ignorant of the truth embodied in sources that only a scholar of his abilities and education is able to interpret and disseminate. For their part, the strict Hādawīs not only held that they were being faithful to their own sources, but that the issues at hand were ultimately about one's political and metaphysical commitment to the cause of the Ahl al-Bayt and as such transcended considerations of learning and scholarship. The punishment meted out to the perpetrators of the riots and those strict Hādawīs highlights the influence Shawkāṇī had garnered with the imam and the extent to which the latter now came to identify with the Traditionist ulema. Hādawism had become a mobilising ideology against the state and its authorities, much as it had always been whenever a rival claimant to the imamate rose to challenge a reigning incumbent, with the exception that now the state was perceived by the Hādawīs to have become Sunnī

[43] The initial reaction of the imam of imprisoning all the parties concerned was common practice for the Qāsimī imams. Justice in the form of physical punishment, exile, execution, financial penalty or release would only come later after the dust had settled.

[44] *Badr*, II: 347.

by allowing Sunnī works to be read in Zaydī mosques and by preventing Zaydī works from being taught there.

On 4 Shawwāl 1216/7 March 1802 the imam ordered nineteen of the imprisoned scholars who had incited the riot to be brought before his palace window where they were severely flogged. On the following day, another forty-two prisoners, this time commoners involved in the riot, were brought out and also flogged. Five of them, who were accused of stealing from al-ᶜUlufī's house, had drums attached to their backs which were beaten while they were paraded around the town. On 27 Dhū al-Qaᶜda/1 April, thirty-two prisoners were manacled, of whom sixteen were exiled to the Red Sea island of Kamarān and the rest were sent to the prison island of Zaylaᶜ. All were to die in exile, including al-Nuᶜmī who passed away sometime before 1220/1805.[45] The remaining prisoners, who were either ministers or Traditionist scholars, were freed a few days later, making clear which tendency the authorities preferred. Jaḥḥāf says that the action taken by the imam 'resulted in his having strength and inspiring fear and terror. This led people to avoid the roads he took. He could leave his palace with a small retinue and no one would dare look him in the eye'.[46] The imamic gaze was now a Sunnī one, and it was more than thirty-five years before a Hādawī imam again took the reins of power in Sanaa.

The issues being fought over in this episode go back to the time following the Prophet's death. In Yemen, they were brought up whenever Zaydīs clashed with their opponents. What gives these issues currency in late eighteenth-century Yemen, however, is that just as the first three caliphs were seen to have usurped the rights of ᶜAlī, so Shawkānī was perceived as an interloper usurping the authority of the Zaydī-Hādawī scholars within the institutions of the state and in determining doctrine.

Further Hādawī Resistance

Another example of opposition to the Traditionists was when one of Shawkānī's long-standing students, Sayyid Aḥmad b. ᶜAlī, a descendant of al-Mutawakkil Ismāᶜīl, fell into some sort of dispute or competition with other students and felt that Shawkānī had sided with his enemies. As a result, Sayyid Aḥmad took one of Shawkānī's works and spread the word among 'the rabble (*ᶜāmma*) and those fanatics with little knowledge (*al-mutafaqqiha al-muqaṣṣirīn al-mutaᶜaṣṣibīn*)' that it upheld loathsome opinions. The work is not named, but in it Shawkānī had argued that the group that would attain salvation in the hereafter (*al-firqa al-nājiya*) would be the one which clung to the practice (*ᶜamal*) of the Messenger of God and his Companions, and not the people of the various schools of law who all claim that

[45] *Badr*, II: 205–6; The English traveller Viscount Valentia attests to having seen these prisoners, whom he describes as fanatics, in Mocha, see Valentia, *Voyages and Travels*, vol. II, pp. 353–4.
[46] Jaḥḥāf, *Durar nuḥūr*, fols. 223b–224a.

they alone will be saved.[47] In other words, Shawkānī was presented as claiming that only those who follow the Sunna, as the Traditionists understood it, would be saved, and, by implication, the Hādawīs who gave less credence to the Sunnī ḥadīth works and more to their school's doctrines would not. The ramifications of such an allegation were serious indeed since nothing less than eternal salvation was at stake.

The imams Shawkānī served were seen by the Hādawīs to partake of Shawkānī's Traditionist approach and were therefore accused of being anti-Zaydī. In Zaydism, one of the doctrinally valid ways in which to react to what one sees as corrupt or unjust rule is to 'emigrate', performing what is referred to as *hijra*.[48] This is what took place now with many Zaydīs leaving Sanaa and heading to northern tribal areas or to towns like Ṣaᶜda where they attempted to garner support against the regime. The first scholar of note to do this was Sayyid Ismāᶜīl b. Aḥmad al-Kibsī (d. 1250/1834), whose nickname was Mughallis (i.e., the one who tarries) and who 'emigrated' with some of his supporters in 1220/1806 to Ẓafīr Ḥajja where he made his 'summons' (*daᶜā ilā nafsihi*), taking the title al-Mutawakkil ᶜalā Allāh.[49] His 'summons' was not generally recognised except, it seems, by a few in Ṣaᶜda whereupon he left for there and tried on successive occasions to raise the tribes of Baraṭ against the government in Sanaa, apparently without much success. After spending seventeen years in Ṣaᶜda, Mughallis returned to his home town of Hijrat al-Kibs, where he taught and preached, and maintained his claim to the imamate. He died in Dhamār.

Muḥammad b. Ṣāliḥ al-Samāwī (d. 1241/1825)

The most serious attempt to take Shawkānī to task for his Traditionist views came from a strict Hādawī scholar called Muḥammad b. Ṣāliḥ al-Samāwī (d. 1241/1825), who was nicknamed Ibn Ḥarīwah. As explained earlier, Ibn Ḥarīwah regarded Shawkānī's ideas on *ijtihād*, when combined with the power he wielded as chief judge, as a threat to the Hādawī school and a means of empowering himself as the supreme legal authority in Yemen. The scholarly clash came with Shawkānī's

47 *al-Tiqṣār*, pp. 355–6; cf. *Nayl*, I: 163–4.

48 The practice of emigrating (*hijra*) is an established doctrine that was already clearly elaborated by the early Zaydīs. Imam al-Qāsim b. Ibrāhīm held that the Qurᵓānic injunction to the early Meccan Muslims to sever their ties with the unjust and emigrate constituted a permanent obligation for all the faithful, who also had to emigrate from the 'abode of injustice (*dār al-ẓulm*)', understood as the neighbourhood of the wicked and the oppressors, even though the neighbours were nominally Muslims too. Cf. Madelung, *Der Imam al-Qāsim*, pp. 138f.; idem, 'A Muṭarrifī manuscript', reprinted in *Religious Schools and Sects in Medieval Islam* (London: Variorum Reprints, 1985), art. XIX, p. 77.

49 Ismāᶜīl b. Ḥusayn Jaghmān, *al-Durr al-manẓūm fī tarājim al-thalātha al-nujūm*, ed. Zayd al-Wazīr (McLean, Virginia: Markaz al-Turāth waᵓl-Buḥūth al-Yamanī, 2002), pp. 75–84. I am grateful to Zayd al-Wazīr for providing me with a copy of this work which consists of three biographies of the Hādawī scholars Ismāᶜīl b. Aḥmad al-Mughallis, Aḥmad b. ᶜAlī al-Sirājī, and al-Ḥusayn b. ᶜAlī al-Muᵓayyadī. The first revolted against al-Manṣūr ᶜAlī whereas the latter two revolted against al-Mahdī ᶜAbd Allāh. For al-Mughallis's biography see *Badr*, I: 141; *Nayl*, I: 259–61.

writing in 1235/1820 of *al-Sayl al-jarrār* (The Raging Torrent). In it, he provides a line by line critique and refutation of the principal legal manual used by the Zaydīs in Yemen, the *Kitāb al-Azhār*. In writing the *Sayl*, Shawkānī was building on an existing Yemeni tradition of commentaries on the *Kitāb al-Azhār*. Before him, the Traditionists al-Ḥasan al-Jalāl and Ibn al-Amīr wrote similar works, and Shawkānī drew on these, especially Jalāl's *Ḍaw' al-nahār*.[50] It would seem, however, that Shawkānī's criticism was more vehement and thorough than that of his predecessors.

Ibn Ḥarīwah responded to the *Sayl al-jarrār* in a work entitled *al-Ghaṭamṭam al-zakhkhār al-muṭahhir min rijs al-Sayl al-jarrār* (The Vast Ocean which Purifies the Filth of the Raging Torrent). In it, he accuses Shawkānī of plagiarising from al-Jalāl and, more specifically, from Ibn Ḥajar's *Talkhīṣ al-ḥabīr* and *Fatḥ al-bārī*.[51] Ibn Ḥarīwah further claims that Shawkānī is a deviant from the teachings of the Ahl al-Bayt who hates the Prophet's family (*al-ᶜitra*) and suffers from compounded ignorance (*jahl murakkab*).[52] Moreover, in a view shared by some contemporary Hādawīs, Ibn Ḥarīwah holds that Shawkānī was out to undermine the Hādawī school by supplanting the *Kitāb al-Azhār* with his own *fiqh* work, *al-Durar al-bahiyya*, on which he also penned a commentary called *al-Darārī al-muḍiyya*.[53] Ibn Ḥarīwah ends by claiming that Shawkānī properly belongs to the school of Muḥammad b. ᶜAbd al-Wahhāb. Here is what he says:

> And after you have claimed absolute *ijtihād* (*al-ijtihād al-muṭlaq*) and to be competent in all its areas, what is your objective from all the opinions and preferences which you have substantiated in your works? If it is that the people should refer to these for the knowledge which you have and which they do not, then this is the *taqlīd* which you forbade! The *muqallid* is free to choose; if he prefers your opinion then he must accept it, and if he prefers the opinion of the Ahl al-Bayt then he must abide by theirs. So what does your *ijtihād* amount to – assuming it is correct – except the *ijtihād* of one among the *mujtahids*? We have not known a single *mujtahid* from this community who claimed that it is incumbent [on others to] accept his opinion or his *ijtihād*, and that it is forbidden to accept the *ijtihād* of anyone else, except those whose school you have joined, by whom I mean the Najdī [Muḥammad b. ᶜAbd al-Wahhāb] and Ḥasan b. Khālid...
>
> Among the things that the Najdī has said is that he is right in matters of dispute (*masāʾil al-khilāf*) and that the others are in error. With this he made licit the shedding of the blood of Muslims and the taking of their wealth. You belong to this school in claiming that you are right in disputed matters and that others are in error. Because of this you wish to defile the opinions of the Ahl al-Bayt by attributing these to error and you take it upon yourself to circulate your works and opinions and claim that these are the truth.[54]

Ibn Ḥarīwah paid for his principled stance with his life, leaving the *Ghaṭamṭam* unfinished. An event which took place in Mocha precipitated this. It is reported

50 Cf. *Badr*, II: 223. 51 *Ghaṭamṭam*, vol. I (*muqaddima*), pp. 65–74, 132–3.
52 Ibid., p. 53. 53 Ibid., p. 50.
54 Ibid., pp. 128–9. Al-Ḥasan b. Khālid (d. 1234/1819) was a Traditionist *sayyid* from Hijrat Ḍamad in ᶜAsīr. He appears to have shared Shawkānī's views and was the main advisor to and judge under Sharīf Ḥamūd, who ruled much of the Tihāma until Muḥammad ᶜAlī's troops finally defeated him; cf. *Nayl*, I: 323–7.

that a number of Westerners (*ifranj*) who were in the port town attacked a *sharīfa* (a descendant from the Prophet's family) from Taᶜizz, wanting to rape her. She screamed for help, and a *faqīh* from Sanaa who was in Mocha on his way to pilgrimage in Mecca fought with one of the Westerners, stabbing him. The people of Mocha took hold of the *faqīh* and handed him over to the governor who then sent him in chains to Sanaa where he apparently remained in prison. Ibn Ḥarīwah was asked for his opinion on this affair and he wrote a vituperative answer in which he criticised Imam al-Mahdī ᶜAbd Allāh for holding the *faqīh*, who had done an honourable deed, and for the lamentable state of affairs and his laxity in religious matters. This antagonised al-Mahdī, and a number of jurists took advantage of this and goaded the imam to punish Ibn Ḥarīwah for his insolence. On 16 Dhū al-Ḥijja 1240/1 August 1825, the imam ordered that Ibn Ḥarīwah be taken from his house. He was then paraded through the streets of Sanaa with drums attached to his back and was whipped and pelted with refuse. After this, he was sent to the island prison of Kamarān and shortly thereafter brought back to prison in Hodeida. Some scholars (no names are mentioned) issued a *fatwā* for his execution, and he was beheaded on 10 Muḥarram 1241/25 August 1825. His body was crucified and it is said that his head continued to recite verses from the Qurʾān well after the event.[55]

Though the dating of Ibn Ḥarīwah's execution to 10 Muḥarram is a topos, given that it is intended to coincide with al-Ḥusayn's death in Karbala, and as such the date must be apocryphal, the story has become the stuff of legend and modern politics among Hādawīs in Yemen. They consider him a martyr (*shahīd*) who was killed by an oppressive ruler and point the finger of blame at Shawkānī for the *fatwā*. In discussing this matter, the modern scholar Aḥmad al-Shāmī reports that Shawkānī said in his last will and testament that he would forgive all who transgress against him, except those who accuse him of having had a hand in Ibn Ḥarīwah's death. Yet, al-Shāmī adds, it is impossible to believe that Shawkānī could not at least have saved him from this fate given the privileged status he enjoyed in al-Mahdī ᶜAbd Allāh's court.[56] Be that as it may, Ibn Ḥarīwah's execution became a cause célèbre and led to serious attempts to topple the existing order.

Sayyid Aḥmad b. ᶜAlī al-Sirājī (d. 1248/1832)

The Hādawī revolts continued after Mughallis. In Ṣafar 1247/July 1831[57] one of Sanaa's leading Hādawī scholars, Sayyid Aḥmad b. ᶜAlī al-Sirājī (d. 1248/1832), emigrated from Sanaa, again with a number of students and supporters, because of the state's oppression (*ẓulm*) and the mismanagement of the religious endowments (*awqāf*), among other matters. Before al-Sirājī could make the 'summons' he

[55] Cf. *Nayl*, II: 274–9; al-ᶜAmri, *al-Imām al-Shawkānī*, pp. 269–72; Aḥmad al-Shāmī, *Nafaḥāt wa lafaḥāt min ʾl-Yaman* (Beirut: Dār al-Nadwa al-Jadīda, 1988), pp. 401–5.

[56] al-Shāmī, *Nafaḥāt wa lafaḥāt*, p. 404.

[57] There is some confusion about the exact date of al-Sirājī's emigration in revolt from Sanaa. Some sources claim it was in 1247/1831 and others claim it was two years later in 1249/1833; cf. *Nayl*, I: 151; al-Jirāfī, *al-Muqtaṭaf*, p. 263; al-ᶜAmrī, *Miʾat ᶜām*, p. 237; Jaghmān, *al-Durr al-manẓūm*, pp. 49–52, 88.

traveled to Hijrat Kibs to discuss matters with Mughallis in order to clarify the matter of who was to be imam, since the latter had earlier claimed the title for himself. The result of the discussions appears to have been that Mughallis desisted from his claim, thus allowing al-Sirājī to make his own 'summons'.[58] That al-Sirājī felt it necessary to seek Mughallis's permission is indicative of the fact that Hādawīs considered that the legitimate imams were not those in Sanaa. It is as if a parallel imamate existed, one with greater claims to legitimacy than that in Sanaa but politically and militarily ineffectual. One senses this also in Hādawī historical works, like Majd al-Dīn al-Muʾayyadī's *al-Tuḥaf sharḥ al-zalaf* or Ismāʿīl Jaghmān's *al-Durr al-manẓūm*, which provide their own lists of 'legitimate' imams, ignoring totally that there were rulers in Sanaa who claimed to be imams and held the reins of effective power.

A short while after his trip to Hijrat al-Kibs, al-Sirājī made his 'summons' and rose in rebellion against al-Mahdī ʿAbd Allāh (d. 1251/1835), claiming the imamate for himself with the backing of the tribes of 'Khawlān, Arḥab, Nihm and others from the lands of Ḥāshid and Bakīl'.[59] The rallying point of al-Sirājī's revolt was the execution a few years earlier in 1241/1825 of Shawkānī's bitter enemy Ibn Ḥarīwāh.[60] The Hādawī ire against Shawkānī is reflected in the following lines from a poem written by one of al-Sirājī's supporters and biographers, Ismāʿīl Jaghmān.[61]

They have killed Muḥammad b. Ṣāliḥ [Ibn Ḥarīwāh] insolently // and he is the critical and perspicacious imam
He has no blemish other than silencing // the Nāṣibīs whom he describes as impudent
He loved Ṭāhā [the Prophet], the *waṣī* [ʿAlī], and Fāṭima // and their boys who are the pride of the proud
his edifice for the Āl [the family of the Prophet] is glorious and lofty // [it is] the *Ghaṭamṭam* [Ibn Ḥarīwāh's commentary attacking Shawkānī's *al-Sayl al-jarrār*] which abounds in [goodness] for men
in it is the proof from the Book and Sunna // to which both the nomads and the urban folk have witnessed
the riffraff have gathered in quite a gathering // seeking [to please] the Ghimr [Imam al-Mahdī ʿAbd Allāh], and they are duffers
they tortured him, may evil befall them for their deed // it is fitting for us to seek revenge from them
it is necessary for us to punish them for their actions // repeatedly, till the tyrant/butcher tires of them
[we will] parade the despot as the oppressed // one was paraded, him [Shawkānī] and his *Sayl al-jarrār*
[even] in disgrace this [crime] will never be undone // and let the pious be optimistic.[62]

[58] Jaghmān, *al-Durr al-manẓūm*, p. 89.
[59] *Nayl*, I: 151; al-Jirāfī, *al-Muqtaṭaf*, p. 263; *Ḥawliyyāt Yamāniyya*, pp. 60–2; al-ʿAmrī, *Miʾat ʿām*, pp. 236–9. The Hādawī mentor of those who rebelled against al-Mahdī ʿAbd Allāh and later against his son al-Manṣūr ʿAlī was Qāḍī ʿAbd al-Raḥmān b. ʿAbd Allāh al-Mujāhid (d. 1252/1836); cf. *Nayl*, II: 33–4.
[60] Cf. al-Jirāfī, *al-Muqtaṭaf*, p. 263.
[61] For Jaghmān's biography, see *Nayl*, I: 270–3.
[62] Jaghmān, *al-Durr al-manẓūm*, pp. 100–1.

Al-Sirājī's revolt ended in failure because the tribes who had come with him to attack Sanaa abandoned him, allegedly after being paid off by al-Mahdī ᶜAbd Allāh. In 1248/1832 he was assassinated, and his supporters claim that his assassin was an agent sent by 'the government of Sanaa' (*dawlat Ṣanᶜāʾ*).[63] In Hādawī terms, the expression *dawlat Ṣanᶜāʾ* denotes an illegitimate regime in power because it is confined to one location and transmits none of the universalistic attributes of an imamic appellation.

Despite al-Sirājī's failure a number of his students were now active in the mosques of Sanaa, especially in the Qubbat al-Mahdī Mosque by the Sāʾila (the dry river bed running through the city). These students and scholars met in the month of Rabīᶜ (presumably al-Awwal) in the year 1249/1833 and secretly gave their allegiance (*bayᶜa*) to Sayyid ᶜAbd Allāh b. al-Ḥasan b. Aḥmad b. al-Mahdī al-ᶜAbbās (d. 1256/1840), who was an eminent student of the religious sciences and a scion of the Qāsimī family from a branch which had been superseded in rule by another headed by al-Manṣūr ᶜAlī b. al-Mahdī al-ᶜAbbās.[64]

The Hādawī Restoration: Imam al-Nāṣir ᶜAbd Allāh b. al-Ḥasan (d. 1256/1840)

Shawkānī passed away late in 1250/1834 and the last imam he served, al-Mahdī ᶜAbd Allāh, died a year later on 6 Shaᶜbān 1251/27 November 1835.[65] In a fashion now consistent with precedent, al-Mahdī's son ᶜAlī became imam on the day after his father's death and took the title al-Manṣūr; the post of *Qāḍī al-Quḍāt* was inherited by Shawkānī's brother Yaḥyā (d. 1267/1851). For a while, it seemed as if the order established by Shawkānī, with its network of judges and students, would continue.

Al-Manṣūr ᶜAlī's reign lasted just over one year, however, ending with a rebellion of his troops because of a delay in the payment of their wages.[66] Late on

63 Ibid., p. 92; cf. al-ᶜAmrī, *Miʾat ᶜām*, pp. 236–9.

64 *Ḥawliyyāt*, p. 60. Among the other Hādawīs who also 'emigrated' from Sanaa was Sayyid Ḥusayn b. ᶜAlī al-Muʾayyadī, who left for Ṣaᶜda in 1251/1835 after he was invited by its people to perfom the obligation of 'ordaining the proper and forbidding the improperʾ; cf. *Nayl*, I: 392–4, *Nayl*, II: 89–90; Jaghmān, *al-Durr al-manẓūm*, pp. 104–16. Al-Muʾayyadī, however, did not claim the imamate for himself. Other Hādawīs in Sanaa who were active in their opposition to the rule of al-Mahdī ᶜAbd Allāh were Qāḍī ᶜAbd Allāh b. ᶜAlī al-Ghālibī and Sayyid ᶜAbd al-Karīm Abū Ṭālib. Their main teacher was imam Aḥmad al-Sirājī, who in turn was taught by ᶜAbd al-Raḥmān b. ᶜAbd Allāh al-Mujāhid.

65 Al-Jirāfī considers al-Mahdī ᶜAbd Allāh to have been 'the last imam of the Qāsimī state to have had the [qualities] of complete authority and leadership'; cf. *al-Muqtaṭaf*, p. 264.

66 The story behind the rebellion is complicated. It would seem that some tribes from Baraṭ and Arḥab under the leadership of Ḥusayn b. Yaḥyā b. ᶜAbd Allāh al-Baraṭī attacked the fortress of ᶜUṭṭān south-west of Sanaa and began causing troubles in the area in the hope that they would be paid off by the imam. Al-Manṣūr ᶜAlī refused to pay them, and instead called upon the tribes of Khawlān to come to his aid against the Baraṭīs and Arḥabīs. The arrival of Khawlān, however, corresponded with a period of tension between the imam and his troops because of a delay in the payment of their wages. The troops in fact had cut the road in front of the imam upon his return

Wednesday 3 Dhū ᵓal-Qaᶜda 1252/9 February 1837 the soldiers, led by a slave commander named Farḥān Ṣāliḥ al-ᶜUlufī,[67] attacked al-Manṣūr's palace, Bustān al-Mutawakkil, and imprisoned him and his uncle Muḥammad. The chronicle *al-Ḥawliyyāt Yamāniyya* states that a consensus had developed, presumably among the troops, that Sayyid ᶜAbd Allāh b. al-Ḥasan would be made imam. Upon this, Sayyid ᶜAbd Allāh b. al-Ḥasan, who had been secretly nominated imam four years before by a group of Hādawī students and scholars, made his *daᶜwa* and took the title 'al-Nāṣir'.[68] Nearly ninety years after Imam al-Mahdī al-ᶜAbbās's accession, which ushered in the dominance of Traditionist scholars, the strict Hādawīs finally had an imam in power. They now sought to redress the wrongs they felt had been done in the past, and in particular by Shawkānī.

Unlike the imams who preceded him, al-Nāṣir ᶜAbd Allāh was a scholar in his own right. He was well versed in the Islamic sciences and especially in Zaydī works. Though not a *mujtahid*, he acted more like the paragon of a Zaydī imam since he gave the Friday sermon and led the communal prayers himself.[69] According to the *Ḥawliyyāt*, many were pleased at al-Nāṣir's accession thinking he would be a 'renewer' (*mujaddid*) who would enforce the Sharīᶜa. Until he assumed the mantle of the imamate, he had been the prayer leader in the Qubbat al-Mahdī mosque, where he had a circle of students and scholars who shared his strict Hādawī views. With his assumption of power, these supporters now came to the forefront in the imamate's judicial and ruling structures.

The extent to which this new elite wished to eradicate the traces left by the old guard can be seen in a series of actions taken by al-Nāṣir. In addition to imprisoning the previous imam, al-Manṣūr ᶜAlī, and his uncle Muḥammad, al-Nāṣir imprisoned all the governors, *waqf* administrators (*nuẓẓār*), and judges, including Shawkānī's brother Yaḥyā, his son Aḥmad as well as his students (e.g., Muḥammad b. al-Ḥasan al-Shijnī). The *Ḥawliyyāt* mentions that the intention was to replace all these with new people, presumably ones who were Hādawī in orientation, such as Sayyid Muḥammad b. ᶜAbd al-Rabb (d. 1262/1846), who was appointed chief judge in the *dīwān*.[70]

Al-Nāṣir's antagonism toward his predecessors, and Shawkānī in particular, took extreme proportions. He ordered Jews to stand over the grave of al-Mahdī ᶜAbd Allāh and read the Torah, and initiated plans to exhume Shawkānī's corpse and burn it.[71] However, he abandoned the idea of exhumation on the advice of certain learned people. There was also fear that the tribe of Khawlān, to

from Friday prayers and were under the impression that the Khawlānī tribesmen had been called in to replace them. Faced with this threat, the troops then revolted and replaced al-Manṣūr ᶜAlī with al-Nāṣir.

[67] Slaves often carried the last name of their masters as in the case here with Farḥān who was owned by someone from the al-ᶜUlufī family.

[68] For a full description of the coup against al-Manṣūr ᶜAlī, see *Ḥawliyyāt*, pp. 70–2. Also see al-Kibsī, *al-Laṭāᵓif al-saniyya*, pp. 303–5.

[69] For his biography and education, see *Nayl*, II: 70–3. Also see al-Jirāfī, *al-Muqtaṭaf*, p. 264, and *Ḥawliyyāt*, pp. 73–4.

[70] *Ḥawliyyāt*, pp. 73–4; *Nayl*, II: 282–3. [71] *Ḥawliyyāt*, pp. 73.

which Shawkānī had belonged, would attack Sanaa if the exhumation was carried out.[72]

Al-Nāṣir's attempts to punish anti-Hādawī scholars and judges did not end here. After waging a campaign in Lower Yemen against a number of recalcitrant tribes, and also against an Egyptian army which was now in control of the Tihāma and Taᶜizz, he returned to Sanaa, defeated in 1253/1837.[73] Once in Sanaa, al-Nāṣir sought to rid himself once and for all of his predecessor and rivals, the former Imam al-Manṣūr ᶜAlī and his uncle Muḥammad, by having them executed. To accomplish this, al-Nāṣir felt he needed the support of the leading scholars, judges and notables of Sanaa. He therefore invited them to his *dīwān*, but soon realised that they would not grant him what he desired. He desisted from carrying out the executions because rumours began circulating that such an act would lead to civil unrest. He was obviously in a weak position and could neither garner the support he needed nor impose his wishes by fiat. This is in marked contrast to his predecessors who were able to have their Hādawī critics silenced either through execution, as in the case of Ibn Ḥarīwāh, or through exile and imprisonment on the Red Sea islands of Zaylaᶜand Kamarān, as in the case of Ismāᶜīl al-Nuᶜmī.

Thwarted by those assembled before him, al-Nāṣir claimed that he had invited the scholars to his palace in order to diminish the number of judges, who had become too numerous. To accomplish this, he posed a legal question about the validity of prayer in mosques that had been built by oppressive rulers (*al-ẓalama*). The answer each scholar gave would determine whether he remained in his post. The author of the *Ḥawliyyāt*, who is narrating the story, makes it clear that he finds the question risible and indicative of al-Nāṣir's stupidity (*ḥumq*). He says that the Zaydīs were never troubled by this issue and pray in, among other places, the Great Mosque of Sanaa, parts of which were built by the Ṣulayḥids, who were Ismāᶜīlī. The question, however, is telling of al-Nāṣir's strict Shīᶜite views, since what in fact he was asking was whether Zaydīs were allowed to pray in non-Zaydī mosques. In other words, were Sunnī mosques to be considered valid places of worship?

The scholars were not put to the test on this issue because Aḥmad b. Zayd al-Kibsī (d. 1271/1854),[74] one of those present, was able to give an answer which appears to have circumvented the matter and avoided causing embarrassment to the imam. From the perspective of Hādawī law, the question seems unusual since Zaydīs have been known to pray in mosques regardless of their original builders.

72 As mentioned already, Shawkānī was of the *qāḍī* estate and therefore would not be considered properly a tribesman. However, he did hail from Shawkān, which was in Khawlān territory, and as such would have had some claims to the protection of that tribe. It is unlikely that this protection would extend posthumously. The threat of tribal attack may have been made by pro-Shawkānī scholars who wished to frighten al-Nāṣir into desisting from the exhumation.

73 Cf. *Ḥawliyyāt*, pp. 75–85; ᶜAbd al-Ḥamīd al-Biṭrīq, *Min tārīkh al-Yaman al-ḥadīth: 1517–1840* (n.p.: Maᶜhad al-Buḥūth wa'l-Dirāsāt al-ᶜArabiyya, 1969), pp. 62–87; al-Kibsī, *al-Laṭā'if al-saniyya*, pp. 304–5; al-ᶜAmrī, *Mi'at ᶜām*, pp. 258–67.

74 See his biography in *Nayl*, I: 101–4. His entry offers a good example of a scholar who was well versed in both the Zaydī as well as the Sunnī ḥadīths.

This is corroborated by the *Sharḥ al-Azhār* in which it is stated that the imam is explicitly forbidden to tamper with a mosque either built or in any way modified by someone unjust or oppressive.[75] Zaydī history, however, does offer examples of Zaydī imams destroying mosques built by those they considered heretics, as when al-Manṣūr ᶜAbd Allāh b. Ḥamza (d. 614/1217) ordered the demolition of the Mutarrifī mosque in Sanāᶜin 611/1214–5 after destroying their principal centre, the *hijra* of Waqash.[76] It was perhaps to this tradition of extreme Zaydī intolerance that al-Nāṣir was alluding in his question. It seems, however, that al-Nāṣir was again thwarted in his desire to punish the Sunnī Traditionist scholars.

The matter did not end here. On the following day, al-Nāṣir sent two of his supporters, Qāḍī Ismāᶜīl Jaghmān and Sayyid Yaḥyā b. Muḥammad al-Akhfash (d. 1262/1845),[77] to test the judges and decide for themselves who would be stripped of their posts. The author of the *Ḥawliyyāt* tells us that they proceeded to find fault with certain judges on such grounds as 'he knows the Sunna of the Messenger of God whereas for us only the *madhhab* (i.e., the Hādawī school) is valid', and 'he loves the Companions of the Prophet'.[78] Jaghmān was a strict Hādawī, and one can imagine him leading this purge of judges; al-Akhfash, however, had been Shawkānī's student and protégé, and it is not likely that he would have participated in such activity. So, this report is dubious. But whether historically true or not, the story does reflect the intense antagonism between strict Hādawīs and Traditionists in Sanaa at the time.

In the month of Rabīᶜ al-Awwal 1256/May 1840, al-Nāṣir was ambushed and brutally killed in Wādī Ḍahr by Ismāᶜīlīs of the Hamdān tribe. He had ruled for a period of three years and four months, and his death signaled the end of the last serious Hādawī challenge to the predominance of the Traditionist scholars and jurists, who consisted mostly of Shawkānī's students. The upper hand now returned to the Traditionists, who, despite the period of great turmoil that Yemen was to witness (a period referred to in the Arabic sources as 'the period of disorder', *fatrat al-fawḍā*), were to dominate the judicial scene and irrevocably diminish the influence of Hādawism in Yemen.

The Period of Disorder

The imamate in Sanaa effectively lost the coastal regions of the Tihāma from 1832 onward and would never recover them. This was severe blow to the government's treasury which relied heavily on revenues generated from trade in the Tihāmī ports. In a letter written in 1818 to Khalīl Bāshā – the commander of Muḥammad ᶜAlī's forces, who occupied the Tihāma on two separate occasions from 1811 till 1819 and from 1832 till 1840 – Shawkānī urged him to lower the 200,000 riyals in

[75] Cf. *Sharḥ al-Azhār*, vol. IV, p. 558.

[76] Wilferd Madelung, 'The origins of the Yemenite Hijra', in Alan Jones (ed.), *Arabicus Felix* (Reading: Ithaca Press, 1991), p. 32.

[77] Cf. *Nayl*, II: 400; *al-Tiqṣār*, p. 437.

[78] *Ḥawliyyāt*, p. 88.

remittances the Egyptians demanded from the imamate's treasury for the return of the coastal region. He argued that without the ports of the Tihāma the imamate could not pay the sum demanded because the state's expenditures far outstripped its revenues from the highlands.[79] The Tihāma was returned to the imamate in 1819, only to be occupied again by the Egyptians in 1832. Eventually, the Egyptians left the Tihāma in 1840, leaving it under the control of the ruler of Abū ᶜArīsh, Sharīf Ḥusayn b. ᶜAlī Ḥaidar (d. 1293/1876). He was to control it until 1849 when troubles led him to invite the Ottomans to re-occupy it.

In Sanaa a number of imams succeeded each other at short intervals. After al-Nāṣir's death al-Hādī Muḥammad b. al-Mutawakkil Aḥmad (d. 1259/1843) took control in Sanaa.[80] He ruled for nearly four years and led a series of campaigns in Lower Yemen, most famously bringing to an end the rebellion led by a Sufi called Faqīh Saᶜīd in the region of Ibb. Al-Hādī was succeeded by ᶜAlī b. al-Mahdī ᶜAbd Allāh, who had already ruled previously under the title al-Manṣūr. His reign lasted two-and-a-half years until he was ousted by his cousin, al-Mutawakkil Muḥammad b. Yaḥyā, who had made an alliance with Sharīf Ḥusayn. The pact broke down within two years and al-Mutawakkil led a force into the Tihāma to regain control over it from the Sharīf. A series of battles ensued in which al-Mutawakkil was ultimately defeated, forcing him to flee back to Sanaa. Sharīf Ḥusayn, however, was unable to regain full control and this led him to formally invite the Ottomans to claim the region for themselves. The Ottomans dispatched 3,000 soldiers who arrived in Hodeida in Jumādā al-Ūlā 1265/April 1849. The Sharīf was given a stipend and was allowed to retire in Mecca where he later died. In June al-Mutawakkil Muḥammad traveled to Hodeida in order to come to terms with the Ottoman commanding officer. Yemen was declared part of the Ottoman empire and al-Mutawakkil its representative in the highlands.

An Ottoman force of 1,500 men entered Sanaa on 6 Ramaḍān 1265/26 July 1849, but no sooner had they arrived than the people revolted, surrounding the force and the imam in the citadel.[81] ᶜAlī b. al-Mahdī ᶜAbd Allāh was called upon by the notables to make his 'summons' and he claimed the imamate for the third time, taking the title al-Hādī. The new imam made arrangements for the Ottoman force to return to the Tihāma and a few months later had his predecessor, al-Mutawakkil, executed.[82] Al-Hādī gave up his claim to the imamate after nine months, however, because of a rival claimant called al-Manṣūr Aḥmad b. Hāshim al-Waysī.[83] The latter took Sanaa but his rule did not endure for more than a few months and ᶜAlī b. al-Mahdī ᶜAbd Allāh was again asked in Rabīᶜal-Ākhir 1267/February 1851 to become imam for the fourth time. Four months later, while the imam was on campaign in Lower Yemen, his cousin Ghālib, the son of the slain al-Mutawakkil, claimed the imamate in Sanaa, taking the title al-Hādī. The rest of the 1850s were taken up with at least six rivals each claiming the imamate for themselves. Authority in Sanaa finally devolved to two successive local shaykhs,

[79] Cf. Maḥmūd (ed.), *Dhikrayāt al-Shawkānī*, pp. 182–5. [80] *Nayl*, II: 226–8.
[81] *Hawliyyāt*, pp. 175–7. [82] Ibid., pp. 183–4; *Nayl*, II: 347. [83] *Nayl*, I: 235–41.

Aḥmad al-Ḥaymī and Muḥsin Muʿīd.[84] With this the Qāsimī state came to an end. The rule of the shaykhs lasted until the Ottomans were finally recalled to occupy Sanaa in 1269/1872 to end the period of disorder.[85] Shawkānī's intellectual legacy and the example he set would live on in his written works and with the generations of students he educated. The next chapter will explore his legacy in modern Yemen.

[84] Cf. Mermier, *Le Cheikh de la nuit*, pp. 42–54.

[85] Yemen's history in the second half of the nineteenth century is sketchy, and the Yemeni sources are sparse, no doubt a reflection of the troubled times and the absence of central authority. Recently, scholars, such as Thomas Kühn and Isa Blumi, have begun to study the Ottoman archival sources on Yemen and their results will hopefully fill in the existing lacunae.

CHAPTER 7

Shawkānī's Legacy

> [Shawkānī], the imam of the Sunnī *mujtahids* of his epoch, the Judge of Judges, the Shaykh al-Islam.
> Ismāᶜīl al-Akwaᶜ[1]

> May God protect us and you from Shawkānī's cutting swords.
> ᶜAbd al-Salām al-Wajīh[2]

The nineteenth and twentieth centuries mark a significant rupture in Yemeni history as in other countries of the Middle East. This break with the past is distinguished by the direct intervention of imperial states in local affairs (the British seize Aden in 1839 and the Ottomans are in control of the highlands by 1872) and by the emergence of nationalism and a centralised state. The nature of politics, social dynamics and intellectual life are altered irrevocably in modern times. There are, however, important continuities with the Qāsimī period, namely, an continuing relationship between Traditionist scholars and the state as well as debates over *madhhab* identity, the role religious scholars ought to have in governance and the nature of rule more generally. Consequently, Shawkānī's intellectual project and the example he set personally remain central features in the religious politics of modern Yemen.

Since the republican revolution in 1962 Shawkānī has been repeatedly lionized by the Yemeni republic and by its jurists and intellectuals, all of whom have included him in the state's pantheon of heroes. The largest public hall in Sanaa, and therefore probably in Yemen, is named 'Shawkānī Hall' (it is in the police academy). One of Sanaa's main avenues running off Zubayrī Street in the direction of the old airport is called Muḥammad b. ᶜAlī al-Shawkānī Street. Schools and religious institutes bear his name as well. The Yemen Centre for Research and Studies, an official state organ modelled on the Centre National de Recherches Scientifique in France, organised a conference on Shawkānī in February 1990 and published some of its papers. One of these was entitled 'Shawkānī's liberated thought and his liberation from the *madhāhib*'; another was entitled 'Imam

[1] *Hijar al-ᶜilm*, IV: 2251.
[2] ᶜAbd al-Salām al-Wajīh, *Aᶜlām al-muᵓallifīn al-Zaydiyya* (Amman: Muᵓassasat al-Imām Zayd b. ᶜAlī al-Thaqāfiyya, 1999), p. 123.

Shawkānī Street (author)

Muḥammad b. ᶜAlī al-Shawkānī, the scholar, the *mujtahid*, the Qurʾānic exegete'.[3] The republican literature on this servant of the Qāsimī imams is large.

In order to understand how this came to pass, one must look at Shawkānī's legacy, at how his 'students'[4] propagated his ideas and works, and at the juridical and political roles they have played in the last century of Yemeni history. One must look at the Ḥamīd al-Dīn imamate (the last before the republic was established) to see the extent to which their forms of rule were influenced by the general shift towards Sunnism described in earlier chapters, and by the Ottomans who ruled highland Yemen from 1872 till 1918. One must also look at the way Shawkānī's life and works have been depicted in recent times, how he has been re-invented, and for what reasons. These enquiries illuminate much about how contemporary Yemeni intellectuals define religious identity and reappropriate 'tradition' for political and nationalist ends.

Shawkānī's legacy in the last two centuries of Yemeni intellectual and juridical history has been monumental. His injection of Sunnī Traditionist ideas, and legal and educational methodologies into the Zaydī scholarly milieu has irrevocably changed Zaydism, and prevented renewal of its pre- and early-Qāsimī agenda. Zaydism has not been able to escape either his looming intellectual presence or the forms of government he envisaged and embodied during his period as chief judge. This legacy was perpetuated by his students, who played important political roles in the period of turmoil which set in after his death.[5] The Ottomans, who were invited to rule in Sanaa so as to end the state of disorder which prevailed from the late 1840s till the early 1870s, attempted to introduce administrative and legal reforms – associated with the *Tanẓīmāt* and the *Majalla* – which attracted certain members of the learned elite, many of whom were Shawkānī's students. The reforms initiated by the Ottomans appear, however, to have failed, largely because they were not accepted by the local population.[6]

After the Ottomans left, Shawkānī's 'generational students' continued to occupy important posts in the Ḥamīd al-Dīn imamate, later to be called the Mutawakkilite

[3] Muḥammad Muṣṭafā Balḥāj, 'al-Taḥarrur al-fikrī wa ʾl-madhabī ᶜinda al-imām al-Shawkānī', *Dirāsāt Yamaniyya*, 40 (1990), 247–59; Ibrāhīm ᶜAbd Allāh Rufayda, 'al-Imām Muḥammad b. ᶜAli al-Shawkānī al-ᶜālim al-mujtahid al-mufassir', *Dirāsāt Yamaniyya* 40 (1990), 284–342.

[4] In referring to Shawkānī's students, I am not only referring to those who studied with him directly. I also include in this category his 'generational students', i.e., those who studied with his immediate students and in turn their students and who avowedly claim to adhere to Traditionist views. A number of contemporary scholars in Yemen refer to themselves in these terms. For example, Muḥammad b. Ismāᶜīl al-ᶜAmrānī, an eminent muftī and scholar in Sanaa today calls himself 'a third generation student of Shawkānī's'. By this, he means that two scholars separate him, in *ijāza* terms, from Shawkānī.

[5] A good example of such a scholar in the nineteenth century is Aḥmad b. Muḥammad al-Kibsī (d. 1316/1899); cf. Muḥammad b. Muḥammad Zabāra, *Nuzhat al-naẓar fī rijāl al-qarn al-rābiᶜ ᶜashar* (Sanaa: Markaz al-Dirāsāt waʾl-Abḥāth al-Yamaniyya, 1979), pp. 143–5 (hereinafter *Nuzhat al-naẓar*); *Hijar al-ᶜilm*, IV: 1792–3.

[6] Cf. Thomas Kühn, 'Ordering the past of Ottoman Yemen, 1872–1914', *Turcica* (2002), forthcoming; idem, 'Clothing the "uncivilized": military recruitment in Ottoman Yemen and the quest for "native" uniforms, 1880–1914', in Suraiya Faroqhi and Christoph K. Neumann (eds.), *Costume and Identity in the Ottoman Empire* (Istanbul: Simurg Publishers, forthcoming).

Kingdom of Yemen. They played a seminal role in giving expression to modern notions of Yemeni nationalism. After the 1962 revolution, which ended the rule of the Ḥamīd al-Dīn imams and with it a millennium of Zaydī rule in Yemen, Shawkānī's importance assumed even greater proportions. Since then, republicans have continuously evoked his works and memory in a conscious effort to undermine the doctrinal legitimacy of the Zaydī imamates of the past, and Zaydism itself. In republican writings he is presented as a model jurist, who upheld and promulgated a 'moderate' (*muᶜtadil*) and a 'liberated' (*mutaḥarrir*) version of Islam which, it is claimed, informs republican Islam and state ideology.

Linked to the ways Shawkānī is depicted has been the rise in tensions in modern times between the two estates of men of religion, the *qāḍī*s and the *sayyid*s. In part, this is probably due to the Zaydī requirement that the imam must be a *sayyid* and that *sayyid*s are perceived to have dominated Yemeni social and political life until recent times. Since the revolution, the political fortunes of certain *qāḍī* families have risen significantly, and members of these, like the Akwaᶜs and Iryānīs, have levelled attacks against Zaydism and the *sayyid*s. For instance, Ismāᶜīl al-Akwāᶜ has claimed that the Zaydī imams and the *sayyid*s throughout their history in the country wittingly monopolised all knowledge and power while keeping the remaining population in ignorance so as to ensure obedience.[7] In al-Akwaᶜ's reconstruction of Yemeni history, Shawkānī is a central figure not only because he was a very learned *qāḍī* with whom al-Akwaᶜ identifies socially, but also because he 'resisted' the Zaydīs. Zayd al-Wazīr, a *sayyid*, has refuted al-Akwaᶜ's claims by highlighting the number of learned *qāḍī*s who flourished and were indeed fêted under imamic rule. In completing his rebuttal, al-Wazīr remarks pointedly that Shawkānī had argued that persons of the lowly estates (e.g., butchers, weavers, barbers) should not engage in scholarly activities as they would bring disrepute to the scholars. In other words, it was Shawkānī, not the imāms and *sayyid*s, who had argued for keeping certain people ignorant.[8]

These modern polemics can often mislead an observer into exaggerating the historical tensions between the two learned estates. More generally, the histories that contemporary Yemenis pen often project backwards current political concerns and can have a distorting effect.[9] Although no *qāḍī* ever became imam, many *qāḍī*s, including Shawkānī, were highly influential in Yemeni politics. Yemeni history also provides ample evidence of *qāḍī*s who were devoted to Zaydī teachings and were among their chief propagators. In Shawkānī's writings there is no clear evidence of such tension between *qāḍī*s and *sayyid*s, or more broadly the Qaḥṭānīs and ᶜAdnānīs; as he proudly points out in his autobiography, he came from a family

[7] *Hijar al-ᶜilm*, III: 1668–9.

[8] Yaḥyā b. Muḥammad al-Miqrāʾī, *Maknūn al-sirr fī taḥrīr naḥārīr al-Sirr*, Zayd al-Wazīr (ed.) (McLean, VA: Markaz al-Turāth waʾl-Buḥūth al-Yamanī, 2002), pp. 8–20; cf. *Adab al-ṭalab*, pp. 129–31.

[9] Yohanan Friedmann has highlighted a similar distorting phenomenon in modern Indian historiography in its treatment and depiction of Shaykh Aḥmad Sirhindī (d. 1034/1624) as a religious reformer in Mughal times; cf. Yohanan Friedmann, *Shaykh Aḥmad Sirhindī* (New Delhi: Oxford University Press, 2000), pp. 87–111.

of *qāḍī*s who were also staunch supporters of the imams. It would be incorrect therefore to reduce the development and elaboration of his anti-Zaydī views to his being a *qāḍī*.

Studying Sunnī works and other Sunnī developments

Yemeni biographical dictionaries of the last two centuries give the sense that Traditionist scholars such as Ibn al-Amīr and Shawkānī caused a rupture in the educational curricula pursued by highland scholars: becoming learned now *necessarily* entailed studying Sunnī works, especially the Sunnī canonical ḥadīth collections, alongside Zaydī books.[10] Echoing Shawkānī's preference for the science of ḥadīth and the cardinal role it had in his teachings, ᶜAbd Allāh b. ᶜAbd al-Karīm al-Jirāfī, a twentieth-century scholar and a scion of Shawkānī's school says:

> The science of ḥadīth is a science of great worth and importance. Scholars have said that it is the most elevated of sciences, of most certain foundation, of greatest benefit and of greatest reward . . .[11]

Yet another development was that these scholars, but also at times imams, were given the epithet 'renewer' (*mujaddid*) or 'renewer of the century' (*mujaddid al-qarn*), which had not been employed in traditional Zaydism.[12] A further new development was that a succession of scholars, starting with Shawkānī's son Aḥmad, assumed the title of Shaykh al-Islām, a practice that lasted well into modern times.[13] In addition, students began writing eulogistic works (something resembling a hagiography) about a single great teacher, for example *al-Tiqṣār*, which al-Shijnī dedicated to Shawkānī or the *Tuḥfat al-ikhwān*, which al-Jirāfī dedicated to al-Ḥusayn b. ᶜAlī al-ᶜAmrī.[14] These give an elaborate biography of the teacher, and list his own teachers, the books he studied and who his students were. In addition, they report notable incidents and stories in the teacher's life. This constituted a new genre in the Zaydī context, where similar, though not identical, types of written works had been produced about the imams.[15]

Scholars generally became more ḥadīth-oriented and were concerned to acquire licences (*ijāza*) in both the *musalsalāt* ḥadīths and the works which fell under the

[10] The main biographical dictionaries for this period are Muḥammad Zabāra's *Nayl al-waṭar* and *Nuzhat al-naẓar* as well as ᶜAbd Allāh b. ᶜAbd al-Karīm al-Jirāfī's *Tuḥfat al-ikhwān*.

[11] ᶜAbd Allāh b. ᶜAbd al-Karīm al-Jirāfī, *Tuḥfat al-ikhwān bi-ḥilyat ᶜallāmat al-zamān* (Cairo: al-Maṭbaᶜa al-Salafiyya, 1365/1946), pp. 39–40, (hereinafter *Tuḥfat al-ikhwān*).

[12] *Tuḥfat al-ikhwān*, p. 20; al-Laknawī, *Nuzhat al-khawāṭir*, vol. VII, p. 270.

[13] Cf. *Tuḥfat al-ikhwān*, pp. 20, 25; *Nuzhat al-naẓar*, pp. 438–9; Aḥmad b. Muḥammad al-Jirāfī, *Ḥawliyyāt al-ᶜallāma al-Jirāfī*, Ḥusayn al-ᶜAmrī (ed.) (Beirut: Dār al-Fikr al-Muᶜāṣir, 1992), pp. 211f.

[14] For a list of such books, which were written in Yemen, see *Tuḥfat al-ikhwān*, pp. 5–6.

[15] A notable exception to this is the hagiographic account by Sayyid Yaḥyā b. al-Mahdī b. al-Qāsim al-Ḥusaynī of the life of his shaykh and founder of a moderate Sufī order amongst the Zaydīs, Ibrāhīm b. Aḥmad al-Kaynaᶜī (d. 793/1391), entitled *Ṣilat al-ikhwān fī ḥilyat barakat ahl al-zamān*, ms. Milan, Ambrosiana, no. D 222. However, being a Sufistic work it constitutes an exception in itself in Zaydī writings.

rubrics of *masmūʿāt* or *marwiyyāt*.[16] Highland Yemeni scholars desired more than ever to belong to a wider, Sunnī, world where such licences were issued, linking scholars to others beyond their local region or tradition. In the biography of nearly every scholar mentioned in *Nuzhat al-naẓar*, the last great Yemeni biographical dictionary of the scholars of the fourteenth century AH (published in 1979), the *ijāzas* they received are mentioned in detail. Earlier biographical dictionaries, such as *Maṭlaᶜ al-budūr*, do not make such systematic mention of *ijāzas*. Earlier Zaydī scholars, it seems, were locally trained and more interested in acquiring the standard works of the Hādawī school. The educational system after Ibn al-Amīr and Shawkānī became effectively Sunnī, as evinced by Ibn al-Amīr when he says:

> When I realized that the *ijāza* was one of the ways taken by the Sunnī scholars, a path among the paths of action which is the way to paradise, I expended my utmost in reading its books [i.e., books of *ijāzas*], amassing the pearls from its sea.[17]

Here is an explicit acknowledgement that Zaydī scholars discovered a wider, more developed world of scholarship with more authoritative epistemological and pedagogical methodologies than those traditionally found in the highlands. Zaydism, in its older forms, seems to have been considered too parochial by these scholars.

This is not to say that staunch adherents of Hādawism were no longer found in the highlands in the post-Shawkānī period. Muḥammad b. ᶜAbd Allāh al-Wazīr (d. 1308/1891) is a good example of a scholar who was in the Hādawī mould, despite having studied with Shawkānī.[18] He made his 'summons', declaring himself Imam al-Manṣūr in 1270/1854. This was a period of great political instability, during which a number of men claimed to be imams within a divided Yemen. Al-Manṣūr al-Wazīr's domains were confined to his home area of Wādī al-Sirr, where it is said that he 'ordained the good and prohibited the evil'.[19] Being imam in a single valley did not diminish him or the institution of the imamate; what mattered was that he considered himself the righteous ruler.

Another Hādawī in this period was al-Hādī Sharaf al-Dīn b. Muḥammad (d. 1307/1890). He made his 'summons' in 1296/1879 and based himself in Ṣaᶜda. From here he waged a war against the Ottomans until his death.[20] Imam Sharaf al-Dīn's son, Muḥammad, was also a Hādawī but in his later years developed an affinity for the Sunna and rejected *taqlīd*. He refused to become imam after his

[16] A *musalsal* Tradition is one in which a ḥadīth is transmitted from a teacher to student accompanied by some saying or action. The *masmūᶜāt* are works which the student either reads to or 'hears' from his teacher. The *marwiyyāt* are works that have not been read or studied with the teacher, but whose *isnād* the one receiving an *ijāza* can transmit.

[17] *Tuḥfat al-ikhwān*, p. 39.

[18] Cf. Muḥammad b. Ismāᶜīl al-Kibsī, *Jawāhir al-durr al-maknūn wa ᶜajāʾib al-Sirr al-makhzūn*, Zayd al-Wazīr (ed.) (n.p.: Manshūrāt al-ᶜAṣr al-Ḥadīth, 1988), pp. 169–234.

[19] *Nuzhat al-naẓar*, pp. 539–40. For his *sīra* see al-Kibsī, *Jawāhir al-durr*. Another example of a Hādawī scholar in this period is Zayd b. Aḥmad al-Kibsī (d. 1316/1898), cf. *Nuzhat al-naẓar*, pp. 301–3.

[20] *Nuzhat al-naẓar*, p. 313; *Hijar al-ᶜilm*, IV: 1983–4; Muḥammad Zabāra, *Aʾimmat al-Yaman biʾl-qarn al-rābiᶜ ᶜashar liʾl-hijra* (Cairo: al-Maṭbaᶜa al-Salafiyya, 1376/1956), vol. I, pp. 7f.

father's death and this opened the way for Muḥammad b. Yaḥyā Ḥamīd al-Dīn to make his 'summons', taking the title al-Manṣūr. Muḥammad Sharaf al-Dīn became the imam's deputy in Ṣaʿda and held this post until Imam Yaḥyā Ḥamīd al-Dīn (d. 1948) 'turned the imamate into a kingship', whereupon he retired to a life of scholarship in al-Madān.[21]

One cannot claim that all those who advocated Traditionist views were pro-Ottoman and against the imams, nor can one claim that all Hādawīs refused to collaborate with, or accept posts from, the Ottomans. Sayyid Aḥmad b. ʿAbd Allāh al-Kibsī, for example, was a ḥadīth scholar who fought alongside Imam Yaḥyā in the war against the Ottomans. After the truce of Daʿʿān (1911) he was ordered by the imam to be a preacher and teacher in Hijrat Sināʿ, south of Sanaa. Later, in 1925, he was appointed to teach ḥadīth works in Sanaa's *al-Madrasa al-ʿIlmiyya*, a school established in 1924 to train jurists. Whilst in Sināʿ, al-Kibsī compiled a work of ḥadīths entitled *al-Amāna* in whose introduction he laments the fact that non-Zaydī texts, namely the ḥadīth collections, were still being ignored by strict Hādawīs. Echoing Shawkānī he says:

> I have excluded from my book all ambiguous ḥadīths which require great effort to interpret. What has spurred me to compile it is that the people of our age avoid the books of the [Muslim] nation (*qawm*; i.e., the Sunnī collections) because these contain ḥadīths which are suspected to contradict Zaydism (*madhhab al-ʿAdliyya*). So they have stopped reading the beneficial ḥadīths in these works, fearing the rise of doubts in their hearts from certain obscure ḥadīths (*al-mutashābiha*), which they do not know how to interpret and which only the very knowledgeable can safely understand literally. So my intention with this abridgment is to bring the beginner closer [to ḥadīth] and to remind the graduate [of it] and to make known the ḥadīths of the Lord of Messengers which have sound chains of transmission.[22]

His use of the word *qawm* is significant, not only because it intimates a pan-Islamic sentiment but also because it suggests that Zaydism is somewhat parochial. Such statements foreshadow how the more universal Traditionist discourse would later be seen to fit with ideas about a unified Yemeni nation, transcending differences between Zaydīs and Shāfiʿīs.

Scholars were now being trained fully in Sunnism as well as in traditional Zaydī works. It remained up to individuals whether to claim allegiance to one tradition or the other, or to choose which of the two was appropriate in a given context. Often a scholar's denomination is unequivocal and can be detected from formulae embedded in his biographical entry: 'gave preference to proof-texts' (*murajjiḥ liʾl-dalīl*), for example, or 'he inclined to the Sunna and gave preference to proof-texts' (*māla ilā al-sunna wa tarjīḥ al-dalīl*) imply the person was a Traditionist.[23] Such statements as 'he based himself on the *madhhab*' (*kāna ʿalā ʾl-madhhab*) or 'he ordained the good and prohibited the evil', by contrast, would denote a Hādawī scholar. One can also look at the books a scholar has studied and with whom.

[21] *Hijar al-ʿilm*, IV: 1985–6; *Nuzhat al-naẓar*, p. 532; *Tuḥfat al-ikhwān*, pp. 118–19.
[22] *Nuzhat al-naẓar*, pp. 106–7. [23] Cf. *Nuzhat al-naẓar*, p. 158.

A certain degree of hybridisation is evident in some scholars who uphold Zaydī credal beliefs, like the doctrine of the imamate, while applying Traditionist legal methodologies in deriving legal rulings – Aḥmad al-Kibsī seems to fall into this category. What is incontrovertible is that Sunnī works were being widely studied and the appeal of the science of ḥadīth was widespread, even among some who considered themselves Hādawīs.[24]

Muftī Aḥmad Zabāra's General Licence

The developments mentioned above can be illustrated from the 'general license' (*ijāza ᶜāmma*) which the late Grand Muftī of Yemen, Sayyid Aḥmad b. Muḥammad Zabāra (d. 2000), issued to petitioning scholars from around the world. Muftī Zabāra was born into a scholarly family of *sayyids*. His father, Muḥammad b. Muḥammad (d. 1380/1961), was the author of numerous Yemeni chronicles and biographical collections, and held important posts in the reign of Imam Yaḥyā Ḥamīd al-Dīn. The latter allowed him to publish several Yemeni works, namely those by Shawkānī and other Traditionists, in Egypt in the 1920s and 1930s in a bid to portray Zaydism as doctrinally and juridically close to Sunnism (we shall say more on this later).[25] Aḥmad b. Muḥammad, the recently deceased Grand Muftī, was born on 21 Dhū ᵓal-Ḥijja 1325/25 January 1908, and was likewise an official in the court of Imam Aḥmad Ḥamīd al-Dīn (d. 1962), whose daughter he married.[26] After the revolution and the ensuing civil war, which resulted in the permanent establishment of the republic, President ᶜAbd al-Raḥmān b. Yaḥyā al-Iryānī (r. 1967–74) asked him to become the muftī of Sanaa. This post was later formalised with the establishment of *Dār al-Iftāᵓ* – translated on his official letter-head as 'Casuistry House' – and he took on the official title of Grand Muftī (*al-muftī al-ᶜāmm*) of the republic, the form used on his letter-head and stamp.[27]

Zabāra's *ijāza* opens a window onto the educational curriculum of a Zaydī scholar in the early decades of the twentieth century. By tracing and cross-referencing the biographies of the scholars whom Zabāra mentions, a picture can be formed of what was being taught from the latter half of the nineteenth century through the first half of the twentieth. The *ijāza* shows that Zabāra had not only studied the major Zaydī-Hādawī texts but also many important Sunnī ones, in particular the ḥadīth collections and the works produced by Shawkānī and other Yemeni Traditionists. What is more remarkable is that contemporary Sunnī Muslims consider Zabāra to have held one of the most 'elevated' chains of transmission (*sanad ᶜālī*) to such works as the *Ṣaḥīḥayn*. This is because only two

[24] A good example of such a person is Imam Muḥammad b. Yaḥyā Ḥamīd al-Dīn, who was a Hādawī but nonetheless studied Sunnī works too; cf. ᶜAlī b. ᶜAbd Allāh al-Iryānī, *Sīrat al-imām Muḥammad b. Yaḥyā Ḥamīd al-Dīn*, Muḥammad Ṣāliḥiyya (ed.), 2 vols. (Amman: Dār al-Bashīr, 1996), vol. I, pp. 26–31.

[25] *Nuzhat al-naẓar*, p. 585; cf. *Hijar al-ᶜilm*, II: 588–602.

[26] Cf. *Hijar al-ᶜilm*, II: 603–10.

[27] *Nuzhat al-naẓar*, pp. 148–51.

individuals separate him from Shawkānī, who, in turn, is considered to have had a very 'elevated' *isnād*.[28] Hence, Zabāra's *ijāza*s were much sought after by Sunnī scholars worldwide. The Muftī issued his licences in template format, with blanks at the top and bottom where the name and professional background of the supplicant receiving the *ijāza* were to be filled in.

Zabāra's importance for contemporary Sunnīs raises several questions. How 'Zaydī' was the Ḥamīd al-Dīn imamate if its leading jurists were also fully educated as Sunnīs? Did the Ḥamīd al-Dīn imams deliberately put to use Shawkānī's Traditionist legacy in accommodating modern concepts of nationalism, Arab nationalism and pan-Islamism? Did the competence in reformist Traditionist methodologies and discourses of scholars assist the Ḥamīd al-Dīns in presenting Zaydism to the larger Sunnī world? To what extent was all this useful in bridging the gap between Shāfiᶜīs and Zaydīs within Yemen? Zabāra's education may perhaps explain how he has been able to hold key posts in the pre-revolutionary Zaydī imamate as well as in the republic without feeling compromised by these two very different forms of government, and despite the republic's major claim to legitimacy being the imamate's overthrow.

In his *ijāza*, Zabāra lists all the works he studied and with which teachers. Then he gives his chains of transmission to a number of registers (*thabat*) or books of *isnād*s for which he himself has received an *ijāza*. It is this last category which links him to the major Islamic corpus of written works and ḥadīths, both Zaydī and Sunnī. Two of these registers may be marked out for special mention: Shawkānī's *Itḥāf al-akābir*, which has been discussed in chapter three, and Qāḍī Muḥammad b. Aḥmad Mashḥam's *Bulūgh al-amānī min ṭuruq asānīd kutub Āl man unzilat ᶜalayhi al-mathānī*, which is a Zaydī compilation.[29]

The two most striking features in Zabāra's *ijāza* are the pre-eminent place of Shawkānī's students in it as his teachers, and the great number of Sunnī works studied. Respectfully, Zabāra begins the list with his father, who in scholarly families was often a child's first teacher, as in Shawkānī's case. After this, the list of teachers is organised not chronologically, but loosely according, it seems, to the scholarly importance of a given teacher. The second teacher mentioned, and therefore the most important, is Qāḍī al-Ḥusayn b. ᶜAlī al-ᶜAmrī (d. 1361/1942). Zabāra says he attached himself (*lāzama*) to him for ten years, covering among other works the six Sunnī canonical ḥadīth collections, *Sharḥ al-Azhār*, al-Sayāghī's *Rawḍ al-naḍīr* and Shawkānī's *Fatḥ al-qadīr*.

A second generation Shawkānī student, al-ᶜAmrī was considered a Shaykh al-Islām and was a prominent judge in Sanaa during the period of Ottoman rule. The

28 Cf. Ḥusām al-Dīn b. Salīm al-Kīlānī, *al-Amālī fī aᶜlā al-asānīd al-ᶜawālī* (Aleppo: Dār al-Qalam al-ᶜArabī, n.d.), p. 23. I was informed in the late 1990s that only one living member of the Ahdal family in Zabīd has a more 'elevated' *isnād* to Shawkānī, with remarkably only one person separating them. The 'elevation' of an *isnād* is a function of the number of persons in the chain separating the author of a given work from its living transmitter, each of whom form either end of the chain. The smaller the number of persons the more 'elevated' the *isnād*.

29 Muḥammad b. Aḥmad Mashḥam (d. 1182/1768–9), cf. *Nashr*, II: 412f.

Ottomans appointed him supervisor of religious endowments (*nāẓir al-awqāf*) in Sanaa and he later played a crucial role in mediating between the Ottomans and Imam Yaḥyā during the two uprisings of 1904 and 1911. After the treaty of Daᶜᶜān was concluded (1911), one of Imam Yaḥyā's prerogatives was the appointment of judges in the Zaydī areas of Yemen. In some sense this signalled the re-establishment of a Qāsimī-like state with religious posts becoming available. Imam Yaḥyā could nominate the president and members of a court of appeals in Sanaa (*al-maḥkama al-sharᶜiyya al-istiᵓnāfiyya*) and al-ᶜAmrī was appointed as its first president. Reminiscent of Shawkānī's role, al-ᶜAmrī's duties included overseeing the judgements of all the judges in Sanaa and those in the Zaydī regions.[30] This new position seems to have combined very naturally certain Qāsimī interests in state-centred legitimacy and justice with modern bureaucratic concepts. Al-ᶜAmrī's appointment, however, also marked the beginning of a long relationship between the al-ᶜAmrī family and the Ḥamīd al-Dīn imams. Al-ᶜAmrī's son, ᶜAbd Allāh b. al-Ḥusayn would later become Imam Yaḥyā's first secretary, and was assassinated with him in 1948. ᶜAbd Allāh's son, Muḥammad, would in turn become one of Imam Aḥmad's principal secretaries. In the republican era another of ᶜAbd Allāh's sons, Ḥusayn, continued the family's tradition in government service by taking up several ministerial positions, and more recently was Yemen's representative in London.

The continuity of the Āl al-ᶜAmrī's official service from Ottoman times to the end of the Ḥamīd al-Dīn imamate deserves noting. It confirms the point, already made by Messick, about educational, legal and bureaucratic continuities from the Ottoman period into that of the Ḥamīd al-Dīn imamate.[31] In fact continuities extend further. And what to Messick, with an interest mainly in Lower Yemen, seems simply 'Zaydī' tradition, is to those interested in Zaydism in Upper Yemen, a final parting of ways. The traditional Zaydism of the Ḥamīd al-Dīn period is in fact the Zaydism only of the Qāsimīs. The Āl al-ᶜAmrī were scions of the Shawkānī school, and their patronage by the Ḥamīd al-Dīns underscores a much longer continuity, namely the patronage of Traditionist jurists by the rulers. A longer continuity yet is the domination of the post-revolutionary religious and judicial structures by these scholars.

Perhaps Zabāra's most eminent teacher after Ḥusayn al-ᶜAmrī was Qāḍī Yaḥyā b. Muḥammad al-Iryānī (d. 1362/1943), also a second generation student of Shawkānī's.[32] Muftī Zabāra mentions how he was taught Bukhārī's *Ṣaḥīḥ* by al-Iryānī in his father's house during the nights of Ramaḍān. Among the other works he studied with him were al-Suyūṭī's *al-Itqān fī ᶜulūm al-Qurᵓān* and Shawkānī's *Tuḥfat al-dhākirīn*. Al-Iryānī was famous for the lessons he gave in Shawkānī's *Nayl al-awṭār*, Jalāl's *Ḍawᵓ al-nahār* and Ibn al-Amīr's *Minḥat al-ghaffār* at the

30 Cf. *Nuzhat al-naẓar*, pp. 265f.; al-Jirāfī, *Ḥawliyyāt*, pp. 115–16, 181–2.
31 Messick, *Calligraphic State*, pp. 107–8 and passim.
32 *Nuzhat al-naẓar*, pp. 635–42; *Hijar al-ᶜilm*, I: 71–7. Al-Iryānī was a famous poet and a prominent figure in Muḥammad Zabāra's historical works. He can be seen as a representative figure of the period who differed at times with Imam Yaḥyā's policies, sending him critical poems.

Filayḥī mosque, all of which Zabāra attended. This study circle was unambiguously Traditionist and is remembered fondly by contemporary republican jurists such as Muḥammad b. Ismāʿīl al-ʿAmrānī, as a locus of anti-Hādawī legal thought. After Mufti Zabāra completed his studies with al-Iryānī, which lasted six years, a 'banquet of termination' (*walīmat khatm*) was held in his father's house. It was attended by all the pupils and some of the teachers and friends, and during it poetry was recited and Zabāra received a general licence from al-Iryānī.

Qāḍī Yaḥyā al-Iryānī was born in the Hijrat Iryān, a border region between the Zaydī Upper Yemen and Shāfiʿī Lower Yemen. Imam Yaḥyā appointed him judge in Ibb in 1919. He held this post until 1926 when problems with the strict Hādawī governor of Dhamār, Sayyid ʿAbd Allāh b. Aḥmad al-Wazīr (d. 1948), led to his dismissal. In 1931, however, Imam Yaḥyā reappointed him a member of the Sanaa court of appeals, whose president was the Traditionist scholar Sayyid Zayd b. ʿAlī al-Daylamī (d. 1366/1947). Two years later, al-Iryānī was promoted to president of the court, and held this post until his death in 1943.[33]

One can see from the biographies of men like al-ʿAmrī and al-Iryānī that the politico-juridical alliances forged between Traditionist scholars and the rulers already in Shawkānī's time continued to be a feature of the twentieth century. Furthermore, the links of certain families with the central government administration were strong. Families, such as the ʿAmrīs, Kibsīs and Jirāfīs, in the Ottoman and Ḥamīd al-Dīn period alike, represent, as it were, a 'civil service'. All of them had access to the Ḥamīd al-Dīn court and their advice was often taken seriously. Strict Hādawī scholars, by contrast, were excluded and some were imprisoned by Imam Yaḥyā. The reason for this was probably that their loyalty could not be assured, in part because they would insist on Yaḥyā's upholding the stipulations of the Hādawī imamate. If they happened to be *sayyid*s who could independently rally support, they constituted a real threat. At least two examples of this can be found in the biographical dictionaries. The first is Imam Yaḥyā's defeat and banishment of al-Ḥasan b. Yaḥyā al-Ḍaḥyānī (d. 1343/1924), a rival claimant to the imamate who was widely reckoned to be more learned than he.[34] The second is Yaḥyā's imprisonment of Muḥammad b. Ibrāhīm al-Muʾayyadī (d. 1381/1961–2) for over thirty years because of his great popularity and influence in the Ṣaʿda region.[35] Popularity had become politically unacceptable.

Imam Yaḥyā Ḥamīd al-Dīn (r. 1322–1367/1904–1948)

Conflicting opinions are invariably given by Yemenis about Imam Yaḥyā's religious and legal orientation. Muṭahhar al-Iryānī, a famous contemporary Yemeni

[33] *Nuzhat al-naẓar*, p. 635; Yaḥyā b. Muḥammad al-Iryānī, *Kitāb Hidāyat al-mustabṣirīn bi-sharḥ ʿuddat al-hiṣn al-ḥaṣīn* (Sanaa: n.d.), pp. 9–27.

[34] Cf. *Nuzhat al-naẓar*, pp. 241–9; *Hijar al-ʿilm*, I: 131–3.

[35] Cf. *Nuzhat al-naẓar*, pp. 397–8; *Hijar al-ʿilm*, III: 1434–5; Aḥmad b. Muḥammad al-Wazīr, *Ḥayāt al-amīr ʿAlī b. ʿAbd Allāh al-Wazīr* (n.p.: Manshūrāt al-ʿAṣr al-Ḥadīth, 1987), pp. 383–4.

poet, describes him as having been a religious moderate (*muʿtadil dīniyyan*) and a scholar in his own right, but continues to say that Yaḥyā was a Zaydī in political terms (*Zaydī siyāsiyyan*). By contrast, Zayd al-Wazīr, a contemporary Yemeni intellectual and writer, says that Imam Yaḥyā was Hādawī in applying the Sharīʿa but politically a Sunnī, because he favoured a monarchic system of rule.[36] Ismāʿīl al-Akwaʿ mentions that as a young man Yaḥyā had inclined to the science of the Sunna (i.e., ḥadīth) and was greatly influenced by his teacher Aḥmad b. ʿAbd Allāh al-Jindarī (d. 1337/1918), a Traditionist scholar.[37] This annoyed his father, Imam al-Manṣūr Muḥammad b. Yaḥyā Ḥamīd al-Dīn (d. 1322/1904), who, by contrast, was a strict Hādawī. One incident highlights this feature of Imam Muḥammad's views. A downpour one day led to water seeping through the roof of his library, and a number of books were ruined. The imam claimed that had Ibn al-Amīr's *Subul al-salām* not been in the room (his son Yaḥyā had acquired a copy from Jindārī) this would not have happened.[38] In other words, ruination was the consequence of studying Traditionist books.

Al-Akwaʿ says that upon becoming imam, Yaḥyā ceased manifesting his proclivity for ḥadīth for fear of being attacked by Zaydī *muqallidūn*, and continually combined the mid-day and afternoon prayers (*al-jamʿ bayna al-ṣalātayn*) as a sign of his adherence to the Hādawī school.[39] The issue is obviously blurred in post-revolutionary writings which depict the Ḥamīd al-Dīn imams as reactionary, obscurantist and fanatically Zaydī. Interestingly, this depiction was corroborated by the Lebanese traveler Ameen Rihani who visited Imam Yaḥyā in 1922. Of his rule Rihani says:

> he invoked the creed of his ancestors against the Shawafeʿ (Sunnis) of the Tihama as well as against the Idrisi . . . I am also of the belief that if the Imam Yahya's rule were not sectarian, were purely civil, he would realise his highest political ambition without having to wage war, and call it a *jehad*, against his fellow Muslems. The Shawafeʿ would then have no grievance against him – would cease to be a weapon in the hands of his enemies – would, in fact become his greatest supporters.[40]

Not hiding his dislike of the Zaydīs, Rihani says in another passage that 'the Zaydi . . . is the most exclusive, not to say fanatical, of all Muslems'.[41]

Certainly, Shāfiʿīs, especially the Shāfiʿī peasantry in coastal and Lower Yemen, did not like Imam Yaḥyā's rule, mainly because of the corrupt taxation policies of his administrators and army. But Rihani's assertion that his rule was sectarian and true to the creed of his ancestors is not entirely correct. Yaḥyā's rule does not fit the Zaydī tradition neatly and exclusively. Partly because it had to contend with forces the Zaydī imamate had never encountered and also because Yaḥyā opted in the end for dynastic forms, it comprised a composite of elements. In some respects,

36 These statements are based on personal communications with the author by both individuals.
37 For al-Jindārī biography, see *Nuzhat al-naẓar*, pp. 97–104. 38 *Hijar al-ʿilm*, III: 1696.
39 Ibid., III: 1696–7.
40 Ameen Rihani, *Arabian Peak and Desert* (Delmar, New York: Caravan Books, 1983), pp. 115–16.
41 Ibid., p. 97.

it obviously did conform to Zaydism. Rihani describes a scene in which Imam Yaḥyā was dispensing justice in a mode reminiscent of the rule of the early Zaydī imams.

> There, under the Tree of Justice, was the Image of Perfection, seated on a stool, with one indigo soldier to his right bearing high the sword of State and another to his left holding over his head one of the Imamic umbrellas. Before him sat cross-legged on the ground a scribe, and around him was a crowd of people of every rank and class, in turbans and shawls of all colours as well as in rags, waiting to be heard. And everyone was heard... Two full hours sat the Image of Perfection under the Tree of Justice, and then... he went on his regular daily tour of the city, preceded by a platoon of the soldiery and accompanied by a multitude of his beloved subjects. After the tour, he goes [sic] into a mosque for the noon prayer and then returns to his home for the noonday meal. His return was heralded as usual with drum and bugle, and the indigos shouted at the top of their lungs the Yo-ho-haw of the national anthem. The sky-blue and belaced *mazallah* (parasol) held by a soldier marked his place in the heart of the procession.[42]

Yaḥyā here resembles an ideal Zaydī imam, interacting personally and immediately with his people on a frequent and regular basis. Yet Rihani's account also depicts some of the symbolic trappings which were established by the Qāsimīs in the eighteenth century, such as umbrellas, drums, seals, flags and standards, a panoply absent in early Zaydī imamates.[43] In addition, Yaḥyā's imamate had administrative institutions, e.g., a Shaykh al-Islām[44] and a standing army,[45] which are equally reminiscent of the eighteenth century. Moreover, his state incorporated several modern aspects, such as a 'hybrid' educational system based, in part, on the one the Ottomans left behind,[46] and ministries, such as a ministry of education and a ministry of health which were headed by his sons.

Imam Yaḥyā was a scholar, a *mujtahid*, unlike his eighteenth- and nineteenth-century predecessors, who ruled during Shawkānī's tenure as *qāḍī al-quḍāt*. He adjudicated cases personally and issued legal 'choices' (*ikhtiyārāt*) which superseded those of the established Hādawī school. The *ikhtiyārāt* had a reflexive quality in that they confirmed the *mujtahid* status of the imam issuing them. A form of legal rulings by imams to be enforced by judges, the *ikhtiyārāt* have a long history among the Zaydīs in Yemen. Al-Manṣūr ᶜAbd Allāh b. Ḥamza (d. 614/1217), for example, issued a set of these in a work entitled *al-Ikhtiyārāt al-Manṣūriyya*.[47] Al-Mutawakkil Ismāᶜīl (d. 1087/1776) also issued *ikhtiyārāt* in a work entitled *al-Masāʾil al-murtaḍāt fīmā yaᶜtamiduhu al-quḍāt*.[48]

42 Ibid., p. 104. 43 Cf. ibid., pp. 90–1.

44 The Shaykh al-Islām's duties were not specified. He appears to have been an aid and advisor to the imam in issuing letters and judgements.

45 Imam Yaḥyā established a regular army (*al-Jaysh al-Niẓāmī*) which was trained by Ottoman officers who chose to stay in Yemen after 1918. It was armed with the weapons inherited from the Ottomans and with new purchases from Italy. He also had an irregular force called the *al-Jaysh al-Difāʿī* or *al-Barrānī* which consisted mainly of tribal levies.

46 Messick, *Calligraphic State*, pp. 107–10.

47 Cf. al-Ḥabshī, *Muʾallafāt ḥukkām al-Yaman*, p. 38.

48 al-Ḥabshī, *Muʾallafāt ḥukkām al-Yaman*, p. 142; ms. Sanaa, Gharbiyya Library, *majmuᶜ* no. 19, fols. 104–6. Dr. Ḥusayn al-ᶜAmrī kindly provided me with a copy of these *ikhtiyārāt* with a commentary

When appointing judges to the various provinces and towns of Yemen, Imam Yaḥyā would issue them a letter of appointment in which he stated which laws were to be applied and what the judge's duties were. In one such a letter, dated Ramaḍān 1343/April 1925, Muḥammad b. Ḥusayn al-Kibsī (d. 1358/1940) was appointed as chief judge of the governorate of Hodeida. Al-Kibsī's biography provides another interesting example of a scholar who was an official under the Ottomans and later became a judge under Imam Yaḥyā.[49] Among the issues covered in the letter are the following:

> He [al-Kibsī] should perform the affairs of the Sharīᶜa and establish its straight and exalted paths by separating adversaries and making the one who is wronged win . . . He should rely in his judgements on what accords with the texts of the Noble *madhhab* [i.e., the Hādawī school], except in those matters where we have a 'choice'. [In such cases] agreement with the 'choice' is the path to be followed. Our 'choices' – and all kindness is from God – have clear proof, and the great and honourable [scholars] of religion have inclined to them . . . We have ordered him . . . to obey God and to obey us, to comply with our commands and prohibitions and to ordain the good and prohibit the evil . . . He must be committed to providing easy access [to himself] . . . and to refrain from imposing monetary penalties. We forbid him, as we prohibit all our judges and governors, from doing this. Should a matter arise requiring this [i.e., a monetary penalty], this should be presented to us and [judgement] will be based on our response. He is not to take anything from the adversaries in the name of wages, and this holds for all judges of districts and sub-districts; we have provided them with enough [wages] to suffice them. Brother Muḥammad [al-Kibsī] – may God pardon him – should know that we have entrusted him with all the judges of the governorate who are to refer to him immediately. He must tell them what he sees to be good, supervise all their activities and prevent actions which do not conform to God's wishes and our wishes. Likewise, he should inform us and the governorate's governor if he should know of a saying or action of a district administrator which is not satisfactory . . . He must uphold the rules of God's Sharīᶜa and make them the arbiter in all incidents. He must teach the ordinary folk the morals of religion and what God has commanded regarding prayers and ablution . . . He must guide people to what will make them like the rule of the Prophet's family, informing them of the expected reward and victory which comes through loving and heeding them . . . In the event of a case arising which necessitates imposing a legal punishment entailing an execution, the severance of a body part or a canonical punishment, then we command him to take permission from us [in this] and to present the judgement to us [before applying the penalty].[50]

Imam Yaḥyā's judicial system was hierarchically ordered, but ultimately tied every judge and potentially every judgement to himself. It was a micro-managed system and the role of men like Ḥusayn al-ᶜAmrī, the president of the court of appeals

by al-Mutawakkil entitled *Kitāb Taftīḥ abṣār al-quḍāt ilā azhār al-masāʾil al-murtaḍāt ikhtiyārāt amīr al-muʾminīn al-Mutawakkil ᶜalā Allāh . . .*, cf. ms. Sanaa, Gharbiyya Library, *ᶜilm kalām* no. 134.

[49] *Nuzhat al-naẓar*, p. 522.

[50] Dr Ḥusayn Al-ᶜAmrī kindly provided me with a copy of this letter. Similar letters can be found in al-ᶜAlīmī, *al-Taqlīdiyya waʾl-ḥadātha*, pp. 272–5 and Sālim, *Wathāʾiq Yamaniyya*, pp. 357, 359.

(the *qāḍī al-quḍāt* of earlier days), was not clearly defined. He acted as an aide to the imam, who was himself a judge and a *mujtahid*.

The *ikhtiyārāt* that Imam Yaḥyā issued were promulgated gradually, corresponding to actual cases that were brought before him and recurring issues which needed definitive guidelines for resolution. They all fall under the rubric of transactional law (*muᶜāmalāt*) and lists of these 'choices' were drawn up and sent to judges throughout Yemen.[51] They were the fruits of the imam's own *ijtihād* and by definition they either contradicted an established opinion in the Hādawī law books or provided an opinion not contained there. By promulgating the *ikhtiyārāt*, Imam Yaḥyā achieved several aims. The *ikhtiyārāt* helped, at least, in dealing with real problems facing the judiciary. For example, one 'choice' provides clear terms for when a woman can have her marriage annulled in the event of a husband absenting himself: The marriage may be ended if no one has heard from him in four years and he, or members of his family, have not provided the wife with any form of sustenance. Another prohibits all legal ruses (*ḥiyal*) that were intended to suspend the law of pre-emption (*shufᶜa*). Yet another states that written documents are to be accepted as authoritative in court if the author is known to others for his probity or if the script itself is self-evidently ancient, thereby securing the document's authenticity.[52]

At least one of the 'choices' had national political dimensions and implied clearly to Yemenis that Imam Yaḥyā was not in legal terms a strict Hādawī.[53] This *ikhtiyār* stipulates that 'equality' (*kafāʾa*), as a condition for enacting a marriage contract, has no validity if the woman has attained maturity and consented. Hādawī law stipulates that 'equality of descent' (*al-kafāʾa fī ʾl-nasab*) is a condition in marriage.[54] In practice, this often had the effect of prohibiting men who were not *sayyid*s from marrying women of the Prophet's family and created a source of tension, largely theoretical it seems, between the *sayyid*s and the *qaḍī*s. The latter, since the revolution, have presented this condition as an example of the racism of the Hādawīs.[55] By effectively repealing it with his *ikhtiyār*, Imam Yaḥyā signalled that differences in origin among Yemenis would have no legal consequences – all Yemenis were equal before the law.

Imam Yaḥyā's *ikhtiyārāt* were eventually put in verse form and were commented on by Qāḍī ᶜAbd Allāh b. ᶜAbd al-Wahhāb al-Shamāḥī (d. 1406/1985). This work was published in 1356/1937 in Sanaa by the Ministry of Education Press (Maṭbaᶜat al-Maᶜārif), a hold-over from Ottoman days. In his commentary, al-Shamāḥī offers the legal arguments and textual bases for the *ikhtiyārāt*. Interestingly, the *Ṣaḥīḥayn*

51 See, for example, ᶜAlīmī, *al-Taqlīdiyya waʾl-ḥadātha*, pp. 258–9.

52 ᶜAbd Allāh b. ᶜAbd al-Wahhāb al-Shamāḥī, *Ṣirāṭ al-ᶜārifīn ilā idrāk ikhtiyārāt amīr al-muʾminīn* (Sanaa: Maṭbaᶜat al-Maᶜārif, 1356/1937), pp. 31–3.

53 A noteworthy example of a leading Shāfiᶜī scholar who commented approvingly on Imam Yaḥyā's *ikhtiyārāt* is ᶜAbd al-Raḥmān b. ᶜAlī al-Ḥaddād (d. 1340/1922) whose commentary entitled *al-Intiṣārāt naẓm al-ikhtiyārāt* is extant in the ms. Sanaa, Gharbiyya Library, *majmūᶜ* no. 11, fols. 81–3; cf. Messick, *Calligraphic State*, pp. 48, 272 fn. 30.

54 Cf. *Azhār*, p. 108; *Sharḥ al-Azhār*, vol. II, pp. 303–5.

55 Cf. al-Maqbalī, *al-ᶜAlam al-shāmikh*, pp. 282–5; *Hijar al-ᶜilm*, II: 1104–6 and III: 1247–52.

are constantly cited and the opinions of Ibn al-Qayyim, al-Maqbalī and Shawkānī are highlighted and cited on certain issues.[56] Only the opinions of Imam Zayd b. ᶜAlī receive special attention from among the Zaydī imams, and those of al-Hādī are ignored completely. Given that these *ikhtiyārāt* superseded Hādawī views, the lapse in mentioning al-Hādī's opinions is not unusual. However, given the importance of the politics of citation in this legal tradition, it is noteworthy that the opinions of Ibn al-Qayyim and Shawkānī are mentioned because it shows the extent to which Imam Yaḥyā was willing to depart from his own school's teachings.

In al-Shamāḥī's introduction, one sees that the concept of nationalism had crept into Yemeni legal discourse. He tries to appeal to Zaydī tradition to justify rulings which contradict those of the school, but he also makes appeal to Yemeni nationalism and the fact that Yemen, through the imams, has not succumbed to adopting positive laws of foreign origin, as other Muslim nations have.

> We, the Yemeni nation (*umma*), thank God for the success granted by Him and His guidance for making the Qurʾān and the Sunna of the chosen Messenger a law (*qānūn*) unto us whose authority we only obey and are guided solely by its proofs [which have been] preserved among us by the Prophet's family (*al-ᶜitra al-nabawiyya*) and the Fāṭimī descendants until this crucial time when many peoples have been overcome by whims (*ahwāʾ*) and deviation from religion towards laws which are like the web of a spider, but even more fragile. God, who is most kind, has protected our Yemeni people (*shaᶜbunā al-Yamanī*) from the flow of this sweeping torrent through the son of the Seal of Prophets Abī Shams al-Dīn Aḥmad, our lord, Commander of the Faithful, al-Mutawakkil ᶜalā Allāh Yaḥyā b. Muḥammad, son of God's Messenger. He has renewed (*jaddada*) through his determination and knowledge that which has been extinguished from the distinguishing features of the Muḥammadan lordly religion. Treading the path of his forefathers, which is connected to his grandfather al-Muṣṭafā – May God's blessings and prayers be upon him – and who are the lords of valour and purity. For he [i.e., Imam Yaḥyā], may God support him and reward him for [his actions on behalf of] Islam, has risen to renew (*tajdīd*) [the religion] through the sword and the pen, rendering judgement to the Qurʾān among his people, his community and himself in all that is specific and general. He has made it what lowers, raises, brings near, renders far, the educator, and that which restrains. [Legal aspects of] social interaction (*al-muᶜāmalāt*) are a necessity for life and also for the foundations of this society (*arkān hādhā al-mujtamaᶜ*). The Legislator (*al-shāriᶜ*) has not neglected anything, for he has lit the way of interaction and the manner in which it is to be conducted. And by this light, the ulema of the Zaydī school have been guided, as others have been too, to establish principles (*uṣūl*), branches (*furūᶜ*) and issues (*masāʾil*) in [the realm of] social interaction which are clearer in the sky of the true Islamic Sharīᶜa than the sun at mid-day. It is incumbent on the Yemeni community and their imams to accept and adhere in knowledge and in practice to what they have established as issues and to their proofs. They are not to restrict ideas from roaming the realm of examination (*naẓar*), *ijtihād*, and making choices (*ikhtiyār*) and criticism, given that every *mujtahid* is correct (*kull mujtahid muṣīb*). 'This is God's bounty, He awards it to whomever He pleases' (LXII: 4). We mention this since the Commander

56 Cf. al-Shamāḥī, *Ṣirāṭ al-ᶜārifīn*, pp. 6, 17, 24, 33, 51; also see al-ᶜAmrānī, *Niẓām al-qaḍāʾ*, pp. 225f.

> of the Faithful, may God support him, has ordered adhesion (*ilzām bi-mulāzamat*) to the Noble School [i.e., the Hādawī school] in all [rules of] interaction except in certain issues. [In these exceptional matters] his mind, and the vastness of the circle of his knowledge, have led him to exempt them on the basis of derived proof from the Book and the Sunna, as is the prerogative of any *mujtahid*. He is a just imam who watches over the interests of his community (*umma*) and the defence of his people (*sha*ᶜ*b*) and nation (*waṭan*).[57]

Messick has described how Imam Yaḥyā reacted to nationalist ideas by, among other things, authorizing the writing and publication of official national histories of Yemen, using forms and idioms which were completely new.[58] Until ᶜAbd al-Wāsiᶜ b. Yaḥyā al-Wāsiᶜī's 'unofficial' history, published in 1346/1927–8, historical writing was localised to a geographical region or town, to scholars of a *madhhab*, to an individual or was delimited by a fixed period of time. These new histories conceived of Yemen as a single cohesive geographical and cultural unit – as a nation.

It is clear that Imam Yaḥyā had to contend with currents in the wider Islamic and Arab worlds. Rihani had come to Yemen to promote Arab nationalist ideas and got a hearing from the imam, though to little practical effect. Pan-Islamic ideas appear to have been given more serious consideration. By allowing certain Traditionist works to be published in Cairo, it appears that Imam Yaḥyā was promoting the notion that the Zaydīs were a 'moderate' sect no different in essence from the Sunnī *madhhab*s. This deliberately contrived conception of Zaydism as a 'fifth Sunnī school', or as being 'moderate', continues to pervade modern writing on Yemen.[59] It trades on crucial areas of ambiguity, minimising the fundamental differences between Zaydī and Sunnī theology, namely the importance of the doctrine of the imamate, as well as notable differences in normative rulings, especially in the realm of the ᶜ*ibādāt* (ritual law).

The roots of this argument probably lie in the publication of the works of the Traditionists Ibn al-Wazīr and al-Maqbalī in the first years of the twentieth century by Egyptians in Cairo. These immediately received the attention and praise of modern Islamic reformers such as Rashīd Riḍā, and were seen to represent a spirit of openness in Zaydism which had continuously allowed for the practice of *ijtihād*.[60] This, it was argued, would in turn allow for the much needed reform (*iṣlāḥ*) and renewal (*tajdīd*) of Islam in modern times. Ibn al-Wazīr's work entitled *Īthār al-ḥaqq* ᶜ*alā al-khalq* was published as early as 1318/1900 and was very favourably reviewed in Riḍā's journal *al-Manār*.[61] Eleven years later, in 1911, al-Manār Press published an edition of al-Maqbalī's *al-*ᶜ*Alam al-shāmikh* and its

[57] al-Shamāḥī, *Ṣirāṭ al-*ᶜ*ārifīn*, pp. 3–4.
[58] Messick, *Calligraphic State*, pp. 123–31; cf. *Hijar al-*ᶜ*ilm*, I: 368–9.
[59] Cf. Serjeant, 'The Zaydīs', p. 285; al-ᶜAmrī, *The Yemen*, pp. 115–16.
[60] For a study of how Riḍā appropriated and reformulated certain concepts Shawkānī had used see Ahmad Dallal, 'Appropriating the past: twentieth-century reconstruction of pre-modern Islamic thought', *Islamic Law and Society* 7 (2000), 325–58.
[61] Ḥusayn al-ᶜAmrī, *al-Manār wa'l-Yaman* (Damascus: Dār al-Fikr, 1987), pp. 42–3; cf. *al-Manār*, no. 1 (1318), 16.

addendum *al-Arwāḥ al-nawāfikh*. In 1915 Riḍā expressed great enthusiasm for Shawkānī's works and listed him in a lineage of Traditionist scholars whose works 'provided the best substance for effecting reform'.[62] Here is what he says:

> No one emerged after Ibn Ḥazm excelling or equaling him in terms of breadth of knowledge and strength of argument . . . except Shaykh al-Islām, the renewer of the seventh century, Aḥmad Taqī al-Dīn b. Taymiyya. . . . [Then] the imam Abū ᶜAbd Allāh Muḥammad b. al-Qayyim inherited the knowledge of his teacher [Ibn Taymiyya] and was his elucidator. . . . The most beneficial work by a supporter of the Sunna which was thereafter produced is *Fatḥ al-bārī sharḥ ṣaḥīḥ al-Bukhārī* by the all encompassing ocean of the Sunna, the *ḥāfiẓ*, Aḥmad b. Ḥajar al-ᶜAsqalānī. . . . Also among the most beneficial books in ḥadīth-based law is *Nayl al-awṭār fī sharḥ Muntaqā al-akhbār*, as is *Irshād al-fuḥūl fī taḥqīq ᶜilm al-uṣūl* on the principles of jurisprudence, both of which are by the great imam, the renewer and *mujtahid* of Yemen of the twelfth century Muḥammad b. ᶜAlī al-Shawkānī.[63]

The conjuncture of discourses and interests between modernising Islamic reformers and Traditionist scholars in Yemen did not escape the attention of the imam nor that of certain Yemeni ulema, who would now consciously highlight this.

Riḍā felt that Imam Yaḥyā was the ideal candidate for the caliphate after the abdication of the last Ottoman sultan in 1924. Yaḥyā, he argued, was of impeccable Qurayshite descent, was a *mujtahid* and most importantly had maintained his country's independence from Western occupation and influence.[64] It is not clear how Imam Yaḥyā reacted to Riḍā's views. He may have toyed with the idea of being caliph, for several types of coins were minted as early as 1344/1925 which bore the inscription 'minted in the Abode of the Mutawakkilite Caliphate, Sanaa Yemen' (*ḍuriba bi-dār al-khilāfa al-Mutawakkiliyya Ṣanᶜāʾal-Yaman*).[65]

Riḍā met with Yemenis such as ᶜAbd al-Wāsiᶜal-Wāsiᶜī (d. 1379/1960), who were actively publishing Zaydī works in Cairo, namely *Kitāb al-Azhār* and its principal commentary the *Sharḥ al-Azhār*, both published in 1921.[66] His spirit of reform greatly influenced such men as Muḥammad Zabāra and Imam Yaḥyā's son Muḥammad (d. 1350/1928). These two embarked on a grand project of publishing

[62] It must be noted that a number of Shawkānī's and Ibn al-Amīr's treatises were also first published in Egypt in 1343/1924 and later 1346/1927 by Muḥammad Munīr at Idārat al-Ṭibāᶜa al-Munīriyya. These appeared, along with other works by Traditionists such as Ibn Taymiyya, in two volumes entitled *Majmūᶜat al-rasāʾil al-Munīriyya*. Munīr was Rashīd Riḍā's brother-in-law and an Azharī scholar himself.

[63] Al-ᶜAmrī, *al-Manār*, pp. 374–5, 118–23. *Al-Manār* also had an article praising Ibn al-Amīr's *Subul al-salām* which was first published in 1344/1926, cf. al-ᶜAmrī, *al-Manār*, pp. 126–7.

[64] Henri Laoust, *Le Califat dans la Doctrine de Rašīd Riḍā*, (Beirut: n.p., 1938), pp. 6, 90, 92, 119–20.

[65] Cf. Chester Krause *et al.* (eds.), *Standard Catalog of World Coins* (Iola, Wisconsin: Krause Publications, 1998), pp. 1749–51. Imam Aḥmad issued a number of coins with the same inscription.

[66] al-ᶜAmrī, *al-Manār*, p. 124; *Tuḥfat al-ikhwān*, p. 94; *Nuzhat al-naẓar*, p. 411; *Hijar al-ᶜilm*, III: 1675. There is some discrepancy over the publication date of these works. In the *Sharḥ al-Azhār* it is stated that ᶜAlī Yaḥyā al-Yamānī paid the costs of its publication and that it was published in Egypt with Maṭbaᶜat Sharikat al-Tamaddun in 1332/1914, cf. vol. I, p. 1. It is noteworthy that the manuscript copy on which the edited edition of *Sharḥ al-Azhār* was based was none other than Shawkānī's own personal copy of the work.

ᶜImādī coin, obverse (author)

ᶜImādī coin, reverse (author)

the works of the Yemeni Traditionists. Starting in 1929, they published Shawkānī's biographical dictionary *al-Badr al-ṭāliᶜ*, followed by his *Tuḥfat al-dhākirīn* and *al-Fatḥ al-qadīr*. Zabāra also published Ibn al-Wazīr's *al-Burhān al-qāṭiᶜ*, *Tarjīḥ asālīb al-Qurʾān ᶜalā asālīb al-Yūnān*, *al-Rawḍ al-bāsim* and finally Ḥusayn al-Sayāghī's commentary on Zayd b. ᶜAlī's *Majmūᶜ* entitled *al-Rawḍ al-naḍīr* as well as a collection of treatises entitled *Majmūᶜat al-rasāʾil al-Yamaniyya*.[67] Ismāᶜīl al-Akwaᶜ says that the publication of these works 'had a great influence in making Yemen known to Muslim scholars elsewhere, and led them to believe that the Zaydī *madhhab* was not very different from that of Ahl al-Sunna'.[68]

The argument that the Zaydī-Hādawī school was like Sunnism continued to be made by Yemeni scholars throughout the Ḥamīd al-Dīn imamate. In 1950 Qāḍī Muḥammad al-ᶜAmrānī, for example, published an article entitled *al-Zaydiyya fi ʾl-Yaman* in which he says '... the Ḥanafī *madhhab* and the Hādawī *madhhab* are brothers. Indeed, I can state to the reader that the Ḥanafī *madhhab* is closer to the Zaydī or Hādawī *madhhab* than it is to the Ḥanbalī *madhhab*'.[69] Drawing on the Traditionist legacy, he says later in the same article:

> ... the Zaydīs in Yemen are not as many, who are ignorant of their state and law, imagine. Indeed, if they practised *taqlīd* they would be imitating the imams of their school, which does not exclude them from the schools of their brothers the Sunnīs, especially the Ḥanafīs. As for those who practise *ijtihād* and become liberated (*taḥarrarū*), such as the *ijtihād* of al-Wazīr, al-Maqbalī, al-Amīr, al-Jalāl and al-Shawkānī, no one knows the worth of these ulema except after becoming knowledgeable in all their precious works. They are like the scholars who belong to the other Muslim schools in being faithful to the Rightly Guided caliphs, and in glorifying them as the ministers and supporters of the Prophet – may His peace and blessings be upon him. Those who seek to diminish their worth either belong to the ignorant masses or the fanatical elite.[70]

It is obvious that by focusing on the legacy of their Traditionists, Yemenis were now claiming an identity of interests and ideology with a wider, pan-Islamic movement of reform. Yemen was not a cultural backwater but at the forefront of judicial and religious change.

Imam Yaḥyā held a pragmatic view of the Traditionist legacy and its scholars, who had a long history of working for the state. Though a Zaydī imam, he does not appear to have been dogmatic or to have based his policies on strict Hādawī beliefs. ᶜAbd Allāh al-Shamāḥī, whom we saw earlier writing on the imam's *ikhtiyārāt*, claims in a historical work published after the revolution that Imam Yaḥyā encouraged and supported Traditionist ulema until the Saudi–Yemeni war of 1934,

---

67 Cf. *Hijar al-ᶜilm*, III: 1741.

68 *Hijar al-ᶜilm*, II: 590–1. Elsewhere, al-Akwaᶜ says that this impression is a great delusion because these Traditionists had severed their ties with the Zaydī-Hādawī *madhhab* by rejecting *taqlīd*; cf. Ismāᶜīl al-Akwaᶜ, *al-Zaydiyya nashʾatuhā wa muᶜtaqadātuhā* (Beirut: Dār al-Fikr al-Muᶜāṣir, 1993), p. 40.

69 Muḥammad b. Ismāᶜīl al-ᶜAmrānī, *al-Zaydiyya biʾl-Yaman*, reprint, (Sanaa: Maktabat Dār al-Turāth, 1990), p. 9. This article was first published in the journal *Risālat al-Islām* (Cairo: Dār al-Taqrīb, 1369/1950).

70 al-ᶜAmrānī, *al-Zaydiyya*, p. 14.

because of their social weakness and politically subservient attitudes. After the war, in which the Yemenis were defeated in the Tihāma, Shamāḥī says that the imam veered in the direction of conservative Zaydism because of the support the northern Zaydī tribes had offered him during the war.[71] This is a dubious claim, first because the relevance of Zaydism to the tribes is not immediately evident, and second because it is not borne out by the facts. Imam Yaḥyā continued to appeal to his Shāfiᶜī subjects by celebrating with them the first Friday of the month of Rajab, which is believed to be the day on which the Prophet invited Yemenis to accept Islam. This was intended to balance Hādawī celebrations of Yawm al-Ghadīr and the Tenth of Muḥarram. Furthermore, the Traditionist judges were maintained in their posts after 1934, as in the case of Qāḍī Yaḥyā al-Iryānī, who continued to teach Sunnī works in mosques and schools, namely the works of Shawkānī and Ibn al-Amīr which were also taught at *al-Madrasa al-ᶜIlmiyya*.[72] It is true, however, that Imams Yaḥyā and Aḥmad both felt the teaching of Shawkānī's *al-Sayl al-jarrār* was problematic because of its thoroughgoing critique of the Hādawī school and they feared this would stir public passions.[73]

Becoming a Dynasty: The Issue of *Wilāyat al-ᶜAhd*

As was mentioned earlier, Zaydīs have consistently opposed the idea of kingship (*mulk*) and that an incumbent imam should officially nominate his successor. Interestingly, this is reflected on two of Imam Yaḥyā's coins, minted in the early years of his rule, which bear the inscription, 'There is no God but God, Kingship belongs to God, Lord of the worlds' (*lā ilāha ilā Allāh al-mulk li-llāh rabb al-ᶜālamīn*).[74] In practice, it has often been the case that son succeeded father, though the process was never formalised except in the eighteenth-century Qāsimī state. Under Imam Yaḥyā, however, an effort was undertaken to nominate his son Aḥmad as crown prince (*walī al-ᶜahd*). It is also notable that Imam Yaḥyā, who at first was loath to assume the title of 'His Majesty the King' (*jalālat al-malik*), later accepted its usage in reference to himself. These two instances provide an example of a shift in conceptions of rule which took place at this time and signal another departure from traditional Zaydism.

Muḥammad Zabāra, who wrote a chronicle of Imam Yaḥyā's reign, reports that in 1342/1923 the governor of Sanaa, the commander of its garrison and the governor of Bilād al-Rūs raised with Imam Yaḥyā the matter of nominating his eldest son Aḥmad as successor to the supreme imamate (*al-imāma al-sharᶜiyya al-ᶜuẓmā*).

71 ᶜAbd Allāh al-Shamāḥī, *al-Yaman al-insān waʾl-ḥaḍāra* (Beirut: Manshūrāt al-Madīna, 1985), pp. 190, 194f.

72 Cf. Ismāᶜīl al-Akwaᶜ, *al-Madāris al-islāmiyya fī ʾl-Yaman* (Beirut: Muʾassasat al-Risāla, 1986), pp. 404–6.

73 *Qāḍī* Muḥammad al-ᶜAmrānī, for example, was prohibited by imam Aḥmad from teaching the *Sayl* in the Filayḥī mosque (taped interview with *Qāḍī* ᶜAmrānī); cf. Aḥmad, *Min aᶜlām al-Yaman*, p. 72.

74 Cf. Krause, *Standard Catalog* (1998), p. 1747.

Yaḥyā answered that it was up to them to pursue the matter, given that it was a known fact that the supreme imamate was a matter for the great ulema to decide. In Muḥarram 1343 / August 1924, a group of Aḥmad's retainers asked many of the great ulema of the age for their opinion in the matter. All those who were asked were Shawkānī students who held official positions in government, such as Ḥusayn al-ᶜAmrī, Zayd al-Daylamī and ᶜAbd Allāh al-Yamānī. On 20 Muḥarram 1343 / 21 August 1924, these scholars collectively issued a statement arguing for the nomination of Aḥmad as *walī al-ᶜahd*. The language of the statement is purely Sunnī. Among the claims they make is that there is a consensus among Muslim scholars which necessitates the designation of an imam who will act as the Prophet's successor (*ajmaᶜū ᶜalā ījāb naṣb imām khalīfatan li-rasūl Allāh*). The statement also argues for obedience to rulers and cites ḥadīths such as 'obey those who perform the prayer duty among you', 'obey those who establish amongst you the Book of God', 'the one who dislikes a matter in his commander must be patient; should he rebel against a sultan even [the breadth of] one hand-span, he will die a death of the Jāhiliyya', and 'the one who wishes to divide this nation, and they are many, sever their heads with a sword'. The statement then adopts nationalistic and anti-imperialist terms by asserting that the best means of protecting Yemen's bounties, which the imams of the Prophet's House have preserved from the depredations of foreign states, whose only aim is to spread corruption and to divide Muslims, is to maintain the post of imam among Imam Yaḥyā's children. These ulema finally advise Imam Yaḥyā to designate his son, Sayf al-Islām Aḥmad, as successor and they state explicitly that such designation is consistent with the teachings of the four Sunnī schools.[75]

Imam Yaḥyā initially reacted to this recommendation with caution, because he knew it contravened the tenets of the Hādawī school. *De facto*, however, Aḥmad was henceforth called *walī al-ᶜahd*, a first in recent Zaydī history. Some Zaydī scholars objected to the innovation and were critical of Imam Yaḥyā for remaining silent about it.[76] Surprisingly, however, direct written criticism came from a group of ulema in Calcutta, India, who possibly considered the caliphate to reside in Yemen. They sent a letter to Imam Yaḥyā and the Yemeni people in which they found fault with the imam for nominating a successor, arguing that the imamate in Yemen is not a hereditary institution and, more specifically, that Aḥmad's morals make him unfit to rule the Yemeni people.[77] Again Imam Yaḥyā did not react to this but appointed his son to official military and governorate posts in a bid to show that Aḥmad was indeed fit.

Another innovation that drew the censure of some ulema was Imam Yaḥyā's adopting the title of 'His Majesty the King of the Mutawakkilite Kingdom of Yemen' as well as calling Yemen a kingdom (*mamlaka*). The first time this title was officially used was apparently in the treaty which Yemen signed with Italy

[75] Zabāra, *Aʾimmat al-Yaman biʾl-qarn al-rābiᶜ ᶜashar*, vol. II, pp. 106–10.
[76] Cf. *Hijar al-ᶜilm*, II: 822 and I: 190; al-Wazīr, *Ḥayāt al-amīr*, pp. 209–10.
[77] For the text of this letter see *Hijar al-ᶜilm*, II: 822–6. The link between the Indian scholars and Yemen which led to this statement being issued is not yet established.

on 24 Ṣafar 1345 / 2 September 1926. The governor of Taᶜizz, ᶜAlī b. ᶜAbd Allāh al-Wazīr (d. 1367/1948), is reported to have reacted to this by saying, 'We did not fight the Turks for the sake of a kingdom, for they were kings; [we fought] for an Islamic caliphate'.[78] It is reported that Imam Yaḥyā calmed some of the fears by explaining that such usage did not change the essence of his rule and was intended to accommodate international requirements.

Another indication of this shift in the nature of the forms of Ḥamīd al-Dīn rule can be gleaned from a passage in two different editions of al-Wāsiᶜī's 'unofficial' history entitled *Tārīkh al-Yaman*. In the first edition published in 1346/1928, al-Wāsiᶜī says the following:

Notice

> The kings of this age are given the title *His Majesty King so and so*. However, because the people of good taste feel dejected at the use of this title, I have avoided using the title *His Majesty* in this book when referring to our Lord the Imam of Yemen. He does not approve of it [anyway], because of his great godliness, knowledge, merit and his fidelity to the character of his ancestor the Lord of Messengers – may God's peace and blessing be upon him. I have restricted myself to using the title he uses for himself and the title of his early forefathers, the imams of Yemen: Commander of the Faithful, The Trusting in Allāh Lord of the Worlds. The exception is what I found in the Italian treaty which I have rendered as it was written.[79]

Interestingly, in the second edition of al-Wāsiᶜī's history, published in 1367/1948, this notice has been removed. The ellipsis was not merely intentional; rather, the matter of imams being called kings was no longer a public issue.

Imam Ahmad's Reign (r. 1367–1382/1948–1962)

Imam Yaḥyā was assassinated in 1948, and for three weeks a 'Constitutional government' ruled in Sanaa, headed by Imam ᶜAbd Allāh b. Aḥmad al-Wazīr. The new regime aimed to establish a more representative form of government and claimed it rejected the autocratic ways of the Ḥamīd al-Dīn imams. Aḥmad vowed to avenge his father's murder and declared himself imam, taking the title al-Nāṣir.[80] He attacked Sanaa, deposed its fledgling government and allowed his tribal supporters to loot the city. The rival imam and some of the main leaders of

[78] al-Wazīr, *Ḥayāt al-amīr*, pp. 212, 298. Another scholar who is reported to have objected as well is ᶜAlī b. Ḥusayn al-Shāmī (1372/1952), saying that the word 'majesty' belongs to God alone and that even God had not used the plural pronoun We (*naḥnu*) which Imam Yaḥyā was now using.

[79] al-Wāsiᶜī, *Tārīkh al-Yaman* (1346/1927–8 ed.), p. 279. I would like to thank Paul Dresch for pointing this 'notice' out to me.

[80] An exchange of telegrams took place between the Imam ᶜAbd Allāh al-Wazīr and Imam Aḥmad that shows clearly the dynastic conception of rule which Imam Aḥmad now subscribed to. Claiming to be the rightful imam, al-Wazīr asked Aḥmad to offer his allegiance and the latter gave a vituperative response, beginning with a list of his forebears who were imams. Cf. *Hijar al-ᶜilm*, II: 838–9.

the constitutional government were executed, a good number were imprisoned, and Aḥmad set up his capital in Taʿizz, where until recently he had been governor.

Aḥmad's reign can be seen as an extension of his father's, except that Yemen had to contend with the forces of the outside world, especially the turbulent politics of the Arab world, to a much greater extent than before. Aḥmad had to operate much more like an Arab statesman, and traditional notions of being imam of the Zaydīs or caliph of Islam were no longer meaningful. The opposition forces that played a role in his father's demise, the Free Yemenis, were directly influenced by ideas of reform and progress from abroad. As pointed out earlier, this influence goes back to the 1920s, to such men as Muḥammad Zabāra who had traveled to Egypt, Mecca and Jerusalem where they met Muslim reformers like Riḍā and Shawkat ʿAlī. Furthermore, the Muslim Brotherhood in Egypt had sent a representative, al-Fuḍayl al-Wartalānī, to effect reform in Yemen, and he played a key role in advising the Free Yemenis.[81] The world had changed and impinged much more directly on Yemen.

Recognising this, Imam Aḥmad initially promised constitutional reforms. His first official announcement upon taking power stated that his rule would be based on an ordered consultative government (*ḥukūma shūrawiyya munaẓẓama*), and that he would establish a Higher Islamic Council (*majlis Islāmī aʿlā*) which would include ministers, notables, ulema, literary figures and tribal leaders. Little came of it, however. It is important nonetheless that he recognised that new forms and idioms of rule had to be used and perhaps instituted. His choice, however, fell on an avowedly monarchic system of rule. That Yemen was a kingdom was now taken for granted. His first official statement, indeed, was addressed from the 'court of His Majesty Imam Aḥmad son of Imam Yaḥyā son of Muḥammad Ḥamīd al-Dīn, the venerated King of Yemen'. The first Yemeni coinage with the inscription 'the Mutawakkilite Kingdom of Yemen' was issued by him in the year of his accession.[82] The 3rd of Jumādā al-Ulā, the day of his accession, became a national holiday called the 'Day of Victory' (ʿĪd al-Naṣr).[83] His son al-Badr Muḥammad was called *walī al-ʿahd* from a very early date after 1948, and the imam's brother, al-Ḥasan, was designated prime minister.[84]

Yet Aḥmad remained in some respects a Zaydī imam. He was considered a scholar but not of his father's stature. He issued *ikhtiyārāt*, some of which restated

[81] Cf. J. Leigh Douglas, *The Free Yemeni Movement* (American University of Beirut Press, 1987).

[82] Cf. Krause, *Standard Catalog* (1998), pp. 1750–1. [83] Cf. *Hijar al-ʿilm*, pp. 841–6.

[84] Cf. Aḥmad b. Muḥammad al-Shāmī, *Imām al-Yaman Aḥmad Ḥamīd al-Dīn* (Beirut: Dār al-Kitāb al-Jadīd, 1965), pp. 12–13. In the preface, dated 1954, Aḥmad Muḥammad Nuʿmān (d. 1997), who was an important figure among the Free Yemenis, says that al-Badr was referred to by then as *walī al-ʿahd*. It is also interesting to note that Nuʿmān here praises Imam Yaḥyā for bringing to Yemen such modern reforms as establishing ministries, a council of ministers, a formalised system of succession, a royal court, modern schools, hospitals, systems of communication, newspapers, publishing, international diplomatic relations, bringing in some of the modern sciences as well as foreign experts and technical consultants, and sending delegations of students abroad. He then goes on to praise Imam Aḥmad for building on and expanding these reforms and for making the system of rule stronger than it had been before. Yemen, he says, has become a member of the international community of nations under these imams.

those made by his father. They are most notable, however, for the added rights he gives women in matters of marriage annulment, divorce and inheritance. In this regard, Ismāᶜīl al-Akwaᶜclaims that Aḥmad opposed his father's opinion on the invalidity of *kafāʾa fī ʾl-nasab*, confirming it instead as a condition for enacting a valid marriage. Furthermore, Ismāᶜīl al-Akwaᶜdepicts Aḥmad as having been a fanatical Zaydī, oppressing the Shāfiᶜī population of the Tihāma during his campaigns against the Zarānīq tribe (1927–1929), ordering that *ḥayya ᶜalā khayr al-ᶜamal* be said in the call to prayer and demolishing the dome over Aḥmad b. Mūsā al-ᶜUjayl's tomb in Bayt al-Faqīh.[85] This assessment, like that of many post-revolutionary republican authors, is too polemical and skews reality by depicting the rule of the Ḥamīd al-Dīns as determined more by doctrine and sectarian sentiments than by pragmatism and *Realpolitik*. It is not evident that Imam Aḥmad took decisions along sectarian lines. His actions in the Tihāma were taken while he was crown prince, and they were directed at a rebellious tribe that was presumed to have British support from Aden. It is doubtful whether his admittedly brutal policies in this instance were motivated by religious zeal.

In looking at Imam Aḥmad's judicial and administrative appointments, one sees that they did not conform to a clearly defined policy of favouring Zaydīs exclusively. Loyalty was an important determinant, as was the fear of rival contenders or possible opponents with an independent power base, much as it had been in his father's reign. He would not forget that the al-Wazīrs, who were *sayyid*s and had been appointed governors, had led the plot to assassinate his father. This made him wary of appointing *sayyid*s of politically influential families to high administrative posts. The picture which emerges is not one of a transparent system that conformed either to ideological or doctrinal considerations; it was, to say the least, opaque. Sayyid Yaḥyā b. Muḥammad b. al-ᶜAbbās (d. 1962), for example, had been one of Imam Yaḥyā's judges and military commanders. He was loyal and sided with Imam Aḥmad in 1948, playing an important role in defeating the constitutional forces, and was therefore rewarded with the presidency of Sanaa's court of appeals. Al-Akwaᶜreports that Sayyid Yaḥyā was an ᶜAdnānī fanatic who was in favour of the *kafāʾa fī ʾl-nasab* and had opposed the appointment of Qaḥṭānīs to high posts, namely that of Qāḍī Aḥmad b. Aḥmad al-Sayāghī, who was the imam's representative in Ibb.[86] Again, however, this claim is misleading since it does not seem that Imam Aḥmad was prejudiced against those of Qaḥṭānī descent in deciding his appointments. A number of them, including Shāfiᶜīs, were given posts by him. Al-Sayāghī, for example, had been appointed commander of the governorate of Ibb by Imam Yaḥyā in 1357/1938, and because of his loyalty in 1948 he was reappointed by Imam Aḥmad as his representative there and held the post until 1961.[87]

[85] *Hijar al-ᶜilm*, II: 817, 828.
[86] *Hijar al-ᶜilm*, II: 1104; cf. *Nuzhat al-naẓar*, pp. 643–4. Sayyid Yaḥyā and his grandson were shot dead by a republican officer on 26 September 1962.
[87] *Hijar al-ᶜilm*, III: 1533f.

By contrast with Sayyid Yaḥyā's appointment, that of Qāḍī ᶜAbd al-Raḥmān b. Yaḥyā al-Iryānī (later President of the republic from 1967 till 1974), who belonged to the lineage of Shawkānī students and was a supporter of the Free Yemenis, deserves noting. Imam Aḥmad made him member of the judicial council (*al-hayʾa al-sharᶜiyya*) in Taᶜizz, a post he held till the 1962 revolution despite his collaboration with the constitutional government in 1948 and with a failed attempt to depose the imam in 1955. Both times he was imprisoned but was later released and reinstated in his post. Court politics and intrigues, rather than ideology, offer reasonable explanations for Aḥmad's policies.

Codifying Hādawī Law

Despite the efforts by Shawkānī to establish his own authoritative legal text, based on a direct interface with the Qurʾān and ḥadīth, and the considerable influence of his Traditionist students, Hādawī law remained the 'official' law of Yemen through the twentieth century. The weight of tradition and that all jurists in the northern highlands were initially taught Hādawī law explain the endurance of this *madhhab*. Hādawism, after a millenium in the highlands, was too deeply entrenched and integral to the religious identity of a great number of Yemenis. Because of this, its agreed upon rules gave coherence and determinacy to the legal order, characteristics that were not obvious in the system of autonomous *mujtahid*s envisaged by Shawkānī. Moreover, to revoke it completely would require considerable coercive force, a feature which no state had until the modern republic. Therefore, the influence of the Traditionists in actual legal practice is only tangible in the 'choices' of the imams and the claims the latter made to rise above sectarian differences. In concrete terms, Traditionism was an ideological posture adopted by certain scholars and revealed itself in the anti-*madhhab* claims they made, the sources they cited, the scholarly cliques they established, and the forms of rule they sanctioned.

During the reigns of Imams Yaḥyā and Aḥmad, attempts were made to present Hādawī law in simplified terms and code-like structures. These attempts are first reflected in the last major commentary on *Kitāb al-Azhār* of the twentieth century. This is the four volume work by Qāḍī Aḥmad b. Qāsim al-ᶜAnsī (d. 1390/1970) entitled *al-Tāj al-mudhhab li-aḥkām al-madhhab* (The Gilded Crown regarding the Judgements of the School). It was published in stages over a period from 1938 until 1947 and reflected several significant developments. In the preface, the author states that he wrote it in order to make it easier for students to study law because the compendium which was traditionally used, the *Sharḥ al-Azhār*, had become too cumbersome. Its study, he says, demanded a great deal of time from students because of all its marginal glosses, and its extensive listing of opinions and differences among the various schools of law rarely occur and are no longer relevant. He, therefore, sought to simplify matters and present them in an organised fashion by dividing the book into two clearly delineated sections: the first on the *ᶜibādāt* and the second on the *muᶜāmalāt*.[88] Each section is then divided into numbered subsections for easy reference and cross-referencing.

Another novel feature of the work is the author's use of footnotes, a first in Hādawī commentaries, which elucidate points in the text or make cross-reference to other relevant subsections. Furthermore, the author points out in the footnotes whenever an opinion in the text corresponds to one of Imam Yaḥyā's *ikhtiyārat* and justifies this by saying:

> So as to complete the benefit [of this work], we have deemed it necessary to decorate this crown [i.e., this book] with the jewels of the *ikhtiyārāt* of the Imam of our age, our Lord, the Commander of the Faithful al-Mutawakkil ᶜalā Allāh Yaḥyā... He has ordered adherence to the Noble School in all transactions barring those matters where his knowledge in the sciences has led him to make exceptions for the benefit of all and in accordance with proofs from the Book and Sunna. [This is] as it should be with any *mujtahid* and just imam, who is concerned with the welfare of his subjects and who looks after the rights of his community. This is why the Noble School has stipulated that a condition for a proper 'summons' (*daᶜwa*) to the imamate – as we shall see in *siyar* [i.e., public law] sub-section 456 – is that it should be made by a *mujtahid* in the sciences. This condition does not mean that he [i.e., the imam] should be able to impose the Sharīᶜa in accordance with its laws, since he can do this through *taqlīd*. Rather, what is meant by the stipulation of *ijtihād* is that he should be just, not a fanatic of one school or sect. Only the *mujtahid* can be like this. And the one who is like this is the one who fulfils the Prophetic role, who interprets it, ruling by its sanctions and will [therefore] be accepted by Muslims regardless of their school affiliation as long as they disregard obdurateness and make justice their guide to the Book of God and the Sunna of his Prophet – may God's blessings and prayers be upon him.[89]

The *ikhtiyārāt* were thereby directly incorporated into a code-like version of Hādawī law. By denoting his *mujtahid* status, they acted to reinforce the imam's claim to being a 'full imam' in accordance with Hādawī stipulations. But by the same token, they were also was intended to show that he transcended sectarian differences.

A second work which had even more the qualities of a code was commissioned by Imam Aḥmad. This work is entitled *Kitāb Taysīr al-marām fī masāʾil al-ahkām liʾl-bāḥithīn waʾl-ḥukkām* and was produced by the three scholars, Qāsim b. Ibrāhīm, ᶜAlī b. ᶜAbd Allāh al-Ānisī and ᶜAbd Allāh b. Muḥammad al-Sarḥī. Although completed in 1951, the work was not published until after the revolution and appears to have been used in manuscript form until then.[90] This work deals exclusively with transactional law, and though based on the sections in *Kitāb al-Azhār*, it is presented in simple and clear Arabic as a numbered code without any explanation of the legal arguments underpinning the rules. In the preface, the authors explain that they wrote the work because Imam Aḥmad felt that legal questions were too numerous for a jurist to master, that only a few men knew how to apply judgements properly, and that many judges, even those who had studied law, would often make mistakes. The *Taysīr* was therefore intended as a quick and

[88] al-ᶜAnsī, *al-Tāj al-mudhhab*, vol. I, pp. 4–5. [89] Ibid., vol. II, pp. 13–14 fn. 1.
[90] al-ᶜAlīmī, *al-Taqlīdiyya waʾl-ḥadātha*, p. 129.

easy reference for judges. The authors also argue that though the work is based on a *Kitāb al-Azhār* and its *Sharḥ*, Zaydism is much like the other Sunnī schools and, moreover, all the imams of the schools were *mujtahid*s and therefore their opinions are correct.[91]

It is interesting to note that in many respects the 1962 revolution caused no rupture in legal practice. The civil war years (1962–70) were a period of judicial stasis, and no significant reforms took place other than the closing down of *al-Madrasa al-ᶜIlmiyya*. This was done by the Republic's first minister of education, Qāsim Ghālib Aḥmad, a Shāfiᶜī from Lower Yemen, who justified this on grounds that *al-Madrasa al-ᶜIlmiyya* was a bastion of Zaydī thought, reproducing Zaydī jurists.[92] The net effect was that no jurists were trained until the creation of the Higher Institute of Justice (*al-Maᶜhad al-ᶜĀlī li'l-Qaḍā'*) in the early 1980s.[93] Judges trained under the Ḥamīd al-Dīns continued to run the judicial structures of the state and continue doing so today. It was not until 1971 that the Ministry of Justice issued a list of 68 rulings (*qarārāt*), and judges were instructed to follow these.[94] A full third of the *qarārāt* were identical to the Ḥamīd al-Dīn *ikhtiyārāt*. The *Tāj al-mudhhab* was assigned to students at Sanaa University's faculty of law in the early 1970s, and the *Taysīr al-marām* was published and is presently taught in the *Maᶜhad al-ᶜĀlī li'l-Qaḍā'*. In other words, the works which were produced under the Ḥamīd al-Dīns were incorporated into the Republic's educational curricula, though these now also include a greater number of Sunnī works as well as modern legal textbooks.

By 1975, measures were being taken to establish legal codes similar to those in other Arab countries, especially those of Egypt. A commission of eleven members was established, and foreign advisors, mainly Sudanese and Egyptian, were recruited to help in drafting new codes. The first of these was the civil code of 1979. A public prosecutor's office (*al-niyāba al-ᶜāmma*) was also established, as was a Higher Judicial Council (*al-Majlis al-Qaḍā' al-ᶜĀlī*) to act as the supreme court. The process of instituting and making acceptable these new forms of law and procedure is still unfolding. Many of the jurists who were trained in the Ḥamīd al-Dīn era view them with suspicion, preferring to use the old manuals and commentaries.

The 1962 Revolution

The political and religious rhetoric which the Free Yemenis, such as Muḥammad Maḥmūd al-Zubayrī and Muḥammad Aḥmad Nuᶜmān, had leveled against the Ḥamīd al-Dīns whilst in opposition became part of official state propaganda against

91 Qāsim b. Ibrāhīm *et al.*, *Kitāb Taysīr al-marām* (Sanaa: Manshūrāt al-Madīna, 1986), pp. 5–6.

92 al-Akwaᶜ, *al-Madāris al-islāmiyya*, p. 406.

93 In the early 1970s, a faculty of law (*kulliyyat al-sharīᶜa wa'l-qānūn*) was established at the University of Sanaa, but its graduates were not considered sufficiently qualified to act as judges by the existing judicial hierarchy who were trained under the old system, mainly in *al-Madrasa al-ᶜIlmiyya*; cf. al-ᶜAlīmī, pp. 174–5.

94 *Qarārāt wizārat al-ᶜadl* (Sanaa: 1971); cf. al-ᶜAmrānī, *Niẓām al-qaḍā'*, pp. 233–44 and Wizārat al-ᶜAdl, *Majallat al-buḥūth wa'l-aḥkām al-qaḍā'iyya* 1(1980).

the *ancien régime*, whose defenders during the civil war (1962–1970) were labeled royalists (*malakiyyūn*). The Ḥamīd al-Dīns and the Zaydī imams of past eras were castigated for being despotic, racist, sectarian and anti-egalitarian. The new revolutionary leadership was made up of several distinct groups: military officers, modern educated political activists, tribal leaders, and ulema who were mainly from the *quḍāt* estate. In the first five years after the revolution the decision-making processes were dominated by military officers and modern-educated political activists, who had Egyptian military and political backing.[95] Men like Vice-President ᶜAbd al-Raḥmān al-Bayḍānī and Minister of Education Qāsim Ghālib Aḥmad took the lead in the ideological fight against the royalists. Among other things these men criticized the *sayyid*s for being the historical oppressors of the Southern Arabs, the Qaḥṭānīs, and on these grounds a number of *sayyid*s were summarily executed or persecuted.

Al-Bayḍānī, an Egyptian-born Shāfiᶜī whose family was originally from al-Bayḍāʾ in Yemen, had been involved with the Free Yemenis before the revolution and was noted for his vitriolic attacks against the *sayyid*s broadcast from Cairo's Voice of the Arabs radio station.[96] The Free Yemeni leader, Qāḍī Muḥammad Maḥmūd al-Zubayrī, had also engaged in the Qaḥṭānī versus ᶜAdnānī debate but had tempered his attack against the *sayyid*s by focusing more on the Ḥamīd al-Dīn family, arguing that there were poor *sayyid*s who suffered equally at the hands of the royal family.[97] Al-Zubayrī seems to have objected to the crudeness of al-Bayḍānī's rhetoric and therefore refused to cooperate with him whilst still in opposition in Egypt.[98]

Al-Zubayrī can be seen to represent the ulema members among the early republican leadership. In his writings, he attacked the Ḥamīd al-Dīn regime and the Zaydī imams for being obscurantist and reactionary, and for being sectarian by stressing differences between Zaydīs and Shāfiᶜīs, giving preference to the former. He is also perhaps the first to have mentioned Shawkānī and Ibn al-Amīr in this context. An example of al-Zubayrī's critique can be found in one of his pamphlets entitled 'The Imamate and its menace to Yemeni Unity'. Here he presents the view that the imams had throughout Yemeni history played a divisive role, splitting regions and tribes and discriminating against the Shāfiᶜī population. He further claims that they circumscribed the practice of *ijtihād*, and incited the tribes against such *mujtahid*s as Ibn al-Amīr and Shawkānī. This was not so; in fact, the imams, who ruled in the time of Ibn al-Amīr and Shawkānī, had done the very opposite by providing both with protection and support. Furthermore, al-Zubayrī's pamphlet implies that *mujtahid*s like Ibn al-Amīr and Shawkānī were politically

95 A good account of the events which took place during and after the revolution can be found in J. E. Peterson, *Yemen: The Search for a Modern State* (London: Croom Helm, 1982).

96 Cf. Douglas, *The Free Yemeni Movement*, pp. 234–7; Aḥmad al-Shāmī, *Riyāḥ al-taghyīr fī 'l-Yaman* (Jeddah: al-Maṭbaᶜa al-ᶜArabiyya, 1984), pp. 17–37.

97 Cf. R. B. Serjeant, 'The Yemeni Poet al-Zubayrī and his polemic against the Zaydī imāms', *Arabian Studies* 5 (1979), 87–130; Douglas, *The Free Yemeni Movement*, pp. 220–1.

98 Peterson, *Yemen*, p. 85.

opposed to the Zaydī imams. This again is a fabrication since both men, though at times critical of certain measures taken by the imams, had accepted posts in their governments. It appears that what was at issue here was al-Zubayrī's need to find historical figures who had in their time opposed Hādawī teachings and with whom he could identify. By doing this, he could present himself, and like-minded ulema, as latter-day equivalents of figures like Shawkānī.

Republican intellectuals obviously needed exemplary predecessors, especially non-*sayyid* ones, and found them in the Traditionist scholars of the past. In doing this they obscured the crucial fact that though these scholars had opposed Hādawī law and theology, they had not opposed the imams politically – indeed, Shawkānī was explicit that rebellion against rulers, even those who were tyrants, was not allowed. The reconstruction of Yemeni history by the republican intellectuals remains crudely instrumental; its aim is to garner legitimacy for the nationalist revolution by fabricating a native genealogy for republican ideas which it presents as forever being rooted in Yemen's soil.

Qāsim Ghālib Aḥmad, the modern-educated Shāfiᶜī Minister of Education, took up al-Zubayrī's views and was perhaps the first after the revolution to raise the banner of Ibn al-Amīr and Shawkānī as opponents of the imams. He wrote what is possibly the first book to be published under the Republic (in 1964), entitled *Ibn al-Amīr wa ᶜaṣruhu: ṣūra min kifāḥ shaᶜb al-Yaman* (Ibn al-Amīr and his Epoch: an illustration of the struggle of the Yemeni people). In it he presents Ibn al-Amīr as a fervent antagonist of the Zaydī imamate who tries to unite the Yemeni people by calling them back to the Qurʾān and Sunna.[99] The book crudely attempts to 'republicanise' Yemeni history by appealing to the notion of a 'people' who are represented by Ibn al-Amīr in their fight against imamic oppressors. Ibn al-Amīr was a *sayyid* and it appears that Aḥmad's intention was to present royalist *sayyid*s with an example of one of their own who was purportedly against the imams. Ultimately, however, by virtue of being a *sayyid*, Ibn al-Amīr was not a model with whom most republicans could fully identify; a non-*sayyid* had to be found to fill this role and the focus shifted to Shawkānī.

Aḥmad's second work, which followed up on some of the themes already stated in his earlier one, was entitled *Min aᶜlām al-Yaman: shaykh al-islām al-mujtahid Muḥammad b. ᶜAlī al-Shawkānī* (One of the Distinguished of Yemen: the Shaykh al-Islām, the *Mujtahid*, Muḥammad b. ᶜAlī al-Shawkānī). Here, Shawkānī is presented in a similar light to Ibn al-Amīr: as an anti-Zaydī *ᶜālim* trying to unite Yemenis by preaching *ijtihād* and a return to the Qurʾān and Sunna. The thorny issue of Shawkānī's acceptance of the position of *qāḍī al-quḍāt* is dismissed with the claim that he accepted the post because he wanted to spread his liberating message. In appointing him, Aḥmad claims, the imams sought to conceal themselves behind his fame and uprightness as well as to occupy their subjects with his message of *ijtihād*.[100] Republicans were obviously also attracted to him because

[99] Qāsim Aḥmad *et al.*, *Ibn al-amīr wa ᶜaṣruh*, 2nd ed. (Sanaa: Wizārat al-Iᶜlām waʾl-Thaqāfa, 1983), p. 155.

[100] Aḥmad, *Min aᶜlām al-Yaman*, p. 17.

of his critical stance toward the Zaydī-Hādawī school and his advocacy of a return to the Qur'ān and the Sunnī ḥadīth collections as the only sources of law. They depicted him as an enemy of the imams who was able to separate the power of legislation (*tashrīᶜ*) from their grip, returning it 'to God's Book and the Sunna of His Prophet', sources all Yemenis consider to be authoritative.[101] Linked to this was Shawkānī's criticism of the established *madhāhib*, a criticism one could invoke to transcend religious differences and establish unity among Yemenis.[102] Again, what remained unstated was that the process by which this took place entailed a rejection of Hādawī teachings in favour of Sunnī ones. Unity, therefore, would be clearly one-sided.

Unlike the earlier work on Ibn al-Amīr, Aḥmad's antipathy for *sayyids* becomes evident here. He refers to Shawkānī's South Arabian stock, and draws his intellectual lineage to include al-Ḥasan b. Aḥmad al-Hamdānī (d. circa 336/947) and Nashwān al-Ḥimyarī (d. 573/1178), both famous Yemenis, of South Arabian stock, who held critical stances toward the Zaydī imams. Aḥmad says in this regard:

> ... al-Shawkānī, like al-Hamdānī and Nashwān al-Ḥimyarī and others is proud of Yemen and of Yemen's free-thinking ulema. They [all] wish the unity of Yemen.[103]

In doing this, Aḥmad inserted Shawkānī into a 1960s polemic against the 'northern Arabs', the ᶜAdnānī Hāshimīs, who were depicted as having divided a naturally united Yemen and exploited in particular the Shāfiᶜī populations and regions.[104]

Although historically untenable, Aḥmad's characterisation of Shawkānī and Ibn al-Amīr as courageous opponents of the imams and Zaydism has pervaded modern Yemeni political rhetoric.[105] As such, both scholars have been used effectively as anti-imamic symbols in republican ideology. The republican ulema felt, however, that Aḥmad's characterisation and use of Shawkānī was too crudely functional, and that his works were full of obvious errors. Qāḍī Muḥammad b. Ismāᶜīl al-ᶜAmrānī, for example, says of Aḥmad's book on Shawkānī that the reader should beware as 'it contains... historical errors and attacks on the people of Shawkānī's era and on the society and judges of that period'.[106] Aḥmad was not a member of the republican ulema or the *quḍāt* estate, and one senses that the latter resented his appropriation of Shawkānī since they felt themselves to be the heirs of his legacy as his disciples and students. We see in the 1970s and 1980s a number of historical works written by these ulema and by scions of *quḍāt* families which appropriate Shawkānī in ways reflecting their own concerns and are, in certain respects, more historically informed than Aḥmad's works.

The year 1967 was a watershed in Yemeni politics, as it was in other countries of the Arab world. It spelt the end of Egyptian influence and of the ideology

101 Ibid., p. 35.
102 Cf. ᶜAbd Allāh al-Baraddūnī, *al-Yaman al-jumhūrī* (Beirut: Dār al-Fikr al-Muᶜāṣir, 1994), p. 199.
103 Ibid., p. 38. 104 Ibid., p. 20.
105 Cf. Ḥārith al-Shawkānī, 'al-Malakiyya fikra wa laysat ᶜirqan aw sulāla', *al-Ṣaḥwa* 326 (Sanaa, 1992), p. 4; Muḥammad Zabāra, 'Ra'y al-imām al-Shawkānī fī 'l-Rāfiḍa', *al-Ṣaḥwa* 328 (Sanaa, 1992), p. 4.
106 This is a gloss written in al-ᶜAmrānī's copy of the book (photocopy in my possession).

promoted by such men as al-Bayḍānī and Aḥmad. In their stead, republican ulema now came to the fore, as seen in the elevation of Qāḍī ᶜAbd al-Raḥmān al-Iryānī to the office of president of the presidential council of the republic. Men like al-Iryānī, Muḥammad and Ismāᶜīl al-Akwaᶜ, and Muḥammad al-ᶜAmrānī had a profound knowledge of Yemeni history and of the role men like Shawkānī played in it. And unlike modern-educated political activists, they did not wish to condemn the past in its entirety; they were culturally and educationally products of the imamic era. One sees in their written works, therefore, an attempt to distinguish between the rule of different imams and a more historically grounded attempt to situate scholars like Shawkānī in the political and social configurations of his time.

Republican ulema depict the period of Shawkānī's tenure as *qāḍī al-quḍāt* as one of juridical autonomy, when he and jurists more generally were free to impose the sanctions of the Sharīᶜa with the result that order and justice prevailed.[107] Muḥammad al-Akwaᶜ, for example, has this to say about this period:

> The mutual trust between al-Mahdī [ᶜAbd Allāh] and his peer Shawkānī was one reason why the foundations of his kingdom became firm . . . As to what transpired between Shawkānī and [society's] other strata, in whose lead were the ulema, the leaders and the other members of the imam's family, they all trusted him in regard to their honour, dignity and corporate duties. Likewise, all the people felt secure about their property and lives and there was complete conviction in society that Shawkānī was the sole valve [securing] all this . . . In Shawkānī's age the arts and sciences flourished and opened their sleeves, spreading especially the science of the Sunna, the sciences of the Prophetic ḥadīth and the science of its transmitters. The lighthouse of the Sunna was raised and the collections of the *Ṣiḥāḥ* and *Sunan* were taught in the congregational mosques and in smaller mosques after [a period] when their voice had been low or totally absent.[108]

Al-Akwaᶜ goes on to describe how Shawkānī's school (*madrasat al-Imām al-Shawkānī*) went on to produce a multitude of ulema who were judges and muftīs all upholding the science of the Sunna. They were, he says, a living example of rectitude, honesty, purity and justice and among their benefits was:

> that relations between Zaydī and Shāfiᶜī ulema became harmonious in all regions, as in the towns of Zabīd, Taᶜizz, Ibb and other places. Visits were exchanged and they studied with each other by reading, teaching, auditing and through *ijāza*s. They became loving brothers drinking from the same source – that of the school of [the Prophet] Muḥammad b. ᶜAbd Allāh, may God's blessings and peace be upon him.[109]

One can see that al-Akwaᶜ is describing a vision of society in which the ulema govern. Moreover, he exults in the role Shawkānī and his students have played in sustaining the more profound religious and intellectual unity of Yemen despite the country's political upheavals. His vision is ultimately a reflexive one too, since he and other Shawkānī students now held many of the country's leading administrative and judicial posts.

[107] Cf. al-ᶜAmrānī, *Niẓām al-qaḍā'*, pp. 244–5, 271–4.
[108] al-Akwaᶜ, *Ḥayāt ᶜālim wa amīr*, p. 62. [109] Ibid., p. 63.

A younger generation of Yemeni scholars, who can be described as the intellectuals of the republican state, have also focused on Shawkānī, writing studies of his life and works and depicting him as a religious, legal and educational reformer for having advocated the practice of *ijtihād* and the rejection of *taqlīd*. An example of this is the work by ᶜAbd al-Ghanī al-Sharjī, one time chairman of the department of education at Sanaa University, entitled *Imām al-Shawkānī ḥayātuhu wa fikruhu* (Imam Shawkānī: his life and thought).[110] In it al-Sharᶜabī describes Shawkānī's pedagogical views as laid out in his work *Adab al-ṭalab* and situates him among those who contributed to the movement of Islamic awakening (*al-yaqẓa al-Islāmiyya*). The work is in essence an extended eulogy of the man and al-Sharᶜabī concludes that, if taken seriously, Shawkānī's comprehensive vision of Islamic education could redress many of the faults in the modern and westernised system of education, which suffers from confusion and loss of identity. He does not, however, explain how this can be brought about.

Another eminent Yemeni intellectual who has written on Shawkānī is ᶜAbd al-ᶜAzīz al-Maqāliḥ, rector of Sanaa University and director of the Yemen Centre for Research and Studies. In his work entitled *Qirāʾa fī fikr al-Zaydiyya waʾl-Muᶜtazila* (A Reading in the Teachings of the Zaydiyya and the Muᶜtazila), al-Maqāliḥ entitles the section in which he writes about Shawkānī *Salafiyyūn lākin aḥrār* (Salafīs But Free Thinkers). The term *aḥrār* is republican and denotes that Shawkānī is to be considered a forebear of the Free Yemenis who led the opposition to the imamate. Here al-Maqāliḥ reviews *Adab al-ṭalab* and accepts uncritically all that Shawkānī says about his opponents, a feature he shares with all the non-Yemeni and Yemeni authors who have written on Shawkānī (except for the Hādawīs of course). He comes to the conclusion that Shawkānī was an 'Islamic thinker who fought fanaticism and the sectarian attitudes which divided Muslims and violated the Islamic creed' and asserts that he devoted his life to 'liberating mankind's thinking from the prison of *taqlīd* and fanaticism'.[111] Al-Maqāliḥ then justifies Shawkānī's acceptance of an official post in the imamic government by referring to Ayatollah Khomeini. He explains that Khomeini made it an obligation to accept office if in so doing the scholar can make Islam and Muslims victorious or if he can curb acts of injustice. Shawkānī, al-Maqālīḥ says, was therefore justified in taking up an official post since his aim was to eliminate fanaticism and to establish justice, both of which he accomplished by becoming *qāḍī al-quḍāt* and by having good relations with the imams.[112] The only criticism al-Maqāliḥ levels at Shawkānī comes from a passage in *Adab al-ṭalab* in which the latter argues that the people of lowly professions, such as tailors, bloodletters and butchers should not study the religious sciences or frequent the ulema since this would lead them to becoming haughty and ultimately would reflect badly on the

110 ᶜAbd al-Ghanī b. Qāsim al-Sharjī, *Imām al-Shawkānī ḥayātuhu wa fikruhu* (Beirut: Muʾassasat al-Risāla, 1988).
111 ᶜAbd al-ᶜAzīz al-Maqāliḥ, *Qirāʾa fī fikr al-Zaydiyya waʾl-Muᶜtazila* (Beirut: Dār al-ᶜAwda, 1982), p. 225.
112 Ibid., pp. 236–7.

ulema as a whole.[113] Al-Maqāliḥ laments that Shawkānī was not able to transcend social and class distinctions which contradict the egalitarian spirit of Islam, but exonerates him for being a product of the imamic age in which such attitudes were prevalent. He ends by praising the September revolution for finally getting rid of all discrimination and making education a right for all citizens regardless of social origin.[114]

Perhaps, the most prolific Yemeni to write about Shawkānī is Ḥusayn al-ᶜAmrī, a scion of the Āl al-ᶜAmrī whom we saw earlier playing an important role in perpetuating the Shawkānī legacy as well as holding important posts in the governments of the Ḥamīd al-Dīn imams. Al-ᶜAmrī's writings are the most historically informed, though they pursue rather the same view as the republican writings on Shawkānī described above. He depicts him as a liberated and fair (*munṣif*) thinker, a leader of his generation (*raʾid ᶜaṣrih*), and reformer calling for the reawakening and unity of the Muslim *umma* through *ijtihād*.[115] Moreover, al-ᶜAmrī is quick to condemn Shawkānī's Hādawī opponents; he sees him as having 'led the *free* Zaydīs... and faced *fanatics* who were for the most part supported by the rabble'.[116] The question of whether Shawkānī is a Zaydī at all is not clarified by al-ᶜAmrī, and it is only Ismāᶜīl al-Akwaᶜ who unequivocally says that the Traditionist scholars of Yemen, from Ibn al-Wazīr down to Shawkānī, 'had severed their ties with the Zaydī-Hādawī school after rejecting *taqlīd*.[117]

It is this element of rupture, however, which makes the Traditionist so appealing to republican authors who wish to dissociate the new era from the imamic past which had based itself on Hādawī teachings. Moreover, republicans have highlighted the legacy of the Traditionist scholars because of its appeal in the wider Muslim world, where they are seen as pre-modern reformers and renewers whose views presaged concerns of the modern period. Shawkānī's works are read and referred to everywhere in the Sunnī world, and through him republicans have sought to make wider claims for Yemen's cultural and historical importance as a place of learning from which ideas of universal relevance emerged.

Shawkānī's Influence on Yemeni Law

The Republic's leading jurists claim that Shawkānī's legal opinions have been very influential in the reform and development of modern Yemeni law. It has already been noted that under President ᶜAbd al-Raḥmān al-Iryānī the Ministry of Justice promulgated a set of sixty-eight rulings which were binding on the judges of the Republic. Qāḍī Muḥammad al-ᶜAmrānī has pointed out that fifteen of the sixty-eight rulings correspond exactly with Shawkānī's opinions, and some of these have

[113] Cf. *Adab al-ṭalab*, p. 129. [114] al-Maqāliḥ, *Qirāʾa fī fikr al-Zaydiyya*, pp. 241–3.
[115] Cf. Al-ᶜAmrī, *The Yemen*, part two; idem, *al-Imām al-Shawkānī*; idem, 'Ḥarakat al-tajdīd waʾl-iṣlāḥ fī ʾl-Yaman fī ʾl-ᶜaṣr al-ḥadīth', *al-Ijtihād* 9 (1990), 175–94.
[116] al-ᶜAmrī, *The Yemen*, pp. 115–16 (the emphasis is mine).
[117] al-Akwaᶜ, *al-Zaydiyya*, p. 40.

enormous practical significance.[118] For example, 'rule 21' denies the neighbour the right of pre-emption (*shufᶜa*) and accords it only to the partner in ownership. This is in direct contradiction to Hādawī law which does accord the neighbour this right.[119] Shawkānī restricted the right of pre-emption by excluding the neighbour on the basis of *ḥadīths* found in the *Ṣaḥīḥayn* and the *Sunan* of Abū Dāwūd and Ibn Mājah.[120] In the years after the revolution, when Sanaa was growing rapidly, in part because of rural–urban migration, 'rule 21' allowed for the relatively quick sale of land by denying neighbours the right to interfere.[121] Both the 1979 Yemen Arab Republic's civil code and the 1992 civil code of the Republic of Yemen have maintained that pre-emption is a right accorded solely to a partner and not to a neighbour.[122] Though this rule of pre-emption can be found in Shāfiᶜī legal texts for example, what is notable is that Shawkānī's opinion is invoked to give it legitimacy.

Qāḍī Muḥammad b. Ismāᶜīl al-Ḥajjī, who headed the commission of jurists who drew up the 1979 civil code, and who describes himself as belonging to '*madhhab* al-Shawkānī', stated that the methodology used in drafting the civil code was consistent with Shawkānī's legal methodology. The commission, according to al-Ḥajjī, looked at the legal opinions of all the Islamic schools of law and chose only that which conforms with the Qurʾān and Sunna. Furthermore, al-Ḥajjī stated that many of Shawkānī's opinions influenced the 1979 civil code, e.g. the division of contracts into the two categories of *ṣaḥīḥ* (valid) and the *bāṭil* (null and void) instead of the Hādawī division of contracts into the three categories of *ṣaḥīḥ*, *bāṭil* and *fāsid* (invalid).[123] Although one can differ with al-Ḥajjī about the extent of Shawkānī's actual influence on the 1979 civil code, given that it is remarkably similar to the modern Egyptian civil code, it is worth noting the importance al-Ḥajjī gives to al-Shawkānī's *imprimatur*.[124]

*Fatwā*s have been another means through which Shawkānī's opinions have been made relevant in Yemeni legal life. This has been accomplished mainly through the medium of the radio, and more recently television. In 1969 ᶜAbd al-Raḥmān al-Iryānī set up a radio programme called *Fatāwā* on which jurists read out their *fatwā*s in answer to questions sent them by the public.[125] Muḥammad b. Ismāᶜīl al-ᶜAmrāni has been issuing his *fatwā*s for the last three decades on this programme. His *fatwā*s, he says, conform to Shawkānī's *ijtihād* methodology. Here is a recent *fatwā* he gave in answer to a question about whether a man and a woman had the right to marry if they were nursed by the same wet-nurse only once. The answer:

[118] al-ᶜAmrānī, *Niẓām al-qaḍāʾ*, pp. 232–44. [119] Cf. al-ᶜAnsī, *al-Tāj al-mudhhab*, vol. III, p. 9.
[120] Cf. Shawkānī, *al-Sayl al-jarrār*, vol. III, pp. 171–2.
[121] This is based on an interview with Qāḍī Muḥammad al-Ḥajjī, Vice-President of the Higher Judicial Council.
[122] Cf. *al-Qānūn al-madanī*, Yemen Arab Republic (n.p.: 1979), p. 677; *al-Qarār al-jumhūrī bi 'l qānūn raqm 19 li-sanat 1992 bi-isdār al-qanūn al-madanī* 19, Republic of Yemen, (n.p.: Muʾassasat 14 October, 1992), p. 207.
[123] Cf. *al-Qānūn al-madanī* (1979), p. 174.
[124] This information is based on an interview held with al-Ḥajjī.
[125] Cf. Brinkley Messick, 'Media muftis: radio fatwas in Yemen', in Muhammad Masud *et al.* (eds.), *Islamic Legal Interpretation* (Cambridge: Harvard University Press, 1996), pp. 310–20.

> If you want the *fatwā* in accordance with the Zaydī-Hādawī *madhhab*, then the marriage is prohibited because their only [prohibiting] condition is the arrival of the milk to the abdomen, even if only once. And if you want the answer in accordance with the Shāfiᶜī *madhhab*; the Shafiᶜīs say that the marriage is not prohibited unless they have suckled five times, because of a ḥadīth from ᶜĀᵓisha [the Prophet's wife] that 'five nursings prohibit'. This corresponds to Shawkānī's *madhhab*. So, you are free to choose between the two. As to my opinion, [I say that] only five [nursings] prohibit because the ḥadīth which specifies the five is sound (*ṣaḥīḥ*). And God knows best.[126]

The importance of this *fatwā* does not simply lie in the fact that Shawkānī's opinion on the matter is stated, which it often is, but also in that his methodology is being applied. The *muftī* justifies his opinion through a ḥadīth that has a high degree of authority and is drawn from the Sunnī collections. Therefore, not only is the *muftī* offering the questioner authoritative proof, but he is also extracting the proof for himself from a principal source – the Sunna. One can also see in this *fatwā* how Shawkānī's opinion on the matter, as well as the *muftī's*, is presented as transcending the sectarian differences between Zaydīs and Shāfiᶜīs because of its substantiation by a sound Tradition which supersedes the opinion of any one school of law. Note also, that this *fatwā*, like most others which conform to Shawkānī's methodology, legitimates Sunnī ḥadīth works as the authoritative source for the Sunna while Zaydī texts remain unmentioned.

A Coincidence of Views

The attraction of republican authors and jurists to the Traditionist scholars, and in particular to Shawkānī, is shared by many in Saudi Arabia. The Traditionist Yemeni view of Islam bears a close resemblance to Wahhābism, despite certain important differences. This fact has not gone unnoticed by ulema in both countries. ᶜAbd al-Raḥmān al-Iryānī has even levelled the accusation at a Saudi prince that he published one of Shawkānī's works under Muḥammad b. ᶜAbd al-Wahhāb's name.[127] More specifically, and perhaps more honestly, Saudi Arabian universities have in the past two decades produced a significant number of works which focus on Shawkānī, highlighting in particular the affinities between Wahhābism and the Traditionist legacy in Yemen.[128]

126 al-ᶜAmrānī read this *fatwā* to me after writing it in preparation for the radio programme.

127 ᶜAbd al-Raḥmān al-Iryānī (ed.), *Majmūᶜat rasāᵓil fī ᵓilm al-tawḥīd* (Damascus: Dār al-Fikr, 1983), pp. 148–9.

128 Cf. Muḥammad Ḥasan al-Ghamārī, *al-Imām al-Shawkānī mufassiran* (Jeddah: Dār al-Shurūq, 1981); Ṣāliḥ Muḥammad Muqbil, *Muḥammad b. ᶜAlī al-Shawkānī wa juhūduh al-tarbawiyya* (Beirut: Dār al-Jīl, 1989); Nūmsūk, *Manhaj al-imām al-Shawkānī*; Ṣāliḥ b. ᶜAbd Allāh al-Ẓabyānī, 'Ikhtiyārāt al-imām al-Shawkānī al-fiqhiyya', Ph.D. thesis, Imam Muḥammad b. Saᶜūd Islamic University (1411/1990). The last work mentioned is over two thousand pages long and can be more properly considered to be a traditional super commmentary on Shawkānī's *Nayl al-awṭār* and *al-Sayl al-jarrār*.

The relationship between Saudi Arabia and Yemen is too complex to enter into here, but nonetheless it is important to highlight the extent to which the Saudis have been able to propagate their views in Yemen, not least by focusing on the Traditionist legacy.[129] The Saudis have officially had a significant presence in Yemen since the early 1970s. They have funded the establishment and running of the 'scientific institutes' (*al-maᶜāhid al-ᶜilmiyya*), a parallel system to the national schools, which place greater emphasis on the study of religious subjects. The curricula of these institutes can definitely be categorised as Traditionist. Muḥammad Ṣubḥī Hallāq, a Syrian member of the Muslim Brotherhood presently living in exile in Yemen, teaches at one of these institutes in Sanaa, which significantly is called the Muḥammad b. ᶜAlī al-Shawkānī Institute. He has been prolific in editing all of Shawkānī's major works and smaller treatises. Saudi universities have also graduated Yemeni students in the religious sciences who have returned to Yemen and spread Traditionist views. The most notable example is the late Muqbil al-Wādiᶜī, a graduate of the Islamic University of Medina. He had based himself in his home village of Dammāj, which is close to the town of Ṣaᶜda, establishing there a seminary for ḥadīth studies. Since his return, he engaged in virulent attacks against the Zaydīs, amongst others, through the medium of cassette tapes and written works. Al-Wādiᶜī's students, who call themselves Salafīs, have gone to other regions of Yemen where they have established their own centres of instruction and become sermoners and imams of mosques.[130] Among these is one Shaykh ᶜAqīl b. Muḥammad al-Maqṭarī, who is presently based in Taᶜizz. Al-Maqṭarī is a great devotee of Shawkānī's and has edited a number of his treatises. When a leading member of the Salafīs was questioned about the specific appeal of Shawkānī, he answered that Shawkānī was a great Salafī and a *mujaddid*. He also added that giving the example of Shawkānī was very effective in helping convince Yemenis, especially in the rural areas, of their teachings because like them Shawkānī was a Yemeni who was also a Salafī.[131]

The Zaydī Reaction

Republican state ideology, which, as we have seen, valorises the Traditionist legacy and excoriates certain Zaydī-Hādawī elements of the past, has led to the effective political and social marginalisation of the Zaydī ulema. With few notable exceptions, these have not benefited in terms of administrative or political appointments.

[129] I am using the term 'Saudi' in a very general sense. Depending on the context, it may refer to official persons and efforts but also to unofficial people who may have studied in Saudi Arabia or maintain contacts there.

[130] Cf. Bernard Haykel, 'The Salafis in Yemen at a crossroads: an obituary of Shaykh Muqbil al-Wādiᶜī of Dammāj (d. 1422/2001)', *Jemen Report* 1 (2002), 28–31.

[131] Based on an interview with Mr. ᶜAlī al-Kawl, the financial director in Sanaa of the Yemeni Wisdom Benevolent Association (*Jamᶜiyyat al-Ḥikma al-Yamaniyya al-Khayriyya*), which is run by the Salafīs.

Zaydīs often speak of a combined onslaught by the state and by the Wahhābīs whose influence has been especially significant in Ṣaᶜda province. The only organised effort by Zaydīs to reclaim influence has come belatedly with the establishment of Ḥizb al-Ḥaqq (The Party of Truth) in 1990. Al-Ḥaqq's general secretary, Sayyid Aḥmad b. Muḥammad b. ᶜAlī al-Shāmī, does not mince words in explaining why the party was established. He says:

> Wahhābism is a child of imperialism and is its spear-head in our country. Both are one and the same thing. How do we stand up to an enemy we don't see? We are seeing imperialism in our country in its Islamic guise. In reality, we are fighting something which is more dangerous than imperialism: its legitimate son. Wahhābism is readying conditions in order to colonise us indirectly for [the] imperialist [cause].[132]

And:

> Look, Saudi Arabia is pouring lots and lots of money into Yemen to promote its own version of Wahhābī Islam. This is actually an irrational and uncompromising version of our religion, which we can do without. So, we need to counter those efforts . . . and to fight intellectual advances by Wahhābism into Yemen.[133]

It is implicit in these statements that the republican government has allowed this to take place and is therefore guilty by association. Politically, al-Ḥaqq has proved ineffectual. They won only two seats in the 1993 parliamentary elections and none in 1997. In part, this is due to the ambiguous nature of a Zaydī political party operating in a republican context. In an unsuccessful attempt to clarify matters al-Shāmī and other Zaydī scholars issued a statement (*bayān sharᶜī*) in which they abandoned the very institution of the imamate.[134] Here they argued that the imamate is a historical construct whose time has passed and no longer has any present-day validity. They state that the most important matter for the present age is to attend to the welfare (*ṣalāḥ*) and the betterment (*iṣlāḥ*) of the conditions of the Muslim community, which alone has the right to appoint a leader, who is not an imam in the strict sense, but a hired servant (*ajīr*). Finally, they state that this protector may be descended from any lineage and may belong to any race as long as the affairs of the *umma* are safe and sound.[135] An institution that once defined Zaydism was thus done away with in a few pages. Not all Hādawī scholars agree with this, and some therefore remained formally outside the party. Ḥizb al-Ḥaqq maintained that it represented a Yemeni view of Islam, but without the imamate it was difficult for outsiders to understand what that view consisted of.

[132] Muḥammad ᶜIzzān (ed.), *al-ᶜAllāmā al-Shāmī: Ārāʾ wa mawāqif* (Amman: Maṭābiᶜ Sharikat al-Mawārid al-Ṣināᶜiyya al-Urduniyya, 1994), pp. 89 and see 87–90.

[133] *Yemen Times*, 1 July 1992, cited in Dresch and Haykel, 'Stereotypes and political styles: Islamists and tribesfolk in Yemen', *IJMES* 27.4 (1995), 412.

[134] *al-Waḥda*, no. 26, 28 November 1990; cf. Bernard Haykel, 'Rebellion, migration or consultative democracy? The Zaydis and their detractors in Yemen', in Rémy Leveau *et al.* (eds.), *Le Yémen Contemporain* (Paris: Karthala, 1999).

[135] Cf. ᶜIzzān (ed.), *al-ᶜAllāmā al-Shāmī*, p. 90.

Institute of al-Shahīd al-Samāwī (author)

Ideologically, the response of Zaydīs to the Sunnī onslaught has been meagre. They have tried to fight back through the publication of books and pamphlets and the setting up of schools and institutes where Zaydī works are taught.[136] Ṣaᶜda has been their most active centre, though schools have also been established in Sanaa and the Wādī Jawf. It is interesting to look at some of the symbols they have used. They have, for example, established a teacher training institute in Ṣaᶜda which is called Maᶜhad al-Shahīd al-Samāwī (The Institute of the Martyr al-Samāwī). The person referred to here is Shawkānī's opponent, Muḥammad b. Ṣāliḥ al-Samāwī or Ibn Ḥarīwah, who was executed at the order of al-Mahdī ᶜAbd Allāh and, the Zaydīs claim, with Shawkānī's fervent approval. They have also edited and published Ibn Ḥarīwah's critical response to Shawkānī's *al-Sayl al-jarrār*, entitled *al-Ghaṭamṭam al-zakhkhār*. In so doing, they hope to undermine the state's most praised scholar and to present an alternative vision to that generally accepted. On the whole, their efforts have been defensive and are on terms set by the state. The story of Shawkānī and the Zaydī-Hādawīs continues to unfold, but the outcome appears to have been determined in the late eighteenth century when the state chose to support the Traditionist scholars – for reasons that in the modern era are all too obvious.

[136] Bernard Haykel, 'Recent publishing activity by the Zaydis in Yemen: a select bibliography', *Chroniques Yéménites* 9 (2002), 225–30.

Conclusion

> It has become a common practice that if one mentions a ḥadīth of the Messenger of God another asks: Is this a sound or a weak Tradition? This practice [of asking] has even become widespread among the masses.[1]

Recent scholarship has focused on the ways Shīʿīs have managed the divide that separates them from the Sunnī majority. Devin Stewart, for example, provides a study on Twelver Shīʿī legal responses to the rise of the Sunnī legal schools. He argues that with the rise of the *madhhab* system Sunnīs developed and used the principle of consensus (*ijmāʿ*) to exclude and stigmatise non-Sunnīs and that Twelver Shīʿī jurists reacted in three distinct ways to this feature of Sunnī law. Some Shīʿīs conformed to the Sunnī theory of *ijmāʿ* and outwardly passed themselves off as Sunnīs of the Shāfiʿī school. A second group adopted the concept of *ijmāʿ* but modified it in order to maintain a separate but parallel Twelver school of law. The last group, that of the Akhbārīs, rejected *ijmāʿ* and all rationalist juristic methods of the Sunnīs, preferring to adhere to a literal interpretation of Shīʿite ḥadīth texts.[2] A second study by Rainer Brunner details the mainly twentieth-century process of rapprochement that has taken place between Twelvers and Sunnīs, animated to a large degree by a modern ecumenical spirit.[3]

Neither of the above-mentioned approaches helps explain the rise in pre-modern times of the Sunnī Traditionists amongst the Zaydīs in Yemen. In the first place, the process this study has sought to outline involved an abandonment of Zaydism by the Traditionists for theological and legal reasons, and the Traditionists did not posit an accommodationist position between theirs and that of the sect and school

[1] Muqbil al-Wādiʿī, *Tarjamat Abī ʿAbd al-Raḥmān Muqbil b. Hādī al-Wādiʿī* (Sanaa: Maktabat Ṣanʿāʾal-Athariyya, 1999), pp. 10–11.

[2] Devin Stewart, *Islamic Legal Orthodoxy: Twelver Shiite Responses to the Sunni Legal System* (Salt Lake City: University of Utah Press, 1998). The Akhbārīs resemble the Traditionists in their hermeneutic approach to law that insists on a literal interpretation and reliance on ḥadīth sources. The driving force behind this may be the same, namely a desire to attain and claim certainty for their respective views. The similarity, however, ends insofar as the Akhbārīs reject *ijtihād* and refuse to label their endeavours as such, whereas the Traditionists insist that their efforts fall under this label. Each group also refers to different works of ḥadīth and in matters of theology are very distinct.

[3] Rainer Brunner, *Annäherung und Distanz: Schia, Azhar und die Islamische Ökumene im 20. Jahrhundert* (Berlin: Klaus Schwarz, 1996).

they were born into. Second, the Traditionists did not reject Zaydism because they felt stigmatised by the Sunnīs nor did they do this in order to initiate a rapprochement between the sects of Islam. Rather, they were animated by a genuine desire to obtain, inasmuch as is humanly possible, certainty of God's will, this being the path to salvation. In order to do this, they argued that one had to adhere to the Traditionist principles of interpretation of the most authoritative sources of revelation, namely the Qur$^{\circ}$ān and the Sunnī canonical ḥadīth collections. It is this yearning for certainty and their disillusionment with the interpretive methods and opinions of *all* the established schools of law, and in particular those of the Hādawī school, that I feel best explains their scholarly and political endeavours. In short, they claimed that an opinion based on the argument 'according to Bukhārī: "the Prophet said x" ' trumped the Hādawī one that bases itself on the assertion that 'the school's opinion is y because Imam al-Hādī held this view'. In this, the Traditionists rejected the guiding role that Zaydism accords to the imams of Ahl al-Bayt as the appointed leaders of the Muslim community. Authority for them lay with the scholars of ḥadīth whereas the Zaydīs found this with their imams. Consequently, their respective interpretive methodologies were fundamentally incommensurable and a clash was inevitable, especially once the political authorities began to favour one side over the other.

Shawkānī's importance lies in that he represents the culmination of the Traditionist enterprise in Yemen, or what Michael Cook has labelled 'the Sunnisation of Zaydism'.[4] His extensive writings crystallised the teachings of the Traditionists and completed the attack on the Zaydī-Hādawī school which was begun by Ibn al-Wazīr in the ninth/fifteenth century. Shawkānī's influence was made all the greater because of the alliance the Qāsimī imamate had forged with the Traditionists in his lifetime. As the chief judge of the imamate for four decades, he was able to implement his ideas and form a cohort of like-minded scholars who would carry on his legacy into modern times. The eighteenth-century transformation of the imamate into a dynastic and patrimonial state coincided with the rise of Traditionist scholars in Sanaa's religious circles, and a symbiotic relationship developed between the two. One the one hand, the state provided appointments and on the other the scholars accorded it legitimacy despite its doctrinal shortcoming as viewed from the Zaydī perspective. By the same token, the Traditionists became the upholders and implementers of the Sharī^{c}a and the imams were more properly seen as sultans in the Sunnī tradition: rulers who must, in theory at least, defer to the scholars in matters of religion. This local transformation and the tensions it engendered mirror the much larger Islamic dispute between Sunnīs and Shī^{c}īs over the nature of legitimate rule and rightful succession after the death of the Prophet.

[4] Cook, *Commanding Right and Forbidding Wrong*, pp. 247–51. According to Valerie Hoffman, a comparable transformation in the direction of Sunnism occured among Ibāḍī scholars in the nineteenth century, in particular after Zanzibar came under the control of the Sultans of Oman. Cf. Valerie J. Hoffman, 'Nineteenth-century Ibadi discussions on religious knowledge and Muslim Sects', paper presented at the Middle East Studies Association Conference, 2001.

This remarkable feature of Qāsimī religious politics is a result of the character of the state at this historical juncture. Large tax-generating areas were inhabited by Shāfiᶜī Sunnīs whose scholars, a number of whom were also Traditionists, maintained close links with the Traditionists of Upper Yemen. A similar, though not identical, discursive tradition united the Shāfiᶜīs and the Traditionists, or put differently, they were loosely part of the same interpretive community. This was not the case between the Shāfiᶜīs and Zaydīs who were theologically and legally, in particular in matters of ritual law, at some distance from each other. The seventeenth-century Zaydī claim that the Shāfiᶜīs be considered 'infidels of interpretation' (*kuffār taʾwīl*) shows this to be the case. By the eighteenth century, this labelling of Shāfiᶜīs had not only become a moot point, but it was flatly rejected by the Traditionists in Sanaa. This endeared the Traditionists of Upper Yemen to the Shāfiᶜīs in Lower Yemen and the Tihāma, and the praise that the al-Ahdal scholars lavished on Shawkānī is an important token of this. But the abandonment of strict Hādawism by the eighteenth-century Qāsimī imāmate was not due entirely to the perceived sensibilities of its Shāfiᶜī subjects nor was it inevitable. Many strict Hādawīs continued to clamour for a return to the teachings of the early Qāsimī imams and sought by all means available to them to make this happen, including the initiation of rebellious riots in the streets of Sanaa. The Qāsimī imams, beginning with al-Mahdī al-ᶜAbbās, took deliberate steps that led ultimately to the Sunnisation of state structures. This policy was due to the need felt by the imams to have scholars who would both legitimise dynastic succession as well as run a government bureaucracy. With their insistence on being ruled by a righteous imam, Traditional Zaydī scholars were not as amenable as the Traditionists and represented a constant source for rebellion.

Shawkānī and Islamic Reform

Not wishing to treat eighteenth-century Islamic reformers as constituents of an undifferentiated phenomenon, this book has sought to delineate in fine detail the life and work of a single reformist scholar within his local context and intellectual tradition. It is this book's premise that this is the proper backdrop for understanding any given reformer, and only with this established can one venture to make broader comparisons and intellectual taxonomies. Though certainly aware of the reformist ideas that other scholars were engaged in, whether in Medina, Najd or India, Shawkānī's principal sources of inspiration in the formulation of his ideas on reform were the works of the Traditionist scholars of Yemen. This, however, is not to say that he was not influenced by outsiders, a fact that would be impossible in the eighteenth century given the quantity of written sources and outside contacts available to him. Furthermore, the notion that reform could be effected through *ijtihād* and that certain elements of tradition could be rejected by labelling these *taqlīd* practices was the common property of Islamic jurists for centuries before Shawkānī. And the fact that many scholars were invoking *ijtihād* in the eighteenth century does not justify categorising these as a homogeneous group since important doctrinal differences are evident in their teachings.

An important example of such a difference can be gleaned from a comparison on a particular point between the scholar Muḥammad Murtaḍā al-Zabīdī (d. 1205/1791) and Shawkānī, both of whom are often mentioned in the same breath as representatives of eighteenth-century reformism.[5] Al-Zabīdī had a close relationship with the Ottomans and is known to have written a treatise in defense of the Ḥanafī *madhhab* against Traditionist adversaries, proving that its teachings were grounded in sound ḥadīths.[6] As we have seen in his attacks on all the schools of law, it is inconceivable for Shawkānī to have done the same. Yet another difference relates to the attacks on the monistic ideas of Muḥyī al-Dīn Ibn al-ᶜArabī and the antinomian practices associated with certain Sufi orders, two intertwined topics that a number of eighteenth-century reformers, whether in Medina or in India, wrote on at considerable length. The Upper Yemeni highlands did not have institutionalised Sufi brotherhoods and consequently the Yemeni Traditionists dealt with either issue in a perfunctory manner.[7] Shawkānī, for instance, argued against those who perform reprehensible practices at grave sites, but his treatise on the subject was written in the context of a Wahhābī military threat to the imamate.

All this is not to deny that important doctrinal similarities appear to exist between the Yemeni Traditionists and reformers in other parts of the Islamic world. One example of this is the attack on the fanaticism and dissension that ensues from strict adherence to the *madhhab*, a consequence of the establishment of the schools of law.[8] This important feature of Islamic reformism, however, is not specific to the eighteenth-century, whether in Yemen or elsewhere, and should not lead to the conclusion that the teachings of the scholars of this period constitute a novel or innovative moment in the history of Islam.

In the Yemen, something novel did take place in the eighteenth century and this can only be deduced if one weaves together political and intellectual history. The transformation of the Zaydī Qāsimī imamate into a dynastic state that was served by Sunnī Traditionist scholars is an unprecedented phenomenon in the history of Zaydism in Yemen. This alliance unleashed considerable potentials, to be seen mainly in Shawkānī's teachings and written works, the example he set of a state dominated by a *mujtahid* and a pedagogical template for reproducing scholars like himself.

5 Fazlur Rahman, *Islam* (University of Chicago Press, 1979), pp. 196–7.

6 Stefan Reichmuth, 'Murtaḍā Az-Zabīdī (d. 1791) in biographical and autobiographical accounts', *Die Welt des Islams* 39 (1999), 83.

7 Shawkānī's principal work condemning Ibn al-ᶜArabī's monism is *al-Ṣawārim al-ḥidād al-qāṭiᶜa li-ᶜalāʾiq arbāb al-ittiḥād* and consists of an abridged and verbatim copy of Ṣāliḥ al-Maqbalī's treatment of the subject in his *al-ᶜAlam al-shāmikh*. Al-Maqbalī wrote his work while living in Mecca where the influence of Ibn ᶜArabī's teachings was apparently a hotly contested issue.

8 Compare, for instance, Shawkānī's views with those of Ṣāliḥ b. Muḥammad al-Fullānī (d. 1218/1803) as described by J. O. Hunwick, 'Ṣāliḥ al-Fullānī (1752/3–1803): the career and teachings of a West African ᶜĀlim in Medina', in A. H. Green (ed.), *In Quest of an Islamic Humanism* (American University in Cairo Press, 1986), pp. 139–54.

At the core of his teachings lay a set of simple and elegant ideas: *ijtihād* is not only possible for latter-day Muslims, it is mandated by God; jurists with the requisite and attainable training must interface directly with the primary sources of revelation and can ignore the opinions of earlier scholars if they feel these are not substantiated by the revealed sources; through *ijtihād*, Muslims can rid themselves of the ills they are facing and these are wholly due to the practice of *taqlīd*. In formulating these ideas, Shawkānī was unaware of the European enlightenment and perceived no intellectual threat to the world of Islam from Europe. He was cognisant of the military and commercial presence of Europeans in Egypt (e.g., Napoleon's invasion) and in the Red Sea and Indian Ocean, and may even have met with European emissaries of the various trading companies (Dutch, English and French) or renegade sailors who had converted to Islam and sought refuge in Yemen. There is, however, no evidence in his writings of any appreciation for ideas that are not entirely part of the Islamic intellectual tradition. For him, the sources of Muslim weakness were intrinsic insofar as they were to be found in the erroneous beliefs and practices of Muslims themselves. Reforming these in light of his interpretive methodology would lead to a reformed order in which the Sharīᶜa is applied and Islam's glory regained.

The widespread appeal of Shawkānī's ideas and written works since his death is attributable to a variety of factors. First, he was perhaps the last great figure in a long line of Traditionist scholars, both Yemeni and non-Yemeni, at the dawn of the modern age. He was not only prolific in his output, but also synthetic and lucid in style. A teacher at the Nadwat al-ᶜUlamāᵓ seminary in Lucknow, India, mentions that he assigns Shawkānī's *Fatḥ al-Qadīr* when teaching *tafsīr* because all one's requirements can be found therein, whether on points of grammar or exegesis through ḥadīth. Second, Shawkānī's biography, as it is told by himself or his students, is a success story. He was able to promote and implement his views and defeat his strict Zaydī enemies. Third, his arguments on how to reform Islamic society have resonated with the concerns of many modern Sunnī reformers, the most prominent of whom were Siddīq Ḥasan Khān in India and Rashīd Riḍā in Egypt, both of whom spread Shawkānī's name far and wide through the medium of the printing press. But Riḍā and many modern Yemenis of the Ḥamīd al-Dīn and the republican periods have appropriated Shawkānī in an iconic fashion, projecting onto him their modern anxieties and using his prestige to give weight to their arguments. Such misappropriation is lamentable perhaps, but, by invoking Shawkānī, moderns can attack 'tradition' and re-invent themselves in ways more suitable to their time.

Bibliography

References in Arabic

ᶜAbd al-Qādir b. Badrān, *al-Madkhal ilā madhhab al-imām Aḥmad*, Beirut: Dār al-Kutub al-ᶜIlmiyya, 1996.

al-Ahdal, ᶜAbd al-Raḥmān, *al-Nafas al-Yamānī*, Sanaa: Markaz al-Dirāsāt waʾl-Abḥāth al-Yamaniyya, 1979.

Aḥmad, Qāsim Ghālib, *Min aᶜlām al-Yaman: shaykh al-islām al-mujtahid Muhammad b. ᶜAlī al-Shawkānī*, Cairo: Maṭābiᶜ al-Ahrām al-Tijāriyya, 1969.

Aḥmad, Qāsim Ghālib *et al.*, *Ibn al-Amīr wa ᶜaṣruhu*, 2nd ed., Sanaa: Wizārat al-Iᶜlām waʾl-Thaqāfa, 1983.

al-Akhfash, Ṣalāḥ b. al-Ḥusayn, *Masʾalat al-ṣaḥāba*, ms. Sanaa, Gharbiyya Library, *majmūᶜ* no. 124, fols. 28–35. In its margin is ᶜAbd Allāh b. ᶜAlī al-Wazīr's *Irsāl al-dhuʾāba*.

al-Akwaᶜ, Ismāᶜīl b. ᶜAlī, *Hijar al-ᶜilm wa maᶜāqiluh fī ʾl-Yaman*, 5 vols., Beirut: Dār al-Fikr al-Muᶜāṣir, 1995.

——, *al-Madāris al-islāmiyya fī al-Yaman*, Beirut: Muʾassasat al-Risāla, 1986.

——, *al-Zaydiyya nashʾatuhā wa muᶜtaqadātuhā*, Beirut: Dār al-Fikr al-Muᶜāṣir, 1993.

al-Akwaᶜ, Muḥammad b. ᶜAlī, *Ḥayāt ᶜālim wa amīr*, Sanaa: Maktabat al-Jīl al-Jadīd, 1987.

——, *Ṣifa min tārīkh al-Yaman al-ijtimāᶜī wa qiṣṣat ḥayātī*, n.p.: n.d.

al-ᶜAlawī, ᶜAlī b. Muḥammad, *Sīrat al-Hādī ilā al-ḥaqq Yaḥyā b. al-Ḥusayn*, Suhayl Zakkār (ed.), Beirut: Dār al-Fikr, 1981.

al-ᶜAlīmī, Rashād Muḥammad, *al-Taqlīdiyya waʾl-ḥadātha fī ʾl-niẓām al-qānūnī al-Yamanī*, Cairo: Maṭābiᶜ al-Shurūq, n.d.

Amīn, Aḥmad, *Zuᶜamāʾal-iṣlāḥ fī ʾl-ᶜaṣr al-ḥadīth*, Cairo: Maktabat al-Nahḍa al-Miṣriyya, 1948.

al-Amīr, Muḥammad b. Ismāᶜīl, *Dīwān al-Amīr al-Ṣanᶜānī*, 2nd ed., Beirut: Manshūrāt al-Madīna, 1986.

——, *Irshād dhawī al-albāb ilā ḥaqīqat aqwāl Muḥammad b. ᶜAbd al-Wahhāb*, ms. Sanaa, Gharbiyya Library, *majmūᶜ* no. 107, fols. 131–42.

____, *Irshād al-nuqqād ilā taysīr al-ijtihād*, Muḥammad Ṣubḥī Ḥallāq (ed.), Beirut: Muʾassasat al-Rayyān liʾl-Ṭibāʿa, 1992.

____, *Jawāb fīmā yustaḥsan min tawẓīf al-khārijīn ilā ʾl-bawādī li-taʿlīm al-ṣalāt*, ms. Sanaa, Gharbiyya Library, *majmūʿ* no. 39.

____, *Masāʾil ʿilmiyya*, Sanaa: Maktabat al-Irshād, n.d.

____, *Minḥat al-ghaffār ʿalā ḍawʾal-nahār*, in the margins of Ḥasan al-Jalālʾs *Ḍawʾal-nahār*, 4 vols., Sanaa: Majlis al-Qaḍāʾ al-Aʿlā, n.d.

____, *al-Qawl al-mujtabā fī taḥqīq mā yaḥrum min al-ribā*, ʿAqīl al-Maqṭarī (ed.), Sanaa: Maktabat Dār al-Quds, 1992.

____, *al-Rawḍa al-nadiyya fī sharḥ al-tuḥfa al-ʿalawiyya*, n.p.: al-Maktaba al-Islāmiyya, n.d.

____, *Risāla ḥawl madhhab Ibn ʿAbd al-Wahhāb*, ms. Sanaa, Sharqiyya Library, *majmūʿ* no. 1, fols. 29–37.

____, *Subul al-salām sharḥ Bulūgh al-marām*, 4 vols., Beirut: Dār al-Kitāb al-ʿArabī, 1987.

____, *Uṣūl al-figh al-musammā ijābat al-sāʾil sharḥ bughyat al-āmil*, Beirut: Muʾassat al-Risāla, 1986.

al-ʿAmrānī, Muḥammad b. ʿAlī, *Itḥāf al-nabīh bi-taʾrīkh al-Qāsim wa banīh*, ms. personal library of Muḥammad b. Ismāʿīl al-ʿAmrānī; and ms. Sanaa, Gharbiyya Library, *tārīkh*, no. 77.

al-ʿAmrānī, Muḥammad b. Ismāʿīl, *Niẓām al-qaḍāʾ fī ʾl-Islām*, Sanaa: Maktabat Dār al-Jīl, 1984.

____, *al-Zaydiyya biʾl-Yaman*, reprint, Sanaa: Maktabat Dār al-Turāth, 1990. (First published in journal *Risālat al-Islām*, Cairo: Dār al-Taqrīb, 1369/1950.)

al-ʿAmrī, Ḥusayn b. ʿAbd Allāh, *Fatrat al-fawḍā wa-ʿawdat al-Atrāk ilā Ṣanʿāʾ*, Damascus: Dār al-Fikr, 1986.

____, 'Ḥarakat al-tajdīd waʾl-iṣlāḥ fī ʾl-Yaman fī ʾl-ʿaṣr al-ḥadīth', *al-Ijtihād* 9 (1990), 175–94.

____, *al-Imām al-Shawkānī rāʾid ʿaṣrih*, Damascus: Dār al-Fikr, 1990.

____, *al-Manār waʾl-Yaman*, Damascus: Dār al-Fikr, 1987.

____, *Maṣādir al-turāth al-Yamanī fī ʾl-matḥaf al-Barīṭānī*, Damascus: Dār al-Mukhtār, 1980.

____, *Miʾat ʿām min tārīkh al-Yaman al-ḥadīth*, Damascus: Dār al-Fikr, 1988.

____, *al-Muʾarrikhūn al-Yamaniyyūn fī ʾl-ʿaṣr al-ḥadīth*, Beirut: Dār al-Fikr al-Muʿāṣir, 1988.

____, *al-Umarāʾ al-ʿabīd waʾl-mamālīk fī ʾl-Yaman*, Beirut: Dār al-Fikr al-Muʿāṣir, 1989.

al-ʿAmrī, Ḥusayn b. ʿAbd Allāh and al-Jirāfī, Muḥammad b. Aḥmad, *al-ʿAllāma waʾl-mujtahid al-muṭlaq al-Ḥasan b. Aḥmad al-Jalāl*, Beirut: Dār al-Fikr al-Muʿāṣir, 2000.

Anonymous, *Ḥawliyyāt Yamāniyya*, ʿAbd Allāh al-Ḥibshī (ed.), Sanaa: Dār al-Ḥikma al-Yamāniyya, 1991.

al-Ansārī, Zakariyya b. Muḥammad, *Ghāyat al-wuṣūl*, Cairo: Maṭbaʿt Muṣṭafā al-Bābī al-Ḥalabī, 1360/1941.

al-ʿAnsī, Aḥmad b. Qāsim, *al-Tāj al-mudhhab li-aḥkām al-madhhab*, 4 vols., Sanaa: Maktabat al-Yaman al-Kubrā, n.d.

al-ʿAqīlī, Muḥammad b. Aḥmad, *Tārikh al-Mikhlāf al-Sulaymānī*, 2 vols., Jāzān: Sharikat al-ʿAqīlī, 1989.

al-ʿArashī, Ḥusayn b. Aḥmad, *Kitāb Bulūgh al-marām fī sharḥ misk al-khitām*, Beirut: Dār Iḥyāʾ al-Turāth al-ʿArabī, n.d.

al-Ashʿarī, Abū ʾl-Ḥasan, *Kitāb Maqālāt al-islāmiyyin*, Helmut Ritter (ed.), Wiesbaden: Franz Steiner, 1963.

al-Bahkalī, ʿAbd al-Raḥmān b. Aḥmad, *Nafḥ al-ʿūd fī sīrat dawlat al-Sharīf Ḥamūd*, Muḥammad b. Aḥmad al-ʿAqīlī (ed.), Riyadh: Maṭbūʿāt Dārat al-Malik ʿAbd al-ʿAzīz, 1982.

al-Bakrī, Ṣalāḥ, *Tārīkh Ḥaḍramawt al-siyāsī*, 2 vols., Cairo: Maṭbaʿat Muṣṭafā al-Bābī al-Ḥalabī, 1956.

Balḥāj, Muḥammad Muṣṭafā, 'al-Taḥarrur al-fikrī wa ʾl-madhhabī ʿinda al-imām al-Shawkānī', *Dirāsāt Yamaniyya* 40 (1990), 247–59.

al-Baraddūnī, ʿAbd Allāh, *al-Yaman al-jumhūrī*, Beirut: Dār al-Fikr al-Muʿāṣir, 1994.

al-Biṭrīq, ʿAbd al-Ḥamīd, *Min tārīkh al-Yaman al-ḥadīth: 1517–1840*, n.p.: Maʿhad al-Buḥūth waʾl-Dirāsāt al-ʿArabiyya, 1969.

al-Dijwī, Yūsuf, 'al-Ḥukm ʿalā al-Muslimīn biʾl-kufr', *Nūr al-Islām* 4.3 (Cairo, 1352/1933), 170–82.

al-Ghamārī, Muḥammad Ḥasan, *al-Imām al-Shawkānī mufassiran*, Jeddah: Dār al-Shurūq, 1981.

al-Ḥabshī, ʿAbdullāh b. Muḥammad, *Muʾallafāt ḥukkām al-Yaman*, Elke Niewohner-Eberhard (ed.), Weisbaden: Otto Harrassowitz, 1979.

al-Hādī Yaḥyā b. al-Ḥusayn, *Durar al-aḥādīth al-nabawiyya biʾl-asānīd al-Yaḥyawiyya*, Yaḥyā al-Faḍīl (ed.), Beirut: Muʾassasat al-Aʿlamī liʾl-Maṭbūʿāt, 1982.

——, *Kitāb al-Aḥkām fī ʾl-ḥalāl waʾl-ḥarām*, 2 vols., n.p., 1990.

——, *Kitāb al-Muntakhab wa yalīh kitāb al-funūn*, Sanaa: Dār al-Ḥikma al-Yamāniyya, 1993.

al-Ḥajrī, Muḥammad b. Aḥmad, *Majmūʿ buldān al-Yaman wa qabāʾilihā*, 2 vols., Sanaa: Wizārat al-Iʿlām waʾl-Thaqāfa, 1984.

——, *Masājid Ṣanʿāʾ*, 2nd ed., Beirut: Dār Iḥyāʾal-Turāth al-ʿArabī, 1398/1978.

al-Ḥarīrī, Muḥammad, *Dirāsāt wa buḥūth fī tārīkh al-Yaman al-islāmī*, Beirut: ʿĀlam al-Kutub, 1998.

al-Ḥaymī, Muḥammad b. Luṭf al-Bāriʾ, *al-Rawḍ al-bāsim fī mā shāʿa fī quṭr al-Yaman min al-waqāʾiʿ waʾl-aʿlām*, ʿAbd Allāh al-Ḥibshī (ed.), Sanaa: Maṭābiʿ al-Mufaḍḍal, 1990.

al-Ḥibshī, ʿAbd Allāh b. Muḥammad, *Dirāsāt fī ʾl-turāth al-Yamanī*, Beirut: Dār al-ʿAwda, 1977.

——, *Maṣādir al-fikr al-ʿarabī al-islāmī fī ʾl-Yaman*, Sanaa: Markaz al-Dirāsāt al-Yamaniyya, n.d.

——, *al-Ṣūfiyya waʾl-fuqahāʾ fī ʾl-Yaman*, Sanaa: Maktabat al-Jīl al-Jadīd, 1976.

——, 'Thabat bi-muʾallafāt al-ʿallāma Muḥammad b. ʿAlī al-Shawkānī,' *Dirāsāt Yamaniyya* 3 (1979), 65–86.

Hilāl, Ibrāhīm Ibrāhīm, *al-Imām al-Shawkānī waʾl-ijtihād waʾl-taqlīd*, Cairo: Dār al-Nahḍa al-ʿArabiyya, 1979.

——, *Min niqāṭ al-iltiqāʾ bayna al-imāmayn Muḥammad ʿAbduh waʾl-imām al-Shawkānī*, Cairo: Maktabat al-Nahḍa al-Miṣriyya, 1987.

——, *Umanāʾ al-sharīʿa liʾl-imām al-Shawkānī*, Cairo: Dār al-Nahḍa al-ʿArabiyya, n.d.

Ḥumaydān b. al-Qāsim b. Yaḥyā, *Majmūʿ al-sayyid Ḥūmaydān*, ms. London, British Library, no. OR. 3959.

al-Ḥusayn b. Badr al-Dīn, *Kitāb Shifāʾ al-uwām fī aḥādīth al-aḥkām*, 3 vols., n.p.: Jamʿiyyat ʿUlamāʾ al-Yaman, 1996.

al-Ḥusayn b. al-Qāsim, *Adāb al-ʿūlamāʾ wa ʾl-mutaʿallimīn*, Sanaa: al-Dār al-Yamaniyya li ʾl-Nashr wa ʾl-Tawzī, 1987.

——, *Ghāyat al-sūl fī ʿilm al-uṣūl*, in *Majmūʿ al-mutūn al-hāmma*, Sanaa: Maktabat al-Yaman al-Kubrā, 1990, pp. 227–300.

——, *Kitāb Hidāyat al-ʿuqūl ilā ghāyat al-sūl fī ʿilm al-uṣūl*, 2 vols., n.p.: al-Maktaba al-Islāmiyya, 1401/1981.

al-Ḥusaynī, Aḥmad, *Muʾallafāt al-Zaydiyya*, 3 vols, Qom: Maṭbaʿat Ismāʿīliyyan, 1413/1993.

Ibn Abī ʾl-Rijāl, Aḥmad b. Ṣāliḥ, *Iʿlām al-muwālī bi-kalām sādatihi al-aʿlām al-mawālī*, ms. London, British Library, no. OR 3852, fols. 36–59.

——, *Maṭlaʿ al-budūr wa majmaʿ al-buḥūr*, 4 vols., ms. photocopy, New Sanaa University Library.

——, *Tafsīr al-sharīʿa li-wurrād al-sharīʿa*, ms. London, British Library, no. OR 3852, fols. 5–35.

Ibn Bahrān, Muḥammad b. Yaḥyā, *Matn al-kāfil*, in *Majmūʿ al-mutūn al-hāmma*, Sanaa: Maktabat al-Yaman al-Kubrā, 1990, pp. 301–30.

Ibn Daybaʿ, ʿAbd al-Raḥmān b. ʿAlī al-Shaybānī, *Taysīr al-wuṣūl ilā jāmiʿ al-uṣūl min ḥadīth al-rasūl*, 4 vols., Beirut: Dār al-Fikr, n.d.

Ibn Ḥazm, Ali b. Ahmad, *al-Iḥkām fī uṣūl al-aḥkām*, 2 vols., Beirut: Dār al-Kutub al-ʿIlmiyya, n.d.

——, *al-Muḥallā biʾl-āthār*, Abd al-Ghaffār al-Bindārī (ed.), 12 vols., Beirut: Dār al-Kutub al-ʿIlmiyya, 1988.

Ibn Miftāḥ, ʿAbd Allāh, *Kitāb al-Muntazaʿ al-mukhtār min al-ghayth al-midrār al-mufattiḥ li-kamāʾim al-Azhār fī fiqh al-aʾimma al-aṭhār*, 4 vols., reprint of Yemeni Ministry of Justice, Cairo: Maṭbaʿ at Sharikat al-Tamaddun, 1332/1914 (= *Sharḥ al-Azhār*).

Ibn Muzaffar, Yaḥyā b. Aḥmad, *Kitāb al-Bayān al-shāfī al-muntazaʿ min al-burhān al-kāfī*, 4 vols., Sanaa: Maktabat Ghamḍān li-Iḥyāʾ al-Turāth al-Yamanī, 1984.

Ibn al-Ṣalāḥ, *ʿUlūm al-hadith*, Nūr al-Dīn ʿItr (ed.), Damascus: Dār al-Fikr, 1984.

Ibn Taymiyya, Aḥmad, *Iqtiḍāʾ al-ṣirāṭ al-mustaqīm mukhālafat aṣḥāb al-jaḥīm*, Aḥmad Ḥamadī (ed.), Jeddah: Maktabat al-Madanī, n.d.

——, *Majmū*ᶜ *fatāwā Shaykh al-Islām Aḥmad b. Taymiyya*, ᶜAbd al-Rahmān b. Muḥammad b. Qāsim (ed.), 27 vols., Rabat: al-Maktab al-Taᶜlīmī al-Saᶜūdī bi'l-Maghrib, n.d.

——, *al-Wāsiṭa bayna al-ḥaqq wa'l-khalq*, in *Majmūᶜat al-tawḥīd*, ᶜAlī b. ᶜAbdullāh al-Rathānī (sponsor), Damascus: al-Maktab al-Islāmī, 1381/1962.

al-Iryānī, ᶜAbd al-Raḥmān (ed.), *Majmūᶜat rasā'il fī ᶜilm al-tawḥīd*, Damascus: Dār al-Fikr, 1983.

al-Iryānī, ᶜAlī b. ᶜAbd Allāh, *Sīrat al-imām Muḥammad b. Yaḥyā Ḥamīd al-Dīn*, 2 vols., Muḥammad Ṣāliḥiyya (ed.), Amman: Dār al-Bashīr, 1996.

al-Iryānī, Yaḥyā b. Muḥammad, *Kitāb Hidāyat al-mustabṣirīn bi-sharḥ ᶜuddat al-hiṣn al-ḥaṣīn*, Sanaa: n.d.

ᶜĪsawī, Aḥmad and Muḥammad al-Malīḥ (eds.), *Fihris makhṭūṭāt al-maktaba al-Gharbiyya bi'l-Jāmiᶜ al-Kabīr bi-Ṣanᶜā'*, Alexandria: Mansha'at al-Maᶜārif, n.d.

Isḥāq b. Yūsuf, *al-Tafkīk li-ᶜuqūd al-tashkīk*, ms. Sanaa, Gharbiyya Library, *ᶜilm kalām* no. 33.

——, *al-Wajh al-ḥasan al-mudhhib li'l-ḥazan*, Sanaa: Maktabat Dār al-Turāth, 1990.

Ismāᶜīl, Shaᶜbān Muḥammad, *al-Imām al-Shawkānī wa manhajuhu fī uṣūl al-fiqh*, Manama: Qatar University, 1989.

ᶜIzzān, Muḥammad (ed.), *al-ᶜAllāmā al-Shāmī: Ārā' wa mawāqif*, Amman: Matābiᶜ Sharikat al-Mawārid al-Ṣināᶜiyya al-Urduniyya, 1994.

al-ᶜIzzī, ᶜAbd Allāh, *ᶜUlūm al-ḥadīth ᶜinda al-Zaydiyya wa'l-muḥaddithīn*, Amman: Mu'assasat al-Imām Zayd b. ᶜAlī al-Thaqāfiyya, 2001.

Jaghmān, Ismāᶜīl b. Ḥusayn, *al-Durr al-manẓūm fī tarājim al-thalātha al-nujūm*, Zayd al-Wazīr (ed.), McLean, Virginia: Markaz al-Turāth wa'l-Buḥūth al-Yamanī, 2002.

Jaḥḥāf, Luṭf Allāh b. Aḥmad, *Durar nuḥūr al-ḥūr al-ᶜīn fī sīrat al-imām al-Manṣūr*, ms. Sanaa, Gharbiyya Library, *tārīkh* no. 86 (photocopy kindly provided by ᶜAbd Allāh al-Ḥibshī).

al-Jalāl, al-Ḥasan b. Aḥmad, *Ḍaw' al-nahār al-mushriq ᶜalā ṣafaḥāt al-Azhār*, 4 vols., Sanaa: Majlis al-Qaḍā' al-Aᶜlā, n.d.

——, 'Risāla fī ᶜadam taqrīr al-Bāniyān (al-Hunūd) aw ahl al-dhimma fī 'l-Yaman', Ḥusayn b. ᶜAbd Allāh al-ᶜAmrī (ed.) in Ḥusayn b. ᶜAbd Allāh al-ᶜAmrī and Muḥammad b. Aḥmad al-Jirāfī, *al-ᶜAllāma wa 'l-mujtahid al-muṭlaq al-Ḥasan b. Aḥmad al-Jalāl*, Beirut: Dār al-Fikr al-Muᶜāṣir, 2000, pp. 469–76.

al-Jarmūzī, al-Muṭahhar b. Muḥammad, *al-Jawhara al-munīra fī akhbār mawlāna wa-imāminā al-imām al-Mu'ayyad bi-Allāh Muḥammad*, ms. Sanaa, Sharqiyya Library, nos. 2133 and 2134.

——, *Kitāb al-Nubdha al-mushīra ilā jumal min ᶜuyūn al-sīra*, ms. photo-reproduction, Sanaa: Maktabat al-Yaman al-Kubrā, n.d.

al-Jāsir, Ḥamad, 'al-Imām Muḥammad b. ᶜAlī al-Shawkānī wa mawqifuhu min al-daᶜwa al-salafiyya al-iṣlāḥiyya', *al-Dirᶜiyya* 8 and 10 (Riyadh, 2000), 9–16, 13–19.

____, 'al-Ṣilāt bayn Ṣanᶜāʾ wa-l-Dirᶜiyya', *al-ᶜArab* 22 (Riyadh, 1987), pp. 433–49.
al-Jirāfī, ᶜAbd Allāh b. ᶜAbd al-Karīm, *al-Muqtaṭaf min tārīkh al-Yaman*, Beirut: Manshūrāt al-ᶜAṣr al-Ḥadīth, 1987.
____, *Tuḥfat al-ikhwān bi-ḥilyat ᶜallāmat al-zamān*, Cairo: al-Maṭbaᶜa al-Salafiyya, 1365/1946.
al-Jirāfī, Aḥmad b. Muḥammad, *Ḥawliyyāt al-ᶜallāma al-Jirāfī*, Ḥusayn al-ᶜAmrī (ed.), Beirut: Dār al-Fikr al-Muᶜāṣir, 1992.
Kamālī, Muḥammad, *al-Imām Aḥmad b. Yaḥyā al-Murtaḍā*, Sanaa: Dār al-Ḥikma al-Yamāniyya, 1991.
Khān, Muḥammad Ṣiddīq Ḥasan, *Abjad al-ᶜulūm*, 3 vols., Damascus: Dār al-Kutub al-ᶜIlmiyya, 1978.
____, *Ḥuṣūl al-maʾmūl min ᶜilm al-uṣūl*, Istanbul: Maṭbaᶜat al-Jawāʾib, 1296/1879.
____, *al-Rawḍa al-nadiyya sharḥ al-Durar al-bahiyya*, Ḥasan Ḥallāq (ed.), 2 vols., Beirut: Dār al-Nadā, 1993.
____, *al-Tāj al-mukallal*, Beirut: Dār Iqraʾ, 1983.
Khaṭīb al-Tibrīzī, Muḥammad b. ᶜAbd Allāh, *Mishkāt al-maṣābīḥ*, Muḥammad al-Albānī (ed.), 3 vols., Damascus: al-Maktab al-Islāmī, 1961.
al-Kibsī, Muḥammad b. Ismāᶜīl, *Jawāhir al-durr al-maknūn wa ᶜajāʾib al-Sirr al-makhzūn*, Zayd al-Wazīr (ed.), n.p.: Manshūrāt al-ᶜAṣr al-Ḥadīth, 1988.
____, *al-Laṭāʾif al-saniyya fī akhbār al-mamālik al-Yamaniyya*, n.p.: Maṭbaᶜat al-Saᶜāda, n.d.
al-Kīlānī, Ḥusām al-Dīn b. Salīm, *al-Amālī fī aᶜlā al-asānīd al-ᶜawālī*, Aleppo: Dār al-Qalam al-ᶜArabī, n.d.
al-Laknawī, ᶜAbd al-Ḥayy b. Fakhr al-Dīn, *al-Iᶜlām bi-man fī tārīkh al-Hind min al-aᶜlām*, 8 vols., Rāʾī Barīlī: Maktabat Dār ᶜArafāt, 1413/1992–3 (= *Nuzhat al-khawāṭir wa-bahjat al-masāmiᶜ waʾ-l-nawāẓir*).
Maḥmūd, Ṣāliḥ Ramaḍān (ed.), *Dhikrayāt al-Shawkānī: rasāʾil liʾl-muʾarrikh al-Yamanī Muḥammad b. ᶜAlī al-Shawkānī*, Beirut: Dār al-ᶜAwda, 1983.
____, *Majmūᶜat al-rasāʾil waʾl-masāʾil al-Najdīya*, 4 vols., Cairo: Maṭbaᶜat al-Manār, 1346/1928.
al-Manṣūr ᶜAbd Allāh b. Ḥamza, *Kitāb al-Shāfī*, 4 vols. in 2, Sanaa: Maktabat al-Yaman al-Kubrā, 1986.
al-Manṣūr, Muḥammad b. Muḥammad, *al-Kalima al-shāfiya fī ḥukm mā kāna bayn al-imām ᶜAlī wa Muᶜāwiya*, n.p.: Dār al-Ḥaḍāra, 1992.
al-Manṣūr al-Qāsim b. Muḥammad, *al-Irshād ilā sabīl al-rashād*, Muḥammad ᶜIzzān (ed.), Sanaa: Dār al-Ḥikma al-Yamāniyya, 1996.
____, *al-Iᶜtiṣām bi-ḥabl Allāh al-matīn*, 5 vols., Sanaa: Maktabat al-Yaman al-Kubrā, 1987.
____, *Kitāb al-Asās li-ᶜaqāʾid al-akyās*, Muḥammad al-Hāshimī (ed.), Ṣaᶜda: Maktabat al-Turāth al-Islāmī, 1994.
____, *Kitāb al-Asās li-ᶜaqāʾid al-akyās*, Albert Nadir (ed.), Beirut: Dār al-Ṭalīᶜa, 1980.
____, *Kitāb Ḥatf anf al-āfik*, ms. private library of Sayyid Muḥammad b. al-Ḥasan al-ᶜUjrī in Ḍaḥyān.

al-Maqāliḥ, ᶜAbd al-ᶜAzīz, *Qirāʾa fī fikr al-Zaydiyya waʾl-Muᶜtazila*, Beirut: Dār al-ᶜAwda, 1982.

al-Maqbalī, Ṣāliḥ b. Mahdī, *al-ᶜAlam al-shāmikh*, Sanaa: al-Maktaba al-Yamaniyya liʾl-Nashr waʾl-Tawzīᶜ, 1985.

——, *Kitāb al-Abḥāth al-musaddada fī funūn mutaᶜaddida*, Damascus: Dār al-Fikr, 1982.

——, *Kitāb al-Arwāḥ al-nawāfikh*, Sanaa: al-Maktaba al-Yamaniyya liʾl-Nashr waʾl-Tawzīᶜ, 1985.

——, *al-Manār fī ʾal-mukhtār min jawāhir al-Baḥr al-zakhkhār*, 2 vols., Beirut: Muʾassasat al-Risāla, 1988.

al-Maqḥafī, Ibrāhīm Aḥmad, *Muᶜjam al-buldān waʾl-qabāʾil al-Yamaniyya*, Sanaa: Dār al-Kalima, 1988.

al-Miqrāʾī, Yaḥyā b. Muḥammad, *Maknūn al-sirr fī taḥrīr naḥārīr al-Sirr*, Zayd al-Wazīr (ed.), McLean, VA: Markaz al-Turāth waʾl-Buḥūth al-Yamanī, 2002.

al-Mīthāq al-Waṭanī (Yemeni National Charter), n.d., n.p.

al-Muʾayyad Aḥmad b. al-Ḥusayn, *Sharḥ al-tajrīd fī fiqh al-Zaydiyya*, ms. photo-reproduction, 3 vols., Damascus: Dār Usāma, 1985.

al-Muʾayyad Yaḥyā b. Ḥamza, *al-Risāla al-wāziᶜa liʾl-muᶜtadīn ᶜan sabb ṣaḥābat sayyid al-mursalīn*, Sanaa: Maktabat Dār al-Turāth, 1990.

al-Muʾayyidī, Majd al-Dīn b. Muḥammad, *Lawāmiᶜ al-anwār*, 3 vols., Ṣaᶜda: Maktabat al-Turāth al-Islāmī, 1993.

——, *Tuḥaf sharḥ al-zalaf*, n.p., n.d.

Muḥammad b. ᶜAbd al-Wahhāb, *Kitāb al-Tawḥīd*, Beirut: al-Maktab al-Islāmī, 1408/1988.

Muḥammad b. al-Ḥasan b. al-Qāsim, *Kitāb Sabīl al-rashād ilā maᶜrifat rabb al-ᶜibād*, Sanaa: Dār al-Ḥikma al-Yamāniyya, 1994.

al-Muḥibbī, Muḥammad, *Khulāṣat al-athar fī aᶜyān al-qarn al-ḥādī ᶜashar*, 4 vols., n.p., n.d.

Muqbil, Ṣāliḥ Muḥammad, *Muḥammad b. ᶜAlī al-Shawkānī wa juhūduh al-tarbawiyya*, Beirut: Dār al-Jīl, 1989.

al-Murtaḍā, Aḥmad b. Yaḥyā (= Ibn al-Murtaḍā), *Kitāb al-Azhār fī fiqh al-aʾimma al-aṭhār*, 5th ed., n.p., 1982.

——, *Kitāb al-Baḥr al-zakhkhār*, photoreprint of 1366/1947 ed., 6 vols. (incl. *muqaddima*), Sanaa: Dār al-Ḥikma al-Yamāniyya, 1988.

——, *Kitāb al-Qalāʾid fī taṣḥīḥ al-ᶜaqāʾid*, Albert Nader (ed.), Beirut: Dār al-Mashriq, 1985.

——, *Minhāj al-wuṣūl ilā miᶜyār al-ᶜuqūl fī ᶜilm al-uṣūl*, Aḥmad al-Mākhidhī (ed.), Sanaa: Dār al-Ḥikma al-Yamāniyya, 1992.

——, *al-Munya waʾl-amal fī sharḥ al-milal waʾl-niḥal*, Muḥammad Mashkūr (ed.), Beirut: Dār al-Nadā, 1990.

Mūṣallilī, Aḥmad, *al-Uṣūliyya al-islāmiyya: dirāsa fī ʾl-khiṭāb al-īdiyūlūjī waʾl-siyāsī ᶜinda Sayyid Qutb*, n.p.: al-Nāshir, 1993.

al-Mutawakkil Ismāᶜīl b. al-Qāsim, *al-Jawāb al-muʾayyad biʾl-burhān al-ṣarīḥ ᶜalā ᶜadam al-farq bayna kufr al-taʾwīl waʾl-taṣrīḥ wa ḥukm al-bughā ᶜalā al-madhhab al-ṣarīḥ*, ms. Milan, Ambrosiana, no. D 244, IX.

____, *Kitāb al-ᶜAqīda al-ṣaḥīḥa*, Sanaa: Maktabat Dār al-Turāth, 1990.

____, *Kitāb Taftīḥ abṣār al-quḍāt ilā azhār al-masāʾil al-murtaḍāt ikhtiyārāt amīr al-muʾminīn al-Mutawakkil ᶜalā Allāh*, ms. Sanaa, Gharbiyya Library, *ᶜilm kalām*, no. 134.

al-Nadwī, Muḥammad Akram, *Nafaḥāt al-Hind waʾl-Yaman bi-asānīd al-shaykh Abī ʾal-Ḥasan*, Riyadh: Maktabat al-Imām al-Shāfiᶜī, 1998.

al-Nāṭiq biʾl-Ḥaqq Yaḥyā b. al-Ḥusayn al-Hārūnī, *Kitāb al-Taḥrīr*, 2 vols., Muḥammad ᶜIzzān (ed.), Sanaa: Maktabat Badr, 1997.

al-Nawbakhtī, al-Ḥasan b. Mūsā, *Kitāb Firaq al-Shīᶜa*, Helmut Ritter (ed.), Istanbul: Maṭbaᶜat al-Dawla, 1931.

al-Nuᶜmī, Aḥmad b. Aḥmad, *Ḥawliyyāt al-Nuᶜmī al-Tihāmiyya*, Ḥusayn al-ᶜAmrī (ed.), Damascus: Dār al-Fikr, 1987.

al-Nuᶜmī, Ḥusayn, *Maᶜārij al-albāb fī manāhij al-haqq wa ʾl-sawāb*, Riyadh: Maktabat al-Maᶜārif, 1985.

al-Nuᶜmī, Ismāᶜīl b. ᶜIzz al-Dīn, *al-Sayf al-bātir al-mudīʾ li-kashf al-īhām wa ʾl-tamwīh fī Irshād al-ghabī*, ms. Sanaa, Gharbiyya Library, *majmūᶜ* no. 188, fols. 1–36 and *majmūᶜ* no. 91, fols. 55–77.

Nūmsūk, ᶜAbd Allāh, *Manhaj al-imām al-Shawkānī fī ʾl-ᶜaqīda*, Riyadh: Maktabat Dār al-Qalam, 1994.

Qāsim b. Ibrāhīm *et al.*, *Kitāb Taysīr al-marām*, Sanaa: Manshūrāt al-Madīna, 1986.

al-Rabaᶜī, Mufarriḥ b. Aḥmad, *Sīrat al-amīrayn al-jalīlāyn al-sharīfayn al-fāḍilayn*, Riḍwān al-Sayyid and ᶜAbd al-Ghanī ᶜAbd al-ᶜĀṭī (eds.), Beirut: Dār al-Muntakhab al-ᶜArabī, 1993.

al-Rathānī, ᶜAlī b. ᶜAbdullāh (sponsor), *Majmūᶜat al-tawḥīd*, Damascus: al-Maktab al-Islāmī, 1381/1962.

al-Rāziḥī, ᶜAlī Aḥmad (ed.), *al-Majmūᶜa al-fākhira*, Sanaa: Dār al-Ḥikma al-Yamāniyya, 2000.

Rufayda, Ibrāhīm ᶜAbd Allāh, 'al-Imām Muḥammad b. ᶜ Alī al-Shawkānī al-ᶜālim al-mujtahid al-mufassir', *Dirāsāt Yamaniyya* 40 (1990), 284–342.

al-Ruqayḥī, Aḥmad *et al.*, *Fihrist makhṭūṭāt maktabat al-Jāmiᶜ al-Kabīr Ṣanᶜāʾ*, 4 vols., Damascus: Maṭbaᶜat al-Kātib al-ᶜArabī, 1984.

Saḥūlī, Yaḥyā b. Ṣāliḥ, *Fatāwā*, ms. Princeton University Library, no. 3181 (Yahuda Section).

Sālim, Sayyid Muṣṭafā, *al-Fatḥ al-ᶜUthmānī al-awwal liʾl-Yaman*, 3rd ed., Cairo: Maṭbaᶜat al-Jabalāwī, 1977.

____, *Takwīn al-Yaman al-ḥadīth*, 3rd ed., Cairo: Maṭbaᶜat Madbūlī, 1984.

____, *Wathāʾiq Yamaniyya: dirāsa wathāʾiqiyya tārīkhiyya*, 2nd ed., Cairo: al-Maṭbaᶜa al-Faniyya, 1985.

al-Samāwī, Muḥammad b. Ṣāliḥ, *al-Ghaṭamṭam al-zakhkhār al-muṭahhir li-riyāḍ al-Azhār min āthār al-Sayl al-jarrār*, Muḥammad ᶜIzzān (ed.), 6 vols., Amman: Maṭābiᶜ Sharikat al-Mawārid al-Ṣināᶜiyya al-Urduniyya, 1994.

____, *al-ᶜIqd al-munaẓẓam fī jawāb al-suʾāl al-wārid min al-ḥaram al-muḥarram*, Ismāᶜīl al-Wazīr (ed.), Sanaa: n.p., 1992.

al-Sayāghī, Ḥusayn b. Aḥmad, *Kitāb al-Rawḍ al-naḍīr sharḥ Majmū ͨ al-fiqh al-kabīr*, 4 vols., Sanaa: Maktabat al-Yaman al-Kubrā, 1985.

Sayyid, Ayman Fuʾad, *Maṣādir tārīkh al-Yaman fī ʾl-ͨaṣr al-islāmī*, Cairo: Institut Français d'Archéologie Orientale, 1974.

al-Shamāḥī, ͨAbd Allāh b. ͨAbd al-Wahhāb, *Ṣirāṭ al-ͨārifīn ilā idrāk ikhtiyārāt amīr al-muʾminīn*, Sanaa: Maṭbaͨat al-Maͨārif, 1356/1937.

——, *al-Yaman al-insān waʾl-ḥaḍāra*, Beirut: Manshūrāt al-Madīna, 1985.

al-Shāmī, Aḥmad b. Muḥammad, *Imām al-Yaman Aḥmad Ḥamīd al-Dīn*, Beirut: Dār al-Kitāb al-Jadīd, 1965.

——, *Nafaḥāt wa lafaḥāt min ʾl-Yaman*, Beirut: Dār al-Nadwa al-Jadīda, 1988.

——, *Riyāḥ al-taghyīr fī ʾl-Yaman*, Jeddah: al-Maṭbaͨa al-ͨArabiyya, 1984.

al-Shāmī, Aḥmad b. Muḥammad b. ͨAlī, *Ārāʾ wa mawāqif*, Amman: Maṭābiͨ Sharikat al-Mawārid Ṣināͨiyya al-Urduniyya, 1994.

Sharaf al-Dīn, Aḥmad Ḥusayn, *Tārīkh al-fikr al-islāmī fī ʾl-Yaman*, n.p.: Maṭbaͨat al-Kaylānī, 1968.

——, *al-Yaman ͨabr al-tārīkh*, Cairo: Maṭbaͨat al-Sunna al-Muḥammadiyya, 1964.

al-Sharafī, Aḥmad b. Muḥammad, *Kitāb ͨUddat al-akyās fī sharḥ maͨānī al-Asās*, 2 vols., Sanaa: Dār al-Ḥikma al-Yamāniyya, 1995.

al-Sharjī, Aḥmad b. Aḥmad, *Ṭabaqāt al-khawāṣ ahl al-ṣidq waʾl-ikhlāṣ*, Sanaa: Dār al-Yamaniyya liʾl-Nashr waʾl-Tawzīͨ, 1986.

al-Sharjī, ͨAbd al-Ghanī, *al-Imām al-Shawkānī ḥayātuh wa fikruh*, Beirut: Muʾassasat al-Risāla, 1988.

al-Shawkānī, Ḥārith, 'al-Malakiyya fikra wa laysat ͨirqan aw sulāla', *al-Ṣaḥwa*, no. 326 (Sanaa, 1992), 4.

al-Shawkānī, Muḥammad b. ͨAlī, *Adab al-ṭalab*, Sanaa: Markaz al-Dirāsāt waʾl-Buḥūth al-Yamaniyya, 1979.

——, *al-ͨAdhb al-namīr fī jawāb masāʾil ͨālim bilād ͨAsīr*, in *Kitāb al-Fatḥ al-rabbānī min fatāwā al-imām al-Shawkānī*, Sanaa: al-Maͨhad al-ͨĀlī liʾl-Qaḍāʾ, n.d., pp. 55–94.

——, *al-Badr al-ṭāliͨ bi-maḥāsin man baͨd al-qarn al-sābiͨ*, Muḥammad Zabāra (ed.), 2 vols., photoreprint of 1348/1929 edn, Beirut: Dār al-Maͨrifa, n.d.

——, *Baḥth fī ḥadīth anā madīnat al-ͨilm wa ͨAlī bābuhā*, in *Kitāb al-Fatḥ al-rabbānī min fatāwā al-imām al-Shawkānī*, Sanaa: al-Maͨhad al-ͨĀlī liʾl-Qaḍāʾ, n.d., pp. 207–13.

——, *al-Darārī al-muḍiyya sharḥ al-durar al-bahiyya*, Beirut: Dār al-Jīl, 1987.

——, *Darr al-ṣaḥāba fī manāqib al-qarāba waʾl-ṣaḥāba*, Ḥusayn al-ͨAmrī (ed.), Damascus: Dār al-Fikr, 1984.

——, *al-Dawāʾ al-ͨājil fī dafͨ al-ͨaduw al-ṣāʾil*, in *al-Rasāʾil al-salafiyya fī iḥyāʾ sunnat khayr al-bariyya*, Photoreprint of 1348/1930 ed., Beirut: Dār al-Kutub al-ͨIlmiyya, n.d.

——, *Dīwān al-Shawkānī aslāk al-jawhar waʾl-ḥayāt al-fikriyya waʾl-sīyāsiyya fī ͨaṣrih*, Ḥusayn al-ͨAmrī (ed.), 2nd ed., Damascus: Dār al-Fikr, 1986.

____, *Fatḥ al-qadīr al-jāmiʿ bayna fannay al-riwāya waʾl-dirāya min ʿilm al-tafsīr*, 5 vols., Beirut: Dār al-Maʿrifa, n.d.

____, *al-Fawāʾid al-majmūʿa fī ʾl-aḥādīth al-mawḍūʿa*, Beirut: Dār al-Kitāb al-ʿArabī, 1986.

____, *Ḥall al-ishkāl fī ijbār al-Yahūd ʿalā iltiqāṭ al-azbāl*, Cairo: Dār al-Kutub, microfilm no. 2216, fols. 44b–48b.

____, *al-ʿIqd al-thamīn fī ithbāt wiṣāyat amīr al-muʾminīn*, Sanaa: Maktabat Dār al-Turāth, 1990.

____, *Irshād al-fuḥūl ilā taḥqīq al-ḥaqq min ʿilm al-uṣūl*, Beirut: Dār al-Maʿrifa, n.d.

____, *Irshād al-ghabī ilā madhhab Ahl al-Bayt fī ṣaḥb al-nabī*, ms. personal library of Qāḍī Muḥammad b. Ismāʿīl al-ʿAmrānī.

____, *Irshād al-sāʾil ilā dalīl al-masāʾil, in Kitāb al-Fatḥ al-rabbānī min fatāwā al-imām al-Shawkānī*, Sanaa: al-Maʿhad al-ʿĀlī liʾl-Qaḍāʾ, n.d., pp. 309–28.

____, *Itḥāf al-akābir bi-asnād al-dafātir*, Hyderabad: Maṭbaʿat Majlis Dāʾirat al-Maʿārif al-Niẓāmiyya, 1328/1910.

____, *Kashf al-shubūhāt ʿan al-mushtabihāt* in *al-Rasāʾil al-salafiyya fī iḥyāʾ sunnat khayr al-bariyya*, Beirut: Dār al-Kitāb al-ʿArabī, 1991, pp. 97–126.

____, *Kitāb al-Durr al-naḍīd fī ikhlāṣ kalimat al-tawḥīd*, in *al-Rasāʾil al-salafiyya fī iḥyāʾ sunnat kahr al-bariyya*, Photoreprint of 1348/1930 ed., Beirut: Dār al-Kutub al-ʿIlmiyya, n.d.

____, *Kitāb al-Fatḥ al-rabbānī min fatāwā al-imām al-Shawkānī*, Sanaa: al-Maʿhad al-ʿĀlī liʾl-Qaḍāʾ, n.d.

____, *Matn al-Durar al-bahiyya*, n.p., n.d.

____, *Nayl al-awṭār fī sharḥ muntaqā al-akhbār*, 9 sections in 4 vols., Beirut: Dār al-Fikr, 1989.

____, *Qaṭru al-walī ʿalā ḥadīth al-walī*, Ibrāhīm Hilāl (ed.), Beirut: Dār Iḥyāʾ al-Turāth al-ʿArabī, n.d.

____, *al-Qawl al-maqbūl fī radd khabar al-majhūl min ghayr ṣaḥābat al-rasul*, ms. Sanaa, al-Maʿhad al-ʿĀlī liʾl-Qaḍāʾ.

____, *al-Qawl al-mufīd fī adillat al-ijtihād waʾl-taqlīd,* in *al-Rasāʾil al-salafiyya fī iḥyāʾsunnat khayr al-bariyya*, Beirut: Dār al-Kitāb al-ʿArabī, 1991, pp. 191–251.

____, *Rafʿ al-khiṣām fī ʾl-ḥukm bi-ʿilm al-ḥukkām*, Aḥmad al-Wādiʿī (ed.), Sanaa: Maktabat al-Irshād, 1997.

____, *Rafʿ al-rība fīmā yajūz wa mā lā yajūz min al-ghība*, ʿAqīl al-Maqṭarī (ed.), Beirut: Dār Ibn Ḥazm, 1992.

____, *al-Ṣawārim al-ḥidād al-qāṭiʿa li-ʿalāʾiq arbāb al-ittiḥād*, Muḥammad al-Ḥallāq (ed.), Sanaa: Dār al-Hijra, 1990.

____, *al-Sayl al-jarrār al-mutadaffiq ʿalā ḥadāʾiq al-Azhār*, Maḥmūd Zāyid (ed.), 4 vols., Beirut: Dār al-Kutub al-ʿIlmiyya, 1985.

____, *al-Tuḥaf fī madhāhib al-salaf*, in *al-Rasāʾil al-salafiyya fī iḥyāʾ sunnat khayr al-bariyya*, Beirut: Dār al-Kitāb al-ʿArabī, 1991, pp. 127–42.

——, *Tuḥfat al-dhākirīn bi-ᶜUddat al-ḥiṣn al-ḥaṣīn min kalām sayyid al-mursalīn*, Beirut: Dār al-Fikr, n.d.

——, *Wabl al-ghamām ᶜalā Shifāʾal-uwām*, in al-Ḥusayn b. Badr al-Dīn, *Kitāb Shifāʾ al-uwām fī ahādīth al-ahkām*, 3 vols., n.p.: Jamᶜiyyat ᶜUlamāʾ al-Yaman, 1996.

——, *Wabl al-ghamām ᶜalā Shifāʾal-uwām*, Muḥammad Ḥallāq (ed.), 2 vols., Cairo: Maktabat Ibn Taymiyya, 1416/1996.

al-Shijnī, Muḥammad, *Ḥayāt al-imām al-Shawkānī al-musammā Kitāb al-Tiqṣār*, Muḥammad b. ᶜAlī al-Akwaᶜ (ed.), Sanaa: Maktabat al-Jīl al-Jadīd, 1990.

Ṣubḥī, Aḥmad Maḥmūd, *al-Zaydiyya*, 2nd ed., Cairo: al-Zahrāʾ liʾl-Iᶜlām al-ᶜArabī, 1984.

Sulaymān b. Saḥmān (ed.), *al-Hadiyya al-saniyya waʾl-tuḥfa al-Wahhābiyya al-Najdiyya*, Cairo: al-Manār Press, 1342/1923.

Taqī, ᶜIzz al-Dīn Ḥasan (ed.), *Kitāb al-Fatāwā al-sharᶜiyya waʾl-ᶜilmiyya waʾl-dīniyya li-ᶜulamāʾ al-diyār al-Yamaniyya*, Sanaa: Maktabat al-Irshād, n.d.

al-Tāzī, ᶜAbd al-Hādī, 'al-Nuṣūṣ al-ẓāhira fī ijlāʾal-Yahūd al-fājira li-Aḥmad Abī ʾl-Rijāl,' *al-Baḥth al-ᶜIlmī*, (Rabat: al-Maᶜhad al-Jāmiᶜī liʾl-Baḥth al-ᶜIlmī, Jāmiᶜat Muḥammad al-Khāmis), 32 (1981), 15–35.

al-Thawra, (official newspaper of the Yemen Arab Republic), archived in Sanaa: al-Markaz al-Waṭanī liʾl-Wathāʾiq.

al-Wādiᶜī, Muqbil, *Tarjamat Abī ᶜAbd al-Rahmān Muqbil b. Hādī al-Wādiᶜī*, Sanaa: Maktabat Ṣanᶜāʾ al-Athariyya, 1999.

al-Wajīh, ᶜAbd al-Salām, *Aᶜlām al-muʾallifīn al-Zaydiyya*, Amman: Muʾassasat al-Imām Zayd b. ᶜAlī al-Thaqāfiyya, 1999.

al-Wāsiᶜī, ᶜAbd al-Wāsiᶜ b. Yaḥya, *Tārīkh al-Yaman*, Cairo: al-Maṭbaᶜa al-Salafiyya, 1346/1927–8.

——, *Tārīkh al-Yaman*, reprint of 1367/1948 edn (Cairo: Maṭbaᶜat Ḥijāzī), Sanaa: Maktabat al-Yaman al-Kubrā, 1991.

al-Wazīr, ᶜAbd Allāh b. ᶜAlī, *Tārīkh ṭabaq al-ḥalwā wa ṣuḥāf al-mann waʾl-salwā*, Muḥammad Jāzim (ed.), Sanaa: Markaz al-Dirāsāt waʾl-Buḥūth al-Yamanī, 1985.

al-Wazīr, Aḥmad b. ᶜAbd Allāh, *Tārīkh Banī al-Wazīr*, ms. Milan, Ambrosiana, no. D 556.

al-Wazīr, Aḥmad b. Muḥammad, *Ḥayāt al-amīr ᶜAlī b. ᶜAbd Allāh al-Wazīr*, n.p.: Manshūrāt al-ᶜAṣr al-Ḥadīth, 1987.

al-Wazīr, Ibrāhīm b. Muḥammad, *al-Falak al-dawwār fī ᶜulūm al-ḥadīth waʾl-fiqh waʾl-āthār*, Muḥammad ᶜIzzān (ed.), Sanaa: Dār al-Turāth al-Yamanī, 1994.

——, *al-Qaṣīda al-bassāma*, Zayd al-Wazīr (ed.), forthcoming.

al-Waẓir, Muḥammad b. Ibrāhīm, *al-ᶜAwāṣim waʾl-qawāṣim fī ʾl-dhabbi ᶜan sunnati Abī ʾl-Qāsim*, Shuᶜayb al-Arnaʾūṭ (ed.), 9 vols., Beirut: Muʾassasat al-Risāla, 1992.

——, *al-Rawḍ al-bāsim fī ʾl-dhabbi ᶜan sunnati Abī ʾl-Qāsim*, 2nd ed., Sanaa: al-Maktaba al-Yamaniyya liʾl-Nashir waʾl-Tawzīᶜ, 1985.

Wizārat al-ᶜAdl (Ministry of Justice), *Qarārāt wizārat al-ᶜadl*, Sanaa, n.p., 1971.

——, *Majallat al-buḥūth waʾl-aḥkām al-qaḍāʾiyya al-Yamaniyya* 1 (1980).

al-Wushalī, Ismāʿīl b. Muḥammad, *Dhayl nashr al-thanāʾ al-ḥasan*, Muḥammad al-Shuʿaybī (ed.), Sanaa: Maṭābiʿ al-Yaman al-ʿAṣriyya, 1982.

Yaḥyā b. al-Ḥusayn, *Ghāyat al-amānī fī akhbār al-quṭr al-Yamānī*, Saʿīd ʿĀshūr (ed.), 2 vols., Cairo: Dār al-Kātib al-ʿArabī, 1968.

——, *Kitāb al-Mustaṭāb fī tārīkh ʿulamā al-Zaydiyya al-aṭyāb*, ms. New Sanaa University Library (photocopy).

——, *Yawmiyyāt Ṣanʿāʾ*, ʿAbd Allāh al-Ḥibshī (ed.), Abu Dhabi: Manshūrāt al-Majmaʿ al-Thaqāfī, 1996.

Yaḥyā b. al-Mahdī b. al-Qāsim al-Ḥusaynī, *Ṣilat al-ikhwān fī ḥilyat barakat ahl al-zamān*, ms. Milan, Ambrosiana, no. D 222.

Yemen Arab Republic, *al-Qānūn al-madanī*, n.p., 1979.

Yemen Republic, *al-Qarār al-jumhūrī biʾl-qānūn raqm 19 li-sanat 1992 bi-iṣdār al-qānūn al-madanī*, n.p.: Muʾassasat 14 October, 1992.

Yūsuf b. Yaḥyā Ḍiyāʾ al-Dīn, *Nasmat al-saḥar bi-dhikr man tashayyaʿa wa shaʿar*, Kāmil al-Jabbūrī (ed.), 3 vols, Beirut: Dār al-Muʾarrikh al-ʿArabī, 1999.

Zabāra, Muḥammad, 'Raʾy al-imām al-Shawkānī fī ʾl-rāfiḍa', *al-Ṣaḥwa* 328, (Sanaa, 1992), 4.

Zabāra, Muḥammad b. Muḥammad, *Aʾimmat al-Yaman*, Taʿizz: Matbaʿat al-Nāṣir al-Nāṣiriyya, 1952.

——, *Aʾimmat al-Yaman biʾl-qarn al-rābiʿ ʿashar liʾl-hijra*, 3 vols., Cairo: al-Maṭbaʿa al-Salafiyya, 1376/1956.

——, *Nashr al-ʿarf li-nubalāʾ al-Yaman baʿd al-alf*, vol. I, photoreprint, Sanaa: Markaz al-Dirāsāt waʾl-Buḥūth al-Yamanī, n.d.

——, *Nashr al-ʿarf li-nubalāʾ al-Yaman baʿd al-alf*, vols. 2 and 3, Sanaa: Markaz al-Dirāsāt waʾl-Buḥūth al-Yamanī, 1985. (Originally published as vol. 2 in 1377/1958 in Cairo by al-Maṭbaʿa al-Salafiyya).

——, *Nayl al-waṭar min tarājim rijāl al-Yaman fī ʾl-qarn al-thālith ʿashar*, 2 vols. in one, Sanaa: Markaz al-Dirāsāt waʾl-Abḥāth al-Yamaniyya, n.d.

——, *Nuzhat al-naẓar fī rijāl al-qarn al-rābiʿ ʿashar*, Sanaa: Markaz al-Dirāsāt waʾl-Abḥāth al-Yamaniyya, 1979.

al-Zabīdī, Muḥammad Ḥusayn, 'Makhṭūṭatān minʾ al-Yaman', *al-Mawrid* 3.4, (Baghdad: Ministry of Information, 1974), 187–96.

al-Ẓabyānī, Ṣāliḥ b. ʿAbd Allāh, 'Ikhtiyārāt al-imām al-Shawkānī al-fiqhiyya', Ph.D. thesis, Imām Muḥammad b. Saʿūd Islamic University, 1411/1990.

References in European languages

Abir, Mordechai, *Ethiopia and the Red Sea: The Rise and Decline of the Solomonic Dynasty and Muslim–European Rivalry in the Region*, London: Frank Cass, 1980.

Album, Stephen, *Sylloge of Islamic Coins in the Ashmolean*, vol. 10, Oxford: Ashmolean Museum, 1999.

al-ᶜAmrī, Ḥusayn ᶜAbdullāh, *The Yemen in the 18th & 19th Centuries: A Political and Intellectual History*, London: Ithaca Press, 1985.

Arazi, Albert, 'Ilqām al-ḥajar li-man zakkā sābb abī bakr wa-ᶜumar dʾal-suyūṭī', *JSAI* 10 (1987), 211–87.

Arberry, Arthur J., *The Koran Interpreted*, Oxford: Oxford University Press, 1989.

Arendonk, C. van, *Les Débuts de lʾImāmat Zaidite au Yemen*, trans. Jacques Ryckmans, Leiden: E. J. Brill, 1960.

Aziz, Abdul, *Arms and Jewelry of the Indian Mughals*, Lahore: n.p., 1947.

Becker, Hans *et al.* (eds.), *Kaffee aus Arabien*, Wiesbaden: Franz Steiner, 1979.

Berkey, Jonathan, *The Transmission of Knowledge in Medieval Cairo*, Princeton University Press, 1992.

Bjorkman, Walther, art. 'Shirk', in *EI*[1].

Blackburn, Richard, 'The collapse of Ottoman authority in Yemen', *Die Welt des Islams* 19 (1979), 119–76.

——, 'The era of Imām Sharaf al-Dīn Yaḥyā and his son al-Muṭahhar', *Yemen Update* 42 (2000), 4–8.

Blukacz, François, 'Le Yémen sous l'autorité des imams zaidites au XVIIe siècle: une éphémère unité', *Revue du Monde Musulman et de la Méditerranée* 67 (1993), 39–51.

——, 'Les relations entre le Yémen et l'Inde au XVIIe siècle, extraits de la correspondance entre l'imam zaidite et al-Mutawakkil ᶜalā Llāh Ismāᶜīl b. al-Qāsim et le sultan moghol Awrangzib', mémoire de maîtrise, Université de Paris-Sorbonne (Paris IV), 1992.

——, 'Les relations politiques des imams zaidites du Yémen avec le Hedjaz au XVIIe siècle', mémoire de D.E.A., Université de Paris-Sorbonne (Paris IV), 1993.

Bonnenfant, Guillemette and Paul, *L'Art du Bois à Sanaa*, Aix-en-Provence: Edisud, 1987.

Boxhall, P., 'The diary of a Mocha coffee agent', *Arabian* Studies 1 (1974), 102–18.

Brockelmann, C., *Geschichte der Arabischen Literatur*, 2nd edn, Leiden: E. J. Brill, 1943–9; supplementary volumes, Leiden: E. J. Brill, 1937–42.

Brouwer, C. G., *al-Mukhā*, Amsterdam: D'Fluyte Rarob, 1997.

Brown, Daniel, *Rethinking Tradition in Modern Islamic Thought*, Cambridge University Press, 1996.

Brunner, Rainer, *Annäherung und Distanz: Schia, Azhar und die Islamische Ökumene in 20. Jahrhundert*, Berlin: Klaus Schwarz, 1996.

Calder, Norman, 'Al-Nawawī's typology of *Muftī*s and its significance for a general theory of Islamic law', *Islamic Law and Society* 3 (1996), 137–64.

Chaudhuri, K. N., art. 'Kahwa', in *EI*[2].

Clark, Stuart, 'The *Annales* historians', in Quentin Skinner (ed.), *The Return of Grand Theory in the Human Sciences*, Cambridge University Press, 1985.

Cohen, Mark R., *Under Crescent and Cross: the Jews in the Middle Ages*, Princeton University Press, 1994.

——, 'What was the pact of 'Umar? A literary-historical study', *JSAI* 23 (1999), 100–57.

Cook, Michael, *Commanding Right and Forbidding Wrong in Islamic Thought*, Cambridge University Press, 2000.

——, 'On the origins of Wahhābism', *Journal of the Royal Asiatic Society* 2.2 (1992), 191–202.

Coulson, N. J., *A History of Islamic Law*, Edinburgh University Press, 1978.

Coussonnet, Nahida and Ory, Solange, *Inscriptions de la Mosquée Dhi Bin au Yémen*, Sanaa: Centre Français d'Études Yéménites, 1996.

Crawford, Michael J., *Wahhābī 'Ulamā' and the Law 1745–1932 AD*, M.Phil. thesis, University of Oxford, 1980.

Crone, Patricia, ' "Even an Ethiopian slave": the transformation of a Sunni tradition', *BSOAS* 57 (1994), 59–67.

Dallal, Ahmad, 'Appropriating the past: twentieth-century reconstruction of premodern Islamic thought', *Islamic Law and Society*, 7 (2000), 325–58.

——, 'The origins and objectives of Islamic revivalist thought, 1750–1850', *JAOS* 113 (1993), 341–59.

Das Gupta, Ashin, *Indian Merchants and the Decline of Surat c. 1700–1750*, New Delhi: Manohar Publishers, 1994.

Detalle, Renaud, 'Ghadir and Nushoor in Yemen: Zaydistan votes for Imam Ali', *Yemen Times*, no. 17 (1997), April 28th–4th May.

Donzel, E. J. van, *A Yemenite Embassy to Ethiopia 1617–1649: al-Haymī's Sīrat al-Ḥabasha*, Stuttgart: Steiner, 1986.

Douglas, J. Leigh, *The Free Yemeni Movement*, American University of Beirut Press, 1987.

Dresch, Paul, 'Imams and Tribes: the writing and acting of history in Upper Yemen', in Philip S. Khoury and Joseph Kostiner (eds.), *Tribes and State Formation in the Middle East*, Berkeley: University of California Press, 1990.

——, *Tribes, Government and History in Yemen*, Oxford: Clarendon Press, 1989.

Dresch, Paul and Haykel, Bernard, 'Stereotypes and political styles: Islamists and tribesfolk in Yemen', *IJMES*, 27.4 (1995), 405–31.

Eagle, A. B. R. D., 'Ghāyat al-amānī and the life and times of al-Hādī Yaḥyā b. al-Ḥusayn', M.Litt. thesis, University of Durham, 1990.

Enayat, Hamid, *Modern Islamic Political Thought*, London: Macmillan Education, 1982.

Esposito, John L., *Islam, the Straight Path*, Oxford University Press, 1988.

Fadel, Mohammad, 'The social logic of *Taqlīd* and the rise of the *Mukhtaṣar*', *Islamic Law and Society* 3 (1996), 193–233.

Friedmann, Yohanan, *Prophecy Continuous*, Berkeley: University of California Press, 1989.

——, *Shaykh Aḥmad Sirhindī*, New Delhi: Oxford University Press, 2000.

Gochenour, David Thomas, 'The penetration of Zaydi Islam into early Medieval Yemen', Ph.D. dissertation, Harvard University, 1984.

Goitein, S. D., *Jews and Arabs*, 3rd edn, New York: Schocken Books, 1974.

Goldziher, Ignaz, *Introduction to Islamic Theology and Law*, trans. Andras and Ruth Hamori, Princeton University Press, 1981.

——, *Muslim Studies*, vol. II, trans. S. M. Stern, London: George Allen and Unwin, 1971.

Goron, Stan, *The Coins of the Indian Sultanate*, New Delhi: Munshiram Manoharlal, 2001.

Goswamy, B. N. and Grewal, J. S., *The Mughals and the Jogis of Jakhbar*, Simla: Indian Institute of Advanced Study, 1967.

Gran, Peter, *Islamic Roots of Capitalism*, Syracuse University Press, 1998.

Griffini, Eugenio (ed.), *'Corpus Iuris' di Zaid ibn ᶜAlī*, Milan: Ulrico Hoepli, 1919.

Hagen, Gottfried and Seidensticker, Tilman, 'Reinhard Schulzes Hypothese einer islamischen Aufklärung', *Zeitschrift der Deutschen Morgenländischen Gesellschaft* 148 (1998), 83–110.

Hallaq, Wael B., 'On the origins of the controversy about the existence of *Mujtahids* and the Gate of *Ijtihād*', *Studia Islamica* 63 (1986), 129–41.

——, 'Was the Gate of Ijtihad closed?', *IJMES* 16.1 (1984), 3–41.

Haykel, Bernard, 'Al-Shawkānī and the jurisprudential unity of Yemen', *Revue du Monde Musulman et de la Méditerranée* 67 (1993), 53–65.

——, 'Rebellion, migration or consultative democracy? The Zaydis and their detractors in Yemen', in Rémy Leveau *et al.* (eds.), *Le Yémen contemporain*, Paris: Karthala, 1999.

——, 'Recent publishing activity by the Zaydis in Yemen: a select bibliography', *Chroniques Yéménites* 9 (Centre Français d'Archéologie et de Sciences Sociales de Sanaa, 2002), 225–30.

——, 'Reforming Islam by dissolving the *Madhhabs*: Shawkānī and his Zaydī detractors in Yemen', in Bernard G. Weiss (ed.), *Studies in Islamic Legal Theory*, Leiden: Brill, 2002.

——, 'The Salafis in Yemen at a crossroads: an obituary of Shaykh Muqbil al-Wādiᶜī of Dammāj (d. 1422/2001)', *Jemen Report* 1 (2002), 28–31.

al-Ḥiyed, ᶜAbd Allāh Hāmid, 'Relations between the Yaman and South Arabia during the Zaydī imāmate of Āl al-Qāsim 1626–1732', D.Phil. thesis, University of Edinburgh, 1973.

Hoffman, Valerie J., 'Nineteenth-century Ibadi discussions on religious knowledge and Muslim sects', paper presented at the Middle East Studies Association Conference, 2001.

Hourani, Albert, *Arabic Thought in the Liberal Age*, Cambridge University Press, 1983.

Hunwick, J. O., 'Ṣāliḥ al-Fullānī (1752/3–1803): the career and teachings of a West African ᶜālim in Medina', in A. H. Green (ed.), *In Quest of an Islamic Humanism*, American University in Cairo Press, 1986.

Israel, Jonathan I., *Radical Enlightenment*, Oxford University Press, 2001.

Jackson, Sherman, '*Taqlīd*, legal scaffolding and the scope of legal injunctions in post-formative theory', *Islamic Law and Society* 3 (1996), 165–92.

Keddie, Nikkie, *Sayyid Jamāl ad-Dīn "al-Afghānī"*, Berkeley: University of California Press, 1972.

Kerr, Malcolm, *Islamic Reform*, Berkeley: University of California Press, 1966.

Khan, Sāqi Mustᶜad [sic], *Maāsir-i-ᶜālamgiri* [sic], trans. Jadunath Sarkar, New Delhi: Munshiram Manoharlal, 1986.

Knysh, Alexander, *Ibn ᶜArabi in the Later Islamic Tradition*, Albany: State University of New York Press, 1999.

Kohlberg, Etan, 'Some Imāmī Shīᶜī views on the Ṣaḥābā', *JSAI* 5 (1984), 143–75.

____, 'Some Zaydī views on the Companions of the Prophet', *BSOAS* 39.1 (1976), 91–8.

____, 'The attitude of the Imāmī-Shīᶜīs to the Companions of the Prophet', D.Phil. thesis, University of Oxford, 1971.

____, 'The term "Rāfiḍa" in Imami Shiᶜi usage', *JAOS* 99 (1979), 677–9, repr. in *Belief and Law in Imami Shiᶜism*, Aldershot: Variorum, 1991, art. IV.

Koningsveld, P. S. van *et al.*, Yemenite Authorities and Jewish Messianism, Leiden: Leiden University, 1990.

Krause, Chester *et al.* (eds.), *Standard Catalogue of World Coins*, Iola, Wisconsin: Krause Publications, 1998.

____, *Standard Catalog of World Coins: eighteenth century, 1701–1800*, 2nd edn, Iola, Wisconsin: Krause Publications, 1997.

Kruse, Hans, 'Takfīr und Gihād bei den Zaiditen des Jemen', *Die Welt des Islams* 13–14 (1984), 424–57.

Kühn, Thomas, 'Clothing the "uncivilized": military recruitment in Ottoman Yemen and the quest for "native" uniforms, 1880–1914', in Suraiya Faroqhi and Christoph K. Neumann (eds.), *Costume and Identity in the Ottoman Empire*, Istanbul: Simurg Publishers (forthcoming).

____, 'Ordering the past of Ottoman Yemen, 1872–1914', *Turcica* (2002, forthcoming).

La Roque, *A Voyage to Arabia the Happy*, London: Golden Ball (for G. Strathan and R. Williamson), 1726.

Lachman, Samuel, 'A gold coin of the Zaidī imām al-Mutawakkil al-Qāsim b. al-Ḥusayn', *Numismatic Circular* 98 (1990), 84.

____, 'A ṭughrāᵓ on a gold coin of the Zaidī Imām al-Mahdī al-ᶜAbbās', *Numismatic Circular* 98 (1990), 351.

____, 'The coins of the Zaidī imām al-Mutawakkil ᶜala Allāh Ismāᶜīl b. al-Qāsim', *Numismatic Circular* 97 (1989), 147–50, 183–5.

____, 'The coins of the Zaidī imāms of the period 1224–1265 H/1809–1849', *Numismatic Circular* 98 (1990), 1–7.

____, 'The Egyptian coinage of the 18th century', *Numismatics International Bulletin* 13.1 (1979), 11–14.

____, 'The gold coins of the Zaidī imāms of the 17th to the 19th centuries', *Numismatic Circular* 96 (1988), 211–12.

____, 'The period of the early Qāsimid imāms of the Yemen', *Numismatic Circular* 96 (1988), 39–43.

——, 'The Zaidī imām al-Mahdī Aḥmad b. al-Ḥasan', *Numismatic Circular* 96 (1988), 143–6.

Landau-Tasseron, Ella, 'The cyclical reform: A study of the *Mujaddid* tradition', *Studia Islamica* 70 (1989), 79–117.

——, 'Zaydī imāms as restorers of religion: *Iḥyā'* and *Tajdīd* in Zaydī Literature', *Journal of Near Eastern Studies* 49 (1990), 247–63.

Laoust, Henri, *Essai sur les Doctrines Sociales et Politiques de Taki-D-Din Ahmad b. Taimiya*, Cairo: Imprimerie de l'Institut Français d'Archéologie Orientale, 1939.

——, 'Ibn ᶜAbd al-Wahhāb', in *EI*^{2}.

——, *Le Califat dans la doctrine de Rašīd Riḍā*, Beirut: n.p., 1938.

Lapidus, Ira M., *A History of Islamic Societies*, Cambridge University Press, 1988.

——, *Muslim Cities in the Later Middle Ages*, Cambridge University Press, 1984.

Lowick, Nicholas, 'The Manṣūrī and the Mahdawī Dirham', in *Coinage and History of the Islamic World*, Aldershot: Variorum, 1990, art. IV.

——, 'The mint of Ṣanᶜā': A historical outline', in R. B. Serjeant and R. Lewcock (eds.), *Ṣanᶜā': An Arabian Islamic City*, London: World of Islam Festival Trust, 1983.

MacKenzie, Kenneth, 'Ottoman coins inscribed with a religious title', *Numismatics International Bulletin* 21.7 (1987), 157–9.

Macro, Eric, *Yemen and the Western World*, London: C. Hurst and Company, 1968.

Madelung, Wilferd, 'A Muṭarrifī manuscript', reprinted in *Religious schools and sects in medieval Islam*, Aldershot: Variorum, 1985, art. XIX.

——, *Der Imam al-Qāsim ibn Ibrāhīm und die Glaubenslehre der Zaiditen*, Berlin: Walter De Gruyter, 1965.

——, 'Imāma', in *EI*^{2}.

——, 'The Hāshimiyyāt of al-Kumayt and Hāshimī Shiᶜism', *Studia Islamica* 70 (1989), 5–26.

——, 'The origins of the Yemenite Hijra', in Alan Jones (ed.), *Arabicus Felix*, Reading: Ithaca Press, 1991.

——, *The Succession to Muḥammad*, Cambridge University Press, 1997.

——, 'Zaydī attitudes to Sufism', in Frederick De Jong and Bernd Radtke (eds.), *Islamic Mysticism Contested*, Leiden: Brill, 1999.

——, 'Zaydiyya', in *EI*^{2}.

Margoliouth, D. S., 'Wahhābīya', in *EI*^{1}.

Meissner, Jefferey R., 'Tribes at the core: legitimacy, structure and power in Zaydi Yemen', Ph.D. thesis, Columbia University, 1987.

Mermier, Franck, *Le Cheikh de la nuit*, Paris: Sindbad, 1997.

Messick, Brinkley, Media muftis: radio fatwas in Yemen', in Muhammad Masud *et al.* (eds.) *Islamic Legal Interpretation*, Cambridge: Harvard University Press, 1996.

——, *The Calligraphic State*, Berkeley: University of California Press, 1993.

——, 'The mufti, the text and the world: legal interpretation in Yemen', *Man* (N.S.) 21 (1986), 102–19.

Metcalf, Barbara, *Islamic Revival in British India: Deoband, 1860–1900*, Princeton University Press, 1982.

Mitchell, Richard P. *The Society of the Muslim Brothers*, Oxford University Press, 1993.

Mundy, Martha, *Domestic Government*, London: I. B. Tauris, 1995.

——, 'Ṣanᶜāᵓ dress', in R. B. Serjeant and R. Lewcock (eds.), *Ṣanᶜāᵓ: an Arabian Islamic City*, London: World of Islam Festival Trust, 1983.

——, 'Women's inheritance of land in highland Yemen', in R. B. Serjeant and R. L. Bidwell (eds.), *Arabian Studies* V, London: C. Hurst, 1979.

Nebehay, Stefan, 'Muslimische Münzen aus dem Jemen', in *Jemen: Im Lande der Königen von Saba*, Vienna: Museum für Völkenkunde, 1989.

Niebuhr, M., *Travels through Arabia and other Countries in the East*, 2 vols., trans. Robert Heron, Edinburgh: R. Morison and Son., 1792, photoreprint, Reading: Garnet Publishing, 1994.

Nini, Yehuda, *The Jews of the Yemen: 1800–1914*, London: Harwood Academic Publishers, 1991.

O'Fahey, R. S., *Enigmatic Saint: Ahmad Ibn Idris and the Idrisi Tradition*, Evanston, Illinois: Northwestern University Press, 1990.

O'Fahey, R. S. and Radtke, Bernd, 'Neo-Sufism reconsidered', *Der Islam* 70.1 (1993), 52–87.

Peskes, Esther, *Muḥammad b. ᶜAbdalwahhāb im Widerstreit*, Beirut: Orient-Institut, 1993.

Peters, Rudolph, 'Erneuerungsbewegungen im Islam vom 18. bis zum 20. Jahrhundert und die Rolle des Islams in der neueren Geschichte', in Werner Ende and Udo Steinbach (eds.), *Der Islam in der Gegenwart*, Munich: Beck, 1984.

——, 'Idjtihād and Taqlīd in 18th and 19th century Islam', *Die Welt des Islams* 20 (1980), 131–45.

Peterson, J. E., *Yemen: the search for a modern state*, London: Croom Helm, 1982.

Philby, H. St. J. B., *Arabia*, London: Ernest Benn, 1930.

Playfair, R., *A History of Arabia Felix or Yemen*, Byculla: Education Society Press, 1859.

Radtke, Bernd, *Authochthone islamische Aufklärung im 18. Jahrhundert*, Utrecht: Houtsma Stichting, 2000.

Rahman, Fazlur, *Islam*, University of Chicago Press, 1979.

——, 'Revival and Reform in Islam', in P. M. Holt *et al.* (eds.), *The Cambridge History of Islam*, 2 vols. in four, Cambridge University Press, 1977.

Raymond, André, 'Le café du Yémen et l'Égypte (XVIIème–XVIIIème siècles)', *Chroniques Yéménites* 3 (1995), 16–25.

Reichmuth, Stefan, 'Murtaḍā Az-Zabīdī (d. 1791) in biographical and autobiographical accounts', *Die Welt des Islams* 39 (1999), 64–102.

Renaud, Etienne, 'Histoire de la pensée religieuse au Yémen', in Joseph Chelhod (ed.), *L'Arabie du Sud: Histoire et Civilisation*, vol. II, Paris: G.-P. Maisonneuve et Larose, 1984.

Rentz, George, 'The Wahhābīs', in A. J. Arberry (ed.), *Religion in the Middle East*, 2 vols., Cambridge University Press, 1969.

Rihani, Ameen, *Arabian Peak and Desert*, Delmar, New York: Caravan Books, 1983.

Sadan, Joseph, 'The "Latrines Decree" in the Yemen versus the Dhimma principles', in Jan Platvoet and Karel van der Toorn (eds.), *Pluralism and Identity: studies in ritual behaviour*, Leiden: E. J. Brill, 1995.

Schacht, Joseph, 'Ahl al-Ḥadīth', in *EI*[2].

——, *An Introduction to Islamic Law*, Oxford: The Clarendon Press, 1982.

——, *The Origins of Muhammadan Jurisprudence*, Oxford University Press, 1950.

——, 'Taklīd', in *EI*[1].

Schultze, Reinhard, 'Das islamische achtzehnte Jahrhundert: Versuch einer historiographischen Kritik', *Die Welt des Islams* 30 (1990), 140–9.

——, 'Was ist die islamische Aufklärung?', *Die Welt des Islams* 36 (1996), 276–325.

Serjeant, R. B. 'The Hindu, Bāniyān, merchants and traders', in R. B. Serjeant and R. Lewcock (eds.), *Ṣanᶜāᵓ: An Arabian Islamic City*, London: World of Islam Festival Trust, 1983.

——, 'The interplay between tribal affinities and religious (Zaydī) authority in the Yemen', in *Customary and Shariᶜah Law in Arabian Society*, Aldershot: Variorum, 1991, art. III.

——, 'The post-medieval and modern history of Sanᶜāᵓ and the Yemen, ca. 953–1382/1515–1962', in R. B. Serjeant and R. Lewcock (eds.), *Ṣanᶜāᵓ: An Arabian Islamic City*, London: World of Islam Festival Trust, 1983.

——, 'The Yemeni poet al-Zubayrī and his polemic against the Zaydī imāms', in R. B. Serjeant and R. Bidwell (eds.), *Arabian Studies* 5, London: C. Hurst, 1979.

——, 'The Zaydīs', in A. J. Arberry (ed.), *Religion in the Middle East*, 2 vols., Cambridge University Press, 1969.

Shivtiel, A. *et al.*, 'The Jews of Ṣanᶜāᵓ', in R. B. Serjeant and R. Lewcock (eds.), *Ṣanᶜāᵓ: An Arabian Islamic City*, London: World of Islam Festival Trust, 1983.

Sivan, Emmanuel, *Radical Islam*, New Haven: Yale University Press, 1990.

Soudan, Frédérique, *Le Yémen ottoman*, Cairo: Institut Français d'Archéologie Orientale, 1999.

Stern, S. M., 'Some unrecognized dirhems of the Zaidis of the Yemen', *Numismatic Chronicle* 9 (1949), 180–8.

Stevenson, Thomas B., *Social Change in a Yemeni Highlands Town*, Salt Lake City: University of Utah Press, 1985.

Stewart, Devin, *Islamic Legal Orthodoxy: Twelver Shiite Responses to the Sunni Legal System*, Salt Lake City: University of Utah Press, 1998.

Stookey, Robert W., *Yemen: The Politics of the Yemen Arab Republic*, Boulder: Westview Press, 1978.

Strothmann, R., *Das Staatsrecht der Zaiditen*, Strassburg: Karl J. Trübner, 1912.
____, 'al-Zaidiyya', in *EI*[1].
Tobi, Yosef, 'The attempts to expel the Jews from Yemen in the 18th century', in Ephraim Isaac and Yosef Tobi (eds.), *Judeo-Yemenite Studies*, Princeton: Institute of Semitic Studies, 1999.
____, *The Jews of Yemen: Studies in their History and Culture*, Leiden: Brill, 1999.
____, 'The Sabbatean activity in Yemen', in *The Jews of Yemen: Studies in their History and Culture*, Leiden: Brill, 1999.
Traini, Renato, *Sources Biographiques des Zaidites*, Paris: Centre National de la Recherche Scientifique, 1977.
Tritton, A. S., *The Rise of the Imams of Sanaa*, Oxford University Press, 1925.
Tuchscherer, Michel, 'Des épices au café, le Yémen dans le commerce international (XVIe–XVIIe siècles)', *Chroniques Yéménites* 4–5 (1996–7), 92–102.
____, *Imams, Notables et Bédouins du Yémen au XVIIIe Siècle*, Cairo: Institut Français d'Archéologie Orientale, 1992.
____, (ed.), *Le Commerce du Café avant l'Ère des Plantations Coloniales*, Cairo: Institut Français d'Archéologie Orientale, 2001.
____, 'Le Commerce en Mer Rouge aux Alentours de 1700', in Yves Thoraval *et al.* (eds.), *Le Yémen et la Mer Rouge*, Paris: Editions L'Harmattan, 1995.
____, Le Yémen et la region de Jāzān au milieu du 18e siècle d'après la Chronique de ᶜAbd al-Raḥmān al-Bahkalī', Thèse (Doctorat de 3e Cycle), Université de Provence Aix-Marseille I, 1985.
Valentia, George, Viscount, *Voyages and Travels to India, Ceylon, the Red Sea, Abyssinia and Egypt*, 3 vols., London: printed for William Miller, 1809.
van Arendonk, C., *see* Arendonk, C. van.
van Donzel, E. J., *see* Donzel, E. J. van.
van Koningsveld, P. S. *et al.*, *see* Koningsveld, P. S. van *et al.*
Voll, John, *Islam: Continuity and Change in the Modern World*, Syracuse University Press, 1994.
____, 'Foundations for renewal and reform', in John L. Esposito (ed.), *The Oxford History of Islam*, Oxford University Press, 1999, pp. 509–47.
____, 'Linking groups in the networks of eighteenth-century revivalist scholars', in Nehemiah Levtzion and John Voll (eds.), *Eighteenth-Century Renewal and Reform in Islam*, Syracuse University Press, 1987.
Ward, Seth, 'A Fragment from an unknown work by al-Ṭabarī on the tradition "expel the Jews and Christians from the Arabian Peninsula (and the lands of Islam)" ', *BSOAS* 53 (1990), 407–20.
Weber, Max, *Economy and Society*, 2 vols., Berkeley: University of California Press, 1978.
Weir, Shelagh, 'Tribe, Hijrah and Madinah in North-West Yemen', in Kenneth Brown *et al.* (eds.), *Middle Eastern Cities in Comparative Perspective*, London: Ithaca Press, 1986.
Wensinck, A. J., *Concordance et Indices de la Tradition Musulmane*, 8 vols., Leiden: E. J. Brill, 1936–88.

——, 'The Refused Dignity', in T. W. Arnold and Reynold A. Nicholson (eds.), *A Volume of Oriental Studies presented to Edward G. Browne*, Cambridge University Press, 1922.

Wiederhold, Lutz, 'Blasphemy against the Prophet Muḥammad and his Companions (*Sabb al-Rasūl, Sabb al-Ṣaḥābah*): the introduction of the topic into Shāfiʿī legal literature and its relevance for legal practice under Mamluk rule', *Journal of Semitic Studies* 42.1 (1997), 39–70.

Winder, R. Baily, *Saudi Arabia in the Nineteenth Century*, New York: St. Martin's Press, 1965.

Zysow, Aron, 'The economy of certainty: an introduction to the typology of Islamic legal theory', Ph.D. dissertation, Harvard University, 1984.

——, 'Ejtehād', in *Encyclopaedia Iranica* 8 (1988), 280–6.

References in Hebrew

Gamliel, Shalom, *ha-Yehūdīm we-ha-Melekh be-Teyman* [*The Jews and the King of Yemen*], 2 vols., Jerusalem: The Shalom Research Center, 1986–7.

Qāfiḥ, Yōsef (Kafih, Joseph), 'Sefer "Dōfī ha-Zeman" le-Rabbī Saʿīd Ṣaʿdīʾ [The Book Dofi-Hazᵉman ("The Chastisements of Time") of R. Saʿid Saʿadiʾ], *Sefunot* 1 (1957), 185–242.

Qoraḥ, 'Amram, *Saʿarat Teyman*, Shimʿōn Greydī (ed.), Jerusalem: Kook, 1954.

Ratzaby, Yehuda (Rasahbi, Judah), 'Galūt Mawzaʿ' ['The Exile of Mawzaʿ: a chapter of Yemenite Jewish history'], *Sefunot* 5 (1961), 337–95.

——, 'Gerūsh Mawzaʿ le-Or Meqōrōt Ḥadashīm' ['The Mawzaʿ Expulsion in the light of New Sources'], *Zion* 37 (1972), 197–215.

Sadan, Yosef, 'Beyn ha-Gzerōt ʿal Yahadūt Teyman be-Sōf ha-Meʾa ha-17 li-"Gzerat ha-Mqammeṣīm" ba-Meʾot ha-18 ve-ha-19' ['The link between the decrees concerning the Yemenite Jews in the seventeenth century and the "Latrine Decree" in the nineteenth century'], in Ezra Fleischer *et al.* (eds.), *Mas'at Moshe*, Jerusalem: The Bialik Institute, 1998, pp. 202–36.

Tobi, Yosef, *'Iyyūnīm Bi-Mgīlat Teyman* [*Studies in a "Megillat Teman"*], Jerusalem: Hebrew University, 1986.

——, 'ha-Nisyōnōt le-Garesh et ha-Yehūdīm mi-Teyman be-Me'a ha-18' ['The Attempts to Expel the Jews from Yemen in the 18th Century'], in Yosef Tobi (ed.), *Le-Rosh Yosef*, Jerusalem: Afikim, 1995, pp. 459–74.

——, (ed.), *Toldot Yehudey Teyman mi-Kitveyhem* [*The History of the Jews of Yemen from their Own Chronicles*], Jerusalem: The Zalman Shazar Center and The Dinur Center, 1979.

Index

Other titles in the series

Popular Culture in Medieval Cairo
Boaz Shoshan
0 521 43209 X

Early Philosophical Shiism
Paul E. Walker *The Ismaili Neoplatonism of Abū Yaᶜqūb al-Sijistāni*
0 521 44129 3

Indian Merchants and Eurasian Trade, 1600–1750
Stephen Frederic Dale
0 521 45460 3

Palestinian Peasants and Ottoman Officials
Amy Singer *Rural Administration around Sixteenth-century Jerusalem*
0 521 45238 4 hardback
0 521 47679 8 paperback

Arabic Historical Thought in the Classical Period
Tarif Khalidi
0 521 46554 0 hardback
0 521 58938 X paperback

Mongols and Mamluks
Reuven Amitai-Preiss *The Mamluk-Īlkhānid War, 1260–1281*
0 521 46226 6

Hierarchy and Egalitarianism in Islamic Thought
Louise Marlow
0 521 56430 1

The Politics of Households in Ottoman Egypt
Jane Hathaway *The Rise of the Qazdağlis*
0 521 57110 3

Commodity and Exchange in the Mongol Empire
Thomas T. Allsen *A Cultural History of Islamic Textiles*
0 521 58301 2

State and Provincial Society in the Ottoman Empire
Dina Rizk Khoury *Mosul, 1540–1834*
0 521 59060 4

The Mamluks in Egyptian Politics and Society
Thomas Philipp and Ulrich Haarmann (eds)
0 521 59115 5

The Delhi Sultanate
Peter Jackson *A Political and Military History*
0 521 40477 0

European and Islamic Trade in the Early Ottoman State
Kate Fleet *The Merchants of Genoa and Turkey*
0 521 64221 3

Reinterpreting Islamic Historiography
Tayeb El-Hibri *Harun al-Rashid and the Narrative of the ʻAbbāsid Caliphate*
0 521 65023 2

The Ottoman City between East and West
Edhem Eldem, Daniel Goffman and Bruce Masters *Aleppo, Izmir, and Istanbul*
0 521 64304 X

A Monetary History of the Ottoman Empire
Sevket Pamuk
0 521 44197 8

The Politics of Trade in Safavid Iran
Rudolph P. Matthee *Silk for Silver, 1600–1730*
0 521 64131 4

The Idea of Idolatry and the Emergence of Islam
G.R. Hawting *From Polemic to History*
0 521 65165 4

Classical Arabic Biography
Michael Cooperson *The Heirs of the Prophets in the Age of al-Maʾmūn*
0 521 66199 4

Empire and Elites after the Muslim Conquest
Chase F. Robinson *The Transformation of Northern Mesopotamia*
0 521 78115 9

Poverty and Charity in Medieval Islam
Adam Sabra *Mamluk Egypt*, 1250–1517
0 521 77291 5

Christians and Jews in the Ottoman Arab World
Bruce Masters *The Roots of Sectarianism*
0 521 80333 0

Culture and Conquest in Mongol Eurasia
Thomas T. Allsen
0 521 80335 7

23988350R00180

Made in the USA
Middletown, DE
10 September 2015